Clinical Applications of Cyberpsychology and Virtual Reality for Mental Disorders

Clinical Applications of Cyberpsychology and Virtual Reality for Mental Disorders

Editor

Stéphane Bouchard

MDPI

Basel • Beijing • Wuhan • Barcelona • Belgrade • Novi Sad • Cluj • Manchester

Editor
Stéphane Bouchard
Department of
Psychoeducation and
Psychology
Université du Québec en
Outaouais
Gatineau, Canada

Editorial Office
MDPI
St. Alban-Anlage 66
4052 Basel, Switzerland

This is a reprint of articles from the Special Issue published online in the open access journal *Journal of Clinical Medicine* (ISSN 2077-0383) (available at: https://www.mdpi.com/journal/jcm/special_issues/cyberpsychology).

For citation purposes, cite each article independently as indicated on the article page online and as indicated below:

Lastname, A.A.; Lastname, B.B. Article Title. *Journal Name* **Year**, *Volume Number*, Page Range.

ISBN 978-3-0365-9286-2 (Hbk)
ISBN 978-3-0365-9287-9 (PDF)
doi.org/10.3390/books978-3-0365-9287-9

Contents

About the Editor

Stéphane Bouchard

Stéphane Bouchard is a full professor at the Université du Québec en Outaouais, where he teaches research methods, clinical psychology nad cyberpsychology. He was a chairholder for 21 years of the Canada Research Chair in Clinical Cyberpsychololgy. As a scientist practitioner, his research shows dedicated attention towards conducting both meaningful clinical applications of cyberpsychology and rigorous science to treat anxiety and other mental disorders. Since 1995, his research projects have involved telepsychotherapy and conducting randomized control trials and processes studies on the efficacy of delivering cognitive-behavior therapy in videoconference, the quality of the working alliance that can be developed in online treatments and documenting the role of telepresence. Another prolific area of expertise involves developing virtual environments to treat anxiety disorders, addictions, body image disturbance and other challenges faced by people with mental disorders. He conducts randomized control trials on the efficacy of interventions based on virtual reality, runs experimental studies to understand to why virtual reality is an effective treatment tool, and try to better understand phenomena of presence and cybersickness. His research lab holds Psyche, the only six-sided total immersion virtual reality system dedicated to mental health research. He has received numerous career awards, including the Prix Adrien Pinard in 2014 for his exceptional contribution to the field of psychology and the Annual Cybertherapy Excellence in Research Award in 2005. He is a dynamic workshop leader and a prolific scholar.

Journal of
Clinical Medicine

MDPI

Article

A Multisite Non-Inferiority Randomized Controlled Trial of the Efficacy of Cognitive-Behavior Therapy for Generalized Anxiety Disorder Delivered by Videoconference

Stéphane Bouchard [1,2,*], Michel J. Dugas [1,2], Geneviève Belleville [3], Frédéric Langlois [4], Patrick Gosselin [5], Geneviève Robillard [1], Giulia Corno [1] and André Marchand [6]

1 Département de Psychologie et de Psychoéducation, Université du Québec en Outaouais, Gatineau, QC J8X 3X7, Canada
2 Centre de Recherche du Centre de Santé et des Services Sociaux de l'Outaouais, Gatineau, QC J8T 4J3, Canada
3 École de Psychologie, Université Laval, Québec, QC G1V 0A6, Canada
4 Département de Psychologie, Université du Québec à Trois-Rivières, Trois-Rivières, QC G8Z 4M3, Canada
5 Département de Psychologie, Université de Sherbrooke, Sherbrooke, QC J1K 2R1, Canada
6 Département de Psychologie, Université du Québec à Montréal, Montréal, QC H2L 2C4, Canada
* Correspondence: stephane.bouchard@uqo.ca; Tel.: +1-819-595-3900 (ext. 2360)

Abstract: Delivering psychotherapy by videoconference has been studied in a number of clinical trials, but no large controlled trial has involved generalized anxiety disorder (GAD). This multicenter randomized controlled non-inferiority trial was conducted to test if cognitive-behavior psychotherapy delivered by videoconference (VCP) is as effective as cognitive-behavior psychotherapy delivered face-to-face, using a strict margin of tolerance for non-inferiority. A total of 148 adults received a 15-session weekly manualized program. The treatment was based on the intolerance of uncertainty model of GAD. The impact of treatment was assessed using primary (GAD severity), secondary (worry, anxiety, and intolerance of uncertainty) and tertiary (general functioning) variables measured before and after treatment and at 6-month and 12-month follow-ups. Results showed that: (a) the treatment was effective; (b) VCP for GAD was statistically non-inferior to face-to-face psychotherapy on primary, secondary and tertiary measures at all assessment points; (c) change in intolerance of uncertainty significantly predicted change in the primary outcome measure over and above important clinical factors common to all psychotherapies (motivation, working alliance, perceived therapist competence, and client satisfaction). These findings support the use of VCP as a promising treatment option for adults with GAD. Clinical trial registry: ISRCTN#12662027.

Keywords: videoconferencing psychotherapy; generalized anxiety disorder; cognitive-behavior therapy; non-inferiority; predictors of outcome

Citation: Bouchard, S.; Dugas, M.J.; Belleville, G.; Langlois, F.; Gosselin, P.; Robillard, G.; Corno, G.; Marchand, A. A Multisite Non-Inferiority Randomized Controlled Trial of the Efficacy of Cognitive-Behavior Therapy for Generalized Anxiety Disorder Delivered by Videoconference. *J. Clin. Med.* **2022**, *11*, 5924. https://doi.org/10.3390/jcm11195924

Academic Editor: Jerzy Samochowiec

Received: 31 August 2022
Accepted: 28 September 2022
Published: 7 October 2022

Publisher's Note: MDPI stays neutral with regard to jurisdictional claims in published maps and institutional affiliations.

1. Introduction

General anxiety disorder (GAD) is a highly common and chronic mental disorder with an estimated lifetime prevalence of 9% and a low rate of spontaneous remission [1–3]. Individuals with GAD experience excessive and uncontrollable anxiety and worry about different events or activities in key spheres of life such as work, health, finances, or family [1]. The prevalence and severity of this disorder are comparable in rural and urban zones, as are its psychosocial characteristics and comorbidity profile [4,5]. Individuals with GAD report high levels of psychological distress, low quality of life and high impairment at work, with high rates of absenteeism and low productivity [6]. Furthermore, patients with GAD are frequent users of healthcare services, leading to major costs to the healthcare system [7].

Cognitive-behavior therapy (CBT), which is considered to be the gold standard therapy for anxiety disorders, is recommended as the first-line treatment for GAD. Indeed, its efficacy and effectiveness for GAD has been extensively demonstrated [8–11]. The conceptual model of GAD proposed by Dugas and his colleagues [12,13] rests on the key role of intolerance of uncertainty (a negative dispositional characteristic arising from a set of catastrophic beliefs about uncertainty and its consequences). Intolerance of uncertainty is theorized to be a key mechanism involved in positive beliefs about worry, cognitive avoidance and chronic anxiety [12–14]. Based on this model, Dugas and colleagues developed a cognitive-behavioral treatment for GAD that is focused on intolerance of uncertainty (IU) and is now commonly referred to as CBT-IU [15]. Several randomized controlled trials have demonstrated the efficacy of CBT-IU for GAD [16–21].

Many individuals, including those with GAD, do not have access to specialized mental health services [22]. People in rural areas can face significant challenges in finding and attending face-to-face psychological services with mental health professionals who often practice in urban areas [5,22–24]. Even in urban areas, it can be difficult to regularly attend psychotherapy sessions because of other barriers to service utilization [24] such as structural barriers (e.g., commuting to the therapist's office), availability of professionals sharing the patient's cultural or ethnic values, or availability of psychotherapists with a specific expertise. The COVID-19 pandemic increased barriers to face-to-face treatment [25] due to recommendations regarding confinement, physical distancing, wearing surgical masks during consultations, etc.

Although telepsychology has traditionally been considered as a solution for providing access to mental health services for people living in rural areas, it is now considered to be a viable alternative to face-to-face psychotherapy [26–31]. Indeed, an increasing number of studies have documented the efficacy and effectiveness of videoconferencing psychotherapy (VCP) for mental health disorders [26,29,30,32,33]. Moreover, a handful of studies have documented the non-inferiority of VCP when compared to gold-standard treatments [34–38]. All reviews have highlighted the need for more randomized controlled trials for mental health disorders that have not yet been studied [26,29,38], such as GAD.

Only two studies have investigated the potential effectiveness of VCP specifically for patients with GAD. In a first uncontrolled study, Griffiths, Blignault and Yellowlees [39] provided CBT to 15 adults suffering from a variety of disorders, including three diagnosed with GAD. Although the overall results showed statistically significant pre to post-treatment differences on measures of anxiety and depression, the authors did not report the specific findings for the participants diagnosed with GAD. Théberge-Lapointe et al. [40] provided CBT-IU to five adults diagnosed with GAD using a multiple baseline design across participants. Their results showed preliminary support for the efficacy of VCP for GAD. Participants' anxiety improved at post-treatment, and gains were maintained at 3- and 12-month follow-ups [40].

In addition to documenting treatment outcome, it is important from a clinical point of view to report information on the predictors of treatment outcome [41,42]. In CBT for anxiety disorders, demographic variables (i.e., age, sex and socioeconomic status) are usually not significant predictors of treatment outcome and treatment adherence [42–47]. Low motivation for treatment and poor working alliance, which are factors common to all psychotherapies, have often been associated with a poorer treatment response [42,48–51]. Change in intolerance of uncertainty, a putative process specific to CBT for GAD, has been shown to mediate treatment outcome and to precede changes in the symptoms of GAD [52]. Predictors of outcome should also be examined when CBT is delivered by VCP to help clinicians adapt their interventions. In their non-inferiority and non-randomized controlled trial, Bouchard et al. [34] and its online supplement found that motivation and working alliance were not statistically significant predictors of improvement for CBT for panic disorder delivered by VCP. As predicted by CBT models of panic disorder, change in dysfunctional beliefs about bodily sensations significantly predicted treatment outcome. No data are available on the predictors of treatment outcome when CBT is delivered by VCP for GAD, and more specifically, whether there is a difference in the role of intolerance of uncertainty when CBT-IU is delivered by VCP or face-to-face.

The objectives of the current study are: (1) to assess with a randomized clinical trial the non-inferiority of CBT-IU for GAD delivered by VCP compared to face-to-face CBT-IU for GAD, and (2) to support findings from studies of face-to-face CBT-IU that show that changes in intolerance of uncertainty are associated with treatment outcome. Based on previous studies, we hypothesized that delivering CBT-IU by VCP would be statistically non-inferior to face-to-face therapy on primary, secondary and tertiary measures. The non-inferiority margin was defined a priori (in the grant application) by a strict and small margin of tolerance for non-inferiority of 10%, or a ε of 0.36 [54], p.16 which, for example, represents a difference in change between the two conditions of no more than 10% on the primary outcome measure. The primary outcome was the severity of GAD as assessed with a standardized structured diagnostic interview. The secondary outcomes were worry, intolerance of uncertainty and overall GAD symptoms. The tertiary outcomes, which focused on generalization of treatment outcome, were depressive mood and quality of life. For the second objective, it was hypothesized that change in intolerance of uncertainty would be significantly associated with treatment outcome, and that this relationship would not be due to shared variance with common therapy factors (motivation, working alliance, perceived therapist's competence and client satisfaction) or the different treatment modalities (VCP or face-to-face therapy). The study was not designed to demonstrate the causal role of change in intolerance of uncertainty (as shown by Bomyea et al. [52]) but to document the relative contribution of specific and non-specific factors associated with the treatment outcomes of CBT-IU.

2. Materials and Methods

2.1. Participants

Participants were 148 adults of White ethnicity who met diagnostic criteria for GAD [1] (excessive anxiety and worry, difficulty to control the worry, anxiety and worry associated with three or more of the six somatic symptoms, significant clinical distress or impairment, and the disturbance not better explained by substance abuse, another medical condition or another mental disorder) as assessed with the diagnostic interview described in Section 2.4.1. Recruitment, which took place from March 2014 to December 2016, was conducted in university-based mental health clinics specialized in anxiety disorders across five of the six largest metropolitan areas in the Province of Quebec, Canada (in alphabetical order: Gatineau, Montréal, Québec, Sherbrooke and Trois-Rivières). Individuals responding to posters or articles in local newspapers, or referred by their doctors or mental health professionals were prescreened over the telephone (verbal consent was obtained prior to beginning the interview) and invited to attend an in-person diagnostic interview. Participants were eligible to take part to the study if they had a primary diagnosis of GAD, were aged between 18 and 75, and were fluent in French. Prior to study enrollment, participant also had to agree to abstain from starting, or refraining from changing, any antidepressant or anxiolytic medications and to not undergo any other psychotherapy during the course of treatment. Participants were excluded from the study if they received CBT in the previous 6 months or if they were taking any anxiolytic or antidepressant medication for less than, respectively, one or three months. Furthermore, individuals who received a secondary diagnosis of bipolar disorder, borderline personality disorder, intellectual disability, psychotic disorder, schizophrenia, substance-related disorder, or who presented firm suicidal intentions or a physical condition making participation in the study inadvisable (e.g., hearing impaired, visual impairment, epilepsy) were ineligible for participation. These eligibility criteria are similar to those used in recent efficacy trials of CBT for GAD [18].

Figure 1 Details the flow of participants from recruitment to follow-up. Intent-to-treat analyses are reported in this article, with data for treatment completers reported in Appendix A. The sample size was established a priori based on a power analysis for non-inferiority trials [53,54].

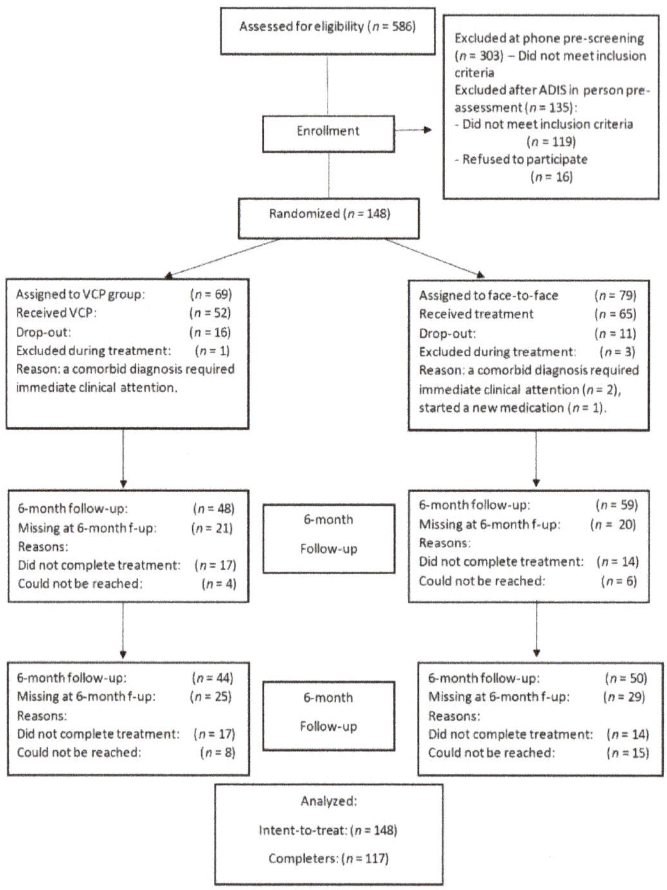

Figure 1. CONSORT flow chart of participation in the randomized control trial.

2.2. Design and Ethics

This study received approval from the Research Ethics Board of the Université du Québec en Outaouais (Gatineau Campus, main research site) as well as from the Research Ethics Board of each participating center. Voluntary and informed consent, ethical reviews, and ethical approvals were performed in accordance with the Declaration of Helsinki of 1975, as revised in 2018, and the ethical standards of the Canadian Tri-Council 2018 policy statement for ethical conduct for research involving humans. Participants did not receive any monetary compensation for participating in this study. Because the cost of the treatment was covered by the research grant, receiving free treatment could be considered as an incentive. Yearly reports were submitted to the Research Ethics Boards, which monitored the study until termination (no adverse events were reported by participants). The study was designed, funded, and conducted in accordance with CONSORT (Consolidated Standards of Reporting Trials) guidelines for trials assessing non-pharmacological treatments and for non-equivalence trials [55,56]. The clinical trial was registered at the time the study received ethical approval and was expected to begin (ISRCTN12662027; https://doi.org/10.1186/ISRCTN12662027 (accessed on 30 August 2022), before participants were allocated to treatment conditions.

2.3. Recruitment and Randomization

All clinical interview sessions occurred in private offices on-campus. The interviews were administered by supervised graduate students in clinical psychology who had completed at least two years of practicum training. In order to assess inter-judge agreement on diagnosis, all clinical interviews were audio recorded. In the absence of a clear diagnostic consensus, a final diagnostic decision was reached after discussion between the interviewer and the senior researcher of the study site. Individuals who were deemed to be eligible to participate were informed of the implications of taking part in the study and signed the study's comprehensive consent form. Recruitment was terminated in accordance with the timetable presented in the research grant to ensure feasibility of the 12-month follow-up.

After providing informed consent, participants were randomized to one of the two treatment conditions: VCP or face-to-face psychotherapy. Randomization was generated before initiating recruitment and was performed using an iPhone generator of random numbers (i.e., 1, 2). A different randomization table was generated for each recruitment site. The study researchers were unaware of treatment allocation. If a participant refused to participate or dropped out of the study, their assignment slot was not reassigned to another participant. A second randomization was performed for participants assigned to the VCP condition in order to determine which distant VCP site would provide psychotherapy. The second randomization followed the same procedure as the first one, with the exception of the use of four randomizing options, numbered 1 to 4 (their local site was excluded from the second randomization). All participants received psychotherapy in an office at the local university-based mental health clinic where they had been recruited and received the diagnostic interview.

2.4. Assessment

All primary, secondary, and tertiary outcome measures were administered at pre-treatment, post-treatment, 6-month follow-up, and 12-month follow-up. All measures have been extensively validated and used in clinical trials. The length of the follow-up was established to provide data on long-term outcome. Follow-ups of 12 months are standard in CBT and feasible within funding constraints. The 6-month follow-up was planned to limit the risks of 12-month attrition and to limit the impact of carrying forward the last available observations for participants who were not able to attend the onsite 12-month diagnostic follow-up interview. Measures not specific to outcome or CBT-IU were: descriptive statistics and treatment motivation (assessed at pre-treatment), working alliance and perceived therapist competence (assessed at mid-treatment [57]). Note that analyses conducted with the measure of working alliance after the first, third and fifth therapy session yielded similar results. Treatment satisfaction was measured at post-treatment. To minimize social desirability, participants were informed that their psychotherapists would not have access to their responses concerning the working alliance and perceived therapist competence. Participants placed the questionnaires in an envelope and in a locked box accessible only to the study researchers. Ratings of treatment fidelity and statistical analyses were performed after the trial was completed. Data were entered at each site and sent to the main study site after the trial was completed for analyses.

2.4.1. Primary Measure: Documenting Efficacy

Anxiety Disorders Interview Schedule for DSM-IV (ADIS-IV). The ADIS-IV [58] was initially used to establish the diagnosis of GAD and to identify other disorders (i.e., other anxiety disorders, mood disorders, obsessive-compulsive disorder, post-traumatic stress disorder, psychotic symptoms, somatization disorders, and substance use disorder). This semi-structured interview is commonly used as a treatment outcome measure in research on GAD. In addition to information about differential diagnosis, the ADIS-IV provides a score of clinical severity for each disorder, ranging from 0 (no symptom, distress or interference) to 8 (severe symptoms, distress or interference). A score of 4 and above warrants a diagnosis. Following the publication of the DSM-5 [1], the ADIS was revised for consistency with the DSM-5's diagnostic criteria. However, the section on GAD was not revised, as its criteria remained unchanged from the DSM-IV to the DSM-5. The ADIS has demonstrated good inter-rater reliability for each anxiety disorder [58]. The ADIS was completed in person by an assessor blind to the treatment condition of the participant. Reassessment by blind raters using audio recordings of a subset of ADIS-IV interviews in this sample confirmed the excellent reliability of GAD scores (intraclass correlation = 0.94, $p < 0.001$).

2.4.2. Secondary Measures: Documenting Self-Reported Symptoms of GAD and IU

Penn-State Worry Questionnaire (PSWQ). The PSWQ [59] is the most widely used measure of excessive worry, which is the central feature of GAD [20,60,61]. The questionnaire includes 16 items rated on a 5-point Likert scale ranging from 1 (not at all typical of me) to 5 (very typical of me). Eleven items are stated in the direction of pathological worry (e.g., « My worries overwhelm me »), while the remaining 5 items are inverted and reverse scored (e.g., « I find it easy to dismiss worrisome thoughts »). The PSWQ has strong internal consistency (Cronbach's alpha of 0.95 [59]). Higher PSWQ scores indicate greater levels of worry.

Worry and Anxiety Questionnaire (WAQ). The WAQ [62] is an 11-item self-report measure of the DSM-IV diagnostic criteria for GAD. Items are rated on a 5-point Likert scale ranging from 0 (not at all) to 8 (very severely), and they reflect both the cognitive and somatic symptoms of GAD. Three items assess cognitive symptoms (excessive or exaggerated worry, duration of excessive worry, difficulty controlling worry), six items assess somatic symptoms (restlessness, being easily fatigued, difficulty concentrating, irritability, muscle tension, sleep disturbance), and one item assesses interference. The WAQ total score is based on a weighted sum score ranging from 0 to 56, and higher WAQ scores indicate more severe GAD symptoms. It has been shown to possess strong internal consistency (Cronbach's alpha of 0.90 [63]).

Intolerance of Uncertainty Scale (IUS). The IUS [64] is a self-report measure consisting of 27 items assessing negative beliefs about, and reactions to, uncertainty. It is a measure of the core variable underlying CBT-IU, not of GAD severity, and it has been shown by Bomyea et al. [52] to mediate treatment outcome. Items are rated on a 5-point scale from 1 (Not at all characteristic of me) to 5 (Entirely characteristic of me), with higher scores reflecting greater intolerance of uncertainty. The IUS has a high internal consistency (Cronbach's alpha of 0.91). The total score is calculated by summing all items, with higher IUS scores indicating stronger intolerance of uncertainty.

2.4.3. Tertiary Measures: Documenting Generalization to General Functioning

Beck Depression Inventory (BDI-II). The BDI-II [65] is one of the most widely used measures for assessing depressed mood. It includes 21 items in which four response options are presented on a 4-point Likert-type scale ranging from 0 to 3, with higher scores corresponding to higher levels of depressive symptoms. Respondents are asked to endorse statements regarding how they have been feeling over the past 2 weeks. The total score can vary from 0 to 63 and the measure has high internal consistency (Cronbach's alpha of 0.90).

World Health Organization Quality of Life (WHO-QOL - Psychological and WHO-QOL - Social relations). The WHO-QOL brief [66] is a self-report questionnaire developed by the World Health Organization that aims to assess quality of life across different cultures. Quality of life is assessed by 6 items documenting psychological health and 6 items documenting social relationships. The WHO-QOL-Psychological scale (Cronbach's alpha of 0.81) and the WHO-QOL-Social relations scale (Cronbach's alpha of 0.71) document global personal and interpersonal functioning with adequate internal consistency; higher scores indicate a higher quality of life in these areas.

2.4.4. General Measures Not Specific to Outcome and CBT-IU

Client Motivation for Therapy Scale (CMTS). Patients' motivation to engage in therapy was assessed using the CMTS [67]. This scale, which is based on Self-Determination Theory [68], is made-up of 6 subscales: intrinsic motivation, integrated regulation, identified regulation, introjected regulation, external regulation and amotivation. The 24 items are scored on a 7-point Likert scale, ranging from 1 (not true at all) to 7 (totally true). The internal consistency of the scale is very good, with an average Cronbach's alpha of 0.84. The total score was calculated as recommended by the authors [67], and a higher score expresses a stronger self-determined motivation to engage in psychotherapy.

Working Alliance Inventory (WAI). The WAI [69], patient-version, is the most widely used instrument for assessing the working alliance. Patients rate how they perceive their working alliance in terms of agreement on psychotherapy goals, psychotherapy tasks and emotional bond with their therapist. The complete patient version consists of 36 items rated on a 7-point Likert scale ranging from 1 (never) to 7 (always). This scale has an excellent Cronbach's alpha of 0.93. Scores range from 36 to 252, and high scores indicate a strong working alliance.

Therapist Competence Scale (TCS). The TCS [70] assesses the patient's perception of their therapist's competence during CBT. The total score on the original version is based on two subscales measuring technical skills and interpersonal skills with 20 items rated on a 7-point Likert scale ranging from 1 (strongly disagree) to 7 (strongly agree). It has been shown to differ from working alliance and patient motivation and to have a strong Cronbach's alpha of 0.87. Higher scores indicate greater therapist competence according to patients.

Client Satisfaction Questionnaire (CSQ). The CSQ [71]. The CSQ is an 8-item self-report questionnaire assessing patient satisfaction with health services. Each item consists of a statement about the services received, and satisfaction is rated on a 4-point Likert scale. The total score ranges between 8 and 32, with higher scores indicating higher satisfaction. Cronbach's alpha is strong at 0.92.

2.4.5. Measures Used for Methodological Purposes

Structured Clinical Interview for DSM–IV Axis-II (SCID-II). The SCID-II [72] is a validated structured interview for assessing personality disorders. In this study, only the borderline personality disorder module was used. A 15-item self-administered questionnaire was first completed by participants to assess possible symptoms of borderline personality disorder, followed by the Borderline Personality Disorder semi-structured interview module of the SCID-II. People with a SCID-II borderline personality diagnosis were excluded from the study.

Adherence to the treatment manual. Psychotherapy sessions were video recorded to assess adherence to the treatment manual. A rating scale was used to document the extent psychotherapists respected the structure of the session (e.g., follow-up of home exercises, addressing intolerance of uncertainty, discussion, planning the upcoming home exercises) and whether each treatment strategy was addressed in the correct module. A quarter of the sessions of participants who completed the trial were randomly chosen, equally in each condition and within each module, to be examined by blind evaluators trained in CBT. Adherence to the treatment manual was calculated based on the frequency an element from the list was checked as being performed according to the manual, with a score of 100% corresponding to complete adherence to the manual.

2.5. *Treatment*

Individuals allocated to face-to-face treatment were greeted at the local site by their assigned psychotherapist, whereas participants assigned to the VCP condition were met by a research assistant who set up the office with the videoconferencing system for VCP with the assigned clinician at the other site (remote site/another city). The research assistant used a remote control to call the remote site, adjust the volume and left the room just before the beginning of the VCP session. The assistant remained nearby and available in case of technical problems or emergencies.

All patients received weekly manual-based CBT based on the IU model of GAD [73,74]. In the face-to-face condition, the patient and psychotherapist met physically in the same room. In the VCP condition, the patient and psychotherapist met online; the patient was in a room at the local site (i.e., the university-based clinic where the patient received the diagnostic interview) and the clinician was in a room in the remote site (i.e., a university-based clinic in another city, where the clinician delivered CBT-IU).

The treatment protocol was identical for both conditions and consisted of 15 weekly, 60-min sessions divided into six modules: (Module 1, Session 1) building a working alliance, a shared case formulation and providing psychoeducation on the symptoms of GAD and the principles of CBT; (Module 2, Session 2) re-evaluating the usefulness of worrying; (Module 3, up to three sessions) increasing tolerance to uncertainty; (Module 4, up to four sessions) improving problem solving and problem orientation; (Module 5, up to four sessions) written exposure to worry; and (Module 6, Sessions 14 and 15) wrap-up and relapse prevention. The use of a treatment manual based on content that must be addressed by module (as opposed to content that must be addressed at each session) allowed for some clinical flexibility in adjusting the pace of treatment while maintaining the delivery of a reproductible validated intervention. Psychotherapists were required to proceed through all six modules and were not allowed to add new material or deviate from the planned sequence; however, they had the freedom to deviate from the expected pace by one or two sessions. A written treatment manual was provided to psychotherapists and to patients, with home exercises scheduled between sessions. Ratings of adherence to the treatment manual were 92.35% (SD = 9.45) in the VCP condition and 94.31% (SD = 8.33) in the face-to-face therapy condition. No significant difference in integrity was found between the two treatment conditions ($t(103) = 1.12$, bilateral $p = 0.267$, partial eta squared = 0.012) or the five sites ($F(4,100) = 1.89$, $p = 0.117$, partial eta-squared = 0.0710).

Psychotherapists were 23 graduate students (91% female) in clinical psychology trained in CBT, who received weekly supervision by the study researchers (six by SB, five by AM, five by GB, four by FL and three by PG, all registered psychologists trained in CBT-IU). One onsite meeting was conducted prior to starting the RCT to review the treatment protocol and ensure the homogeneity of treatment delivery among sites. One hour of the meeting was also devoted to train all staff members on how to use the VCP system. All psychotherapists provided CBT to participants in both conditions (i.e., they were not assigned to provide treatment in only one of the two conditions).

2.6. Material

The technology used for this RCT required dedicated videoconference systems (i.e., not software used on a computer or a portable device), as this technology was the standard in communication security at the time the trial was conducted (standard H.323 with the use of a Gatekeeper). The hardware consisted of Tandberg MXP90 videoconference codec systems in each site allowing data transmission between sites at 1.544 Mbp/s through secured IP link, a 32-inch TV monitor, and a video camera located on the top of the TV monitor. In the VCP condition, the height of the TV monitor and the distance between monitor and patient's chair were intended to replicate the distance and position of a psychotherapist when seated face-to-face. In the event of technical problems, a telephone and a list of telephone numbers of the other university-based clinics were available in all psychotherapy offices. If required, documents could be transmitted by email. The picture-in-picture option was activated on the psychotherapists' videoconference system, and the psychotherapy sessions were recorded on a videorecorder to assess fidelity to the treatment protocol. When psychotherapy was delivered face-to-face, the local videoconference system was turned on (with the TV monitor turned off) to record psychotherapy sessions on the videorecorder.

3. Results

3.1. Statistical Analyses

Data were analyzed using IBM SPSS version 28 (IBM Corp, Armonk, NY, USA, 2021), except for non-inferiority tests which were conducted with jamovi 2.2.5 [75] and the TOSTER module [76] for the lower or upper bound 1-sided significance tests and probability values. Non-inferiority analyses were conducted in accordance with recommendations by Mauri and D'Agostino [77] and Wellek's [53], (p. 16, p. 30) using a strict margin of tolerance for non-inferiority of $\varepsilon = 0.36$ (i.e., $\pm 10\%$) applied to the lower equivalence bound of the TOST equivalence test when VCP showed smaller improvements in comparison to face-to-face or applied to the higher equivalence bound of the TOST equivalence test when VCP showed larger improvements in comparison to face-to-face. The non-inferiority margin was set a priori in the grant proposal based on clinical expertise and Wellek's [53] strict criteria of smallest acceptable difference. Missing data were handled using an intent-to-treat approach, where each missing information was replaced by the last available observation carried forward. This approach is more conservative than analyzing only treatment completers, as it protects against inflation of success rates at post-treatment and follow-ups. The non-completers rate was not statistically different in the two conditions (X2(1) = 1.06, $p = 0.30$). Further comparisons between completers and non-completers revealed no statistical difference on most variables (age, sex, presence or number of comorbid disorders, treatment sites, ADIS-IV, WAQ, and IUS) but significantly lower scores among the non-completers in motivation, PSQW, and measures of quality of life, as well as higher BDI-II scores. Comparisons between completer status and treatment conditions revealed no statistically significant interaction, with all effect sizes being very small (partial eta square range between 0.000 and 0.01). Although the impact of non-completers seemed limited, following recommendations by Mauri and D'Agostino [77], results of the per-protocol treatment completers is also reported for consistency of the non-inferiority tests. As an alternative for handling missing data and covariance among measures over time, Mixed Linear Modeling (MLM) analyses are reported in Appendix A. Analyses on completers are reported in the main text to rely on actual data from participants instead of data estimated by MLM models. Repeated measures ANOVAs with completers and MLM analyses will be given less attention, as their conclusions were consistent with the more conservative approach. The assumption of normality was not met for the outcome measures, which is expected in clinical samples. All analyses were also performed with non-parametric analyses, and all results of the parametric analyses were replicated; parametric analyses are therefore reported here. Mauchly's test for sphericity was sometimes statistically significant; hence, the Greenhouse–Geisser correction to the degrees of freedom was applied to all analyses. Significance levels were set at $p = 0.05$ for the descriptive statistics and the main outcome measure (ADIS-IV), and family-wise Bonferroni corrected for the secondary (PSWQ, WAQ, IUS: $p < 0.05/3 = 0.017$) and tertiary measures (BDI-II, WHO-QOL—Psychological, WHO-QOL—Social relations: $p < 0.05/3 = 0.017$).

To address the second objective of the study, participants with missing data at Session 7 or at post-treatment were excluded from the regression analyses. Changes from pre to post-treatment for the multiple hierarchical regression involving the ADIS-IV and IUS were calculated using residualized change scores (results were similar to those obtained when pre and post scores were used in the regression, but with greater degrees of freedom and power). Predictors of pre/post residualized change on the ADIS-IV entered into the regression were: treatment condition, psychotherapist treatment site, motivation toward therapy at Session 1, working alliance at Session 7, perceived psychotherapist competence at Session 7, client satisfaction at post-treatment and pre/post residualized change in intolerance of uncertainty. The hierarchical regression tested the role of change in intolerance of uncertainty over and above variables that are non-specific to CBT for GAD. A treatment by change in IUS interaction parameter was further used to test for a between-condition difference in the role of cognitive change. The significance level was set at 0.05 for the regression analyses.

3.2. Description of the Sample

Table 1 presents descriptive information for the VCP and face-to-face conditions for the complete intent-to-treat sample. Chi-square tests and Student's t-tests did not reveal pre-existing differences between the two conditions, except for working alliance and perceived therapist competence which reached statistical significance in a direction opposite to the non-inferiority hypotheses (i.e., suggested superiority of VCP over face-to-face therapy) and did not require additional statistical corrections for the non-inferiority tests. There was no statistically significant difference when comparing recruitment sites (i.e., the five centers, with participants assigned to VCP receiving treatment by psychotherapists from other centers) and psychotherapist treatment sites (i.e., the site of the psychotherapists, regardless of treatment modality) on all variables at pre-treatment.

Table 1. Descriptive statistics of the intent-to-treat sample of participants diagnosed with generalized anxiety disorder who received cognitive-behavior therapy either by videoconference (VCP) or face-to-face (FF).

	VCP (n = 69)	FF (n = 79)	Statistical Test (Chi-Square or t Test)
Age, mean (SD)	41.35 (14.80)	39.38 (16.23)	−0.77, $p > 0.05$
Sex (female)	57 (82.60%)	65 (82.30%)	0.003, $p > 0.05$
Presence of at least one comorbid disorder *	36 (52.2%)	44 (55.7%)	0.184, $p > 0.05$
Living alone	15 (21.70%)	8 (10.10%)	3.784, $p > 0.05$
Education High school	12 (17.40%)	13 (16.50%)	0.235, $p > 0.05$
College	21 (30.40%)	27 (34.20%)	
University	36 (52.20%)	39 (49.40%)	
Work status Full-time (35 h or +)	23 (33.30%)	26 (32.90%)	3.694, $p > 0.05$
Part-time (less than 35 h)	23 (33.30%)	23 (29.10%)	
Retirement	9 (13.00%)	11 (13.90%)	
Unemployment	11 (15.90%)	9 (11.4%)	
Other	3 (4.30%)	10 (12.70%)	
Annual income Lower than 29,999$	14 (20.90%)	27 (35.10%)	4.628, $p > 0.05$
(3 refused to answer) 30 k–59,999$	25 (37.30%)	19 (29.70%)	
60 k–89,999$	11 (16.40%)	14 (18.20%)	
90 k and more	17 (25.40%)	17 (22.10%)	
Taking medication	32 (46.4%)	25 (31.6%)	3.38, $p > 0.95$
Previous psychotherapy	49 (71.00%)	57 (72.20%)	0.23, $p > 0.05$
Motivation toward therapy (Session 1)	12.38 (4.60)	12.70 (3.67)	0.46, $p > 0.05$
Working alliance (Session 7)	233.18 (18.05)	225.80 (17.52)	−2.36, $p < 0.05$
Perception of therapist competence (Session 7)	164.00 (12.99)	156.47 (19.32)	−2.49, $p < 0.05$
Client Satisfaction (post-treatment)	28.32 (3.78)	27.77 (3.46)	−0.92, $p > 0.05$

Note. VCP = Videoconference psychotherapy; FF= Face-to-face psychotherapy; SD = Standard deviation. * Participants reported having up to four comorbid conditions and the number specific comorbid conditions were as follows: social anxiety disorder (n = 34), panic disorder (n = 20), agoraphobia (n = 14), major depressive disorder (n = 14), specific phobia (n = 14), obsessive-compulsive disorder or trichotillomania (n = 7), posttraumatic stress disorder (n = 4), other mood disorders (n = 7), eating disorder (n = 1), other (n = 6).

3.3. Main Outcome and Non-Inferiority Analyses

Descriptive statistics at each time point are reported in Table 2, and results of the non-inferiority analyses are reported in Table 3. The repeated measures ANOVAs confirmed statistically significant and large time effects for each variable. Contrasts comparing pre and post-treatment were all statistically significant, and effect sizes were large for the ADIS-IV (pre/post F(1,146) = 211.08, $p < 0.001$, partial eta-squared = 0.59; pre/6-month follow-up F(1,146) = 192.6, $p < 0.001$, partial eta-squared = 0.57; pre/12-month follow-up (1,146) = 191.32, $p < 0.001$, partial eta-squared = 0.57), the PSWQ (pre/post F(1,146) = 177.78, $p < 0.001$, partial eta-squared = 0.55; pre/6-month follow-up F(1,146) = 202.19, $p < 0.001$, partial eta-squared = 0.58; pre/12-month follow-up (1,146) = 191.29, $p < 0.001$, partial eta-squared = 0.57), the WAQ (pre/post F(1,146) = 167.9,

$p < 0.001$, partial eta-squared = 0.54; pre/6-month follow-up F(1,146) = 204.08, $p < 0.001$, partial eta-squared = 0.58; pre/12-month follow-up (1,146) = 187.93, $p < 0.001$, partial eta-squared = 0.56), the IUS (pre/post F(1,146) = 143.21, $p < 0.001$, partial eta-squared = 0.50; pre/6-month follow-up F(1,146) = 165.4, $p < 0.001$, partial eta-squared = 0.53; pre/12-month follow-up (1,146) = 168.83, $p < 0.001$, partial eta-squared = 0.54], the BDI-II (pre/post F(1,146) = 95.14, $p < 0.001$, partial eta-squared = 0.40; pre/6-month follow-up F(1,146) = 108.75, $p < 0.001$, partial eta-squared = 0.43; pre/12-month follow-up (1,146) = 92.97, $p < 0.001$, partial eta-squared = 0.39), the WHO-QOL-Psychological subscale (pre/post F(1,146) = 60.58, $p < 0.001$, partial eta-squared = 0.31; pre/6-month follow-up F(1,146) = 69.42, $p < 0.001$, partial eta-squared = 0.34; pre/12-month follow-up (1,146) = 71.25, $p < 0.001$, partial eta-squared = 0.34], and the WHO-QOL-Social relations subscale (pre/post F(1,146) = 16.42, $p < 0.001$, partial eta-squared = 0.11; pre/6-month follow-up F(1,146) = 30.51, $p < 0.001$, partial eta-squared = 0.18; pre/12-month follow-up (1,146) = 30.6, $p < 0.001$, partial eta-squared = 0.18).

Table 2. Descriptive statistics for variables used in the non-inferiority analyses (intent-to-treat) ($n = 148$).

Variable	Condition	Pre		Post		6-Month F-up		12-Month F-up	
		M	SD	M	SD	M	D	M	SD
ADIS	VCP	5.41	1.07	2.96	1.90	3.25	1.78	3.25	1.78
	FF	5.62	0.90	3.15	1.95	3.17	1.90	3.19	1.85
PSWQ	VCP	66.59	7.27	51.51	11.99	49.27	12.50	49.86	12.37
	FF	66.62	7.31	53.62	11.93	51.92	13.00	52.44	12.73
WAQ	VCP	42.85	6.46	29.87	12.84	28.09	12.71	27.54	12.59
	FF	43.50	6.25	30.20	12.96	29.54	12.06	30.99	11.62
IUS	VCP	85.13	20.54	61.96	23.71	59.51	22.87	58.68	23.20
	FF	87.07	19.33	65.30	22.24	64.34	23.38	62.80	22.58
BDI-II	VCP	21.52	10.93	12.61	11.03	12.68	10.22	12.29	11.03
	FF	21.16	8.96	13.13	11.67	12.19	11.37	13.19	11.03
QOL-Psychol	VCP	11.07	2.23	12.50	2.46	12.65	2.90	12.94	2.95
	FF	10.82	2.20	12.09	2.52	12.66	3.03	12.36	2.87
QOL-Social	VCP	12.22	3.16	13.17	3.44	13.90	3.64	13.80	3.85
	FF	11.84	2.87	12.61	3.11	13.20	3.39	13.19	3.10

Note. M = Mean; SD = Standard deviation; VCP = Videoconference Psychotherapy; FF= Face-to-face; ADIS = Anxiety Disorders Interview Schedule for DSM-IV, PSWQ = Penn-State Worry Questionnaire, WAQ = Worry and Anxiety Questionnaire, IUS = Intolerance of Uncertainty Scale, BDI-II = Beck Depression Inventory-II, QOL-Psychol = WHO-QOL-Psychological subscale, QOL-Social = WHO-QOL-Social relations subscale.

Main effects for all conditions were statistically non-significant (see Table 3), with partial eta-squares of 0.001 for the ADIS-IV, 0.01 for the PSQW, 0.006 for the WAQ, 0.009 for the IUS, 0.000 for the BDI-II, 0.004 for the WHO-QOL-Psychological subscale, and 0.009 for the WHO-QOL-Social relations subscale, respectively.

Time by Condition interaction contrasts comparing CBT-IU delivered by VCP and delivered face-to-face revealed very small effect sizes for all variables: ADIS-IV (pre/post F(1,146) = 0.006, $p = 0.938$, partial eta-squared = 0.000, difference in improvement = −0.03; pre/6-month follow-up F(1,146) = 0.762, $p = 0.384$, partial eta-squared = 0.005, difference in improvement = −0.29; pre/12-month follow-up (1,146) = 0.667, $p = 0.42$, partial eta-squared = 0.005, difference in improvement = −0.27), the PSWQ (pre/post F(1,146) = 0.822, $p = 0.323$, partial eta-squared = 0.007, difference in improvement = 2.1; pre/6-month follow-up F(1,146) = 1.364, $p = 0.245$, partial eta-squared = 0.009, difference in improvement = 2.6; pre/12-month follow-up (1,146) = 1.314, $p = 0.245$, partial eta-squared = 0.009, difference in improvement = 2.5), the WAQ (pre/post F(1,146) = 0.024, $p = 0.877$, partial eta-squared = 0.000, difference in improvement = −0.3; pre/6-month follow-up F(1,146) = 0.159, $p = 0.69$, partial eta-squared = 0.001, difference in improvement = 0.8; pre/12-month follow-up (1,146) = 0.1.907, $p = 0.169$, partial eta-squared = 0.013, difference in improvement = 2.8), the IUS (pre/post F(1,146) = 0.138, $p = 0.711$, partial eta-squared = 0.001, difference in improvement = 1.4; pre/6-month follow-up F(1,146) = 0.593, $p = 0.442$, partial eta-squared = 0.004, difference in improvement = 2.9; pre/12-month follow-up (1,146) = 0.311, $p = 0.578$, partial eta-squared = 0.002, difference in improvement = 2.1), the BDI-II (pre/post F(1,146) = 0.257, $p = 0.613$, partial eta-squared = 0.000, difference in improvement = 0.88; pre/6-month follow-up F(1,146) = 0.006, $p = 0.938$, partial eta-squared = 0.000, difference in improvement = −0.13; pre/12-month follow-up (1,146) = 0.496, $p = 0.482$, partial eta-squared = 0.003, difference in improvement = 1.26), the WHO-QOL-Psychological subscale (pre/post F(1,146) = 0.213, $p = 0.645$, partial eta-squared = 0.002, difference in improvement = 0.14; pre/6-month follow-up F(1,146) = 0.387, $p = 0.535$, partial eta-squared = 0.003, difference in improvement = −0.26; pre/12-month follow-up (1,146) = 0.720, $p = 0.398$, partial eta-squared = 0.005, difference in improvement = 0.37), and the WHO-QOL-Social relations subscale (pre/post F(1,146) = 0.179, $p = 0.673$, partial eta-squared = 0.001, difference in improvement = 0.16; pre/6-month follow-up F(1,146) = 0.347, $p = 0.557$, partial eta-squared = 0.003, difference in improvement = 0.52; pre/12-month follow-up (1,146) = 0.198, $p = 0.657$, partial eta-squared = 0.001, difference in improvement = 0.35).

Table 3. Non-inferiority analyses of a RCT comparing the delivery of psychotherapy by videoconference or face-to-face to patients with generalized anxiety disorder (intent-to-treat) ($n = 148$).

Variable	Outcome Analysis-ANOVA				Non-Inferiority Analysis of the Statistical Interactions with a Strict Margin of Tolerance		
	Time F	Condition F	Interaction		Pre/Post	Pre/6-Month F-up	Pre/12-Month F-up
			F	eta squ.	W	W	W
ADIS	142.772 ***	0.095	0.617	0.004	2.27 **	3.07 **	3.01 **
PSWQ	151.523 ***	1.445	0.995	0.007	−3.16 ***	−3.35 ***	−3.32 ***
WAQ	129.289 ***	0.932	1.325	0.009	2.33 **	−2.57 **	−3.54 ***
IUS	129.984 ***	1.253	0.344	0.002	−2.54 **	−2.94 **	−2.72 **
BDI-II	72.406 ***	0.009	0.440	0.003	−2.66 **	2.25 **	−2.86 **
QOL-Psychol	45.621 ***	0.594	1.113	0.008	2.54 **	−2.75 **	3.03 **
QOL-Social	19.488 ***	1.293	0.182	0.001	2.49 **	2.71 **	2.77 **

Note. ADIS = Anxiety Disorders Interview Schedule for DSM-IV, PSWQ = Penn-State Worry Questionnaire, WAQ = Worry and Anxiety Questionnaire, IUS = Intolerance of Uncertainty Scale, BDI-II = Beck Depression Inventory-II, QOL-Psychol = WHO-QOL-Psychological subscale, QOL-Social = WHO-QOL-Social relations subscale. ANOVA results for the repeated pre–post by condition contrasts are reported in the text. W = Welch's t-test. The value of the W is negative when the test is applied to the lower bound and positive when it is applied to the upper bound. ** $p < 0.017$, *** $p < 0.001$. eta squ = partial eta-squared (a measure of effect size of the differential impact of the treatment from one condition to the other).

The non-inferiority tests (Table 3) showed that the impact of the treatment was statistically non-inferior when delivered by VCP compared to face-to-face for all measures. For the primary measure of efficacy (ADIS-IV), mean scores improved from pre to post-treatment on average by 44.47% in the VCP condition and by 42.44% in the face-to-face condition. Using the cut-off severity score of 4 on ADIS-IV, 68% participants in the VCP condition no longer met diagnostic criteria for GAD (vs. 57% in the face-to-face condition) at post-treatment, 64% (vs. 61%) at 6-month follow-up, and 65% (vs. 62%) at 12-month follow-up. No statistical analyses were conducted on remission rates to avoid redundancy with the ADIS-IV severity scores. A visual representation of the results is provided in Figure 2 in the form of a line chart with 95% confidence intervals and a waterfall bar chart of each individual's change from pre to post-treatment. Only five participants who completed the treatment (one in VCP, four in face-to-face therapy) reported no improvement on the ADIS-IV at post-treatment. The remaining participants with no change illustrate the impact of the intent-to-treat methodology. One participant (in the face-to-face condition) reported a deterioration of 1 point at post-treatment.

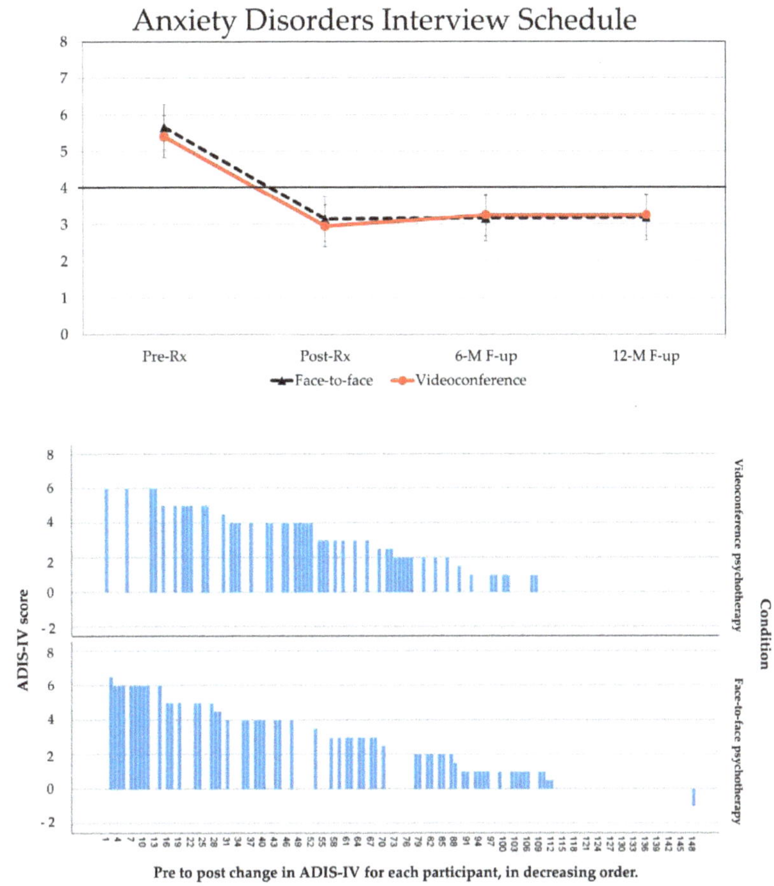

Figure 2. Visual representations of the results on the ADIS-IV primary outcome measure for 148 adults diagnosed with GAD who received cognitive-behavior therapy in videoconference (VCP) or face-to-face, with data aggregated by condition (line-graph, top) and pre to post change data reported for each individual (waterfall bar chart, bottom).

As recommended [77], non-inferiority analyses were also conducted with treatment completers (i.e., per protocol; see also Appendix A for results from MLM analyses). The analyses of the treatment completers sample replicated the results from the intent-to-treat sample, as shown in Table 4, with the exception of the measure of change in global psychological quality of life from pre-treatment to 6-month follow-up. In this case, the probability of the non-inferiority tests was lower than 0.05 ($p = 0.03$) but did not reach the Bonferroni corrected level of significance due to lack of power (see the Figure in Appendix A for a visual illustration of the results). If the tolerance margin for defining a difference as negligible would have been set at 12% instead of 10%, the non-inferiority test would have met the Bonferroni correction. Using the cut-off severity score of 4 on ADIS-IV, 90% participants in the VCP condition no longer met diagnostic criteria for GAD (vs. 67% in the face-to-face condition) at post-treatment, 85% (vs. 72%) at 6-month follow-up, and 87% (vs. 74%) at 12-month follow-up.

Table 4. Non-inferiority analyses for participants who completed the treatment (n = 117).

Variable	Non-Inferiority Analysis of the Statistical Interactions with a Strict Margin of Tolerance		
	Pre/Post W	Pre/6-Month F-up W	Pre/12-Month F-up W
Anxiety Disorders Interview Schedule for DSM-IV	−2.98 **	2.01 *	−1.96 *
Penn-State Worry Questionnaire	−1.87 ***	−4.27 ***	−4.15 ***
Worry and Anxiety Questionnaire	−2.6 **	−3.38 ***	−4.56 ***
Intolerance of Uncertainty Scale	−3.06 **	−3.63 ***	−3.36 ***
Beck Depression Inventory-II	−2.91 **	−2.33 **	−3.12 **
WHO-QOL-Psychological subscale	2.94 **	−1.91 *	3.47 ***
WHO-QOL-Social relations subscale	2.52 **	2.81 **	2.86 **

Note. W = Welch's t-test. The value of the W is negative when the test is applied to the lower bound and positive when it is applied to the upper bound. * $p < 0.5$, ** $p < 0.017$, *** $p < 0.001$.

To document the potential effects of sex, the presence of at least one comorbid disorder, medication use, previous psychotherapy, recruitment site, and psychotherapist site, analyses were conducted by considering these variables as independent factors and repeating the main repeated measures analyses for each factor. The only statistically significant interaction was found for the effect of psychotherapist site for the measures of depressed mood and quality of life in social relations. The statistically significant interaction effects for psychotherapist site did not influence the results of the non-inferiority analyses (i.e., what was statistically significant remained statistically significant, and vice versa), but the findings needed to be investigated. The Time by Treatment condition by Psychotherapist site interaction was statistically significant for the BDI-II (F(8.24,414) = 2.1, p = 0.034, partial eta-squared = 0.06) and the WHO-QOL-Social relations subscale (F(9.66,384) = 1.93, p = 0.042, partial eta-squared = 0.06). Probing the interactions revealed that the Time by Treatment condition interaction contrast was statistically significant for two psychotherapist sites. Face-to-face CBT seemed more impactful on these two measures than VCP when comparing the effect of psychotherapists from the Montréal site to those from the Gatineau site. A detailed exploration of the data revealed that there was less comorbidity in participants treated face-to-face by psychotherapists from the Montréal site (n = 16 co-diagnosed disorders) than from the Gatineau site (n = 26 co-diagnosed disorders). The difference in number of comorbid diagnoses per participant was not statistically significant (F(1,67) = 0.41, p = 0.53, partial eta-squared = 0.006), but the number of comorbid disorders was statistically significantly associated with more severe depressed mood (r = 0.37, p = 0.002) and lower quality of life in social relations (r = −0.28, p = 0.027) at pre-treatment.

3.4. Predictors Change in GAD Severity at Posttreatment

Factors potentially associated with treatment efficacy, as measured by the residualized change in ADIS-IV scores from pre to post-treatment, were examined in a hierarchical regression analysis. The common therapy factors (i.e., motivation, working alliance, perceived therapist competence and client satisfaction) were entered in the first step of the regression. Treatment condition (VCP or face-to-face therapy) and psychotherapist treatment site were also entered as methodological controls. The factor specific to CBT-IU, change in intolerance of uncertainty, was entered in the second step to test its contribution to the regression model over and above the factors entered in the first step. The final regression model was statistically significant (F(7,112) = 10.05, p < 0.001, R^2 = 0.62, Adjusted R^2 = 0.35). The second step in the hierarchical regression significantly contributed to the final model (F change (1,113) = 59.4, p < 0.001, change in R^2 = 0.32). Table 5 details the contribution of each variable to the final model. Consistent with the non-inferiority finding for the Time by Condition interaction with the IUS, testing the direct impact of treatment conditions on the residualized change in intolerance of uncertainty was not statistically significant (F change (1,112) = 0.031, $p = 0.86$, change in $R^2 = 0.00$) and did not reduce the significant role of intolerance of uncertainty in the regression ($t = 6.99$, $p < 0.001$, semi-partial correlation = 0.52). To support the discussion of the findings, Table 6 shows the correlation among the various measures used in the regression. In the hierarchical regression, the role of sex, age, income, education, living alone, medication use, previous psychotherapy and the presence of at least one comorbid disorder were also explored. None of the aforementioned variables significantly predicted outcome or changed the conclusions of the regression analysis.

Table 5. Contribution of non-specific and specific factors of CBT for GAD when delivered by videoconference or face-to-face at the second step of a hierarchical regression predicting improvements in ADIS-IV ratings.

	std Beta	*t*	*sig. p*	*Simple corr.*	*Partial corr.*	*Semi-Partial corr.*
Treatment condition	−0.12	−1.6	0.118	−0.11	−0.15	−0.12
Center providing psychotherapy	−0.03	−0.45	0.657	0.04	−0.04	−0.03
Motivation (Session 1)	−0.05	−0.67	0.502	−0.07	−0.06	−0.05
Working alliance (Session 7)	0.21	1.71	0.087	−0.07	0.16	0.13
Perceived therapists' competence (Session 7)	−0.06	−0.65	0.52	−0.08	−0.06	−0.05
Client satisfaction (at post)	−0.07	−0.64	0.522	−0.19	−0.06	−0.05
IUS Residualized change	0.62	7.71	<0.001	0.60	0.59	0.57

Note. ADIS-IV = Anxiety Disorders Interview Schedule-IV, IUS = Intolerance of Uncertainty Scale.

Table 6. Pearson correlations among the psychological variables used in the hierarchical regression.

	Motivation (Session 1)	**Working Alliance (Session 7)**	**Perceived Therapists' Competence (Session 7)**	**Client Satisfaction (at Post)**	**IUS Residualized Change**
ADIS-IV Residualized change	−0.07	−0.07	−0.08	−0.19 *	0.60 ***
Motivation (Session 1)		0.23 **	0.09	0.16 *	−0.08
Working alliance (Session 7)			0.66 ***	0.67 ***	−0.25 **
Perceived therapists' competence (Session 7)				0.44 ***	−0.14
Client satisfaction (at post)					−0.34 ***

Note. ADIS-IV = Anxiety Disorders Interview Schedule-IV; IUS = Intolerance of Uncertainty Scale. * $p < 0.05$, ** $p < 0.01$, *** $p < 0.001$.

4. Discussion

The motivation for the current study was to show that delivering CBT for GAD by videoconference would not be detrimental or different from delivering it face-to-face. The study was built on a non-inferiority randomized controlled design, with the intent to show VCP's effectiveness at post-treatment and over the long-term using a small margin of tolerance in difference in outcome. Based on previous findings from studies of face-to-face psychotherapy, it was also hypothesized that change in intolerance of uncertainty would make a statistically significant contribution to the prediction of treatment improvement over and above the effect of non-specific predictors of outcome such as motivation, working alliance, perceived therapist competence, and treatment satisfaction.

The sample consisted of adults from five different sites, with clinically severe GAD, significant depressed mood, and high comorbidity rates. CBT-IU led to statistically significant and very large changes on all measures, with statistically significant non-inferiority results based on a margin of tolerance of 10%. The analyses confirmed, with an RCT conducted according to CONSORT guidelines, what has been found in previous clinical trials for other anxiety disorders [30,32,34,77] and other non-anxiety disorders [26,28,33]. In the current study, empirical evidence was obtained for the treatment of GAD. Specifically, treatment efficacy, as measured with severity ratings from the ADIS-IV, was large and maintained at follow-ups. None of the data on the primary measure of efficacy suggested that VCP may be less effective than face-to-face psychotherapy. When the impact of the treatment was compared using two other measures of GAD severity, the PSWQ and the WAQ, the non-inferiority findings remained the same, even after correcting for the number of comparisons. General measures of improvement such a depressed mood and quality of life also revealed a lack of significant difference within the strict margin of tolerance set a priori. The analyses were performed on the intent-to-treat sample and were essentially replicated using the treatment completers sample. Although the results of the current study were somewhat expected given previous findings [16–21], the efficacy of CBT-IU had yet to be conclusively documented with VCP.

Documenting the predictors of change in the severity of GAD was important. The finding that change in intolerance of uncertainty was statistically non-inferior in VCP compared to face-to-face therapy, and significantly associated with treatment success, is consistent with expectations about CBT for GAD [12,52]. In the hierarchical multiple regression predicting change in ADIS-IV scores, change in intolerance of uncertainty was the only statistically significant predictor. The statistically limited role of working alliance, motivation and psychotherapist competence in predicting treatment outcome has sometimes been reported in studies on CBT [34,78] and must not be interpreted negatively. In the current study, these variables were significantly related to client satisfaction and, most importantly in the case of the working alliance, to change in intolerance of uncertainty. Their role must be interpreted in the context of comparing non-specific versus specific predictors of improvement in a manualized treatment for an anxiety disorder. In CBT, working alliance, motivation, competence and satisfaction are considered prerequisites for effective psychotherapy [79]; they enable patients to engage in changing the dysfunctional patterns that maintain their disorder. They are expected to be statistically related to treatment outcome. However, predictors of change based on validated psychopathology models of specific mental disorders should be more important predictors of outcome than non-specific predictors when it comes to treatments based on these models. Until now, that remained to be established with VCP for CBT-IU of GAD. Other forms of psychotherapy and other mental disorders may require a different investment to build, nurture and negotiate ruptures in alliance [57]. In terms of the dynamic mechanisms of CBT, Bouchard et al. [80] analyzed the role of working alliance in VCP and showed that telepresence (the feeling of being in the same psychotherapy room as the therapist) facilitates the development of a sound working alliance, which in turn enables patients and therapists to work on changing the dysfunctional behaviors and mental associations with perceived threat that are required for the reduction in the symptoms of anxiety disorders.

Differential statistical analyses for sex, the presence of a comorbid disorder, taking medication, previous psychotherapy, recruitment site, and psychotherapist site did not reveal any statistically significant difference in VCP versus face-to-face therapy, except for the impact of psychotherapist site on measures of depressed mood and quality of life in interpersonal relations. The relative impact of VCP compared to face-to-face therapy differed on these two variables when comparing two specific sites. These unexpected differences did not influence the conclusions of the main analyses and were observed only on variables measuring the generalization of results. The treatment was manualized, adherence to the manual was excellent, there was no significant psychotherapist site difference in perceived therapist competence, severity of depressed mood, quality of life, treatment outcome on all other variables, or the presence or absence of a comorbid disorder. A potential explanation is that psychotherapists in one center had to deal with slightly less comorbid cases randomly assigned to face-to-face therapy than other centers and conditions. However, the presence of comorbid disorders was not associated with treatment outcome. The impact of comorbidity on how VCP generalizes to factors not specifically targeted in the treatment manual during CBT warrants further investigation.

Contrary to expectations, participants in the VCP condition reported working alliance and perceived psychotherapist competence scores at Session 7 that were significantly higher than those of participants in the face-to-face condition. The statistically significant difference in the strength of the working alliance was not observed in this sample after the first few therapy sessions [81], and it is therefore not likely to be attributable to the effect of randomization. Interestingly, working alliance was significantly and strongly correlated with perceived therapist competence and treatment satisfaction, and to a smaller degree with change in intolerance of uncertainty. Perceived therapist competence was also significantly correlated with treatment satisfaction. In the context of a non-inferiority trial, these results were interpreted as suggesting that VCP may not be less effective than face-to-face CBT (for more on the treatment alliance in VCP, see also [34,82–84]). It is possible that in the current study, which was conducted before the COVID-19 pandemic, patients perceived their psychotherapists as more competent in the VCP condition, because of the additional challenge imposed by the use of technology, which positively impacted their working alliance. Further studies are required to explain why, under some circumstances, working alliance and perceived psychotherapist competence could be stronger after a few sessions in VCP than in face-to-face psychotherapy.

The CBT protocol used in this study focused on intolerance of uncertainty, was based on the 6-module version of CBT-IU, used cognitive restructuring and exposure strategies, and lasted 15 weeks. Can these findings be generalized to variations in CBT for GAD, for example a treatment based on a different theoretical model, e.g., acceptance-based behavior therapy [85], without a problem-solving module, using mostly behavioral experiments [18], or shorter in duration? Empirical findings and replications are always important [86], but the key question is why these variations would be influenced by delivering CBT by videoconference. For psychotherapeutic modalities that may be less compatible with VCP (e.g., group psychotherapy [87]), or for those that place an additional strain on motivation or working alliance (e.g., more intensive treatments), it is imperative to test their effectiveness when using videoconference. For more "standard" treatments, non-inferiority is very likely to be replicated. However, conducting clinical trials to document the efficacy, or non-inferiority, of VCP for other disorders than anxiety-related disorders and major depression remains pressing. Indeed, most studies using videoconferencing have been conducted on anxiety-related disorders and major depression [26,29,30,32,33,88]. The COVID-19 pandemic revealed the relevance of VCP and the lack of information about its efficacy for several disorders. Although not all mental disorders and forms of psychotherapy have solid empirical support when the treatment is delivered face-to-face, there is a need for many more clinical trials using VCP and other eHealth modalities [27].

Research on VCP has significantly evolved from the early clinical trials decades ago [89–91]. Until recently, it was not possible to recommend using the Internet to conduct VCP with sufficient levels of quality and confidentiality. The leap in technology over the last few years, between the moment the current study began and finished, is impressive. It is now possible for patients to receive VCP without having to commute to specific locations where secured and expensive videoconference systems are installed on dedicated communication networks, as was the case for the current study. This turn of events raises questions about the generalizability of our results and suggests several new lines of research. In the current study, the physical settings for the psychotherapy sessions were those one would expect for a mental health clinic. Now, patients can engage in VCP sessions at home, at work between meetings, or in a public café using the free unprotected public Wi-Fi network with a smartphone while simultaneously consulting other information on a laptop. Experimental studies are beginning to examine how to set up VCP to replicate face-to-face communication using computer-based systems (such as replicating direct eye contact [92]) and how these differences in settings can impact the psychotherapeutic process. For example, Grondin et al. [93] reported that altered eye contact in VCP may not be as detrimental as previously believed for the perception of empathy from a psychotherapist. Several practical questions remain unanswered, and these could have an impact on the contexts in which our results could be generalized, such as how to ensure that patients are in an adequate environment for psychotherapy (i.e., no distracting stimuli, secured confidentiality), which software options really make a significant contribution to an optimal experience (e.g., using the picture-in-picture option [94]), or which factors contribute to patients being ready to start their psychotherapy session (e.g., regaining composure in a waiting room before a session [95]). The past experiences of patients and psychotherapists using videoconference also merit study, as attraction to novelty and previous negative experiences with the technology may influence the impact of VCP [96]. Documenting how VCP may reduce barriers for accessing care also deserves to be studied more thoroughly [24].

Additional limitations of this study must be acknowledged. The study was conducted with volunteers of White ethnicity who agreed to be randomized either to face-to-face CBT or CBT by VCP. Results may not fully apply to people from other cultures or who do not have the choice of receiving VCP or not, either because of public health safety recommendations (e.g., imposed confinement due to COVID-19) or lack of a better alternative. In addition, participants were all motivated to engage in psychotherapy, which may not always be the case in routine clinical practice. The CBT-IU treatment protocol [74] used has evolved over the years to focus more specifically on intolerance of uncertainty [18], and treatment strategies such as problem-solving are no longer germane to the protocol. The treatment was delivered by graduate students in clinical psychology, which is a population that has been shown to be able to successfully use VCP to deliver evidence-based treatment [97]. More seasoned psychotherapists may hesitate to use VCP for a variety of reasons [96,98], may diverge from the application of already established treatment manuals to adapt the treatment to their liking [99], or may use exposure strategies less frequently than recommended [100]. The working alliance was measured with the total score, as opposed to focusing on each subscale [101], and according to patients' perspective. Analyses of the psychotherapists' perspective confirmed the quality of the working alliance in our sample [81], but analyses of video recordings of the therapy sessions would reveal much more interesting and nuanced observations of the working alliance, of how ruptures in alliance are handled and of how ruptures in acceptance of VCP technology could impact intersubjectivity and the treatment [102].

5. Conclusions

This study confirmed that CBT for GAD can be effectively delivered using videoconference technology. The nature of the treatment and it processes do not seem to be significantly disrupted when delivered remotely. Studies on VCP pave the way for a paradigm shift with regard to access to psychotherapy. Access to psychotherapy has traditionally been limited to geographical proximity. Patients can now access the psychotherapist of their choice despite geographic limitations. Mental health professionals can practice psychotherapy from their preferred location, including from rural areas with patients in urban centers. Access to a broader set of mental health professionals could help overcome cultural and expertise barriers faced by patients. However, this new situation has created challenges for organizations and governments providing mental health services. Patients can now ask for services from organizations that are not in their catchment area. Professionals can offer services based on their specialized expertise to patients in catchment areas that differ from the one served by their organization. The demands for services that cross legislative barriers will expand. Consequently, researchers will be called upon to provide empirical evidence to guide decisions about for whom VCP is appropriate, when and under which circumstances.

Author Contributions: Conceptualization, S.B., M.J.D., P.G., F.L., G.B., G.R. and A.M.; methodology, S.B., M.J.D., P.G., F.L., G.B., G.R. and A.M.; formal analysis, S.B. and G.C.; investigation, S.B., M.J.D., P.G., F.L., G.B., G.R. and A.M.; data curation, S.B., G.R. and G.C.; writing—original draft preparation, S.B. and G.C., writing—review and editing, S.B., M.J.D., P.G., F.L., G.B., G.C. and A.M.; supervision, S.B., P.G., F.L., G.B. and A.M.; project administration, G.R.; funding acquisition, S.B., P.G., F.L., G.B and A.M. All authors have read and agreed to the published version of the manuscript.

Funding: This research was funded by the Canadian Institutes of Health Research (#176854) and the Canada Research Chairs (#210762, 231039).

Institutional Review Board Statement: The study was conducted in accordance with the Declaration of Helsinki and approved by the Institutional Review Board of all five universities involved under the leadership of the Institutional Review Board of the Université du Québec en Outaouais (UQO protocol #1754). It was approved at UQO on June 5th 2013 and then submitted to each other institution for approval by their own IRB.

Informed Consent Statement: Informed consent was obtained from all subjects involved in the study. See Section 2.2 for more information.

Data Availability Statement: The dataset is not publicly available due to privacy and ethical restrictions. The data for this study are available upon request addressed directly to the Research Ethics Boards of the lead institution (comite.ethique@uqo.ca), which must first approve the request. If the request is approved, anonymized data supporting the conclusions of this manuscript will be made available by the corresponding author.

Conflicts of Interest: Stéphane Bouchard is the President of, and owns equity in, Cliniques et Développement In Virtuo, a spin-off company from the university that distributes virtual environments designed for the treatment of mental disorders. Geneviève Robillard is vice-president of, and owns equity in, Cliniques et Développement In Virtuo. The terms of these arrangements have been reviewed and approved by the Université du Québec en Outaouais in accordance with its conflict of interest policies. The current study does not involve virtual reality. Stéphane Bouchard has received honoraria for presenting research and giving workshops. He also receives royalties from books. The remaining authors report no financial relationships with commercial interests.

Appendix A

Multiple linear mixed (MLM) models were also used to conduct the outcome analyses leading to the non-inferiority analyses, as alternatives to more traditional general linear model repeated measures ANOVAs. The study does not address a multilevel research question [103], but approaching the analyses from the standpoint of multilevel data allows modeling the data without forcing the covariance matrix to sphericity (compound symmetry; i.e., not all participants in each condition are assumed to change in the same way over time and to have similar slopes). MLM also handles missing data with iterative estimation based on available information in the dataset instead of removing participants from the analysis, providing an alternative to intent-to-treat and completers analyses.

The MIXED linear procedure in SPSS 28 was used, with participants' ID as a second-level random effect and Time as a first-level fixed effect with residuals correlated within participants. An unstructured repeated covariance matrix was used for the final analyses, but a first-order autoregressive structure with homogenous variances and a diagonal structure were also tested and were all compared to a compound symmetry structure. The unstructured covariance matrix was theoretically better and provided a better fit to the data based on the AIC and BIC criteria, compared to the alternatives. Models were estimated using restricted maximum likelihood and Satterhwaite approximation. Estimated Marginal Means were computed based on the fitted model of each variable to produce the results illustrated in Figure A1.

Results of Mixed Linear Models with Condition (2) by Time (4) fixed main effects and random intercept for each participant are reported in Table 1. As the study focused on potential differences in treatment modalities, Condition by Time interaction contrasts are reported comparing end-points with pre-treatment. Results closely mirror those reported in the article, with very large treatment effects, and interactions that are not statistically significant and in the same magnitude of those reported in the more traditional analyses.

Table A1. Results of multilevel linear modeling analyses for a randomized control non-inferiority trial comparing the delivery of psychotherapy by videoconference or face-to-face to adults with generalized anxiety disorder ($n = 148$).

Variable	Multi Linear Modeling Tests of Fixed Effects					
	Time F	Condition F	Interaction F	Interaction Contrasts		
				Pre/post	Pre/6-Mo F-up	Pre/12-Mo F-up
ADIS	135.519 ***	2.762	0.519	1.113	0.007	0.012
PSWQ	114.037 ***	3.436	0.938	2.1	1.818	1.192
WAQ	129.011 ***	3.564	1.969	2.99	1.104	3.718
IUS	95.193 ***	5.104 *	0.857	1.66	1.775	0.676
BDI-II	60.481 ***	0.886	1.626	2.097	0.391	1.151
QOL-Psychol	43.106 ***	1.962	1.081	0.521	0.014	0.7
QOL-Social	13.991 ***	2.113	0.269	0.224	0.252	0.072

Note. ADIS = Anxiety Disorders Interview Schedule for DSM-IV, PSWQ = Penn-State Worry Questionnaire, WAQ = Worry and Anxiety Questionnaire, IUS = Intolerance of Uncertainty Scale, BDI-II = Beck Depression Inventory-II, QOL Psycho = WHO-QOL-Psychological subscale, QOL-Social = WHO-QOL-Social relations subscale. * $p < 0.5$, *** $p < 0.001$.

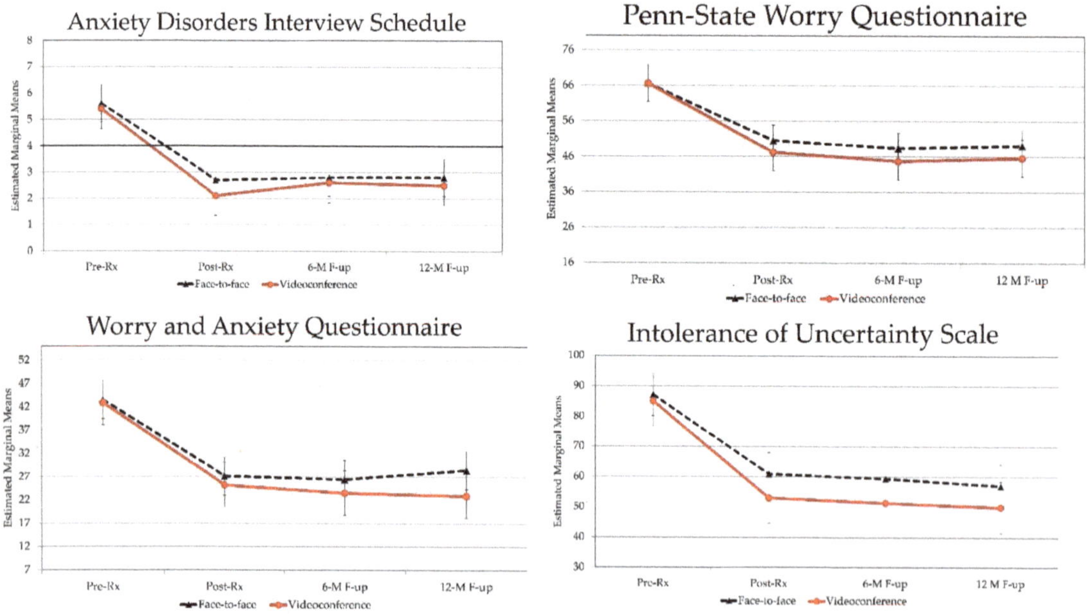

Figure A1. *Cont.*

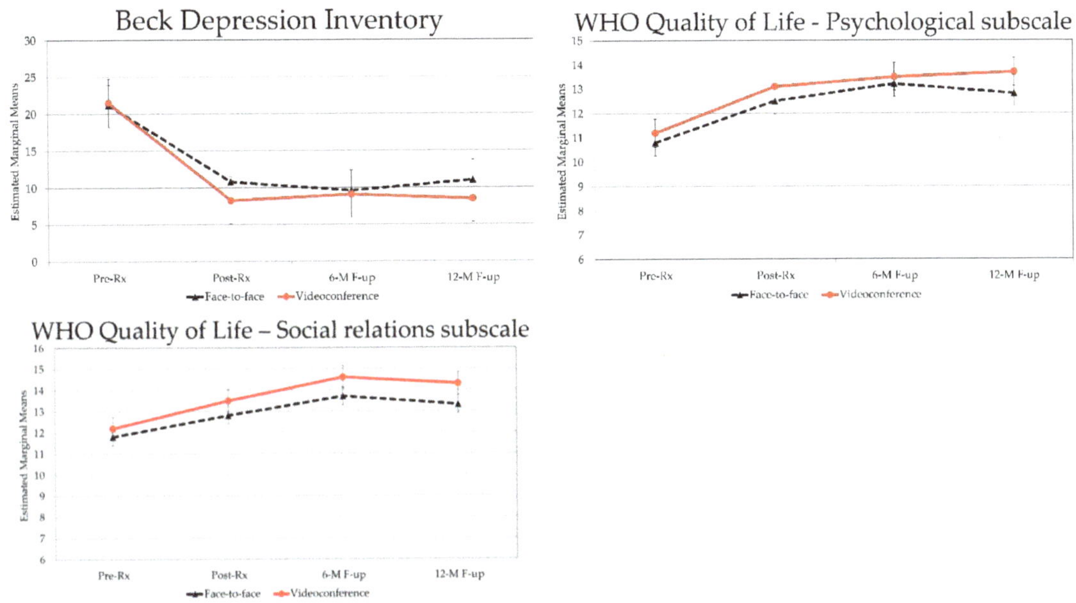

Figure A1. Illustration of the impact of cognitive-behavior therapy delivered by videoconference or face-to-face based on Estimated Marginal Means from Multilevel Linear Models.

References

1. American Psychiatric Association. *Diagnostic and Statistical Manual of Mental Disorders (DSM-5)*; American Psychiatric Association Publishing: Washington, DC, USA, 2013. [CrossRef]
2. Kessler, R.C.; Walters, E.E.; Wittchen, H.-U. Epidemiology. In *Generalized Anxiety Disorder: Advances in Research and Practice*; Heimberg, R.G., Turk, C.L., Mennin, D.S., Eds.; The Guilford Press: New York, NY, USA, 2004; pp. 29–50.
3. Tyrer, P.; Baldwin, D. Generalised anxiety disorder. *Lancet* **2006**, *368*, 2156–2166. [CrossRef]
4. Rueter, M.A.; Holm, K.E.; Burzette, R.; Kim, K.J.; Conger, R.D. Mental health of rural young adults: Prevalence of psychiatric Disorders, comorbidity, and service utilization. *Community Ment. Health J.* **2007**, *43*, 229–249. [CrossRef]
5. Simmons, L.A.; Havens, J.R. Comorbid substance and mental disorders among rural Americans: Results from the national comorbidity survey. *J. Affect. Disord.* **2007**, *99*, 265–271. [CrossRef] [PubMed]
6. Koerner, N.; Dugas, M.J.; Savard, P.; Gaudet, A.; Turcotte, J.; Marchand, A. The economic burden of anxiety disorders in Canada. *Can. Psychol. Can.* **2004**, *45*, 191–201. [CrossRef]
7. Greenberg, P.E.; Sisitsky, T.; Kessler, R.C.; Finkelstein, S.N.; Berndt, E.R.; Davidson, J.R.T.; Ballenger, J.C.; Fyer, A.J. The economic burden of anxiety disorders in the 1990s. *J. Clin. Psychiatry* **1999**, *60*, 427–435. [CrossRef]
8. Bandelow, B.; Sagebiel, A.; Belz, M.; Görlich, Y.; Michaelis, S.; Wedekind, D. Enduring effects of psychological treatments for anxiety disorders: Meta-analysis of follow-up studies. *Br. J. Psychiatry* **2018**, *212*, 333–338. [CrossRef] [PubMed]
9. Carl, E.; Witcraft, S.M.; Kauffman, B.Y.; Gillespie, E.M.; Becker, E.S.; Cuijpers, P.; Van Ameringen, M.; Smits, J.A.J.; Powers, M.B. Psychological and pharmacological treatments for generalized anxiety disorder (GAD): A meta-analysis of randomized controlled trials. *Cogn. Behav. Ther.* **2019**, *49*, 1–21. [CrossRef]
10. Carpenter, J.K.; Andrews, L.A.; Witcraft, S.M.; Powers, M.B.; Smits, J.A.J.; Hofmann, S.G. Cognitive behavioral therapy for anxiety and related disorders: A meta-analysis of randomized placebo-controlled trials. *Depress. Anxiety* **2018**, *35*, 502–514. [CrossRef]
11. Cuijpers, P.; Sijbrandij, M.; Koole, S.; Huibers, M.; Berking, M.; Andersson, G. Psychological treatment of generalized anxiety disorder: A meta-analysis. *Clin. Psychol. Rev.* **2014**, *34*, 130–140. [CrossRef]
12. Dugas, M.J.; Gagnon, F.; Ladouceur, R.; Freeston, M.H. Generalized anxiety disorder: A preliminary test of a conceptual model. *Behav. Res. Ther.* **1998**, *36*, 215–226. [CrossRef]
13. Robichaud, M.; Koerner, N.; Dugas, M.J. *Cognitive-Behavioral Treatment for Generalized Anxiety Disorder: From Science to Practice*, 2nd ed.; Routledge: New York, NY, USA, 2019.
14. Hebert, E.A.; Dugas, M.J. Behavioral experiments for intolerance of uncertainty: Challenging the unknown in the treatment of generalized anxiety disorder. *Cogn. Behav. Pract.* **2018**, *26*, 421–436. [CrossRef]
15. Dugas, M.J.; Ladouceur, R. Treatment of GAD: Targeting intolerance of uncertainty in two types of worry. *Behav Modif* **2000**, *24*, 635–657. [CrossRef]

16. Dugas, M.J.; Ladouceur, R.; Léger, E.; Freeston, M.H.; Langolis, F.; Provencher, M.D.; Boisvert, J.-M. Group cognitive-behavioral therapy for generalized anxiety disorder: Treatment outcome and long-term follow-up. *J. Consult. Clin. Psychol.* **2003**, *71*, 821–825. [CrossRef]
17. Dugas, M.J.; Brillon, P.; Savard, P.; Turcotte, J.; Gaudet, A.; Ladouceur, R.; Leblanc, R.; Gervais, N.J. A randomized clinical trial of cognitive-behavioral therapy and applied relaxation for adults with generalized anxiety disorder. *Behav. Ther.* **2010**, *41*, 46–58. [CrossRef]
18. Dugas, M.J.; Sexton, K.A.; Hebert, E.A.; Bouchard, S.; Gouin, J.-P.; Shafran, R. Behavioral experiments for intolerance of uncertainty: A randomized clinical trial for adults with generalized anxiety disorder. *Behav. Ther.* 2022; *advance online publication*. [CrossRef]
19. Gosselin, P.; Ladouceur, R.; Morin, C.M.; Dugas, M.J.; Baillargeon, L. Benzodiazepine discontinuation among adults with GAD: A randomized trial of cognitive-behavioral therapy. *J. Consult. Clin. Psychol.* **2006**, *74*, 908–919. [CrossRef]
20. Ladouceur, R.; Dugas, M.J.; Freeston, M.H.; Léger, E.; Gagnon, F.; Thibodeau, N. Efficacy of a cognitive–behavioral treatment for generalized anxiety disorder: Evaluation in a controlled clinical trial. *J. Consult. Clin. Psychol.* **2000**, *68*, 957–964. [CrossRef]
21. van der Heiden, C.; Muris, P.; van der Molen, H.T. Randomized controlled trial on the effectiveness of metacognitive therapy and intolerance-of-uncertainty therapy for generalized anxiety disorder. *Behav. Res. Ther.* **2012**, *50*, 100–109. [CrossRef] [PubMed]
22. Jensen, E.J.; Wieling, E.; Mendenhall, T. A phenomenological study of clinicians' perspectives on barriers to rural mental health care. *J. Rural Ment. Health* **2020**, *44*, 51–61. [CrossRef]
23. Roufeil, L.; Lipzker, A. Psychology services in rural and remote Australia. *Bull. Aust. Psychol. Soc.* **2007**, *29*, 8.
24. Tambling, R.R.; Hynes, K.C.; D'Aniello, C. Are Barriers to Psychotherapy Treatment Seeking Indicators of Social Determinants of Health? A Critical Review of the Literature. *Am. J. Fam. Ther.* 2021; *advance online publication*. [CrossRef]
25. Bornheimer, L.A.; Verdugo, J.L.; Holzworth, J.; Smith, F.N.; Himle, J.A. Mental health provider perspectives of the COVID-19 pandemic impact on service delivery: A focus on challenges in remote engagement, suicide risk assessment, and treatment of psychosis. *BMC Health Serv. Res.* **2022**, *22*, 718. [CrossRef] [PubMed]
26. Batastini, A.B.; Paprzycki, P.; Jones, A.C.; MacLean, N. Are videoconferenced mental and behavioral health services just as good as in-person? A meta-analysis of a fast-growing practice. *Clin. Psychol. Rev.* **2020**, *83*, 101944. [CrossRef]
27. Bennett, C.B.; Ruggero, C.J.; Sever, A.C.; Yanouri, L. eHealth to redress psychotherapy access barriers both new and old: A review of reviews and meta-analyses. *J. Psychother. Integr.* **2020**, *30*, 188–207. [CrossRef]
28. Joint Task Force for the Development of Telepsychology Guidelines for Psychologists. Guidelines for the practice of telepsychology. *Am. Psychol.* **2013**, *68*, 791–800. [CrossRef] [PubMed]
29. Lin, T.; Heckman, T.G.; Anderson, T. The efficacy of synchronous teletherapy versus in-person therapy: A meta-analysis of randomized clinical trials. *Clin. Psychol. Sci. Pract.* **2022**, *29*, 167–178. [CrossRef]
30. Matsumoto, K.; Hamatani, S.; Shimizu, E. Effectiveness of videoconference-delivered cognitive behavioral therapy for adults with psychiatric disorders: Systematic and meta-analytic review. *J. Med. Internet Res.* **2021**, *23*, e31293. [CrossRef] [PubMed]
31. Song, L.-L.; Foster, C. Patients' and therapists' experiences of CBT videoconferencing in anxiety disorders. *Cogn. Behav. Ther.* **2022**, *15*, E14. [CrossRef]
32. Berryhill, M.B.; Halli-Tierney, A.; Culmer, N.; Williams, N.; Betancourt, A.; King, M.; Ruggles, H. Videoconferencing psychological therapy and anxiety: A systematic review. *Fam. Pract.* **2018**, *36*, 53–63. [CrossRef] [PubMed]
33. Thomas, N.; McDonald, C.; de Boer, K.; Brand, R.M.; Nedeljkovic, M.; Seabrook, L. Review of the current empirical literature on using videoconferencing to deliver individual psychotherapies to adults with mental health problems. *Psychol. Psychother. Theory Res. Pract.* **2021**, *94*, 854–883. [CrossRef] [PubMed]
34. Bouchard, S.; Allard, M.; Robillard, G.; Dumoulin, S.; Guitard, T.; Loranger, C.; Green-Demers, I.; Marchand, A.; Renaud, P.; Cournoyer, L.-G.; et al. Videoconferencing psychotherapy for panic disorder and agoraphobia: Outcome and treatment processes from a non-randomized non-inferiority trial. *Front. Psychol.* **2020**, *11*, 2164. [CrossRef] [PubMed]
35. Liu, L.; Thorp, S.R.; Moreno, L.; Wells, S.Y.; Glassman, L.H.; Busch, A.C.; Zamora, T.; Rodgers, C.S.; Allard, C.; Morland, L.A.; et al. Videoconferencing psychotherapy for veterans with PTSD: Results from a randomized controlled non-inferiority trial. *J. Telemed. Telecare* **2019**, *26*, 507–519. [CrossRef]
36. Morland, L.A.; Greene, C.J.; Rosen, C.S.; Foy, D.; Reilly, P.; Shore, J.; He, Q.; Frueh, B.C. Telemedicine for Anger Management Therapy in a Rural Population of Combat Veterans with Posttraumatic Stress Disorder: A randomized noninferiority trial. *J. Clin. Psychiatry* **2010**, *71*, 855–863. [CrossRef]
37. Morland, L.A.; Mackintosh, M.-A.; Greene, C.J.; Rosen, C.S.; Chard, K.M.; Resick, P.; Frueh, B.C. Cognitive processing therapy for posttraumatic stress disorder delivered to rural veterans via telemental health. *J. Clin. Psychiatry* **2014**, *75*, 470–476. [CrossRef]
38. Morland, L.A.; Mackintosh, M.-A.; Rosen, C.S.; Willis, E.; Resick, P.; Chard, K.; Frueh, B.C. Telemedicine versus in-person delivery of cognitive processing therapy for women with posttraumatic stress disorder: A randomized noninferiority trial. *Depress. Anxiety* **2015**, *32*, 811–820. [CrossRef]
39. Griffiths, L.; Blignault, I.; Yellowlees, P. Telemedicine as a means of delivering cognitive-behavioural therapy to rural and remote mental health clients. *J. Telemed. Telecare* **2006**, *12*, 136–140. [CrossRef]
40. Théberge-Lapointe, N.; Marchand, A.; Langlois, F.; Gosselin, P.; Watts, S. Efficacy of a cognitive-behavioural therapy administered by videoconference for generalized anxiety disorder. *Eur. Rev. Appl. Psychol.* **2014**, *65*, 9–17. [CrossRef]

41. Steketee, G.; Shapiro, L.J. Predicting behavioral treatment outcome for agoraphobia and obsessive compulsive disorder. *Clin. Psychol. Rev.* **1995**, *15*, 317–346. [CrossRef]
42. Taylor, S.; Abramowitz, J.S.; McKay, D. Non-adherence and non-response in the treatment of anxiety disorders. *J. Anxiety Disord.* **2012**, *26*, 583–589. [CrossRef]
43. Hofmann, S.G.; Richey, J.A.; Asnaani, A.; Sawyer, A.T. Avoiding treatment failure in social anxiety disorder. In *Avoiding Treatment Failures in the Anxiety Disorders*; Otto, M.W., Hofmann, S.G., Eds.; Springer Science & Business Media: New York, NY, USA, 2010; pp. 169–184. [CrossRef]
44. Keeley, M.L.; Storch, E.A.; Merlo, L.J.; Geffken, G.R. Clinical predictors of response to cognitive-behavioral therapy for obsessive–compulsive disorder. *Clin. Psychol. Rev.* **2008**, *28*, 118–130. [CrossRef]
45. Taylor, S. *Understanding and Treating Panic Disorder: Cognitive-Behavioural Approaches*; Wiley: Hoboken, NJ, USA, 2000.
46. Watanabe, N.; Furukawa, T.A.; Chen, J.; Kinoshita, Y.; Nakano, Y.; Ogawa, S.; Funayama, T.; Ietsugu, T.; Noda, Y. Change in quality of life and their predictors in the long-term follow-up after group cognitive behavioral therapy for social anxiety disorder: A prospective cohort study. *BMC Psychiatry* **2010**, *10*, 81. [CrossRef]
47. Wolitzky-Taylor, K.B.; Arch, J.J.; Rosenfield, D.; Craske, M.G. Moderators and non-specific predictors of treatment outcome for anxiety disorders: A comparison of cognitive behavioral therapy to acceptance and commitment therapy. *J. Consult. Clin. Psychol.* **2012**, *80*, 786–799. [CrossRef]
48. Buchholz, J.L.; Abramowitz, J.S. The therapeutic alliance in exposure therapy for anxiety-related disorders: A critical review. *J. Anxiety Disord* **2020**, *70*, 102194. [CrossRef] [PubMed]
49. Hofmann, S.G.; Barlow, D.H.; Papp, L.A.; Detweiler, M.F.; Ray, S.E.; Shear, M.K.; Woods, S.W.; Gorman, J.M. Pretreatment Attrition in a Comparative Treatment Outcome Study on Panic Disorder. *Am. J. Psychiatry* **1998**, *155*, 43–47. [CrossRef] [PubMed]
50. Keller, S.M.; Zoellner, L.A.; Feeny, N.C. Understanding factors associated with early therapeutic alliance in PTSD treatment: Adherence, childhood sexual abuse history, and social support. *J. Consult. Clin. Psychol.* **2010**, *78*, 974–979. [CrossRef] [PubMed]
51. Milosevic, I.; Levy, H.C.; Alcolado, G.; Radomsky, A.S. The treatment acceptability/adherence scale: Moving beyond the assessment of treatment effectiveness. *Cogn. Behav. Ther.* **2015**, *44*, 456–469. [CrossRef] [PubMed]
52. Bomyea, J.; Ramsawh, H.; Ball, T.; Taylor, C.; Paulus, M.; Lang, A.; Stein, M. Intolerance of uncertainty as a mediator of reductions in worry in a cognitive behavioral treatment program for generalized anxiety disorder. *J. Anxiety Disord.* **2015**, *33*, 90–94. [CrossRef]
53. Wellek, S. *Testing Statistical Hypotheses of Equivalence and Noninferioty*, 2nd ed.; CRC Press: Boca Raton, FL, USA, 2010.
54. Hauschke, D.; Kieser, M.; Diletti, E.; Burke, M. Sample size determination for proving equivalence based on the ratio of two means for normally distributed data. *Stat. Med.* **1999**, *18*, 93–105. [CrossRef]
55. Boutron, I.; Altman, D.G.; Moher, D.; Schulz, K.F.; Ravaud, P. Statement for randomized trials of nonpharmacologic treatments: A 2017 update and a CONSORT extension for nonpharmacologic trial. *Ann. Intern. Med.* **2017**, *167*, 40–47. [CrossRef]
56. Piaggio, G.; Elbourne, D.R.; Pocock, S.J.; Evans, S.; Altman, D.G. Reporting of noninferiority and equivalence randomized trials: Extension of the CONSORT 2010 statement. *JAMA J. Am. Med. Assoc.* **2012**, *308*, 2594–2604. [CrossRef]
57. Ardito, R.B.; Rabellino, D. Therapeutic Alliance and Outcome of Psychotherapy: Historical Excursus, Measurements, and Prospects for Research. *Front. Psychol.* **2011**, *2*, 270. [CrossRef]
58. Di Nardo, P.A.; Brown, T.A.; Barlow, D.H. *Anxiety Disorders Interview Schedule for DSM-IV (ADIS-IV)*; Oxford University Press: New York, NY, USA, 1994.
59. Meyer, T.J.; Miller, M.L.; Metzger, R.L.; Borkovec, T.D. Development and validation of the Penn State Worry Questionnaire. *Behav. Res. Ther.* **1990**, *28*, 487–495. [CrossRef]
60. Barlow, D.H.; Rapee, R.M.; Brown, T.A. Behavioral treatment of generalized anxiety disorder. *Behav. Ther.* **1992**, *23*, 551–570. [CrossRef]
61. Borkovec, T.D.; Costello, E. Efficacy of applied relaxation and cognitive-behavioral therapy in the treatment of generalized anxiety disorder. *J. Consult. Clin. Psychol.* **1993**, *61*, 611–619. [CrossRef]
62. Dugas, M.J.; Freeston, M.H.; Provencher, M.; Lachance, S.; Ladouceur, R.; Gosselin, P. Le questionnaire sur l'inquiétude et l'anxiété: Validation dans des échantillons non cliniques et cliniques [The Worry and Anxiety Questionnaire: Validation in non-clinical and clinical samples]. *J. Thérapie Comport. Cogn.* **2001**, *11*, 31–36.
63. Sévigny, J.F.; Gilbert, S.; Deguise, S.; Gosselin, P. Relation entre le sentiment d'efficacité parental et les symptômes d'anxiété postnatale chez les mères d'un nouvel enfant. *Sci. Comport.* **2021**, *31*, 18–28. Available online: http://www.science-et-comportement.uqam.ca/AnciensNumeros/V31/022_Article_final.pdf (accessed on 15 January 2022).
64. Freeston, M.H.; Rhéaume, J.; Letarte, H.; Dugas, M.J.; Ladouceur, R. Why do people worry? *Pers. Individ. Differ.* **1994**, *17*, 791–802. [CrossRef]
65. Beck, A.T.; Steer, R.A.; Brown, G.K. *Manual for the BDI-II*, 2nd ed.; The Psychological Corporation: San Antonio, TX, USA, 1996.
66. World Health Organization. *Program on Mental Health: WHOQOL User Manual (Report No. WHO/HIS/HSI Rev. 2012.03)*; World Health Organization: Geneva, Switzerland, 1998.
67. Pelletier, L.G.; Tuson, K.M.; Haddad, N.K. Client Motivation for Therapy Scale: A measure of intrinsic motivation, extrinsic motivation, and amotivation for therapy. *J. Pers. Assess.* **1997**, *68*, 414–435. [CrossRef] [PubMed]
68. Deci, E.L.; Ryan, R.M. Self-Determination Theory. In *Handbook of Theories Social Psychology*; Kruglanski, A.W., Van Lange, P.A.M., Higgins, E.T., Eds.; Sage Publications Ltd.: London, UK, 2014; Volume 1, pp. 416–437. [CrossRef]

69. Horvath, A.O.; Greenberg, L.S. Development and validation of the Working Alliance Inventory. *J. Couns. Psychol.* **1989**, *36*, 223–233. [CrossRef]
70. Paradis, J.; Marcotte-Beaumier, G.; Green-Demers, I.; Dugas, M.J. Validation de l'Échelle de Compétence du Thérapeute auprès de clients atteints du trouble d'anxiété généralisée. *Can. J. Behav. Sci./Rev. Can. Sci. Comport.* **2020**, *52*, 343–348. [CrossRef]
71. Larsen, D.L.; Attkisson, C.; Hargreaves, W.A.; Nguyen, T.D. Assessment of client/patient satisfaction: Development of a general scale. *Eval. Prog. Plan.* **1979**, *2*, 197–207. [CrossRef]
72. First, M.B.; Gibbon, M.; Spitzer, R.L.; Williams, J.B.W.; Benjamin, L.S. *Structured Clinical Interview for DSM-IV Axis II Personality Disorders (SCID-II)*; American Psychiatric Press, Inc.: Washington, DC, USA, 1997.
73. Dugas, M.J.; Bouchard, S. *Traitement Cognitivo-Comportemental du Trouble d'Anxiété Généralisée: Manuel du Thérapeute [Cognitive-Behavioral Treatment of Generalized Anxiety Disorder: Therapist Guide]*; Department of Psychoeducation and Psychology, Université du Québec en Outaouais: Gatineau, QC, Canada, 2013.
74. Dugas, M.J.; Robichaud, M. *Cognitive-Behavioral Treatment for Generalized Anxiety Disorder: From Science to Practice*; Routledge/Taylor & Francis Group: New York, NY, USA, 2007.
75. Jamovi Project. Jamovi (Version 2.2) [Computer Software]. 2021. Available online: https://www.jamovi.org (accessed on 1 June 2022).
76. Lakens, D. Equivalence Tests: A practical primer for t tests, correlations, and meta-analyses. *Soc. Psychol. Pers. Sci.* **2017**, *8*, 355–362. [CrossRef]
77. Mauri, L.; D'Agostino, R.B. Challenges in the design and interpretation of noninferiority trials. *N. Engl. J. Med.* **2017**, *377*, 1357–1367. [CrossRef]
78. Schuster, R.; Fischer, E.; Jansen, C.; Napravnik, N.; Rockinger, S.; Steger, N.; Laireiter, A.-R. Blending Internet-based and tele group treatment: Acceptability, effects, and mechanisms of change of cognitive behavioral treatment for depression. *Internet Interv.* **2022**, *29*, 100551. [CrossRef]
79. Beck, A.; Emery, G.; Greenberg, R. *Anxiety Disorders and Phobias: A Cognitive Perspective*; Basic Books: New York, NY, USA, 1985.
80. Bouchard, S.; Berthiaume, M.; Robillard, G.; Allard, M.; Green-Demers, I.; Watts, S.; Marchand, A.; Gosselin, P.; Langlois, F.; Belleville, G.; et al. The moderating and mediating role of telepresence and cognitive change in cognitive behavior therapy delivered via videoconference. *Clin. Psychol. Psychother.* **2022**. *manuscript submitted for publication.*
81. Watts, S.; Marchand, A.; Bouchard, S.; Gosselin, P.; Langlois, F.; Belleville, G.; Dugas, M.J. Telepsychotherapy for generalized anxiety disorder: Impact on the working alliance. *J. Psychother. Integr.* **2020**, *30*, 208–225. [CrossRef]
82. Norwood, C.; Moghaddam, N.G.; Malins, S.; Sabin-Farrell, R. Working alliance and outcome effectiveness in videoconferencing psychotherapy: A systematic review and noninferiority meta-analysis. *Clin. Psychol. Psychother.* **2018**, *25*, 797–808. [CrossRef]
83. Norwood, C.; Sabin-Farrell, R.; Malins, S.; Moghaddam, N.G. An explanatory sequential investigation of the working alliance as a change process in videoconferencing psychotherapy. *J. Clin. Psychol.* **2021**, *77*, 1330–1353. [CrossRef] [PubMed]
84. Simpson, S.G.; Reid, C.L. Therapeutic alliance in videoconferencing psychotherapy: A review. *Aust. J. Rural Health* **2014**, *22*, 280–299. [CrossRef]
85. Roemer, L.; Orsillo, S.M. An open trial of an acceptance-based behavior therapy for generalized anxiety disorder. *Behav. Ther.* **2007**, *38*, 72–85. [CrossRef]
86. Basile, V.T.; Newton-John, T.; Wootton, B.M. Internet videoconferencing delivered cognitive behavior therapy for generalized anxiety disorder: Protocol for a randomized controlled trial. *Trials* **2022**, *23*, 592. [CrossRef]
87. Banbury, A.; Nancarrow, S.; Dart, J.; Gray, L.; Parkinson, L. Telehealth interventions delivering home-based support group videoconferencing: Systematic review. *J. Med. Internet Res.* **2018**, *20*, e25. [CrossRef]
88. Rees, C.S.; Maclaine, E. A systematic review of videoconference-delivered psychological treatment for anxiety disorders. *Aust. Psychol.* **2015**, *50*, 259–264. [CrossRef]
89. Bouchard, S.; Payeur, R.; Rivard, V.; Allard, M.; Paquin, B.; Renaud, P.; Goyer, L. Cognitive behavior therapy for panic disorder with agoraphobia in videoconference: Preliminary results. *Cyberpsychology Behav.* **2000**, *3*, 999–1007. [CrossRef]
90. Dongier, M.; Tempier, R.; Lalinec-Michaud, M.; Meunier, D. Telepsychiatry: Psychiatric consultation through two-way television. A controlled study. *Can. J. Psychiatry* **1986**, *31*, 32–34. [CrossRef] [PubMed]
91. Dwyer, T.F. Telepsychiatry: Psychiatric consultation by interactive television. *Am. J. Psychiatry* **1973**, *130*, 865–869. [CrossRef]
92. Grondin, F.; Lomanowska, A.M.; Békés, V.; Jackson, P.L. A methodology to improve eye contact in telepsychotherapy via videoconferencing with considerations for psychological distance. *Couns. Psychol. Q.* **2020**, *34*, 586–599. [CrossRef]
93. Grondin, F.; Lomanowska, A.M.; Poiré, V.; Jackson, P.L. Clients in simulated teletherapy via videoconference compensate for altered eye contact when evaluating therapist empathy. *J. Clin. Med.* **2022**, *11*, 3461. [CrossRef]
94. Kemp, J.; Zhang, T.; Inglis, F.; Wiljer, D.; Sockalingam, S.; Crawford, A.; Lo, B.; Charow, R.; Munnery, M.; Takhar, S.S.; et al. Delivery of compassionate mental health care in a digital technology–driven age: Scoping review. *J. Med. Internet Res.* **2020**, *22*, e16263. [CrossRef]
95. Arneill, A.B.; Devlin, A.S. Perceived quality of care: The influence of the waiting room environment. *J. Environ. Psychol.* **2002**, *22*, 345–360. [CrossRef]
96. Békés, V.; Doorn, K.A.-V. Psychotherapists' attitudes toward online therapy during the COVID-19 pandemic. *J. Psychother. Integr.* **2020**, *30*, 238–247. [CrossRef]

97. Rowen, J.; Giedgowd, G.; Demos, A. Effectiveness of videoconferencing psychotherapy delivered by novice clinicians in a training clinic. *Train. Educ. Prof. Psychol.* 2022; *advance online publication*. [CrossRef]
98. Connolly, S.L.; Miller, C.J.; Lindsay, J.A.; Bauer, M.S. A systematic review of providers' attitudes toward telemental health via videoconferencing. *Clin. Psychol. Sci. Pr.* **2020**, *27*, e12311. [CrossRef] [PubMed]
99. Nolet, K.; Corno, G.; Bouchard, S. The adoption of new treatment modalities by health professionals and the relative weight of empirical evidence in favor of virtual reality exposure versus mindfulness in the treatment of anxiety disorders. *Front. Hum. Neurosci.* **2020**, *14*, 86. [CrossRef] [PubMed]
100. Pittig, A.; Kotter, R.; Hoyer, J. The struggle of behavioral therapists with exposure: Self-reported practicability, negative beliefs, and therapist distress about exposure-based interventions. *Behav. Ther.* **2018**, *50*, 353–366. [CrossRef] [PubMed]
101. Marcotte-Beaumier, G.; Bouchard, S.; Gosselin, P.; Langlois, F.; Belleville, G.; Marchand, A.; Dugas, M.J. The role of intolerance of uncertainty and working alliance in the outcome of cognitive behavioral therapy for generalized anxiety disorder delivered by videoconference: Mediation analysis. *JMIR Mental Health* **2021**, *8*, e24541. [CrossRef] [PubMed]
102. Haddouk, L.; Bouchard, S.; Brivio, E.; Galimberti, C.; Trognon, A. Assessing presence in videoconference telepsychotherapies: A complementary qualitative study on breaks in telepresence and intersubjectivity co-construction processes. In *Annual Review of Cyber Therapy and Telemedicine*; Wiederhold, B.K., Riva, G., Bouchard, S., Eds.; IOS Press: Amsterdam, The Netherlands, 2018; pp. 118–123.
103. Monsalves, M.J.; Bangdiwala, A.S.; Thabane, A.; Bangdiwala, S.I. LEVEL (Logical Explanations & Visualizations of Estimates in Linear mixed models): Recommendations for reporting multilevel data and analyses. *BMC Med. Res. Methodol.* **2020**, *20*, 3. [CrossRef]

Journal of
Clinical Medicine

MDPI

Communication

Trainee Therapists' Perceptions of a Blended Intervention to Promote Resilience after a Natural Disaster: A Qualitative Case Study

Vera Békés [1,*], Geneviève Belleville [2], Jessica Lebel [2], Marie-Christine Ouellet [2], Zhaoyi Chen [1], Charles M. Morin [2], Nicolas Bergeron [3,4], Tavis S. Campbell [5], Sunita Ghosh [6], Stephane Bouchard [7], Stéphane Guay [4,8] and Frank P. MacMaster [9]

1 Ferkauf Graduate School, Yeshiva University, 1165 Morris Park Ave, The Bronx, NY 10461, USA; zchen6@mail.yu.edu
2 School of Psychology, Laval University, 2325 Rue de l'Université, Québec, QC G1V 0A6, Canada; genevieve.belleville@psy.ulaval.ca (G.B.); jessica.lebel@psy.ulaval.ca (J.L.); marie-christine.ouellet@psy.ulaval.ca (M.-C.O.); cmorin@psy.ulaval.ca (C.M.M.)
3 Département de Psychiatrie, Centre Hospitalier de l'Université de Montréal, 1000 Rue St-Denis, Montréal, QC H2X 0C1, Canada; n.bergeron@umontreal.ca
4 Department of Psychiatry and Addiction, University of Montreal, 2900 Edouard Montpetit Blvd., Montreal, QC H3T 1J4, Canada; stephane.guay@umontreal.ca
5 Department of Psychology, University of Calgary, 2500 University Dr. NW, Calgary, AB T2N 1N4, Canada; t.s.campbell@ucalgary.ca
6 Faculty of Medicine and Dentistry, University of Alberta, 116 St & 85 Ave, Edmonton, AB T6G 2R3, Canada; sunita.ghosh@ualberta.ca
7 Département de Psychoéducation et de Psychologie, Université du Québec en Outaouais, CISSS de l'Outaouais, 283 Alexandre-Taché Blvd., Gatineau, QC J8X 3X7, Canada; stephane.bouchard@uqo.ca
8 School of Criminology, University of Montreal, 2900 Edouard Montpetit Blvd., Montreal, QC H3T 1J4, Canada
9 Addictions and Mental Health Strategic Clinical Network, Alberta Children's Hospital, 28 Oki Drive NW, Calgary, AB T3B 6A8, Canada; fmacmast@ucalgary.ca
* Correspondence: vera.bekes@yu.edu

Citation: Békés, V.; Belleville, G.; Lebel, J.; Ouellet, M.-C.; Chen, Z.; Morin, C.M.; Bergeron, N.; Campbell, T.S.; Ghosh, S.; Bouchard, S.; et al. Trainee Therapists' Perceptions of a Blended Intervention to Promote Resilience after a Natural Disaster: A Qualitative Case Study. *J. Clin. Med.* **2022**, *11*, 4361. https://doi.org/10.3390/jcm11154361

Academic Editors: Augusto Fusco and Mauro Giovanni Carta

Received: 23 March 2022
Accepted: 18 July 2022
Published: 27 July 2022

Abstract: Background: Natural disasters happen in an increased frequency, and telemental health interventions could offer easily accessible help to reduce mental health symptoms experienced by survivors. However, there are very few programs offered to natural disaster survivors, and no research exists on therapists' experiences with providing blended interventions for natural disaster survivors. Aims: Our qualitative case study aims to describe psychologists' experiences with an online, therapist-assisted blended intervention for survivors of the Fort McMurray wildfires in Alberta, Canada. Method: The RESILIENT intervention was developed in the frames of a randomized controlled trial to promote resilience after the Fort McMurray wildfires by providing survivors free access to a 12-module, therapist-assisted intervention, aiming to improve post-traumatic stress, insomnia, and depression symptoms. A focus group design was used to collect data from the therapists, and emerging common themes were identified by thematic analysis. Results: Therapists felt they could build strong alliances and communicate emotions and empathy effectively, although the lack of nonverbal cues posed some challenges. The intervention, according to participating therapists, was less suitable for participants in high-stress situations and in case of discrepancy between client expectations and the intervention content. Moreover, the therapists perceived specific interventions as easy-to-use or as more challenging based on their complexity and on the therapist support needed for executing them. Client engagement in the program emerged as an underlying theme that had fundamental impact on alliance, communication, and ultimately, treatment efficiency. Therapist training and supervision was perceived as crucial for the success of the program delivery. Conclusions: Our findings provided several implications for the optimalization of blended interventions for natural disaster survivors from our therapists' perspective.

Keywords: telemental health; therapist; blended intervention; alliance; focus group; thematic analysis

1. Introduction

Due to climate change, natural disasters and other extreme events have become more frequent and intense recently [1], and their devastating impact includes various mental health consequences for the survivors [2]. Previous studies estimated that up to forty percent of natural disaster survivors develop some type of mental health symptoms, including post-traumatic stress disorder, depression, and insomnia [3]. Psychotherapy has been found to be effective in the treatment of such problems in the context of natural disasters. For instance, after hurricanes Katrina and Sandy, cognitive-behavior therapy significantly reduced survivors' symptom levels [4,5]. Even though it is essential to be able to provide psychological support after natural disasters, having access to sufficient mental health services at the location of the disaster is often a serious challenge.

Telemental health interventions have many advantages compared to in-person settings, including providing help for those who would not otherwise have access to mental health providers via in-person settings [6,7]. Among telemental health interventions, blended interventions are web-based interventions guided by a therapist that combine the advantages of asynchronous online programs and face-to-face, synchronous, personalized sessions with a therapist [8,9], which may be conducted either over the Internet or in person. Blended interventions have been suggested to have the most benefit by boosting treatment adherence, intensifying the learning process, personalizing and adjusting the intervention content to the client's needs [9], as well as reducing associated therapist time and cost by providing a large proportion of the therapy content on the web to be utilized by the client [8]. Blended interventions appear to have the potential to make telemental health interventions suitable for more clients at lower therapist time and associated costs and may be a candidate for delivering telemental health interventions rapidly after natural disasters. Despite the many advantages of blended interventions over exclusively online, self-help modules, as well as over exclusively face-to-face sessions with a therapist, there are very few existing blended intervention programs providing help for natural disaster survivors.

Telemental health interventions have been underutilized mostly due to negative attitudes and concerns towards some of its aspects (see [10]) before the start of the COVID-19 pandemic. However, the advantages of telemental health interventions have become especially salient during the past months, when the COVID-19 pandemic and the related physical distancing restrictions forced therapists and clients to switch to remote therapy *en masse* [11]. Research suggests that therapists generally hold neutral or positive views of telemental health interventions [12–15]; however, providers are often reluctant to provide telemental health due to concerns and more negative views on it [16–19]. One common concern regards the ability to build therapeutic alliance [10,20–22]. Despite the fact that the quality of working alliance has been found to be excellent in videoconference (see review by [23]) and comparable to in-person therapies (e.g., [24,25]), providers are often worried that they would not be able to build strong rapport and develop alliance remotely [26]. Concerns and negative experiences, on the other hand, have been found to reduce the likelihood of intention to use telemental health in the future [26].

Another major concern regarding the providing of telemental health interventions is whether therapist and client can communicate emotions and empathy effectively remotely [6,27]. Despite research evidence that online channels do not influence emphatic accuracy [28], a common concern is that the online medium prevents the communication of empathy, warmth, and understanding [10]. Consequently, therapists are usually more favorably disposed toward videoconferencing as opposed to telephone or text therapy, as this modality enables them to observe physical cues and thus preserves an important element of in-person therapy [29].

Finally, therapists are also often concerned about the suitability of telemental health interventions to a certain type of clientele and situations [29,30]. Safety and legal concerns are common regarding interventions without physical proximity to the patient, and complex and severe client presentations, such as personality disorder, emotional instability, impulsivity, past suicide attempts, or any crisis situation are often perceived by clinicians as not suitable for telemental health settings [29].

However, we know that the therapists' concerns and perceptions of telemental health vary. Recent studies showed that more previous experience with providing telemental health interventions and a larger teletherapy caseload were associated with more positive views on using telemental health [12,31,32]. Moreover, older therapists, and therapists with more clinical experience also reported more positive experiences with telemental health compared to their younger and less experienced counterparts [16,33].

Fort McMurray Wildfires

On 1 May 2016 in Fort McMurray (Alberta), a major wildfire destroyed approximately 2400 homes and buildings and led to the massive displacement of 88,000 people, making it the most expensive natural disaster in Canadian history at the time. Many individuals faced direct or potential threats to their life or health, were separated from loved ones, and incurred significant losses. Families had to be displaced for several weeks and up to several months. For a report of the evacuees' experiences three months and three years after the fires, see [34].

A year after the disaster, in a representative sample of 1510 evacuees, 38% reported symptom levels indicative of a probable diagnosis of either post-traumatic stress, major depression, insomnia, generalized anxiety, substance use disorder, or a combination of these disorders [35]. In order to provide support to the evacuees with these symptoms, our team of researchers and clinicians gathered an arsenal of well-evidenced CBT strategies into a 12-module online RESILIENT therapy program.

The RESILIENT platform Is a therapist-guided, online self-help treatment; its content was developed following a preliminary study of Fort McMurray residents who were evacuated during the fires, which showed that they had significant symptoms of PTSD, insomnia, and depression after the event [35].

The platform was hosted by Laval University, and the graduate psychology students were included as therapists in the program. A randomized control trial of 136 individuals who participated in the intervention showed that the RESILIENT program was successful and showed large effect sizes of symptom improvement in participants who completed at least half of the treatment. For further details on the RCT, see [36].

The present study aims to learn about the RESILIENT intervention from a different angle, by exploring trainee therapists' first experiences with providing blended therapy for survivors of the Fort McMurray fires, in the context of the RESILIENT program. More specifically, our aims were twofold: (1) To explore therapists' experiences with areas of common concerns described in the literature regarding telemental health services, such as the ability to build alliance online, communicate emotions and empathy, and suitability of remote interventions for all clients; (2) To explore therapists' experiences with delivering the RESILIENT intervention, that is, their views on the intervention content and platform, as well as the training and supervision process.

We used a focus group design to learn about the therapists' experiences. We selected a focus group design because, in contrast with individual interviews, focus groups allow for a discussion between group members, which typically widens the range of responses, brings up forgotten details, or triggers new ideas. In addition, due to the shared experience, the group dynamic often creates a sense of confirmation and of less inhibition in participants to freely share their views [37].

2. Method

2.1. The Resilient Intervention

The intervention was developed for a randomized controlled trial assessing the effectiveness of a blended intervention including online modules and synchronous therapist sessions either by phone or video conference for the evacuees of the Fort McMurray (Alberta, Canada) wildfires. Evacuees completed online symptom assessments, including PTSD (PTSD Symptoms Checklist, PCL-5; [38]), depression (Patient Health Questionnaire—Depression Subscale, PHQ-9, [39]), and insomnia measures (Insomnia Severity Index, ISI; [40]). Participants meeting inclusion criteria were offered free treatment. Inclusion criteria were: (1) significant post-traumatic stress symptoms (PCL $\geq$ 23) or (2) some post-traumatic stress symptoms (PCL $\geq$ 10) and at least mild depressive symptoms (PHQ-9 $\geq$ 5) and/or at least subclinical insomnia symptoms (ISI $\geq$ 8).

The intervention consisted of a therapist-assisted online cognitive-behavior therapy focusing on post-traumatic stress, sleep, and mood. It comprised 12 sessions with modules of psychoeducation about PTSD, sleep and depression, prolonged exposure to avoided situations and memories, sleep management strategies (restriction of time in bed, sleep hygiene education, nightmare image rehearsal), behavioral activation, breathing and mindfulness exercises, cognitive restructuring, and relapse prevention. Participants had to work on each week's session online individually by reading educational material, reflecting on their own experiences by answering questions, planning their homework exercises, and filling out online journals about sleeping, breathing exercises, exposure, and behavior activation. They met a therapist via either videoconference (Skype) or phone, according to the participants' preference, after completing each session to discuss the given topic and review their online work as well as the homework (exercises in-between sessions). Meetings with the therapists were 30 min long, and usually weekly sessions, depending on the participant's online progress. Preliminary results have been previously published in French [41].

2.2. Participating Therapists

Seven clinical psychology graduate students, that is, all the therapists in the program, participated as therapists in the program. All therapists were female with a mean age of 25.86 (range: 22–30, SD = 3.08). None of the therapists had previous experience with remote therapy. Therapists had about 2 years of in-person clinical experience (mean = 2.13 years; range: 0–4.5, SD = 1.67), and only one therapist was beginner. Altogether, 69 clients were invited to participate in the program and were assigned to a therapist; each therapist had 9.75 clients assigned to them on average (range: 3–17, SD = 3.99).

2.3. Procedure and Data Analysis

Two focus groups were conducted to collect data from each participating therapist shortly after the termination of the intervention. Each focus group lasted for 120 min. All 7 therapists provided data about their experiences by participating in the two focus groups (n = 3 and n = 6, two therapists participated in both). The focus groups used a semi-structured interview guide with open questions. Questions focused on general impressions regarding the intervention, perceived challenges for the therapists and the clients, and more specific questions regarding experiences with phone and video conferencing with the clients (such as developing alliance and feeling empathy), the online platform, the content of the intervention, and finally, suggestions for improving the intervention. The focus group interviews were audio recorded and later transcribed. Given the bilingual milieu, where all participants used both English and French in professional and daily communication, the therapists responded in either of these languages within the same group, according to their preferences, or switched from one to the other language as they would naturally do outside of the focus group setting. The possibility to use either English or French allowed participants to express themselves in the language they felt more comfortable with, while not risking hindering the process of understanding. The transcription kept the original languages, and quotes in French were translated to English for the present study.

Two graduate clinical psychology students (who did not participate in the study) conducted thematic analysis on the transcribed data on the guidelines provided by Braun and Clarke (2006). The qualitative analysis included the following phases: (1) generating initial codes, (2) identifying emerging common themes, (3) reviewing the themes, arranging the themes under a priori established categories (building alliance, communicating emotions and feeling empathy, suitability of intervention) as well as defining emerging categories (platform, intervention content, training, and supervision), and (4) finally, refining the definition, specifics of each theme, as well as the thematic map). Illustrative quotes were selected and translated from French to English. Ethical approval for the study was obtained from the Laval University Institutional Review Board, and participants provided informed consent.

3. Results

The themes were categorized under general concerns regarding alliance, communicating emotions and empathy, and suitability (Table 1), and specific issues, including intervention content, platform, and training and supervision (Table 2).

3.1. Alliance and Client Engagement

Despite previous apprehensions, all therapists had generally positive experiences with establishing and maintaining alliance with clients via phone calls and video conferencing (7/7); as one of them described "*It was more rich than I thought, since there was a screen between us, it was interesting to see that I was able to bond with the [clients] even though they were far away, so yes, that surprised me.*" (P1). Most therapists felt that video sessions were more helpful for feeling closer to clients (5/7), and they had positive experiences with phone sessions in general, although some signalled that it took more time to build rapport over the phone (1/7).

Client engagement emerged as a central theme affecting alliance: the therapists felt that they worked well with motivated clients, whereas client non-compliance negatively affected the alliance (7/7). In reaction to issues with engagement, therapists realized that providing regular encouragement, motivation, and checking in were needed to ensure that clients adhered to the intervention (3/7). Moreover, according to the program protocol, in order to maintain client engagement, therapists had to regularly reach out to clients when they had not heard from them. This was frustrating for most therapists and felt like needing to constantly reach out to clients (4/7), which sometimes even felt like they were harassing the clients (2/7). The therapists' impression was that the frequent reaching out process appeared to be frustrating for both them and the clients, and most of the time it did not reach its goal of increasing engagement but most probably negatively affected their alliance.

Table 1. Therapist Experiences with Alliance, Communicating Emotions and Empathy, and Suitability.

Description	N	Supporting Quotes
		Alliance in General
Therapists were able to develop strong alliance both in phone and video sessions	7	"One can create a good therapeutic alliance with the client both by phone or Skype. Active listening and validation of their symptoms make clients already more comfortable with disclosing their feelings." * (P2)
Video helped feeling closer to clients more than phone sessions	5	"I found that over video it was easier (. . .) to feel that you were really there with the client." * (P2)
Phone sessions felt similar to face-to-face	2	"I didn't feel there was a difference to face-to-face, sometimes it [the distance] even helped me personally." * (P1)
Communicating via phone didn't have negative impact on the relationship	2	"I felt that I had a good therapeutic relationship with them, for example in the end it was difficult for them to say "bye," so there was a relationship that had been built." * (P5)
Communicating via phone required longer time to build rapport	1	"I think in the beginning it takes a little bit more time to develop the therapeutic alliance, because you're picking up the phone and all of a sudden you are expected to divulge your whole story to at a random person on the phone." (P4)
		Alliance and Client Engagement
Therapists worked well with those who were motivated and adherent to the program	7	"I found that I had as much empathy as when I saw a client in person. The only thing that affected my ability to be empathetic was with one particular participant. It had been twice that I called her at the time of the appointment and she did not answer and she always postponed the appointment so I was irritated by that so I tell myself that maybe it has affected my ability to be truly empathetic." * (P6)
Reaching out to clients led to frustration on both therapist and client sides and negatively affected alliance	4	"Like I was a mother running after her children pining at them, because I knew it would help them, they just weren't committed to the intervention whatsoever, it was just frustrating the whole time." (P5).
Clients are less engaged if the specific intervention does not match their symptoms	4	"The participants I followed didn't really have the classic symptoms of PTSD necessarily so maybe it was more difficult for them to recognize themselves in like specific categories." (P2)
Regular encouragement needed to increase engagement	3	"Sometimes I went through their answers and gave them little reinforcements. I would tell them that this was a good idea or I would encourage them to go a bit further in their responses." (P2)
Mismatch between client expectation and intervention content led to frictions between therapist and client	3	"They commit to the program, but they don't really know in what they got involved. When they discover that it's a serious program and that we meet with them every week . . . I think it might take too much of their time." * (P3)
Personal contact with therapist improved client engagement	3	"I think (. . .) they really appreciated the opportunity to talk things over." (P6)
Reaching out feels like harassing the client if they do not respond	2	"At some point I was feeling like I was harassing this client who hasn't been answering me."
Challenging to maintain alliance when sessions are too far away in time	1	"When it was difficult to schedule an appointment, it got stretched out. I had one client who (. . .) took really long. It was more difficult, because the alliance was not there anymore (. . .), it was with him that I had to tell him that I had a life too." * (P2)

Table 1. *Cont.*

Description	N	Supporting Quotes
		Communicating Emotions and Empathy
Therapists were able to feel and communicate emotions and empathy	7	"I found that I had just as much empathy as with a client in person." * (P6)
Harder to transmit nonverbal signs	7	"It's a little bit more artificial to say « ok, like, now it's the end » instead of just giving social signs that we are close to the end." (P1)
Nonverbal and social cues were limited even in video conferencing	5	"For example if a person felt uncomfortable and was playing with his pencil, I did not see it on his face as it was too close [to the camera], so maybe there were things I missed." (P5)
Therapists were able to recognize clients' emotions, understand their perspectives, and empathize with their traumatic experiences	4	"I had some doubts [about remote sessions] but speaking to the victims and feeling their emotions through the phone made me want to participate in this project even more; knowing that they really experienced difficult things that affected them a lot, and all that over the phone." * (P2)
Video is better in assessing clients' mental state due to visual information	4	"I had one participant over the phone and obviously, zero nonverbal, it isn't there, at one point she became emotional, and she was crying, but I didn't know she was crying because it was silent. So it was kind of not how you would intervene if it were on video, because you would see that the client was emotional and I would have given her space and let her live these emotions and instead I was like « hello, you still there »" (P5)
Hard to sense the meaning of silences on the phone	3	"You can have silence on [video call], but on the phone you don't know what the person's doing. So I feel like they have to fill more the blank on the phone than when it's face to face." (P1).
Hard to focus, clients tend to chat about other things via phone	3	I think it was harder on the phone for ... to be focused on the content, I think over the phone it was easier to talk about something else. (P2)
Video is better to express empathy	3	"I was wondering, did they feel the non-verbal empathy that we try to show when we are with the person? (...) When they start to cry for example. I felt our silence afterwards was supportive, but I am not sure it worked." * (P1)
Hard to get a sense of the clients' actual surroundings, activity on the phone	2	"You had no idea what they were doing, she could have been watching TV, she could have been doing anything. And well, on Skype I can see, I just felt like it was a lot better on Skype than on the phone." (P5)
Easier to focus on the client and feel empathy on the phone due to decreased therapist anxiety	1	"I may have little performance anxiety but as the person was far away it allowed me to focus on the person, rather than on what I looked like, right? (...) I was more focused on what the person was saying to me, the distance helped me in terms of empathy." * (P1)

Table 1. *Cont.*

Description	N	Supporting Quotes
		Suitability
Clients' presentation of symptoms affects their intervention utilization	7	"The participants I followed didn't really have the classic symptoms of PTSD necessarily, so maybe it was more difficult for them to recognize themselves in like specific categories or specific boxes [in the online modules], which is why it was more difficult for them to understand [the exercise]" (P2)
Clients differ in their commitment to the intervention	7	"I had two or three participants that . . . in a week did sessions 2 to 9 or 2 to 6. I imagine it depends also how committed they are and if they do all the exercises." * (P3)
Lack of accurate expectation of workload in the intervention affected clients' engagement	7	"Some people have never been in therapy, so they don't know what it's like and when they are recruited, we say « oh you want this treatment for insomnia, etc. » and I don't think they expected it to be this big, this demanding. That they would have to monitor many things, be accountable." (P6)
More symptoms/stress leading to dropout	2	"I feel like maybe because they have severe symptoms and they have a lot of things going on in their life, (. . .) they were telling themselves that it was more important than the intervention, so they were putting it on the back burner. It was not their priority so I think it explains a lot of the drop-outs."

Note. * = Translation from the original French.

Table 2. Therapist Experiences with the Content, Platform, and with Training and Supervision.

Description	N	Supporting Quotes
		Intervention Content
		Exposure exercise
Less utilized due to lack of avoidance symptoms	2	"Many of my participants didn't do any exposure because they weren't avoiding anything related to the fires." (P6)
Challenging as it provokes anxiety	2	"The exposure part of the modules, this was challenging, some of them told me that it was hard for them to do [experience] it all over again." (P2)
Clients did not believe it would be useful	2	"It was a challenge for me to try to explain how it would be useful to them if they didn't think it was useful themselves." (P5)
Clients found it helpful	1	"I had two people who found it really useful, it was really really useful, so I think it depends on the person. And they were very surprised at how it helped them." (P1)
Assistance would be helpful	1	"I think sometimes the exposure was (. . .) hard for them to do on their own. Sometimes I wanted them to include somebody that they are comfortable with, but sometimes it was hard. So I think that [it would be helpful] if there was a therapist with them." (P2)

Table 2. *Cont.*

Description	N	Supporting Quotes
		Sleep management (Sleep window, Sleep diary, Nightmare imagery rehearsal exercises)
Sleep diary was hard to follow	6	"I wanted to use it more, but I think sometimes the participants didn't put the right sessions when they filled the entries, so it wasn't always very accurate. So sometimes I wanted to come back to the [sleep] efficiency, but I couldn't. (. . .) It's kind of complicated I think." (P2)
Helpful for those who used it	5	"I only remember a few people who really used the sleep diary and for whom there was no trouble and it was very helpful but not a lot of people did it." (P2)
Sleep diary was helpful in improving sleep	3	"I found the most useful for my participants was the sleep diary for the people that had sleep problems who were really working on improving their sleep." (P4)
Sleep window is difficult to do and requires therapist's explanation	1	"The only section that I found a little bit more difficult, (. . .) was about the sleep window, just because there's tons of noting, there's monitoring, there's adding fifteen minutes here, so it's likI. That was really the only aspect that I felt needed to be explained more in detail to clients (P4)
Sleep diary was not utilized as it felt irrelevant	1	"None of my participants did it and they found it to be really irrelevant." (P5)
Nightmare imagery rehearsal was less utilized due to lack of nightmares	7	"I think only one of them [client] used it because the other ones didn't have nightmares." (P6)
		Behavior Activation (Pleasant activities exercise)
Utilization and adherence varied	5	"Either they use it a lot or they use it for like the first week and then they stop." (P6)
Adaptable, useful, and helped most clients	4	"I think pleasant activities were the most used. They were used by all of my participants. It was something that they can all recognize themselves." (P2)
		Cognitive Restructuring Exercise (Unhelpful thinking styles)
Difficult to do by themselves	4	"I think for some of them [used it], but for others it wasn't natural, some of them don't have access to their other alternative [thought]." (P2)
Challenging to explain	4	"Some participants couldn't recognize their unhelpful thinking styles, so what can you do at that point? You know, you can do nothing if they don't see." (P1)
		Diaphragmatic Breathing and Mindfulness (Calm breathing, Mindfulness mediation exercises)
Diaphragmatic breathing exercise was most helpful	3	"It was the breathing exercises [. . .] that was a really important one for most of my participants" (P7)
Meditation may work better with auditory format	2	"I wonder if it could be an idea to do a recording instead of a text. Because meditation is more of an auditive side than visual." (P6)
Mindfulness meditation was helpful	1	"I feel like the mindfulness exercises really helped a lot of my participants specifically. With one participant she took it and she started journaling with it between the sessions and she told me at the end that it's something she's going to continue to do for the long term because it really helped her." (P5)

Table 2. *Cont.*

Description	N	Supporting Quotes
		Platform
Well-functioning and user-friendly	7	"I thought the platform was great as well. It was visually pleasing, inviting for participants, interactive because there were many things to click on." (P2)
Clients forget to record their exercises	2	I think it was more time consuming or they would do things and they said "Oh! I need to write it down" and then they would forget to write it down once they actually got access to the platform. This is why I suggested keeping a paper journal or an agenda." (P2)
Technical glitches are very frustrating for clients	1	"They would get frustrated or annoyed if they had completed their sleep diary for an entire week and then it didn't save." (P4)
		Therapists Training and Supervision
Therapists needed to get familiar with the content and tools	5	"I felt like I learned a lot since it was only my first year here so I learned a lot on intervention and on CBT in general so it's really enriching for me." (P5)
Supervision was helpful, available for questions	4	"I think that, honestly, it was very useful, very helpful. If I had any questions, I could address them to her [supervisor] directly. (. . .) She helped me deal with that or using it appropriately or how I should be intervening other ways." (P2)
Supervision needed in complicated situations	2	"I found it good . . . Participants sometimes had more complicated situations. So at least we had a different way of thinking about the issue. She [supervisor] could give us clues on what to do." * (P3)
Meaningful training experience for therapists	1	"In general, I felt like it was a really rich experience for me as well, I thought the program was really complete and really rich, I felt like I learned a lot as well since it was only my first year here, so I learned a lot on intervention and on CBT in general so it's really enriching for me." (P5)
Supervision helped keeping frames and communicating expectations	1	"Most of the time, we just postponed it [the session with a participant] to the next week and at some point, I asked [the supervisor] for advice and she told me to ask them to cancel 24 h in advance and be more . . . not strict but have more like a frame on how to do things." (P6)

Note. * = Translation from the original French.

3.2. Communicating Emotions and Empathy

Overall, therapists felt they could adequately sense and communicate emotions and empathy both via video conferencing and phone (7/7). They felt that even when only using audio (phone) and not video, they were able to recognize clients' emotions, understand their perspectives, and empathize with their traumatic experiences (4/7). One therapist reported that phone sessions, compared to face-to-face, made her less stressed and self-conscious, and consequently more focused with the clients, allowing her to develop better empathy.

Despite being comparable in many aspects, video call sessions were viewed as more favorable than phone sessions in general for various reasons. First, the therapists had better experiences with video sessions with regards to communicating empathy, as they felt a "better presence" with clients (3/7). Second, they also felt that it was harder to assess the clients' mental state via phone due to a lack of information about their facial expression (4/7). Third, lacking access to non-verbal cues also limited the therapists' ability to keep the sessions focused on the given topics and not to divert into others (3/7). Some therapists voiced concerns that there might be more distractions around clients during phone session that are hard for the therapist to detect (1/7), and thus sometimes they wondered what the clients were doing during the sessions (2/7).

Despite the overall preference for video calls over phone calls, therapists also experienced its limitations. For example, access to the clients' nonverbal cues were limited to facial expressions and diminished the therapist's ability to transmit nonverbal signs (7/7). Moreover, even though therapists could read and communicate emotions via video call in general, the angle, distance, and resolution of the camera set limits to what the therapists could observe, limiting their access to some nonverbal or social cues (5/7).

3.3. Suitability and Client Engagement

According to the therapists, the single most important factor in the success of the intervention was whether the client was motivated and engaged. In turn, client engagement greatly differed based on certain client and situation characteristics (7/7). Therapists felt that client engagement was often polarized: clients were either motivated and active from the beginning until the end, or were less engaged, non-responsive to emails, missing sessions, and the therapists' efforts to motivate them had a very limited impact on changing this: *"Either they were engaged and following every week or it was difficult to engage them and they would do one to three sessions and then it was very difficult, and it took two or three weeks to do another one and they would always postpone it. So, I think it was the main thing with my participants."* (P6) According to the therapists, clients were less engaged if they did not feel that their symptoms were targeted (4/7), for example, for clients who did not have avoidance symptoms, a central focus of the intervention appeared unrelatable.

Therapists also proposed that the presence of severe symptoms or other ongoing life stressors might have contributed to clients' non-adherence and dropout (2/7): *"I only had one participant that dropped out, and for her I think that her symptoms were really severe and for her to do it by herself on the computer, it was just too much, she told me that the first or second sessions she started having nightmares, felt a lot of anxiety. She had flashbacks again, so I think that's why, she told me that, and she wasn't sure if she wanted to continue or not. And after that she emailed me back and she never answered, so she dropped out after that."* (P5)

Furthermore, mismatch between client expectation and the offered intervention negatively affected client engagement. Most of the time, the client did not expect that the intervention would take so much time, effort, and emotional investment (7/7), *"They didn't know what they were getting into. Even though we told them in the beginning that it was a self-based intervention, I don't think that they knew exactly what it was (...) I don't think that they expected so much work."* (P2)

3.4. Intervention Content

The therapists found the intervention was well-made, the content was clear, well-organized, easy to understand, and that the modules were organized in the right order

(7/7); however, the utilization of the exercises mostly depended on client engagement (7/7). According to therapists, engaged clients claimed that this intervention made a difference in their lives (2/7) and especially appreciated the therapist sessions in addition to the online modules (2/7). The utilization of the exercises also depended on the specific needs and symptoms of the clients, and therapists made efforts to repeat helpful exercises and skip less relevant ones in order to adapt to the client's needs (4/7). *"It was really different from one person to another. I feel like all of my participants had their one or two that they really liked and kept during all the program and I don't believe that any of the intervention wasn't useful, I think it just depends on the fit with the person. Because they are all in themselves relevant, it just depends on the match."* (P1) The clients sometimes focused on a sole exercise, which still led to significant improvements: *"The very use for she was the pleasant activities [behavior activation] and so this is something she really did regularly. So yes, it was helpful and she had issues if I may say, but at the end she had no issues with sleep, and all the things so at the very end she only had to complete the pleasant activities and that was it."* (P1)

The therapists felt that exposure was difficult to do alone (2/7) and in-person assistance would have been helpful for clients (1/7). The insomnia element of the intervention was very helpful for those who had symptoms (5/7), although the online sleep diary was difficult to use (6/7). Behavior activation exercises were popular and helpful in general (4/7). The cognitive restructuring exercise, although the therapists thought it was important, was hard to work with in the blended therapy's frames, as clients would have needed more support to recognize their own maladaptive thoughts and finding alternatives (4/7). The most utilized exercises were the insomnia, behavior activation, and diaphragmatic breathing interventions (4/7); less utilized exercises included nightmare imagery rehearsal, given that very few clients had nightmares (7/7). Utilization of the online tools, for example sleep diary, and anxiety monitoring before and after interventions, greatly varied, and the majority of clients stopped using them after a few times (6/7). For more detailed description of experiences with the specific exercises see Table 2.

3.4.1. Intervention Platform

Therapists agreed that the platform was clear and easy-to-use, visually pleasing, and inviting (7/7), and most therapist did not experience technical problems. However, clients sometimes forgot to enter their exercise data (2/2) and a technical glitch that resulted in losing client data was very frustrating for clients (1/7).

3.4.2. Training and Supervision

Therapists felt they needed to work on getting prepared for providing the intervention by reading and becoming familiar with the content, exercises, online tools, and learnt a lot about therapy principles and practice (5/7) while receiving a meaningful training experience (1/7). The therapists all felt that the supervision was helpful in providing ideas and a new perspective (4/7), as well as support and frames for approaching complicated situations (2/7) and setting boundaries (1/7).

3.5. Underlying Processes: The Role of Client Engagement

In summary of the results, the following underlying process emerged. Client engagement appears to have a fundamental role in the success of the treatment, with regards to developing strong alliance, provide effective communication, and lead to significant symptom improvement. Client engagement, on the other hand, largely depends on the suitability of the intervention for the client. For clients with severe symptoms or symptom profiles that do not match the intervention's focus, or for clients with differing expectations, the intervention proved to be less suitable, leading to a lack of client engagement, which negatively impacted the working alliance and communication between client and therapist and, ultimately, symptom improvement (Figure 1). Moreover, besides suitability to client expectations and symptoms, the utilization and helpfulness of specific exercises greatly varied depending on their suitability to the blended intervention format that heavily relied on asynchronous communication. Some exercises worked well without synchronous therapist support; for example, behavior activation or diaphragmatic breathing, whereas others were challenging to execute without in-person or more synchronous remote support (such as exposure exercise, cognitive restructuring).

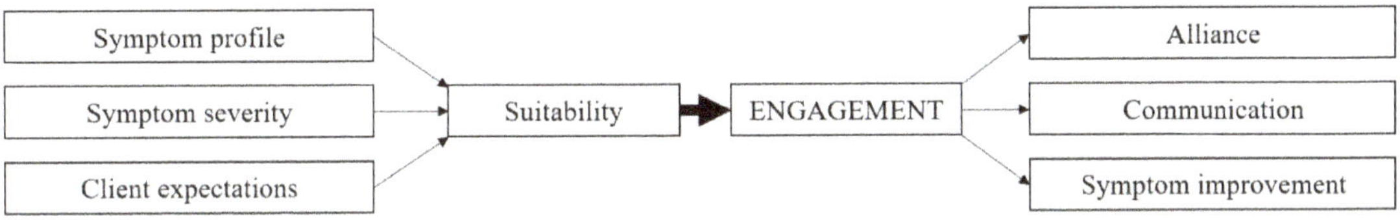

Figure 1. Thematic map of therapists' experiences with alliance, communicating emotions and empathy, and suitability. *Note.* Client engagement was crucial for the success of the treatment, as it tended to lead to stronger alliance, effective communication, and significant symptom improvement. Client engagement, on the other hand, largely depended on the suitability of the intervention for the client. The intervention was less suitable for clients with symptom profiles that did not match the intervention's focus, for clients with severe symptoms, and for clients whose expectations did not match the intervention. Problems with suitability lead to a lack of client engagement, which negatively impacted the working alliance and communication between client-therapist and, ultimately, symptom improvement.

4. Discussion

The present study aimed to explore therapists' experiences with providing telemental health in the context of a blended intervention for survivors of a natural disaster. We found that therapists had an overall positive experience with the ability to build alliance, communicate emotions, and empathize with clients via both phone and video sessions, while they identified special advantages and challenges within each domain. Client engagement emerged as a central underlying theme that was perceived as having a fundamental impact on both the process and the outcome of the intervention. This result is in line with a subsequent quantitative analysis of usage data of by the same participants, where Label and colleagues [42] recently found in the same sample of clients that treatment efficacy (reduction in post-traumatic stress, depression, and insomnia symptoms) was related to the number of modules accessed by the client, which, in turn, was predicted by previous engagement (e.g., number of words entered) in preceding modules.

In our study, client engagement was perceived as depending on (1) the match between the client's symptom profile and the intervention content, (2) symptom severity (overwhelming, severe symptoms often led to disengagement and eventual dropout), and (3) the match between client expectations regarding the program and the actual intervention. Moreover, in our trainee therapists' view, utilization of specific exercises greatly varied based on the difficulty to execute them without direct and synchronous therapist support within the blended intervention paradigm.

4.1. Alliance

Similar to previous findings (e.g., [26]), trainee therapists in the present study had concerns about the ability to build alliance prior to starting the intervention and were pleasantly surprised by the ease of creating bonds remotely. This finding supports the notion that once therapists are effectively engaged in delivering online intervention, their experiences are usually positive with alliance building [10,11]. While creating bonds proved to be easier than expected, trainee therapists still faced various challenges regarding specific aspects of working with clients. They felt that the ability to build alliance greatly depended on the clients' engagement to the program (as seen in previous studies as well, e.g., [43]), and maintaining clients' motivation posed a fundamental challenge to therapists. Based on previous recommendations (e.g., [44]) the study protocol required therapists to reach out to inactive clients regularly in order to maintain engagement; however, this method appeared to be counterproductive, resulted in therapists feeling like they were "chasing the clients", and posed a strain on the alliance on both sides. Eventually, our therapists found different ways to keep clients engaged, tailor-made for each client, which they perceived as more effective.

Moreover, in contrast with earlier findings where the aspect of alliance regarding agreeing on the goals and tasks was found to be higher in online therapies [45], for our trainee therapists this posed a challenge. Since the modules, exercises, and their order had already been pre-established, the therapists had little space to adjust them to the needs of the actual clients, which frequently resulted in a mismatch between client expectations and the delivered intervention. Moreover, since clients were recruited by the RESILIENT program by offering a free intervention for those with above-threshold symptoms, many clients may not have had a strong motivation to begin with, and when faced with the time and emotional investment required by the program, became even less motivated.

Problems with high degrees of non-adherence are common in online interventions [46], and blended interventions' synchronous therapist support component are aimed to address this; however, our results suggest that, in itself, this might not be enough. The clients' specific needs could be better met by making the intervention content and sequence more flexible; this would increase client and therapist agreement on tasks and goals, and consequently, have a positive impact on client engagement. For example, implementing a preliminary phase at the beginning of the intervention where the client's symptoms are assessed, and matching interventions be selected and arranged in the desired order may be helpful. This phase could be either conducted by a therapist or by an online algorithm, or by a combination of both where the therapist is able to adjust the algorithm's recommendations based on a collaborative discussion with the client.

4.2. Communicating Emotions and Empathy

Similar to experiences with alliance, trainee therapists were pleasantly surprised by the ease of communicating and feeling empathy both over the phone and in video calls. Video sessions were perceived as preferable to phone due to the availability of visual information and thus the ability to sense the clients' emotional states and understand their mind states. At the same time, even video calls filtered out the perception of certain nonverbal clues, a common issue that has been raised in previous studies. To address this, Grondin et al. [47] suggested that techniques like exaggeration of nonverbal behaviors and verbal clarification of the client's affective state can facilitate the empathic phenomenon. Moreover, simple technical adjustment in the video camera placement and settings can also increase connection and the perception of nonverbal cues. For example, setting the camera angle in a way that enables eye contact, and selecting the appropriate camera frame (zooming in and out to show the usual head-to-chest versus larger, head-to-waist frame) allows the perception of nonverbal cues while also maintains a sense of psychological connection [48]. Future studies need to explore the utility of these techniques in telemental health.

4.3. Suitability

Previous studies suggested that online interventions might be less suitable for certain clients, for example, those with severe or complex psychopathology and in crisis situations [29]. In our study, although some of the trainee therapists mentioned symptom severity contributing to unsuitability and non-adherence, the relevance of the intervention content to the client appeared to play a more important role in the client–intervention match. As for alliance, our results regarding suitability indicate the need for developing more personalized treatments in telemental health, and specifically, in blended interventions, instead of utilizing a one-size-fits-all approach [49]. Bettering the fit between client needs and expectations and provided content could improve client engagement and adherence, which has been a major challenge in our current as well as in previous studies.

4.4. Helpful Exercises

Therapists perceived certain interventions as better fits, while others as less good fits for blended interventions. Interventions that need strong emotion regulation skills (e.g., in vivo exposure exercises) or ability to critically engage with one's thoughts and beliefs (cognitive restructuring) may be challenging for many clients in a remote setting that heavily relies on independent client work. Providing more synchronous therapist contact, i.e., more frequent sessions, or simplifying these exercises from the given client's treatment protocol could address this problem. Other exercises that need little therapist support but are highly successful (e.g., behavior activation) could also be included in exclusively web-based intervention protocols.

4.5. Professional Support

Training and supervisor support before the preparation and throughout the intervention was perceived as crucial for the trainee therapists, who were young graduate students with relatively little clinical and no telemental health experience. They reported that training and first-hand experience with telemental health positively impacted their attitudes in our study, similarly to earlier findings [11,50]. Since experience with telemental health is also associated with more therapist confidence regarding the ability to build alliance, read emotions, and be emphatic with clients online [26], in order to promote the utilization of telemental health among providers, providing training and ongoing professional support for trainee and novice therapists would be crucial.

4.6. Limitations

As all studies, ours had its limitations as well. First, we had a relatively small sample of participant therapists; however, this is not unusual in qualitative studies. Qualitative inquiry typically uses smaller sample sizes (sometimes even a single participant, [51]) in order to explore a limited number of participants' subjective experiences in depth, in contrast with quantitative studies, where a larger random sample may better represent the views of a general population [52]. Based on this notion, we included a small number of therapists with the specific experience of participating in the RESILIENCE program, instead of a larger sample of therapists with potential experience in other programs. In addition, for a case study like ours, a focus group design with a relatively small number of participants is recommended, where the participants who are all familiar with the case (i.e., the RESILIENT intervention] are able to share experiences and generate ideas together [53]. Therefore, the fact that we could include all the participating therapists in our focus groups could be in fact considered as a strength of the study.

Second, the trainee therapists' experiences with providing telemental health within the context of the RESILIENT intervention in rural Canada might not be transferable to other circumstances. Our trainee therapists were all junior with little or no previous therapy experience, and despite the common view that younger people feel more comfortable using technology, earlier research found that more junior therapists with less clinical experience tend to have *less* positive experiences with providing telemental health compared to their older and more experienced counterparts [16,33]. Therefore, our therapists' perceptions of the intervention may differ from what older and more experienced therapists would experience under the same circumstances. Moreover, our participants, the specific event of the Fort McMurray fires, and the circumstances in our study were also unique, which may further limit the transferability of the findings.

Furthermore, our therapists within the study had some differences, such as their previous clinical experience and present caseload, which might have also impacted their experiences [35]. However, this case study's findings regarding therapist concerns and initial first-hand experiences with blended interventions for natural disaster survivors may still be helpful when preparing for new interventions under different circumstances.

5. Conclusions

The therapists in our case study perceived the blended intervention as a significant mental health tool for survivors of a natural catastrophe. The perceived success of this model encourages the implementation of similar blended interventions for survivors of other natural catastrophes in remote areas, or where psychological help is not readily available, as well as for survivors of other type of traumas who are reluctant to seek help in person, for example, sexual assault victims. However, based on our therapists' experiences, in order to improve the efficiency of such interventions, personalization of the treatment content and sequence, as well as proportion of therapist sessions and web-based content based on client needs, is recommended. Furthermore, providing theoretical and skills-based training in telemental health is recommended to improve the quality of online interventions in crucial areas, such as providing relevant content, building alliance, and specifics of online communication with clients. Our hope is that the accumulating knowledge of the specificities of online interventions for natural disaster survivors will not only inform the development of blended interventions for natural disaster survivors in the future but may also be incorporated in the training of future providers.

Author Contributions: Conceptualization, V.B., J.L. and G.B.; methodology, V.B., J.L. and G.B.; data analysis, Z.C. and V.B.; writing—original draft preparation, V.B.; writing—review and editing, V.B., Z.C., J.L., G.B. and S.B.; funding acquisition, G.B., M.-C.O., C.M.M., N.B., T.S.C., S.B., S.G. (Sunita Ghosh), S.G. (Stéphane Guay) and F.P.M. All authors have read and agreed to the published version of the manuscript.

Funding: This study was funded by a grant from the Operating Grant: Health Effects of the Alberta Wildfires program, supported by the Canadian Institutes of Health Research, Alberta Innovates, and the Canadian Red Cross (#381288).

Institutional Review Board Statement: The study was conducted according to the guidelines of the Declaration of Helsinki and approved by the Research Ethics Committee for Psychology and Education Sciences of Laval University (protocol code 2017-030 Phase II, date of approval: 7 November 2017).

Informed Consent Statement: Informed consent was obtained from all subjects involved in the study.

Data Availability Statement: Not applicable.

Conflicts of Interest: S.B. is President and shareholder of Cliniques et Développement In Virtuo, a clinic that offers psychotherapy services and distributes virtual reality software. All of this is framed by the conflict of interest management policy of the Université du Québec en Outaouais. The other authors declare that they have no conflict of interest.

References

1. Benevolenza, M.A.; DeRigne, L. The impact of climate change and natural disasters on vulnerable populations: A systematic review of literature. *J. Hum. Behav. Soc. Environ.* **2019**, *29*, 266–281. [CrossRef]
2. Makwana, N. Disaster and its impact on mental health: A narrative review. *J. Fem. Med. Prim. Care* **2019**, *8*, 3090. [CrossRef] [PubMed]
3. North, C.S.; Pfefferbaum, B. Mental health response to community disasters: A systematic review. *JAMA* **2013**, *310*, 507–518. [CrossRef] [PubMed]
4. Hamblen, J.L.; Norris, F.H.; Pietruszkiewicz, S.; Gibson, L.E.; Naturale, A.; Louis, C. Cognitive behavioral therapy for postdisaster distress: A community based treatment program for survivors of Hurricane Katrina. *Adm. Policy Ment. Health* **2009**, *36*, 206–214. [CrossRef] [PubMed]
5. Watson, P.J.; Hamblen, J. Assisting Individuals and Communities after Natural Disasters and Community Traumas. In *APA Handbook of Trauma Psychology*; Cook, J., Gold, S., Dalenberg, C., Eds.; American Psychological Association: Washington, DC, USA, 2018.
6. Békés, V.; Grondin, F.; Bouchard, S. Barriers and facilitators to the integration of web-based interventions into routine care. *Clin. Psychol. Sci. Pract.* **2020**, *27*, e12335. [CrossRef]
7. Simpson, S. Psychotherapy via videoconferencing: A review. *Br. J. Guid. Counc.* **2009**, *37*, 271–286. [CrossRef]
8. Erbe, D.; Eichert, H.C.; Riper, H.; Ebert, D.D. Blending face-to-face and internet-based interventions for the treatment of mental disorders in adults: Systematic review. *J. Med. Internet Res.* **2017**, *19*, e6588. [CrossRef]

9. Wentzel, J.; van der Vaart, R.; Bohlmeijer, E.T.; van Gemert-Pijnen, J.E. Mixing online and face-to-face therapy: How to benefit from blended care in mental health care. *JMIR Ment. Health* **2016**, *3*, e4534. [CrossRef]
10. Connolly, S.L.; Miller, C.J.; Lindsay, J.A.; Bauer, M.S. A systematic review of providers' attitudes toward telemental health via videoconferencing. *Clin. Psychol.* **2020**, *27*, e12311. [CrossRef]
11. Békés, V.; Aafjes-van Doorn, K. Psychotherapists' attitudes toward online therapy during the COVID-19 pandemic. *J. Psychother. Integr.* **2020**, *30*, 238. [CrossRef]
12. Békés, V.; Aafjes–van Doorn, K.; Prout, T.A.; Hoffman, L. Stretching the Analytic Frame: Analytic Therapists' Experiences with Remote Therapy during COVID-19. *J. Am. Psychoanal. Assoc.* **2020**, *68*, 437–446. [CrossRef] [PubMed]
13. Damianakis, T.; Climans, R.; Marziali, E. Social Workers' Experiences of Virtual Psychotherapeutic Caregivers Groups for Alzheimer's, Parkinson's, Stroke, Frontotemporal Dementia, and Traumatic Brain Injury. *Soc. Work Groups* **2008**, *31*, 99–116. [CrossRef]
14. Humer, E.; Stippl, P.; Pieh, C.; Pryss, R.; Probst, T. Experiences of Psychotherapists with Remote Psychotherapy during the COVID-19 Pandemic: Cross-sectional Web-Based Survey Study. *J. Med. Internet Res.* **2020**, *22*, e20246. [CrossRef] [PubMed]
15. Van der Vaart, R.; Witting, M.; Riper, H.; Kooistra, L.; Bohlmeijer, E.T.; van Gemert-Pijnen, L.J. Blending online therapy into regular face-to-face therapy for depression: Content, ratio and preconditions according to patients and therapists using a Delphi study. *BMC Psychiatry* **2014**, *14*, 355. [CrossRef]
16. Cioffi, V.; Cantone, D.; Guerriera, C.; Architravo, M.; Mosca, L.L.; Sperandeo, R.; Moretto, E.; Longobardi, T.; Alfano, Y.M.; Continisio, G.I.; et al. Satisfaction degree in the using of videoconferencing psychotherapy in a sample of Italian psychotherapists during Covid-19 emergency. In Proceedings of the 2020 11th IEEE International Conference on Cognitive Infocommunications (CogInfoCom), Mariehamn, Finland, 23–25 September 2020. [CrossRef]
17. Nuttman-Shwartz, O.; Shaul, K. Online therapy in a shared reality: The novel coronavirus as a test case. *Traumatology* **2021**, *27*, 365–374. [CrossRef]
18. Perry, K.; Gold, S.; Shearer, E.M. Identifying and addressing mental health providers' perceived barriers to clinical video telehealth utilization. *J. Clin. Psychol.* **2020**, *76*, 1125–1134. [CrossRef]
19. Topooco, N.; Riper, H.; Araya, R.; Berking, M.; Brunn, M.; Chevreul, K.; Cieslak, R.; Ebert, D.D.; Etchmendy, E.; Herrero, R.; et al. Attitudes towards digital treatment for depression: A European stakeholder survey. *Internet Interv.* **2017**, *8*, 1–9. [CrossRef]
20. Bambling, M.; King, R.; Reid, W.; Wegner, K. Online counselling: The experience of counsellors providing synchronous single-session counselling to young people. *Couns. Psychother. Res.* **2008**, *8*, 110–116. [CrossRef]
21. Becker, E.M.; Jensen-Doss, A. Computer-Assisted Therapies: Examination of Therapist-Level Barriers to Their Use. *Behav. Ther.* **2013**, *44*, 614–624. [CrossRef]
22. Bengtsson, J.; Nordin, S.; Carlbring, P. Therapists' Experiences of Conducting Cognitive Behavioural Therapy Online vis-à-vis Face-to-Face. *Cogn. Behav. Ther.* **2015**, *44*, 470–479. [CrossRef] [PubMed]
23. Norwood, C.; Moghaddam, N.G.; Malins, S.; Sabin-Farrell, R. Working alliance and outcome effectiveness in videoconferencing psychotherapy: A systematic review and noninferiority meta-analysis. *Clin. Psychol. Psychother.* **2018**, *25*, 797–808. [CrossRef] [PubMed]
24. Bouchard, S.; Allard, M.; Robillard, G.; Dumoulin, S.; Guitard, T.; Loranger, C.; Green-Demers, I.; Marchand, A.; Renaud, P.; Cournoyer, L.-G.; et al. Videoconferencing Psychotherapy for Panic Disorder and Agoraphobia: Outcome and Treatment Processes from a Non-randomized Non-inferiority Trial. *Front. Psychol.* **2020**, *11*, 2164. [CrossRef] [PubMed]
25. Watts, S.; Marchand, A.; Bouchard, S.; Gosselin, P.; Langlois, F.; Belleville, G.; Dugas, M.J. Telepsychotherapy for generalized anxiety disorder: Impact on the working alliance. *J. Psychother. Integr.* **2020**, *30*, 208–225. [CrossRef]
26. Sucala, M.; Schnur, J.B.; Brackman, E.H.; Constantino, M.J.; Montgomery, G.H. Clinicians' attitudes toward therapeutic alliance in e-therapy. *J. General Psychol.* **2013**, *140*, 282–293. [CrossRef]
27. Roesler, C. Tele-analysis: The use of media technology in psychotherapy and its impact on the therapeutic relationship. *J. Anal. Psychol.* **2017**, *62*, 372–394. [CrossRef]
28. Reese, R.J.; Mecham, M.R.; Vasilj, I.; Lengerich, A.J.; Brown, H.M.; Simpson, N.B.; Newsome, B.D. The effects of telepsychology format on empathic accuracy and the therapeutic alliance: An analogue counselling session. *Couns. Psychother. Res.* **2016**, *16*, 256–265. [CrossRef]
29. Simms, D.C.; Gibson, K.; O'Donnell, S. To use or not to use: Clinicians' perceptions of telemental health. *Can. Psychol.* **2011**, *52*, 41–51. [CrossRef]
30. Machluf, R.; Abba Daleski, M.; Shahar, B.; Kula, O.; Bar-Kalifa, E. Couples therapists' attitudes toward online therapy during the COVID-19 crisis. *Fam. Process.* **2021**, *61*, 146–154. [CrossRef]
31. Boldrini, T.; Schiano Lomoriello, A.; Del Corno, F.; Lingiardi, V.; Salcuni, S. Psychotherapy during COVID-19: How the clinical practice of Italian psychotherapists changed during the pandemic. *Front. Psychol.* **2020**, *11*, 591170. [CrossRef]
32. Korecka, N.; Rabenstein, R.; Pieh, C.; Stippl, P.; Barke, A.; Doering, B.; Gossmann, K.; Humer, E.; Probst, T. Psychotherapy by telephone or internet in Austria and Germany which CBT psychotherapists rate it more comparable to face-to-face psychotherapy in personal contact and have more positive actual experiences compared to previous expectations? *Int. J. Environ. Res. Public Health* **2020**, *17*, 7756. [CrossRef]
33. Aafjes-van Doorn, K.; Békés, V.; Prout, T.A. Grappling with our therapeutic relationship and professional self-doubt during COVID-19: Will we use video therapy again? *Couns. Psychol. Q.* **2020**, *34*, 473–484. [CrossRef]

34. Thériault, L.; Belleville, G.; Ouellet, M.C.; Morin, C.M. The experience and perceived consequences of the 2016 Fort McMurray fires and evacuation. *Front. Public Health* **2021**, *9*, 641151. [CrossRef] [PubMed]
35. Belleville, G.; Ouellet, M.-C.; Lebel, J.; Ghosh, S.; Morin, C.M.; Bouchard, S.; Guay, S.; Bergeron, N.; Campbell, T.; MacMaster, F.P. Psychological Symptoms Among Evacuees From the 2016 Fort McMurray Wildfires: A Population-Based Survey One Year Later. *Front. Public Health* **2021**, *9*, 444. [CrossRef] [PubMed]
36. Belleville, G.; Ouellet, M.C.; Békés, V.; Lebel, J.; Morin, C.M.; Bouchard, S.; Guay, S.; Bergeron, N.; Ghosh, S.; Campbell, T.; et al. Efficacy of an online treatment targeting PTSD, depression and insomnia after a disaster: A randomized controlled trial. 2022; *Under review*.
37. Steward, D.W.; Shamdasani, P.N. *Focus Groups: Theory and Practice*; Sage: Thousand Oaks, CA, USA, 2014.
38. Weathers, F.W.; Litz, B.T.; Keane, T.M.; Palmieri, P.A.; Marx, B.P.; Schnurr, P.P. The PTSD Checklist for DSM-5 (PCL-5). The National Center for PTSD. 2011. Available online: www.ptsd.va.gov (accessed on 15 April 2021).
39. Kroenke, K.; Spitzer, R.L.; Williams, J.B. The PHQ-9: Validity of a brief depression severity measure. *J. Gen. Intern. Med.* **2001**, *16*, 606–613. [CrossRef]
40. Morin, C.M.; Belleville, G.; Bélanger, L.; Ivers, H. The Insomnia Severity Index: Psychometric indicators to detect insomnia cases and evaluate treatment response. *Sleep* **2011**, *34*, 601–608. [CrossRef] [PubMed]
41. Békés, V.; Belleville, G.; Lebel, J.; Ouellet, M.-C.; Morin, C.M.; Bergeron, N.; Campbell, T.; Ghosh, S.; Bouchard, S.; Guay, S.; et al. L'expérience des thérapeutes concernant un auto-traitement guidé en ligne visant à promouvoir la résilience après une catastrophe naturelle [Therapist experiences about an online guided self-help intervention to promote resilience after a natural disaster]. *Rev. Francoph. Comport. Cogn.* **2020**, *25*, 103–119.
42. Lebel, J.; Flores-Tremblay, T.; Binet, É.; Ouellet, M.C.; Belleville, G. Usage Data of an Online Multidimensional Treatment to Promote Resilience After a Disaster. *Sante Ment. Quebec* **2021**, *46*, 203–227. [CrossRef]
43. Doherty, G.; Coyle, D.; Sharry, J. Engagement with online mental health interventions: An exploratory clinical study of a treatment for depression. In Proceedings of the SIGCHI Conference on Human Factors in Computing Systems, Austin, TX, USA, 5–10 May 2012; pp. 1421–1430. [CrossRef]
44. Kelders, S.M.; Kok, R.N.; Ossebaard, H.C.; Van Gemert-Pijnen, J.E.W.C. Persuasive system design does matter: A systematic review of adherence to web-based interventions. *J. Med. Internet Res.* **2012**, *14*, e152. [CrossRef]
45. Cook, J.E.; Doyle, C. Working alliance in online therapy as compared to face-to-face therapy: Preliminary results. *CyberPsychol. Behav.* **2002**, *5*, 95–105. [CrossRef]
46. Johansson, O.; Michel, T.; Andersson, G.; Paxling, B. Experiences of non-adherence to Internet-delivered cognitive behavior therapy: A qualitative study. *Internet Interv.* **2015**, *2*, 137–142. [CrossRef]
47. Grondin, F.; Lomanowska, A.M.; Jackson, P.L. Empathy in computer-mediated interactions: A conceptual framework for research and clinical practice. *Clin. Psychol.* **2019**, *26*, e12298. [CrossRef]
48. Grondin, F.; Lomanowska, A.M.; Békés, V.; Jackson, P.L. A methodology to improve eye contact in telepsychotherapy via videoconferencing with considerations for psychological distance. *Couns. Psychol. Q.* **2021**, *34*, 586–599. [CrossRef]
49. Titzler, I.; Saruhanjan, K.; Berking, M.; Riper, H.; Ebert, D.D. Barriers and facilitators for the implementation of blended psychotherapy for depression: A qualitative pilot study of therapists' perspective. *Internet Interv.* **2018**, *12*, 150–164. [CrossRef]
50. Békés, V.; Aafjes-van Doorn, K.; Zilcha-Mano, S.; Prout, T.A.; Hoffman, L. Psychotherapists' Acceptance of Online Therapy During the COVID-19 Pandemic: A Machine Learning Approach. *J. Clin. Psychol. Psychother.* **2021**, *28*, 1403–1415. [CrossRef] [PubMed]
51. Crossley, M.L. Childbirth, complications and the illusion of 'choice': A case study. *Fem. Psychol.* **2007**, *17*, 543–563. [CrossRef]
52. Braun, V.; Clarke, V. To saturate or not to saturate? Questioning data saturation as a useful concept for thematic analysis and sample-size rationales. *Qual. Res. Sport Exerc. Health* **2021**, *13*, 201–216. [CrossRef]
53. Creswell, J.W. *Qualitative Inquiry and Research Design: Choosing among Five Traditions*; Sage: Thousand Oaks, CA, USA, 1998.

Journal of
Clinical Medicine

MDPI

Article

Telepsychology in Europe since COVID-19: How to Foster Social Telepresence?

Lise Haddouk [1,*], Carine Milcent [2], Benoît Schneider [3], Tom Van Daele [4] and Nele A. J. De Witte [4]

1 Centre Borelli (UMR9010), Rouen University, 76000 Rouen, France
2 CNRS, Paris School of Economics, 75014 Paris, France
3 2LPN, Université de Lorraine, 56532 Nancy, France
4 Expertise Unit Psychology, Technology and Society, Thomas More University of Applied Sciences, 2018 Antwerp, Belgium
* Correspondence: lise.haddouk@u-paris.fr

Abstract: All over the world, measures were taken to prevent the spread of COVID-19. Social distancing not only had a strong influence on mental health, but also on the organization of care systems. It changed existing practices, as we had to rapidly move from face-to-face contact to remote contact with patients. These changes have prompted research into the attitudes of mental healthcare professionals towards telepsychology. Several factors affect these attitudes: at the institutional and organizational level, but also the collective and personal experience of practitioners. This paper is based on an original European survey conducted by the EFPA (European Federation of Psychologists' Associations) Project Group on eHealth in 2020, which allowed to observe the variability in perceptions of telepsychology between countries and mental healthcare professionals. This study highlights different variables that contributed to the development of attitudes, such as motivations, acquired experience, or training. We found the "feeling of telepresence"—which consists of forgetting to some extent that we are at a distance, in feeling together—and social telepresence in particular as main determinants of the perception and the practice of telepsychology.

Keywords: telepsychology; social telepresence; mental healthcare professionals; training; acceptance

Citation: Haddouk, L.; Milcent, C.; Schneider, B.; Van Daele, T.; De Witte, N.A.J. Telepsychology in Europe since COVID-19: How to Foster Social Telepresence? *J. Clin. Med.* **2023**, *12*, 2147. https://doi.org/10.3390/jcm12062147

Academic Editors: Stéphane Bouchard and Gennaro Ruggiero

Received: 26 September 2022
Revised: 27 February 2023
Accepted: 6 March 2023
Published: 9 March 2023

1. Introduction

Worldwide, actions were taken to avoid the spread of the COVID-19 pandemic caused by SARS-CoV-2. Aside from reducing the virus' expansion, it also led to physical distancing, travel restrictions, and city-wide quarantines [1]. The pandemic context constrained people to being isolated, unemployed, inactive, and with low social support which increased patients' exposure to factors known to exacerbate mental health disorders [2]. Even more so, all of these measures had a tremendous impact on the delivery of healthcare services, including mental healthcare: consulting patients in person became very challenging [3–5]. In addition, under strict infection control, some clinical psychiatrists refused to enter COVID-19 patients' wards [6]. As a result, innovative solutions were needed to address the critical needs of patients. Since the beginning of the pandemic, many healthcare services therefore shifted from in-person to remote patient contact. According to Patel et al. [7], the COVID-19 pandemic has been associated with a marked increase in remote mental health consultation. Telepsychology practices have also increased significantly in the US following the COVID-19 pandemic [8].

For over two decades, research has been carried out, particularly in North America, on the effectiveness of telepsychology services for patients with different types of mental disorders [9–12]. Telepsychology has been defined by the American Psychological Association (APA) in 2013 as: "the provision of psychological services using telecommunication technologies" (https://www.apa.org/practice/guidelines/telepsychology, accessed on 25 September 2022). The pandemic has prompted a sharp increase in telepsychology practice by new practitioners: a recent study among 1791 mental healthcare professionals in the UK revealed a 12-fold increase in the use of telepsychology [13]. A survey in France, conducted in 2021 among 511 psychologists, showed very infrequent use of telepsychology before the crisis (7.1% of psychologists), whereas more than 70% of psychologists used it during the crisis; slightly less than half (45.6%) estimated that they would still use it after the crisis [14]. This development has prompted new research that shows a gradual acceptance of telepsychology [15]. Prior to the COVID-19 pandemic, the use of teleconsultations in psychiatry and psychology was quite limited in Europe, although these practices existed in some hospitals. For example, in France, telepsychiatry practices, i.e., the application of telemedicine to the specialized field of psychiatry, have been regulated by the decree on telemedicine produced in 2010 (https://www.legifrance.gouv.fr/loda/id/JORFTEXT000022932449, accessed on 25 September 2022). On telepsychology and the use of technology in mental healthcare, some guidelines have in the meantime been produced in Europe [16], but not on a large scale.

A key concept in telepsychology is the notion of telepresence, which was born from anecdotal references regarding the feeling of being moved from a local control room to a remote area when using a teleoperator [17]. In telepsychology, the feeling of telepresence is about the quality of the relationship between the patient and the psychologist [18]. It is an important concept to understand relational processes in telepsychology and it consists of forgetting to some extent that we are at a distance, i.e., feeling together [19]. This feeling of telepresence also seems to predict the therapeutic alliance [9]. In cognitive behavioural therapy using video conferencing, the therapeutic alliance was, for example, found to be positively correlated with the level of telepresence felt by patients [9,20]. Similarly, the evaluation of intersubjective qualities of online interactions also appears to be related to the feeling of telepresence [21]. Several research studies have demonstrated a link between the positive emotions felt by patients in CBT videoconference psychotherapy (VCP) and the level of telepresence [18].

A commonly used tool to assess telepresence is the Videoconference Telepresence Scale (VTS), which was proposed in 2006 and revised in 2018 [22]. The scale consists of seven items, which form three subscales: (1) physical presence (whether the user felt actually present in the consultation with the other person), (2) absorption (forgetting that the psychotherapist and the patient are not in the same room), and (3) social presence (feeling that the interlocutor reacts to your presence and having the impression of actively participating in exchanges with the other person) [22]. This study focuses on social telepresence in particular.

Telepresence appears to be a cornerstone of a successful telepractice for both patient and professional [9,20]. Nevertheless, in the context of the COVID-19 pandemic, little is known about the clinical and sociodemographic factors that may have influenced the effectiveness of remote consultations on the patient side [23] or about the factors that affect professionals' perceptions of telepsychology [24]. Recent research, however, not only showed that telepsychology has the potential to improve access to care, but also that providers' attitudes toward this innovation play a crucial role in its adoption. Some studies found that providers had an overall positive attitude toward telepsychology, even despite multiple drawbacks [25]. Additionally, there is a relationship between access to technology, experience and practitioner training on the one hand and acceptability of videoconferencing use on the other hand [24]. Studies have also shown that psychologists' attitudes about telepsychology and subjective norms are associated with the intention to use telepsychology, which in turn is related to experience of clinical work done via telepsychology [26].

Beyond the current health crisis, telepsychology is likely to remain a major component of mental healthcare, as it might help to improve access to mental healthcare and to reduce costs of service delivery [27]. It is therefore critical to determine the impact, potential benefits and disadvantages of telepsychology not only for patients [28], but also for professionals. In general healthcare, previous work has already found that professionals were often concerned about technical and clinical quality, safety, privacy, and accountability [29–31] when opting for tele-health. In this paper, however, we focus particularly on the mental healthcare professionals' point of view on telepsychology. We study the impact of their personal characteristics and training and try to explore them in relation to the concept of telepresence, which has received less attention than acceptance in the literature.

We therefore aim to present results on telepsychology practices in different European countries during the initial lockdown caused by the COVID-19 pandemic, where access to mental healthcare was highly limited. A large international online survey on the use of telepsychology, in this case focused on online psychological consultations during the COVID-19 pandemic, was set up. Qualitative analyses of actual needs and concerns relating to the use of online consultations have already been published [32] as well as quantitative exploratory analyses which primarily aimed to gain insights into determinants of telepsychology (non)adoption and experience [33]. This study builds on this existing work by focusing exclusively on mental healthcare professionals who had adopted the practice of telepsychology, exploring the extent to which differences across countries can be retrieved and investigating social telepresence.

The first goal of this study is to examine determinants of mental healthcare professionals' perception of telepsychology in Europe during the COVID-19 pandemic. The second goal is to investigate the determinants of social telepresence and the role of telepsychology perception in social telepresence. The analysis takes into account personal characteristics such as gender, motivations, prior training, and experience of mental healthcare professionals. In the proposed conceptual model, we assume that the personal characteristics and the level of training in telepsychology of mental healthcare professionals are factors that directly influence the perception of telepsychology, invariant for country. Additionally, we assume that the level of social telepresence experienced by professionals is directly influenced by their motivation for telepsychology, personal characteristics, and level of training in telepsychology. As a result, we also presume indirect effects of training on mental healthcare professionals' perception of telepsychology.

2. Materials and Methods

2.1. Sample

In the context of the COVID-19 pandemic, the EFPA Project Group on e-Health launched a European survey from 18 March to 5 May 2020 on the online practices of mental healthcare professionals. It was conducted through the mailing lists and social media of the European Federation of Psychologists' Associations (EFPA) as well as national psychologists' associations and project collaborators from different countries.

The online survey was designed to assess the extent to which mental health professionals were implementing telepsychology during the COVID-19 pandemic, their experience with this treatment modality and their concerns. Telepsychology was operationalised as online consultations, i.e., digital contact (text, audio, and/or video) for psychological counselling or psychotherapy. The survey was translated into 17 languages by local researchers and professionals in the field of psychology. This study has analysed the perception of social telepresence for mental healthcare professionals in Austria, Belgium, Denmark, Finland, France, Germany, Italy, the Netherlands, Norway, Portugal, Spain, Sweden and the UK, and relied on a subsample of participants who had opted for telepsychology.

2.2. Measures

Dependent variables of interest. The first variable was 'Perception of telepsychology', which was measured using the question "How comfortable do you consider yourself with (the concept of) online consultations". It was scored on a 5-point Likert scale ranging from 1, *'Highly uncomfortable'*, to 5, *'Highly comfortable'*, with higher scores reflecting greater satisfaction and less concern.

The second variable was 'Social telepresence', the feeling of being connected with one another linked to the evaluation of social presence in the VTS. It was measured using the question: "*If you have started online consultations recently, how would you rate your level of telepresence (feeling of being connected with one another) during consultations?*". It was scored on a 5-point Likert scale, ranging from 1, '*Very low*', to 5, '*Very high*'. Higher scores reflected greater satisfaction and less concern about one's social telepresence during telepsychology.

Independent variables of interest. The first set of variables of interest were 'Personal characteristics of mental healthcare professionals'. These included age (five dummy variables with less than 35 years old as the referent category, compared to 35–44, 45–54, 55–60, over 60), gender (0 = male, 1 = female), professional status (five dummy variables with self-employed as the referent category, compared to group practice, health care organization, mental health care organization, other), and professional seniority (years of professional activity as mental healthcare professionals).

The second variable was 'Reasons for telepractice implementation'. There were several possible motivations for mental healthcare professionals to make use of telepsychology. They included: (1) considering it a necessity from a public health point of view; (2) meeting clients' demands; (3) not wanting to lose income; (4) wanting to provide access to care; and (5) being open-minded concerning digital mental health. As for social telepresence, the data only provide this information for mental healthcare professionals who have only newly used telepsychology.

The third set of variables was 'Training'. Telepractice before the pandemic was captured by the following question: "*I have experience with online consultations, prior to the COVID-19 outbreak.*" (0 = no, 1 = yes). Specific training was defined as "*Have you had any specific training concerning online consultations?*" (0 = no, 1 = yes). We ran econometric models to determine the factors that drove this perception. Descriptive data for the sample are presented in Table 1 and in Appendix A.

Table 1. Perception of telepsychology and social telepresence as reported by European mental healthcare professionals, and the correlation between these concepts.

	Perception of Telepsychology			**Social Telepresence**			
Country	**N**	***M***	***SD***	**N**	***M***	***SD***	***r***
Austria	65	3.84	0.89	43	3.97	1.12	0.01
Belgium	556	3.83	0.81	404	3.56	0.88	0.51 **
Denmark	76	4.06	0.79	68	3.99	0.76	0.41 **
Finland	141	3.59	1.03	79	3.47	1.04	0.48 **
France	491	3.94	0.70	222	3.84	0.81	0.41 **
Germany	168	3.97	0.76	92	4.00	0.84	0.23 *
Italy	4604	3.95	0.75	3605	3.75	0.81	0.43 **
Netherlands	81	3.87	0.94	68	3.56	0.97	0.36 **
Norway	258	4.02	0.87	189	3.83	0.76	0.19 **
Portugal	267	4.19	0.69	165	3.86	0.76	0.39 **
Spain	31	4.41	0.50	21	3.85	0.97	0.30
Sweden	395	3.93	0.96	223	3.55	1.00	0.45 **
UK	50	4.03	0.81	28	3.89	0.69	0.54 **

Note. * $p < 0.05$, ** $p < 0.01$.

2.3. Empirical Models

The following models were used:

Y^1_{ij}: Perception of the concept of telepsychology practice in Europe

$$Y^1_{ij} = a(Training)_{ij} + b(Personal\ information\ on\ psychologists)_{ij} + \beta_j + \varepsilon^1_{ij}$$

With i the individual and j the country

Personal characteristics of mental healthcare professionals: age group, gender, self-employed, group practice, healthcare organisation, mental healthcare organisation, years of experience; training including telepractice before the pandemic and specific training; β_j: the country fixed effects, ε^1_{ij}: the error terms

Y_{ij}^2: The social telepresence for new telepsychology users in Europe

$$\begin{aligned} &Y_{ij}^2 \\ &= a(Training)_{ij} + b(Personal\ infomation\ on\ psychologists\ )_{ij} \\ &+c(Motivationfor\ telepractice\ for\ fresh\ psychologists)_{ij} \\ &+d(Perception\ with\ the\ concept\ of\ telepsychology\ practices\ in\ Europe)_{ij} + \beta_j + \varepsilon_{ij}^2 \end{aligned}$$

With i the individual and j the country

Personal characteristics of mental healthcare professionals: age group, gender, self-employed, group practice, healthcare organisation, mental healthcare organisation, years of experience. training, including telepractice before the pandemic and specific training; motivation for telepractice, including perceived public health need, client's demand, not losing income, guaranteeing access, technological interest; β_j: the country fixed effects. ε_{ij}^2: the error terms.

We used an incremental model, which is a form of the hierarchical regression model (in which variables are added or removed from a model in multiple steps), as used, for example, by Clark and Milcent [34]. This model sought to examine the explanatory power of variables that are deemed essential, together with other groups of variables. The interest of this model, compared to the stepwise model, is not to remove non-significant variables, but to test the influence of correlations of internals to one group of variables on variables in a second group. We also used a fixed effect model for nested data: here, mental healthcare professionals belong to one country. So, we have the mental healthcare professional dimension and the country dimension. The nested data here consist of two levels of sampling, with observations sampled at Level One (mental healthcare professionals) nested (or clustered) within units sampled at Level Two (country). Hierarchical linear modelling is used here with fixed effects.

We investigated the determinants that impacted mental healthcare professionals' telepsychology experience, i.e., their perception of the concept of telepsychology practices, as well as the factors that positively impacted "teleperception". The database is a nested panel of data at two levels: respondent and country. The data also showed an unbalanced structure at two levels: the number of respondents per country differs from country to country. We wanted to work at the individual level in order to take advantage of the variability at the individual level. We therefore used a fixed effect model to control for country specificities and to provide a respondent-level analysis: thus, the effect of mental healthcare professionals' specificities on the perception of telepsychology and social telepresence of mental healthcare professionals was identified only by seeing how mental healthcare professionals' specificities changed within a given country. No cross-country information was used in the estimation of these coefficients.

This approach conditioned the sum of an individual's feelings over a country. The fixed effects approach [35–39] controlled for any interaction between the mental healthcare professionals surveyed and the country variables. Each fixed effect probit model was studied through a multiple regression using STATA SE version 16.

3. Results: Perception of Telepsychology

3.1. Descriptive Data

Table 1 reports the descriptive data for the dependent variables in the study, with more details to be found in Appendix A. The dataset was unbalanced, as the number of surveyed mental healthcare professionals varied for each country.

Spain, Portugal, Denmark, and the UK were the countries where mental healthcare professionals felt most comfortable with the notion of telepsychology. On the other hand, Finland, Belgium, Austria, and the Netherlands were the countries where mental healthcare professionals were least comfortable with telepsychology. Higher levels were reported in Germany, Denmark, Austria and the UK. Participants from these countries reported experiencing a higher level of social telepresence during telepsychology, compared to lower levels in Finland, Sweden, the Netherlands and Belgium.

There were clear disparities between countries with regard to the correlations between both concepts. Two atypical situations were Austria (almost zero correlation) and Spain (non-significant correlation). The correlation then oscillated from $r = 0.18$ (Norway) to $r = 0.53$ (United Kingdom). There did not appear to be a relationship between the level of correlation and high or low scores in the perception of telepsychology or social telepresence. We controlled for cross-countries disparities using fixed effect models. The interpretation of the independent variables was then completed as if mental healthcare professionals were similar, regardless the country. This econometric model was used as we had nested panel data at the level of mental healthcare professionals and countries. It allowed to control for country-invariant attributes of participants.

3.2. Do Mental Healthcare Professionals' Characteristics Play into the Perception of Telepsychology?

In this sample, French mental healthcare professionals were mostly women (90%), as was the case in Denmark, Belgium, the Netherlands, and Portugal. In Germany and Spain, the context was quite different with 64% and 68%, respectively, of female mental healthcare professionals. The sample was younger in Belgium, France, and Portugal (41 years old on average), compared to other European countries (49 years old in Austria, Denmark and the UK). In line with this, they had fewer years of professional seniority in Belgium and France (13 years) than what was observed in the samples of other European countries (21 years in Austria and 17 years in Denmark, the UK, and Spain). There was substantial heterogeneity regarding the context of practice across countries. In Italy, 78% of mental healthcare professionals were self-employed, whereas in The Netherlands and Sweden, less than 20% were. In Norway or Finland, one third worked in a health organization (Appendix A). To control for this variability in mental healthcare professionals' practices across countries, we mobilized a fixed effect country model to explore perceptions of telepsychology.

In many applications, including econometrics and biostatistics, a fixed effects model refers to a regression model in which the group means are fixed (non-random) as opposed to a random effects model in which the group means are a random sample from a population. This model captured country specificities in a country-dummy variable. We analysed mental healthcare professionals' perception as if the countries were comparable in terms of specificities. Using a stepwise multiple regression, we first considered only demographic variables. Then, we added practice conditions.

In Tables 2 and 3, a country dummy, a set of variables specific to country that are invariant over time, captured the country fixed effect. There were as many country dummies as countries (and consequently no intercept because of the strict collinearity). Results were calculated from the model based on the independent variables of interest. "Reference" is the reference group used for comparison.

Table 2 Columns (1), (2), and (3) refer to incremental models 1 to 3. Model 1 refers to the Demographic variables included in the personal characteristics of mental healthcare professionals. Model 2 refers to Personal characteristics of mental healthcare professionals. Model 3 refers to Personal characteristics of mental healthcare professionals + Training. Table 2, Column (1) shows that female mental healthcare professionals had a more negative perception of telepsychology. Even after controlling for professional status and professional seniority (in years), a similar result was obtained (Table 2, Column (2)).

Similarly, after adding control for training (telepsychology practice prior to the pandemic and any specific training for telepsychology), the results showed a negative effect of gender on the perception of telepsychology (Table 2, Column (3)). Additionally, Table 2 shows that the seniority of the mental healthcare professionals compared to the youngest (under 35 years old), improved the perception of telepsychology. However, this effect was captured by the effect of training on the perception of telepsychology (Table 2, Column (3)).

Working in a healthcare organisation, rather than being self-employed, made mental healthcare professionals less positive about telepsychology (Table 2, Columns (1) & (2)). However, this effect was captured by the effect of training on the perception of telepsychology (Table 2, Column (3)). The addition of training as a variable removed the effect of work status.

Table 2. Econometric model predicting the perception of telepsychology among European mental healthcare professionals.

	Perception of Telepsychology		
	(1)	(2)	(3)
Mental healthcare professionals' personal characteristics			
<35 years	Reference	Reference	Reference
>35–40 years	0.09 *	0.06	−0.01
	(0.039)	(0.041)	(0.039)
>40–50 years	0.25 **	0.20 **	0.14 **
	(0.043)	(0.052)	(0.050)
>50–55 years	0.13 *	0.14	0.11
	(0.063)	(0.076)	(0.073)
>55 years	0.18 **	0.11	0.10
	(0.056)	(0.086)	(0.081)
Gender: female	−0.25 **	−0.25 **	−0.16 **
	(0.042)	(0.040)	(0.038)
Self-employed		Reference	Reference
Group practice		0.15	0.20 *
		(0.103)	(0.098)
HC organisation		−0.11 *	−0.01
		(0.047)	(0.045)
MHC organisation		−0.12 **	−0.05
		(0.044)	(0.042)
Years of experience		0.00	−0.00
		(0.002)	(0.002)
Training			
Telepsychology practice before the pandemic			0.35 **
			(0.047)
Specific training			0.77 **
			(0.029)
Country Fixed Effects	Yes	Yes	Yes
R-Squared	0.025	0.013	0.109

Notes: *, **: Student's t-test; * $p < 0.05$, ** $p < 0.01$; Standard errors in parentheses. Reference: reference group used for comparisons.

Taken together, the main results suggested that female mental healthcare professionals had a less positive perception of telepsychology and that seniority in the profession and the fact of working independently were related to a more positive perception of telepsychology.

3.3. Does Training Have an Impact on the Perception of Telepsychology?

We studied the effect of training—operationalised as telepsychology practice before the pandemic as well as specific training—with personal characteristics of mental healthcare professionals as a control.

First, in terms of percentages, some figures on mental healthcare professionals who practiced telepsychology before the pandemic. Prior to the COVID-19 outbreak, the percentage of professionals with experience in telepsychology was 58% in Spain and 54% in the UK, respectively. In contrast, less than a quarter of mental healthcare professionals practiced online in Belgium and France. Regarding specific training for telepsychology, very few European countries reported specific training among mental healthcare professionals. In Austria, Finland, and the UK, more than one fifth of respondents had specific training in support of telepsychology. In France, it dropped to less than one in twenty and 6.6% in Belgium (Appendix A). We used an econometric model to control for this country heterogeneity: a country fixed effect model.

Table 3. Econometric model predicting social telepresence in telepsychology and the characteristics of new European mental health professional users.

	Social Telepresence of European Mental Healthcare Professionals New to Telepsychology (Level)				
	(1)	**(2)**	**(3)**	**(4)**	**(5)**
Personal characteristics of mental healthcare professionals					
<35 years	Reference	Reference	Reference	Reference	Reference
>35–40 years	0.06	0.01	−0.01	0.01	0.01
	(0.031)	(0.032)	(0.032)	(0.032)	(0.029)
>40–50 years	0.15 **	0.03	0.01	0.03	−0.01
	(0.034)	(0.041)	(0.041)	(0.041)	(0.037)
>50–55 years	0.18 **	0.07	0.05	0.07	0.03
	(0.049)	(0.061)	(0.060)	(0.060)	(0.055)
>55 years	0.20 **	−0.00	−0.02	0.00	−0.04
	(0.044)	(0.069)	(0.068)	(0.067)	(0.062)
Gender: female	0.10 **	0.08 **	0.11 **	0.12 **	0.15 **
	(0.032)	(0.031)	(0.030)	(0.030)	(0.028)
Self-employed	Reference	Reference	Reference	Reference	Reference
Group practice		−0.05	−0.04	−0.07	−0.11
		(0.078)	(0.077)	(0.076)	(0.070)
HC organisation		−0.15 **	−0.15 **	−0.18 **	−0.19 **
		(0.041)	(0.041)	(0.041)	(0.038)
MHC organisation		−0.18 **	−0.18 **	−0.20 **	−0.20 **
		(0.037)	(0.036)	(0.036)	(0.033)
Professional seniority: Years of activity		0.01 **	0.01 **	0.01 **	0.01 **
		(0.002)	(0.002)	(0.002)	(0.002)
Training					
Telepsychology practice before the pandemic			0.18 **	0.16 **	0.10 **
			(0.036)	(0.036)	(0.033)
Specific training			0.21 **	0.21 **	0.07 **
			(0.022)	(0.022)	(0.021)
Motivations for telepsychology for novel mental healthcare professionals					
Public health				0.19 **	0.12 **
				(0.025)	(0.023)
Client				0.15 **	0.10 **
				(0.026)	(0.024)
Income				−0.12 **	−0.11 **
				(0.028)	(0.026)
Access				0.10 **	0.09 **
				(0.023)	(0.021)
Techno				0.06 *	0.01
				(0.029)	(0.027)
Perception					0.28 **
					(0.009)
Country Fixed Effects	Yes	Yes	Yes	Yes	Yes
R-squared	0.022	0.017	0.037	0.059	0.206

Notes: *, **: Student's *t*-test; * $p < 0.05$, ** $p < 0.01$; Standard errors in parentheses. Reference: reference group used for comparisons.

Controlling for mental healthcare professionals' personal characteristics, training had a very positive impact on the perception of telepsychology.

The training dimension was captured by two proxies in Table 2: (1) Telepractice before the pandemic and (2) Specific training. As shown Table 2, for these two proxies, the coefficients were significant. Then we were able to conclude that not only previous experience (in years) of telepsychology practices impacted the perception of telepsychology positively; but also that specific training in itself improved the perception of telepsychology. This result was found after controlling for the mental healthcare professionals' characteristics. As a sensitivity analysis, we ran the model without any additional control variables. The results were similar.

Results suggested that training—telepsychology practice before the pandemic and specific training—had a positive impact on the perception of telepsychology.

3.4. Do Mental Healthcare Professionals' Personal Characteristics Have an Impact on the Perception of Social Telepresence?

Table 1 shows the number of mental healthcare professionals surveyed by country. As global features, we observed disparities between countries in the level of social telepresence of the mental healthcare professionals, as presented in Table 1. The average was higher in Germany (M = 4.00) and Denmark (M = 3.99), as compared to in Finland (M = 3.47) and Sweden (M = 3.55). The econometric model took these disparities between countries into account.

Table 3 presents the results. Table 3 Columns (1), (2), (3), (4), and (5) refer to incremental models 1 to 5. Model 1 refers to the demographic variables included in the personal characteristics of mental healthcare professionals. Model 2 refers to Personal characteristics of mental healthcare professionals. Model 3 refers to Personal characteristics of mental healthcare professionals + Training. Model 4 refers to Personal characteristics of mental healthcare professionals + Training + Motivations to start telepsychology. Model 5 refers to Personal characteristics of mental healthcare professionals + Training + Motivations to start telepsychology + Perception.

Using a stepwise multiple regression, we showed the relationship between characteristics of professional status, professional seniority (in years), and social telepresence level. The demographic characteristics of mental healthcare professionals—age and gender—played into social telepresence (Table 3, column (1)). However, by adding professional status and professional seniority, we found that only gender affects social telepresence: being a female psychologist positively affected the level of social telepresence (Table 3, column (2)). When we added training, this result remained, as well as when we added reasons to practice telepsychology (Table 3, columns (3) and (4)). Adding perception of telepsychology did not change this result (Table 3, column (5)).

Employment status, however, did affect social telepresence. Compared to self-employed mental healthcare professionals, working in a healthcare organisation reduced the feeling of social telepresence. This result was obtained regardless of the set of variables controlled (Table 3, columns (2)–(5)). Mental healthcare professionals' year of professional seniority positively affected feeling of social telepresence (Table 3, columns (2)–(5)).

Results therefore suggested that mental healthcare professionals' characteristics had an impact on the feeling of social telepresence: what had a positive influence was being a female mental healthcare professional, professional seniority as a mental healthcare professional and being self-employed compared to working in a healthcare organisation.

3.5. Does Training Impact Social Telepresence?

The training dimension was captured by two proxies in Table 3. These two variables, 'Telepsychology practices before the pandemic' and 'Specific training', were significant. The variable present when social telepresence was very high, 'Telepsychology practices before the pandemic' had a coefficient of 0.033 and 'Specific training' had a coefficient of 0.021. We therefore concluded that training had a positive impact on the feeling of social telepresence, even when taking the mental healthcare professionals' personal characteristics into consideration. This could be due to telepsychology experience prior to the pandemic or specific training to prepare for telepsychology. This result remained when controlling for motivations to practice telepsychology. It also held when adding the level of perception of telepsychology in the set of explanatory variables.

Results therefore suggested that the accumulation of different forms of training promoted a sense of social telepresence.

3.6. *Do Personal Motivations Have an Impact on Social Telepresence?*

Looking at the reasons for starting telepsychology, preliminary analyses suggested heterogeneity in mental healthcare professionals' responses across European countries. The public health reason was a major factor for the UK, Belgium, Denmark, and Finland (around 75%). Another major reason was access to healthcare (56%), except for France where the percentage was lower (40%) (See Appendix A) [39]. Reasons such as 'Client's demand' or 'Not losing income' were quoted by a quarter of respondents. Austria, France, and Portugal stand out for the motivation of being open-minded to telepsychology. The model used—a country fixed effect model—allowed us to control for this country heterogeneity. We obtained results as if countries were similar, with the country-dummy variable capturing the national specificities.

In Table 3, Column (4), we focused on reasons for starting telepsychology during the lockdown, considering the public health motivation, client demand, income motivation, healthcare access, and telepsychology openness. In this model, we controlled for mental healthcare professionals' characteristics, and personal training.

We found that some motivations had a positive impact on the social telepresence of the mental healthcare professionals. These motivations were public health, client demand, and access to healthcare (Appendix A). To be open-minded to telepsychology played a role in social telepresence, but this factor was correlated with the perception of telepsychology to explain social telepresence. In other words, when controlling for perception of telepsychology, the open-mindedness to telepsychology reason was not significant anymore (Appendix A). Income-related motivation negatively impacted mental healthcare professionals' feeling of social telepresence.

Results then suggested that income-related motivation worsened the feeling of social telepresence and that being open-minded to telepsychology was correlated with the perception of telepsychology to explain social telepresence.

3.7. *Does the Perception of Telepsychology Impact Social Telepresence?*

Table 3, Column (5) shows that in addition to the other factors that foster social telepresence, a positive perception of telepsychology had a positive impact on the feeling of social telepresence.

Results suggested that the perception of telepsychology had a positive impact on social telepresence.

3.8. *Sensitivity Analysis*

The sample used was an unbalanced dataset. In the sample, the number of observations was much higher in the Italian subsample than for the other countries (Appendix A). We dealt with this using fixed effect models. However, the results may remain debatable. As a sensitivity analysis, we excluded the Italian mental healthcare professionals surveyed from the sample, which allowed us to see how the Italian information affected the average results.

Some results on the mental healthcare professionals' characteristics were not consistent with the results previously found on the whole sample. However, we found that the perception of telepsychology depended significantly and positively on training (telepsychology practices before the pandemic and specific training), as it was found in the whole sample. In the sub-sample of new mental healthcare professionals as users of telepsychology, training and positive perception of telepsychology were important factors to foster social telepresence. This result was in line with what we found in the overall sample. Therefore, we concluded that with or without the Italian subsample, the main results remained.

4. Discussion and Conclusions

In this paper, we studied the determinants of the perception of telepsychology in a large cross-sectional survey study. Subsequently, we analysed the drivers of social telepresence. We observed disparities between countries (Appendix A) and used a fixed effects econometric model to accommodate these. This study, using a fixed effects approach in a large sample of mental healthcare professionals (allowing to eliminate interactions between the surveyed psychologists that were invariant across countries), is an addition to the study of telepsychology in Europe, where many studies on telepsychology focus on clients' perceptions.

Results suggested that female mental healthcare professionals were more likely to have a negative perception of telepsychology, all else being equal. Training—consisting of both telepsychology practice before the pandemic and specific training—was also a key factor impacting perception of telepsychology [40].

The second interest is social telepresence. The feeling of social telepresence appeared to depend on the mental healthcare professionals' personal characteristics. Female mental healthcare professionals had a higher feeling of social telepresence, even after controlling for all other explanatory variables. The reasons for this remain to be explored. Despite the general positive association between perception and social telepresence, women generally tended to have a more negative perception of telepsychology but a higher social telepresence. Could it be that women are more sensitive than men to relational aspects, which would leave them to have a priori reservations about telepsychology while also predisposing them to being more sensitive to the effects of social telepresence? Previous work has already hinted at gender differences in therapeutic relationships, with female therapists being positioned as more emotionally supportive while male therapist could be seen as more goal-oriented [41,42]. Professional situation was also related to social telepresence. According to the results, social telepresence was higher in those self-employed (and therefore probably freer in their choice of practice) and those with professional seniority as mental healthcare professionals (which may give more confidence, and therefore adaptability to changes in this context). Training, in whatever form (personal experience or specific training), also seemed to be a way to foster social telepresence. Finally, motivations for telepsychology adoption and acceptance were also related to social telepresence. Interestingly, financial motivations worsened social telepresence while openness to telepsychology was correlated with a positive perception of telepsychology to explain social telepresence.

These study results ultimately highlighted the role of "telepsychology perception" as a driver of social telepresence. The results also showed a correlation between telepsychology training and a good perception of telepsychology. Findings suggested that appropriate telepsychology training should enhance social telepresence directly and through experience of telepsychology in practice. This factor could therefore improve the acceptance of telepsychology among professionals

This study also has some limitations that require discussion. Since it is a cross-sectional study, findings need to be confirmed in longitudinal and experimental designs. As we aimed for brevity of the entire questionnaire (at that moment in time when mental healthcare professionals were under exceptional pressure due to the pandemic), only one item was used to evaluate an aspect of telepresence. No telepresence scale was included in our questionnaire, so we only evaluated the dimension of social telepresence.

The pandemic was a time when some mental healthcare professionals began an online practice under difficult conditions. Some of them had no prior experience or training in telepsychology. This raises questions about ensuring a clinical and ethical framework under these conditions and improving these critical terms in the future. According to the APA Guidelines for Telepsychology: "Psychologists who provide telepsychology services strive to take reasonable steps to ensure their competence with both the technologies used and the potential impact of the technologies on clients/patients". These are certainly avenues to be explored to strengthen the framework for telepsychology in Europe, including a reflection on adaptations of the training framework to the practice of psychologists. We note that rare initiatives are beginning to appear in Europe, such as the Erasmus Mundus CYBER Master (https://www.cyber-t.eu, accessed on 25 September 2022), which opened its doors in 2022.

In the present context, and given the increase of telepsychology, issues related to the terminology, methodology and ethics of telepsychology are essential. Our results help to promote reflection among professional federations such as EFPA or FFPP (https://ffpp.net/de-la-cyberpsychologie-a-la-teleconsultation, accessed on 25 September 2022) and to build a solid telepsychology framework to support mental healthcare professionals and foster their acceptance of telepsychology.

Author Contributions: Methodology, C.M.; Investigation, B.S., T.V.D. and N.A.J.D.W.; Writing—original draft, L.H., C.M. and B.S.; Writing—review & editing, L.H., C.M., B.S., T.V.D. and N.A.J.D.W.; Supervision, L.H.; Project administration, L.H. All authors have read and agreed to the published version of the manuscript.

Funding: This research received no external funding.

Institutional Review Board Statement: The study was conducted in accordance with the Declaration of Helsinki, and approved by the Ethics Committee of the Department of Applied Psychology at Thomas More University of Applied Sciences (ID1920_16; 18 March 2022).

Informed Consent Statement: Informed consent was obtained from all subjects involved in the study.

Data Availability Statement: The data presented in this study are available on request from the corresponding author.

Conflicts of Interest: The authors declare no conflict of interest.

Appendix A

Table A1. Characteristics of respondents by country: number, average age, gender; type of practice, experience and type of motivation: percentages by country.

Country		Socio-Demographic		Practice Framework					Experience			Motivations to Start Telepsychology				
		Age	Gender (Female)	Self Employed	Group Practice	Health-Care Organisation	Mental-Health-Care Organisation	Other	Years of Experience	Experience in Telepsychology	Specific Training	Public-Health Need	Client's Demand	Nor Losing Income	Guarantee Access	Technological Interest
	N	M	%	%	%	%	%	%	M	%	%	%	%	%	%	%
Austria	65	49.03	83	66	03	09	05	17	21.51	43	23	57	37	31	60	35
Belgium	556	40.34	87	37	06	10	32	14	14.50	22	07	75	30	33	61	23
Denmark	76	49.86	91	66	03	05	09	17	17.18	39	10	74	22	29	59	11
Finland	141	44.01	79	24	01	31	18	28	15.47	44	21	75	21	26	59	22
France	491	41.40	90	46	01	17	13	23	12.58	25	05	49	25	22	39	31
Germany	168	43.47	64	27	05	07	20	41	15.32	27	07	58	29	27	56	26
Italy	4604	43.55	85	78	01	06	06	09	13.98	37	08	60	20	13	53	12
Netherlands	81	40.49	86	17	01	14	62	06	13.99	47	18	90	21	15	70	22
Norway	258	42.81	81	29	04	32	20	14	14.21	33	17	60	22	22	58	24
Portugal	267	39.73	87	47	00	16	09	29	13.26	38	10	63	37	23	53	32
Spain	31	45.77	67	68	06	10	06	10	17.68	58	16	48	35	29	65	29
Sweden	395	42.86	77	18	03	32	34	12	12.42	53	12	57	27	20	50	21
UK	50	48.78	70	48	02	06	14	30	17.78	54	22	78	36	28	50	24

References

1. Hollander, J.E.; Carr, B.G. Virtually perfect? Telemedicine for COVID-19. *N. Engl. J. Med.* **2020**, *382*, 1679–1681. [CrossRef] [PubMed]
2. Moreno, C.; Wykes, T.; Galderisi, S.; Nordentoft, M.; Crossley, N.; Jones, N.; Cannon, M.; Correll, C.U.; Byrne, L.; Carr, S.; et al. How mental health care should change as a consequence of the COVID-19 pandemic. *Lancet Psychiatry* **2020**, *7*, 813–824. [CrossRef] [PubMed]
3. Chevance, A.; Gourion, D.; Gourion, D.; Hoertel, N.; Llorca, P.M.; Thomas, P.; Bocher, R.; Moro, M.R.; Laprévote, V.; Benyamina, A.; et al. Ensuring mental health care during the SARS-CoV-2 epidemic in France: A narrative review. *Encephale* **2020**, *46*, 193–201. [CrossRef] [PubMed]
4. Kozlof, N.; Mulsant, B.H.; Stergiopoulos, V.; Voineskos, A.N. The COVID-19 global pandemic: Implications for people with schizophrenia and related disorders. *Schizophr. Bull.* **2020**, *46*, 752–757. [CrossRef] [PubMed]
5. Garriga, M.; Agasi, I.; Fedida, E.; Pinzón-Espinosa, J.; Vazquez, M.; Pacchiarotti, I.; Vieta, E. The role of mental health home hospitalization care during the COVID-19 pandemic. *Acta Psychiatr. Scand.* **2020**, *141*, 479–480. [CrossRef]
6. Kang, L.; Li, Y.; Hu, S.; Chen, M.; Yang, C.; Yang, B.X.; Wang, Y.; Hu, J.; Lai, J.; Ma, X.; et al. The mental health of medical workers in Wuhan, China dealing with the 2019 novel coronavirus. *Lancet Psychiatry* **2020**, *7*, e14. [CrossRef]
7. Patel, R.; Irving, J.; Brinn, A.; Broadbent, M.; Shetty, H.; Pritchard, M.; Downs, J.; Stewart, R.; Harland, R.; McGuire, P. Impact of the COVID-19 pandemic on remote mental healthcare and prescribing in psychiatry: An electronic health record study. *BMJ Open* **2021**, *11*, e046365. [CrossRef]
8. Sammons, M.T.; VandenBos, G.R.; Martin, J.N.; Elchert, D.M. Follow-up to the first national survey of psychologists during the pandemic. *J. Health Serv. Psychol.* **2020**, *46*, 145–154. [CrossRef]
9. Allard, M.; Bouchard, S.; Marchand, A.; Cournoyer, L.-G.; Green-Demers, I.; Renaud, P. L'efficacité de la psychothérapie pour le trouble panique en vidéoconférence: Réplication et alliance thérapeutique. *Rev. Québécoise Psychol.* **2007**, *28*, 43–64.
10. Bouchard, S.; Paquin, B.; Payeur, R.; Allard, M.; Rivard, V.; Fournier, T.; Renaud, P.; Lapierre, J. Delivering cognitive-behavior therapy for panic disorder with agoraphobia in videoconference. *Telemed. J. E-Health* **2004**, *10*, 13–25. [CrossRef]
11. Doze, S.; Simpson, J.; Hailey Jacobs, P. Evaluation of a telepsychiatry: Psychiatry pilot project. *J. Telemedecine Telecare* **1999**, *5*, 38–46. [CrossRef]
12. Germain, V.; Marchand, A.; Bouchard, S.; Drouin, M.S.; Guay, S. Effectiveness of cognitive behavioural therapy administered by videoconference for post-traumatic stress disorder. *Cogn. Behav. Ther.* **2009**, *38*, 42–53. [CrossRef]
13. Pierce, M.; Hope, H.; Ford, T.; Hatch, S.; Hotopf, M.; John, A.; Kontopantelis, E.; Webb, R.; Wessely, S.; McManus, S.; et al. Mental health before and during the COVID-19 pandemic: A longitudinal probability sample survey of the UK population. *Lancet Psychiatry* **2020**, *7*, 883–892. [CrossRef]
14. Schneider, B.; Truong-Min, E.; Jover, M. Le psychologue face au COVID-19: Enquête exploratoire sur les pratiques en distanciel. *Prat. Psychol.* 2022; *in press*. [CrossRef]
15. Zentner, K.; Gaine, G.; Ethridge, P.; Surood, S.; Abba-Aji, A. Clinicians' Attitudes Toward Telepsychology in Addiction and Mental Health Services, and Prediction of Postpandemic Telepsychology Uptake: Cross-sectional Study. *JMIR Publ.* **2022**, *6*, e35535. [CrossRef]
16. Van Daele, T.; Karekla, M.; Kassianos, A.P.; Compare, A.; Haddouk, L.; Salgado, J.; Ebert, D.D.; Trebbi, G.; Bernaerts, S.; Van Assche, E.; et al. Recommendations for policy and practice of telepsychotherapy and e-mental health in Europe and beyond. *J. Psychother. Integr.* **2020**, *30*, 160–173. [CrossRef]
17. Minsky, M. Telepresence. *Omni* **1980**, *2*, 45–51.
18. Bouchard, S.; Dumoulin, S.; Michaud, M.; Gougeon, V. Telepresence experienced in videoconference varies according to emotions involved in videoconference sessions. *Annu. Rev. Cybertherapy Telemed.* **2011**, *167*, 128–132.
19. Haddouk, L.; Bouchard, S. Concepts actuels en télépsychologie. In *France Collection Cybercultures*; Haddouk, L., Schneider, B., Eds.; Erès Editions: Toulouse, France, 2022; pp. 49–64.
20. Bouchard, S.; Germain, V.; Marchand, A.; Guay, S.; Drouin, M.-S. Assessment of the Therapeutic Alliance in Face-to-Face or Videoconference Treatment for Posttraumatic Stress Disorder. *Cyberpsychology Behav.* **2010**, *13*, 29–35.
21. Haddouk, L.; Bouchard, S.; Brivio, E.; Galimberti, C.; Trognon, A. Assessing presence in videoconference telepsychotherapies: A complementary qualitative study on breaks in telepresence and intersubjectivity co-construction processes. *Annu. Rev. Cybertherapy Telemed.* **2018**, *16*, 118–123.
22. Berthiaume, M.; Bouchard, S.; Brisebois, C.; Robillard, G. The validation of a telepresence scale for psychotherapy delivered in videoconference. *Annu. Rev. Cybertherapy Telemed.* **2018**, *16*, 131–136.
23. Anthony, B. Use of telemedicine and virtual care for remote treatment in response to COVID-19 pandemic. *J. Med. Syst.* **2020**, *44*, 132.
24. Parisi, K.E.; Dopp, A.R.; Quetsch, L.B. Practitioner use of and attitudes towards videoconferencing for the delivery of evidence-based telemental health interventions: A mixed methods study. *Internet Interv.* **2021**, *26*, 100470. [CrossRef]
25. Connolly, S.L.; Miller, C.J.; Lindsay, J.A.; Bauer, M.S. A systematic review of providers' attitudes toward telemental health via videoconferencing. *Clin. Psychol. Sci. Pract.* **2020**, *27*, e12311. [CrossRef] [PubMed]

26. McKee, G.B.; Pierce, B.S.; Donovan, E.K.; Perrin, P.B. Examining models of psychologists' telepsychology use during the COVID-19 pandemic: A national cross-sectional study. *Clin. Psychol.* **2021**, *77*, 2405–2423. [CrossRef]
27. Chen, S.; Jones, P.B.; Underwood, B.R.; Moore, A.; Bullmore, E.T.; Banerjee, S.; Osimo, E.F.; Deakin, J.B.; Hatfield, C.F.; Thompson, F.J.; et al. The early impact of COVID-19 on mental health and community physical health services and their patients' mortality in Cambridgeshire and Peterborough, UK. *J. Psychiatr. Res.* **2020**, *131*, 244–254. [CrossRef] [PubMed]
28. Monagesh, E.; Hajizadeh, A. The role of telehealth during COVID-19 outbreak: A systematic review based on current evidence. *BMC Public Health* **2020**, *20*, 1193. [CrossRef]
29. Greenhalgh, T.; Koh, G.C.H.; Car, J. COVID-19: A remote assessment in primary care. *BMJ* **2020**, *368*, m1182. [CrossRef]
30. Greenhalgh, T.; Wherton, J.; Shaw, S.; Morrison, C. Video consultations for COVID-19. *Br. Med. J. Publ. Group* **2020**, *368*, m998. [CrossRef]
31. Milcent, C.; Zbiri, S. Use of telehealth: Evidence from French teleconsultation for women's healthcare, prior and during COVID-19 pandemic. *Health Serv. Manag. Res.* **2022**, 9514848221115845. [CrossRef]
32. De Witte, N.; Carlbring, P.; Etzelmueller, A.; Nordgreen, T.; Karekla, M.; Haddouk, L.; Belmont, A.; Overland, S.; Abi-Habib, R.; Bernaerts, S.; et al. Online consultations in mental healthcare during the COVID-19 outbreak: An international survey study on professionals' motivations and perceived barriers. *Internet Interv.* **2021**, *25*, 100405. [CrossRef]
33. Van Daele, T.; Mathiasen, K.; Carlbring, P.; Bernaerts, S.; Brugnera, A.; Compare, A.; Duque, A.; Eimontas, J.; Gosar, D.; Haddouk, L.; et al. Online consultations in mental healthcare: Modelling determinants of use and experience based on an international survey study at the onset of the pandemic. *Internet Interv.* **2022**, *30*, 100571. [CrossRef]
34. Clark, A.; Milcent, C. Ownership and hospital behaviour: Employment and Local Unemployment. *Soc. Sci. Med.* **2018**, *202*, 151–161. [CrossRef] [PubMed]
35. Christensen, R. *Plane Answers to Complex Questions: The Theory of Linear Models*, 3rd ed.; Springer: New York, NY, USA, 2002; ISBN 0-387-95361-2.
36. Gujarati, D.N.; Porter, D.C. Panel Data Regression Models. In *Basic Econometrics*, 5th ed.; McGraw-Hill: Boston, MA, USA, 2009; pp. 591–616. ISBN 978-007-127625-2.
37. Hsiao, C. Fixed-effects models. In *Analysis of Panel Data*, 2nd ed.; Cambridge University Press: New York, NY, USA, 2003; pp. 95–103. ISBN 0-521-52271-4.
38. Wooldridge, J.M. Fixed Effects Estimation. In *Introductory Econometrics: A Modern Approach*, 5th ed.; South-Western: Mason, OH, USA, 2013; pp. 466–474. ISBN 978-1-111-53439-4.
39. Allison, P.D. *Fixed Effects Regression Models*; Sage Publications, Inc.: Los Angeles, CA, USA, 2009; ISBN 9780761924975/0761924973.
40. Haddouk, L.; Milcent, C.; Gabri, S. La télépsychologie en France depuis le COVID-19. La formation comme facteur clé de la pratique de la télépsychologie et la satisfaction des psychologues dans les consultations en ligne. In *Télépsychologie. Etat des Lieux et Enjeux*; Haddouk, L., Schneider, B., Eds.; Erès Editions: Toulouse, France, 2022; pp. 225–248.
41. Bhati, K.S. Effect of client-therapist gender match on the therapeutic relationship: An exploratory analysis. *Psychol. Rep.* **2014**, *115*, 565–583. [CrossRef] [PubMed]
42. Loree, A.J.; Caldwell, B.E. Race, Gender, and Therapist Confidence: Effects on Satisfaction with the Therapeutic Relationship in MFT. *Am. J. Fam. Ther.* **2011**, *39*, 307–324.

Journal of
Clinical Medicine

MDPI

Article

Gender Differences in Usage and Subjective Appreciation of an Online Cognitive Behavioral Therapy for Wildfire Evacuees: Descriptive Study

Émilie Binet [1], Marie-Christine Ouellet [1], Jessica Lebel [1], Vera Békés [2], Charles M. Morin [1] and Geneviève Belleville [1,*]

1 School of Psychology, Laval University, 2325 Rue de l'Université, Quebec, QC G1V 0A6, Canada
2 Ferkauf Graduate School, Yeshiva University, 1165 Morris Park Ave, The Bronx, New York, NY 10461, USA
* Correspondence: genevieve.belleville@psy.ulaval.ca

Abstract: Background: Based on the most common psychological difficulties of the evacuees from the 2016 Fort McMurray wildfires in Alberta, Canada, a therapist-guided cognitive behavioral self-treatment was developed. This study aimed to explore how gender influences the usage and subjective appreciation of the RESILIENT online treatment. Methods: Our study included 81 English-speaking evacuees with significant posttraumatic symptoms, or with some posttraumatic symptoms accompanied by at least mild depression symptoms or subclinical insomnia, and who logged into the platform at least once. Various usage and subjective appreciation variables were analyzed, including number of completed sessions, number of logins, number of words per session, perceived efforts, perception of usefulness and intention to continue using the different strategies. Results: No difference was detected in most objective usage indicators. The number of words written in sessions 7 and 10 was significantly greater for women than for men. Regarding subjective appreciation, men had a greater perception of having put strong efforts in the cognitive restructuring strategy, while women reported in a greater proportion that they wanted to continue using physical exercise as a behavioral activation strategy. Conclusions: Our study offers a first look into how women and men use online treatments, and what their preferences are.

Keywords: usage data; gender; online treatment; cognitive behavioral therapy; natural disaster

Citation: Binet, É.; Ouellet, M.-C.; Lebel, J.; Békés, V.; Morin, C.M.; Belleville, G. Gender Differences in Usage and Subjective Appreciation of an Online Cognitive Behavioral Therapy for Wildfire Evacuees: Descriptive Study. *J. Clin. Med.* **2022**, *11*, 6649. https://doi.org/10.3390/jcm11226649

Academic Editor: Elena Tomba

Received: 20 September 2022
Accepted: 8 November 2022
Published: 9 November 2022

1. Introduction

Interest for self-administered therapies delivered online is on the rise. The current COVID pandemic has illustrated the relevance of this type of therapy and its value, particularly in times of high mental health needs but limited resources. Online mental health interventions offer many benefits, such as an increased accessibility and cost-efficiency, e.g., [1] and represent a promising way to provide timely and effective care to as many people as possible after a natural disaster [2]. Many studies have suggested that internet-based cognitive behavioral therapy is effective for treating anxiety disorders, posttraumatic stress disorder (PTSD) and depression [3–6]. Adherence to online treatments (e.g., completing more treatment modules) is associated with increased effectiveness [7,8], as is the frequency of use of cognitive behavioral therapy skills taught in these treatments [9]. This highlights the importance of paying attention to how participants use online treatments, in addition to whether these treatments are effective.

Many authors have suggested that gender plays a role in adherence to online psychological treatments, although the literature on how online treatments are used according to gender is inconsistent. In their systematic review, Beatty and Binnion [10] concluded that available preliminary evidence points to gender being a significant predictor of adherence, although half of the reviewed studies did not reach this conclusion. The large heterogeneity in studies that were included in the review in terms of intervention target and duration, sample size, and definition and measure of adherence warrants cautious interpretation of the results. Many studies suggested that female gender is a significant predictor of adherence for anxiety, stress and depression treatments [11–15]. However, one study evaluating an online treatment for depression found male gender to be a predictor of number of completed modules [16]. Other results suggest that men and women have a similar adherence to anxiety, depression and insomnia online treatments [17–27]. Taken together, these results underline the difficulty of drawing clear conclusions on the effect of gender on treatment usage and the importance of carrying out more studies to evaluate and better understand this effect.

The few studies that have specifically examined the effect of gender on treatment usage were mostly limited to the measurement of objective indicators of treatment use, i.e., number of logins and number of completed modules [7,23]. While these indicators provide valuable information, they do not appear to be sufficient to understand whether men and women use online treatments differently and which adaptations could prove helpful to enhance engagement. Many authors have suggested that user experience is an important therapeutic process to consider in the development of mental health technologies, e.g., [28,29]. A qualitative meta-synthesis on user experience of computerized therapy showed that participants placed a high importance on treatments that are sensitive to their clinical needs and preferences and that include personalized material [30]. Taking user views and perceptions into consideration appears critical to the efficacy of mental health treatments and adherence of participants [28,31], yet participants' subjective appreciation of the content of online treatments (e.g., what they found useful and used the most) has rarely been examined. In order to determine if exploring whether gender-specific treatment adaptations offers clinical value, it is important to first understand if the use of treatment differs between men and women, and to what extent.

Our team has previously developed an online cognitive behavioral intervention (the RESILIENT platform) to address psychological issues in people evacuated from the 2016 Fort McMurray (AB, Canada) forest fires, the costliest disaster in the history of Canada at the time [32]. Following the event, many evacuees reported significant posttraumatic, depressive and insomnia symptoms [33–35]. A randomized controlled trial indicated that the treatment was more effective than a waitlist condition in terms of symptom improvement [36]. In another previously published study, we observed that men and women reacted differently to the treatment [37]. Men showed greater improvements in insomnia severity and in reducing self-blame posttraumatic cognitions than women, in line with other studies that highlighted that men and women may respond differently to treatment after a traumatic event [38–40]. However, it remains unclear if men and women used or interacted with the online treatment differently, thereby explaining different treatment responses.

The purpose of the present study was thus to examine potential gender differences in the use of an online cognitive behavioral therapy using a variety of objective and subjective indicators. This opportunity to explore how men and women interacted with the treatment could improve our understanding of potential gender-specific treatment mechanisms and ultimately allow us to tailor online psychological treatments to optimize efficacy for women and men. The main goal was to examine whether the usage and subjective appreciation of treatment strategies differed between men and women and to explore which indicators are worth further investigating. Our study aimed to answer the four following questions: (1) To what extent did women and men use our online treatment?; (2) Which treatment strategies seemed the most and the least helpful to each gender?; (3) Which strategies were men and women willing to continue using after the treatment?; and (4) How did the perception of the engagement in the therapeutic strategies differ between men and women?

2. Methods

2.1. Participants and Procedure

Participants were English-speaking adults who were evacuated from their homes during the 2016 Fort McMurray wildfires. They were initially recruited by random telephone sampling to participate to the first part of the larger study [13]. A phone survey was conducted from May to July 2017 with 1510 participants to evaluate the most prevalent psychological symptoms in order to create an adapted online psychological treatment. Following the survey, participants who were interested could participate in the longitudinal component of the study, which included four clinical assessments at 6-month intervals over two years (T1-T4). Validated questionnaires administered online assessed posttraumatic, depression and insomnia symptoms. Participants who reported significant posttraumatic symptoms (PTSD Checklist for DSM-5 [PCL-5] $\geq$ 23), or with some posttraumatic symptoms (PCL-5 $\geq$ 10) accompanied by at least mild depression (Patient Health Questionnaire Depression Scale [PHQ-9] score $\geq$ 5) or subclinical insomnia symptoms (Insomnia Severity Index [ISI] score $\geq$ 8) were invited to receive the online treatment. The treatment study included a randomized controlled trial design, and participants were separated into different groups which received treatment at different times over the 1.5-year period (pilot group, treatment group and waitlist group). Over the course of the study (November 2017–May 2019), 81 participants accepted the invitation to participate and logged into the treatment platform at least once. This includes the pilot group (n = 8), which received the treatment between November 2017 and May 2018, the treatment group (n = 32), which received the treatment between May and November 2018, and the waitlist group (n = 26), which received treatment between November 2018 and May 2019. Some participants with newly developed symptoms (n = 15) were included in the waitlist group and received the treatment between November 2018 and May 2019. All of these participants were included in the present study, regardless of the time at which they received treatment, in order to increase statistical power.

2.2. Treatment

The RESILIENT online intervention is a self-directed therapist-assisted treatment. It includes 12 sessions aimed at reducing PTSD, depression and insomnia symptoms. It incorporates several evidence-based cognitive behavioral interventions such as in vivo exposure, sleep restriction and imagery rehearsal therapy (IRT). A detailed list of session content and strategies is provided in Table 1. Access to a session was granted to the participant after the completion of the previous one, and the participant retained access to it afterwards. Each treatment session included reflection questions and practical exercises where participants could write their thoughts or answers. An important part of the treatment was the interactive tools. Participants were instructed to complete the sleep diary every morning, which provided them with an automated calculation of sleep efficiency and sleep window time recommendation each week. The diaphragmatic breathing tool enabled participants to track their progress with this exercise, for which a frequency of twice a day was recommended. The pleasant activities tool consisted of an activity planner to support behavioral activation. Participants were instructed to fill this every week, planning enjoyable activities for the following week. The in vivo exposure tool was used by participants to track their progress with this exercise, with the recommendation of conducting multiple exercises in a week. A cognitive restructuring tool and a problem-solving tool were also proposed to support cognitive therapy techniques and provide problem-solving skills. These could be used by the participant as needed. Table 1 presents the sessions at which the different tools were introduced to participants.

Table 1. Session content, strategies covered and tools introduced.

Session	Session Content	Strategies Covered and Tools Introduced
(1) *Normal reactions to abnormal events*	▪ Overview of treatment ▪ Empowerment ▪ Posttraumatic stress disorder ▪ Resilience ▪ Sleep and insomnia ▪ Daily self-monitoring	▪ Psychoeducation ▪ Self-assessment of symptoms ▪ Daily self-monitoring ▪ Sleep hygiene [a,b] → **Tool introduced:** Sleep diary
(2) *Catching my breath*	▪ Phases of reactions to a natural disaster/traumatic event ▪ Diaphragmatic breathing ▪ Resilience and pleasant activities ▪ Sleep habits	▪ Psychoeducation ▪ Diaphragmatic breathing [a,b] ▪ Pleasant activities [a,b] ▪ Sleep hygiene [b] ▪ Sleep restriction [a,b] → **Tools introduced:** Diaphragmatic breathing tool Pleasant activities tool
(3) *Getting out there*	▪ Avoidance and in vivo exposure ▪ Role of physical activity in building resilience ▪ Sleep habits	▪ Psychoeducation ▪ In vivo exposure [a,b] ▪ Pleasant activities (physical exercise) [b] ▪ Review of previously covered strategies → **Tool introduced:** In vivo exposure
(4) *Thinking out loud*	▪ In vivo exposure ▪ Posttraumatic cognitions	▪ Psychoeducation ▪ ABC mode ▪ In vivo exposure [b] ▪ Cognitive restructuring [a,b] (changing interpretation of events) ▪ Review of previously covered strategies → **Tool introduced:** Cognitive restructuring tool
(5) *Paying attention to how I talk to myself*	▪ Cognitive distortions ▪ Unhelpful internal monologue	▪ Psychoeducation ▪ Cognitive restructuring (challenging cognitive distortions) [b] ▪ Review of previously covered strategies
(6) *Re-connecting with myself and others*	▪ Mindfulness ▪ Social support	▪ Psychoeducation ▪ Mindfulness meditation [b] ▪ Social support optimization [b] ▪ Review of previously covered strategies
(7) *My progress to date*	▪ Overview and assessment of progress ▪ Self-criticism and self-compassion	▪ Self-assessment of symptoms ▪ Psychoeducation ▪ Consolidation of skills ▪ Self-compassion [b] ▪ Review of previously covered strategies

Table 1. *Cont.*

Session	Session Content	Strategies Covered and Tools Introduced
(8) *Revisiting difficult memories*	▪ Posttraumatic memories and exposure ▪ Active problem solving ▪ Social support	▪ Psychoeducation ▪ Imaginal exposure to traumatic memories (writing) [b] ▪ Active problem solving [b] ▪ Social support optimization [b] ▪ Review of previously covered strategies → **Tool introduced:** Problem-solving tool
(9) *Keep moving forward*	▪ Radical acceptance of the past ▪ Posttraumatic memories and exposure	▪ Radical acceptance [b] ▪ Psychoeducation ▪ Imaginal exposure to traumatic memories (writing and reading) [b] ▪ Review of previously covered strategies
(10) *Taking control*	▪ Nightmares and imagery rehearsal therapy ▪ Posttraumatic memories and exposure	▪ Psychoeducation ▪ Imagery rehearsal therapy [b] (taking control of nightmares) ▪ Imaginal exposure to traumatic memories ▪ Review of previously covered strategies
(11) *Looking ahead*	▪ Resilience ▪ Values and life goals	▪ Reflection on one's values, determination of goals and committed actions [b] ▪ Review of previously covered strategies
(12) *Preparing my toolkit for life*	▪ Triggers and other warning signs ▪ Review of progress	▪ Relapse prevention ▪ Self-assessment of symptoms ▪ Review of strategies toolbox

[a] Strategies assessed at session 7; [b] strategies assessed at the end of session 12.

After completing a given session, participants had a contact with their assigned therapist using the modality of their choice (videoconferencing, telephone or email) to discuss treatment content, ask questions and troubleshoot problems with its application. Therapists provided clients with encouragement and evaluated adherence to the treatment strategies as well as the need for reference to specialized crisis services. It was instructed that these calls should last approximately 30 min. The therapists were graduate psychology students who were supervised by a licensed psychologist specialized in the treatment of PTSD (V.B.). Participants were given a period of six months to complete the 12 sessions, with the recommendation of completing one session per week.

2.3. Measures

Sociodemographic information included gender, age, marital status, ethnicity, ethnic origin, immigration status and membership in a First Nation. Gender identity was evaluated with the question "What is your gender?". Participants could select one of the following answers: female, male, non-binary/third gender, prefer to self-describe (specify) and prefer not to say.

Psychological symptom severity was evaluated with validated self-reported questionnaires to determine the eligibility of participants and assess the association of pre-treatment symptom severity with gender. PTSD symptoms were evaluated with the *PTSD Checklist for*

DSM-5 (PCL-5; [41]), depression symptoms with the *Patient Health Questionnaire Depression Scale* (PHQ-9; [42]), and insomnia symptoms with the *Insomnia Severity Index* (ISI; [43]). In these questionnaires, higher scores indicate a greater severity of symptoms.

Treatment usage data related to how participants used the treatment platform. The number of completed sessions, number of logins, number of days between first and last login, mean number of days between logins, number of entries in each of the treatment tools (*sleep diary, diaphragmatic breathing, pleasant activities,* in vivo *exposure, cognitive restructuring* and *problem-solving*) were exported directly from the platform in an Excel sheet.

At session 7 (i.e., at mid-point), participants were asked to evaluate their level of perceived efforts in the five treatment strategies introduced so far: in vivo exposure, pleasant activities, sleep restriction and hygiene, diaphragmatic breathing and cognitive restructuring (presented as two specific strategies: *changing the interpretation of events* and *challenging cognitive distortions*). This self-reported questionnaire included a 5-point Likert scale (from 1 = a little to 5 = very much). An average was computed to represent the overall perceived effort of participants in the first half of treatment.

Text entered by participants, i.e., comments, reflections and answers to questions, was exported directly from the platform, and the number of words (by session and total) was calculated in an Excel sheet (the specific content was not analyzed). The number of words from a participant was available only for the sessions in which they had participated, thus resulting in variation of sample size due to attrition over the course of the sessions. The modality of contact with the therapist, the number of communications with the therapist, total duration of communications and mean duration of communications were also documented.

Subjective appreciation data. At session 12 (i.e., at the end of treatment), participants completed self-report questionnaires that were integrated in the platform to evaluate each of the individual treatment strategies in terms of: if they perceived them as useful (yes or no), if they wanted to continue using them (yes or no) and if they perceived that they put strong efforts into applying them (yes or no). Seventeen strategies were evaluated by participants: sleep hygiene, sleep restriction, pleasant activities, physical activity, social support optimization, diaphragmatic breathing, in vivo exposure, cognitive restructuring (interpretation of events), cognitive restructuring (cognitive distortions), mindfulness practice, self-compassion, active problem solving, imaginal exposure (writing), radical acceptance, nightmare rescripting, imaginal exposure (writing and reading), and values, goals and committed action. Table 1 presents the sessions in which the different strategies were included.

It should be noted that since participants presented with various levels of posttraumatic, depressive and insomnia symptoms, they were instructed not to use the parts of the intervention which did not apply to them. This may have impacted the results (e.g., a participant with low or no insomnia may have fewer entries in the sleep diary, a lower level of perceived efforts in the sleep diary tool and might have scored "no" to the item "I found it useful" for the sleep strategies).

2.4. Data Analysis

Descriptive data was computed separately for men and women. For continuous variables (e.g., number of completed sessions, number of words), means and standard deviations were computed, and for dichotomous variables, frequencies and percentages were computed (i.e., assessment of treatment strategies). *t*-tests were conducted to test for a difference in means between men and women for the variables on a continuous scale, and Chi-square tests of independence were conducted to test for a difference in frequencies for dichotomous variables in men and women when assumptions were met (i.e., sufficient number of participants per cell). Effect sizes were assessed by calculating Hedge's g using means, standard deviations, and sample sizes. The impact of potentially confounding variables (age, marital status, ethnicity, level of education, membership in a First Nation and pre-treatment symptom severity) on significant results was evaluated to increase confidence that the observed effects on usage data was attributable to gender, using *t*-tests for continuous variables and Chi-square tests of independence for nominal variables (when assumptions were met). All analyses were run with SPSS Statistics version 25 using a significance threshold of 0.05.

3. Results

3.1. Sample Description

Table 2 presents the sociodemographic characteristics of the sample, which includes 81 participants who logged into the platform at least once. Participant age ranged from 19 to 71, with a mean age of 45.4 (SD = 11.6). All participants identified as either female (58/81; 71.6%) or male (23/81; 28.4%) gender. Most participants identified as White (71/81; 87.7%), were married or in a relationship (58/81; 71.6%) and had a postsecondary level of education (64/81; 79.0%). *t*-tests and Chi-square analyses revealed no significant differences between men and women in sociodemographic factors (i.e., age, marital status, level of education) and in symptom severity at pre-treatment (see Table 2). Individuals who did not identify as White (n = 9) or who identified as members of a First Nation (n = 4) were not represented in a sufficient number in our sample to test whether those characteristics were statistically associated with gender. However, descriptive data suggested that a greater proportion of women (94.7%) than of men (73.9%) identified as White. It also seemed that a greater number of men (7; 30.4%) than women (1; 1.7%) had an immigration status: four of them self-reported a European origin, two an Asian origin, one an African origin and one did not provide data for origin.

Table 2. Sociodemographic and clinical characteristics of participants.

Sample Characteristics	Total Sample (N = 81)	Men (n = 23)	Women (n = 58)	Group Differences
	M (SD)	M (SD)	M (SD)	
Age	45.4 (11.6)	46.1 (13.5)	45.1 (10.9)	t_{77} = 0.345, p = 0.366
	n (%)	n (%)	n (%)	
Gender				
Female	58 (71.6)	-	-	-
Male	23 (28.4)	-	-	-
Member of a First Nation	4 (4.9)	1 (4.3)	3 (5.2)	-
Ethnicity				-
White	71 (87.7)	17 (73.9)	54 (93.1)	-
Other [a]	9 (11.1)	6 (26.1)	3 (5.2)	-
Immigration status	8 (9.9)	7 (30.4)	1 (1.7)	-
Marital status				χ^2_1 = 0.700, p = 0.403
Single, separated, divorced or widowed	23 (28.4)	5 (21.7)	18 (31.0)	-
Married or partner	58 (71.6)	18 (78.3)	40 (69.0)	-
Education				χ^2_1 = 0.813, p = 0.367
Primary or Secondary	16 (19.8)	6 (26.1)	10 (17.2)	-
Postsecondary	64 (79.0)	17 (73.9)	47 (81.0)	-
Clinical severity scores at pre-treatment				
PCL-5	27.0 (14.8)	31.0 (15.6)	25.3 (15.8)	t_{79} = 1.474, p = 0.072
PHQ-9	10.9 (6.4)	11.7 (6.4)	10.7 (6.4)	t_{79} = 0.598, p = 0.276
ISI	16.9 (5.9)	17.2 (5.5)	16.7 (6.0)	t_{79} = 0.351, p = 0.363

Note: M = mean; SD = standard deviation. Totals did not always reach 100% since participants could choose not to answer (prefer not to say). [a] Including in decreasing proportion, Asian/Middle Eastern/Pacific Islander, Metis, Native North American or North American Indian, African (Northern, Eastern, Central, Western or Southern).

3.2. Impact of Gender on Treatment Usage

3.2.1. Usage Data

Results initially showed that the mean number of days between first and last login was greater for men than women (115.48 days vs. 80.83 days; see Table 3). However, we found an outlier in the men subgroup (i.e., 370 days), which was over three standard deviations above the mean. When removed, the mean for men dropped to 103.91 days (SD = 63.38) and the difference was no longer significant ($t_{78} = 1.576, p = 0.119$). No significant gender differences were found in the number of completed sessions, number of logins, mean number of days between logins and number of entries in tool (total and for each tool). Men reported a higher level of perceived efforts at mid-treatment than women in the cognitive restructuring tool (4.08 vs. 3.38, range: 1–5). A higher level of perceived effort in the cognitive restructuring tool was also found in participants identifying with an ethnicity other than White ($t_{37} = -2.820, p = 0.004$) and in participants with an immigration status $t_{17.313} = -2.896, p = 0.005$). No significant gender differences were found in perceived efforts at mid-treatment overall and for the other tools.

Table 3. Online treatment usage data for men and women ($N = 81$).

	Men (n = 23)	Women (n = 58)	t	p Value
	M (SD)	M (SD)		
Number of completed sessions	8.78 (4.61)	7.21 (4.89)	−1.329	0.188
Number of logins	21.91 (19.44)	20.90 (21.60)	−0.196	0.845
Number of days between first and last login [a]	**115.48 (83.14)**	**80.83 (56.59)**	**2.161**	**0.034**
Mean number of days between logins	9.62 (9.65)	7.61 (8.49)	0.871	0.387
Number of feedback communications with therapist	8.92 (3.53)	6.92 (4.94)	−1.540	0.136
Total duration of feedback communications with therapist (minutes)	293.63 (116.74)	258.84 (161.79)	−0.560	0.579
Mean duration of feedback communications with therapist (minutes)	30.42 (7.90)	30.98 (10.62)	0.178	0.859
Number of entries in tools—Total	29.48 (49.21)	23.47 (29.94)	0.671	0.504
Sleep diary	17.87 (25.19)	13.97 (19.42)	−0.748	0.457
Pleasant activities tool	4.74 (6.70)	4.76 (6.36)	0.012	0.990
Diaphragmatic breathing tool	2.87 (9.63)	1.66 (2.96)	−0.869	0.387
In vivo exposure tool	1.78 (6.86)	1.64 (4.11)	−0.117	0.907
Cognitive restructuring tool	1.17 (4.20)	0.95 (1.75)	−0.343	0.732
Problem solving tool	1.04 (3.54)	0.50 (1.11)	−1.055	0.295
Perceived level of efforts at mid-treatment (1–5)—Overall	3.67 (0.68)	3.44 (0.61)	1.135	0.263
In vivo exposure tool	3.15 (1.41)	2.80 (1.32)	0.791	0.434
Pleasant activities tool	4.00 (0.58)	4.00 (0.91)	0.000	1.000
Sleep diary	1.03 (0.29)	1.28 (0.23)	−0.312	0.756
Diaphragmatic breathing tool	3.85 (0.99)	3.53 (0.86)	1.048	0.301
Cognitive restructuring tool	**4.08 (0.90)**	**3.38 (0.90)**	**2.276**	**0.029**

Note: Significant results ($p < 0.05$) are identified with a bold font. Totals did not always reach 100% since participants could choose not to answer (prefer not to say). Since participants presented with various levels of posttraumatic, depressive and insomnia symptoms, some of them did not use some parts of the intervention which did not apply to them. [a] When removing one outlier in the men subgroup (i.e., 370 days), the mean for men drops to 103.91 days (SD = 63.38) and the difference was no longer significant ($t_{78} = 1.576, p = 0.119$).

Women's preferred mean of communication with the therapist for feedback related to the sessions was by telephone (55.3%), followed by videoconference (34.2%) and email (10.5%). Men's preferred mean of communication was videoconference (56.3%), followed by telephone (31.3%) and email (12.5%). No statistically significant difference was found between genders in mean of communication ($\chi^2(2, N = 54) = 2.730, p = 0.255$), nor in number of communications, total and mean communication duration (see Table 3).

3.2.2. Number of Words

Results for mean number of words per session by gender are presented in Figure 1. t-tests showed that mean number of words per session was higher in women than in men in session 7 ($t_{44} = 2.022, p = .049$) and in session 10 ($t_{37.577} = 2.602, p = 0.013$). In session 7, women wrote a mean of 212 words while men wrote a mean of 136 words, which represents a medium effect size ($g = 0.636$, 95% CI [0.006–1.266]). In session 10, women wrote a mean of 1087 words while men wrote a mean of 390 words, which represents a medium effect size (g = 0.655, 95% CI [0.012–1.297]). No significant gender difference was found in other sessions and in the total number of words. Number of words was associated with level of education, ethnicity, and immigration status. Participants identifying as White wrote a greater number of words in sessions 7 ($t_{18.001}$ = 2.384, p = 0.014) and 10 ($t_{50.844}$ = 2.425, p = 0.009) and participants with an immigration status wrote a lower number of words in session 10 ($t_{44.342}$ = 2.099, p = 0.021).

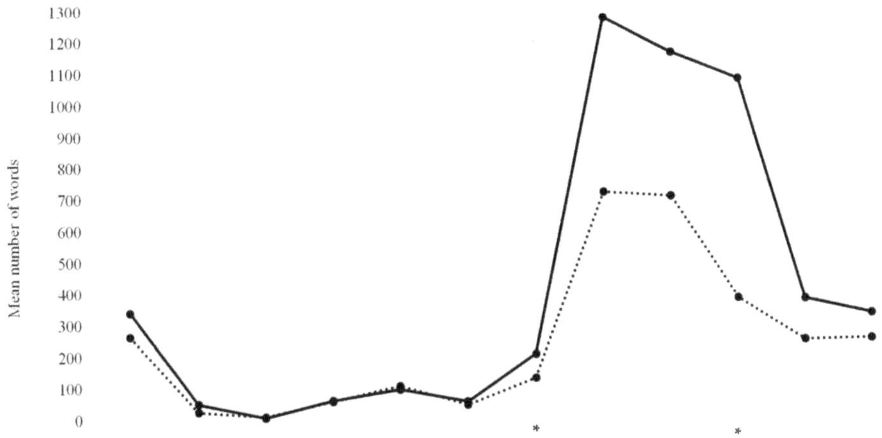

Session number	1	2	3	4	5	6	7	8	9	10	11	12	Total
n	81	64	60	55	50	49	46	45	43	43	42	42	81
Women —•—													
Mean	340	52	9	64	99	62	212	1282	1171	1087	388	344	2728
SD	358.87	78.40	15.76	60.58	67.62	65.30	128.39	1398.79	1279.95	1269.67	275.49	174.61	3674.97
Range (min–max)	0–1954	0–472	0–93	0–182	0–234	0–211	0–550	0–5215	0–5423	0–4272	0–1124	99–711	0–15336
Men ···•···													
Mean	264	27	12	61	111	51	136	726	714	390	258	264	2077
SD	210.44	21.29	13.53	57.55	106.57	53.87	98.24	920.34	787.13	462.23	158.58	289.84	2331.47
Range (min–max)	0–709	0–73	0–56	0–217	0–338	0–211	0–328	0–3510	0–2470	2–1796	1–572	0–1203	0–6973
Hedges's *g*	0.236	0.384	−0.220	0.051	−0.138	0.165	0.636	0.440	0.402	0.655	0.540	0.361	0.194

Figure 1. Means, standard deviations, range and effect sizes for number of words per session by gender. Note. Since participants presented with various levels of posttraumatic, depressive and insomnia symptoms, some of them did not use some parts of the intervention which did not apply to them. * $p < 0.05$.

3.2.3. Subjective Appreciation of Treatment Strategies

Table 4 presents the number of men and women who perceived each of the 17 treatment strategies as useful. The strategies perceived as most useful by women were pleasant activities and diaphragmatic breathing (22/27; 81.5%) followed by values, goals and committed actions (21/27; 77.8%) and cognitive restructuring (*cognitive distortions*) (20/27; 74.1%). The strategies perceived as most useful by men were sleep hygiene, pleasant activities, social support optimization, cognitive restructuring (*interpretation of events* and *cognitive distortions*), mindfulness practice and self-compassion (11/15; 73.3%). Imagery rehearsal therapy, suggested for participants with posttraumatic nightmares, was the strategy perceived as least useful by men and women (respectively 2/15; 13.3% and 4/27; 14.8%). Chi-squared tests did not reveal any statistically significant difference in men and women's perception of the strategies as useful, however many analyses could not be run or may have lacked statistical power due to insufficient number of observations per cell.

Table 4. Subjective appreciation of treatment strategies by gender: perception of usefulness.

Treatment Strategies	Men (n = 15)	Women (n = 27)	$\chi 2$	p Value
Sleep hygiene	11 (73.3%)	16 (59.3%)	-	-
Sleep restriction	9 (60.0%)	12 (44.4%)	0.933	0.334
Pleasant activities	11 (73.3%)	22 (81.5%)	-	-
Physical exercise	10 (66.7%)	18 (66.7%)	0.000	1.000
Social support optimization	11 (73.3%)	19 (70.4%)	-	-
Diaphragmatic breathing	10 (66.7%)	22 (81.5%)	1.167	0.280
In vivo exposure	6 (40.0%)	13 (48.1%)	0.258	0.611
Cognitive restructuring (interpretation of events)	11 (73.3%)	18 (66.7%)	-	-
Cognitive restructuring (cognitive distortions)	11 (73.3%)	20 (74.1%)	-	-
Mindfulness meditation	11 (73.3%)	19 (70.4%)	-	-
Self-compassion	11 (73.3%)	15 (55.6%)	-	-
Active problem solving	9 (60.0%)	18 (66.7%)	0.187	0.666
Imaginal exposure (writing)	7 (46.7%)	16 (59.3%)	0.617	0.432
Radical acceptance	8 (53.3%)	14 (51.9%)	0.008	0.927
Imagery rehearsal therapy	2 (13.3%)	4 (14.8%)	-	-
Imaginal exposure (writing and reading)	7 (46.7%)	16 (59.3%)	0.617	0.895
Values, goals and committed actions	10 (66.7%)	21 (77.8%)	0.616	0.432

Note. Since participants presented with various levels of posttraumatic, depressive and insomnia symptoms, some of them did not use some parts of the intervention which did not apply to them.

The strategies that women most wanted to continue using (Table 5) were physical activity (20/27; 74.1%), followed by pleasant activities (19/27; 70.4%), social support optimization and cognitive restructuring (*cognitive distortions*) (18/27; 70.4%). The strategies that men most wanted to continue using were sleep hygiene, pleasant activities, social support optimization, mindfulness practice and values, goals and committed actions (8/15; 53.3% for all strategies). Imagery rehearsal therapy was the strategy that men and women least wanted to continue (respectively 1/15; 6.7% and 3/27; 11.1%). Chi-squared tests revealed that a greater proportion of women (20/27; 74.1%) than men (6/15; 40.0%) wanted to continue using physical exercise after the intervention ($\chi^2(1, N = 42) = 4.747, p = 0.029$).

Table 5. Subjective appreciation of treatment strategies by gender: intent to continue.

Treatment Strategies	Men (n = 15)	Women (n = 27)	χ^2	p Value
Sleep hygiene	8 (53.3%)	17 (63.0%)	0.371	0.542
Sleep restriction	5 (33.3%)	12 (44.4%)	0.494	0.482
Pleasant activities	8 (53.3%)	19 (70.4%)	1.219	0.270
Physical exercise	**6 (40.0%)**	**20 (74.1%)**	**4.747**	**0.029**
Social support optimization	8 (53.3%)	18 (66.7%)	0.727	0.394
Diaphragmatic breathing	6 (40.0%)	14 (51.9%)	0.543	0.461
In vivo exposure	2 (13.3%)	7 (25.9%)	-	-
Cognitive restructuring (interpretation of events)	7 (46.7%)	14 (51.9%)	0.104	0.747
Cognitive restructuring (cognitive distortions)	7 (46.7%)	18 (66.7%)	1.601	0.206
Mindfulness meditation	8 (53.3%)	14 (51.9%)	0.008	0.927
Self-compassion	6 (40.0%)	12 (44.4%)	0.078	0.780
Active problem solving	7 (46.7%)	12 (44.4%)	0.019	0.890
Imaginal exposure (writing)	3 (20.0%)	7 (25.9%)	-	-
Radical acceptance	5 (33.3%)	9 (33.3%)	0.000	1.00
Imagery rehearsal therapy	1 (6.7%)	3 (11.1%)	-	-
Imaginal exposure (writing and reading)	4 (26.7%)	7 (25.9%)	-	-
Values, goals and committed actions	8 (53.3%)	17 (63.0%)	0.371	0.542

Note. Significant results ($p < 0.05$) are identified with a bold font. Since participants presented with various levels of posttraumatic, depressive and insomnia symptoms, some of them did not use some parts of the intervention which did not apply to them.

Strategies in which participants perceived they had put strong efforts are presented in Table 6. Women reported that they had put strong efforts into pleasant activities (16/27; 59.3%), cognitive restructuring and self-compassion (13/27; 48.1%). Men reported that they put strong efforts into cognitive restructuring (cognitive distortions) (10/15; 66.7%), pleasant activities and cognitive restructuring (8/15; 53.3%). Radical acceptance was the strategy for which men perceived they had put the lowest level of efforts into (0/15; 0.0%), while for women, it was imagery rehearsal therapy (1/27; 3.7%). Chi-squared tests revealed that a greater proportion of men (10/15; 66.7%) than women (9/27; 33.3%) perceived they had put strong efforts into the cognitive restructuring (*cognitive distortions*) strategy ($\chi^2(1, N = 42) = 4.325$, $p = 0.038$).

Table 6. Subjective appreciation of treatment strategies by gender: perception of having put strong efforts.

Treatment Strategies	Men ($n = 15$)	Women ($n = 27$)	χ^2	p Value
Sleep hygiene	5 (33.3%)	10 (37.0%)	0.058	0.810
Sleep restriction	4 (26.7%)	8 (29.6%)	-	-
Pleasant activities	8 (53.3%)	16 (59.3%)	0.138	0.710
Physical exercise	4 (26.7%)	9 (33.3%)	-	-
Social support optimization	5 (33.3%)	9 (33.3%)	0.000	1.00
Diaphragmatic breathing	7 (46.7%)	12 (44.4%)	0.019	0.890
In vivo exposure	3 (20.0%)	8 (29.6%)	-	-
Cognitive restructuring (interpretation of events)	8 (53.3%)	13 (48.1%)	0.104	0.747
Cognitive restructuring (cognitive distortions)	**10 (66.7%)**	**9 (33.3%)**	**4.325**	**0.038**
Mindfulness meditation	5 (33.3%)	10 (37.0%)	0.058	0.810
Self-compassion	3 (20.0%)	13 (48.1%)	-	-
Active problem solving	6 (40.0%)	6 (22.2%)	1.493	0.222
Imaginal exposure (writing)	3 (20.0%)	11 (40.7%)	-	-
Radical acceptance	0 (0.0%)	8 (29.6%)	-	-
Imagery rehearsal therapy	2 (13.3%)	1 (3.7%)	-	-
Imaginal exposure (writing and reading)	1 (6.7%)	9 (33.3%)	-	-
Values, goals and committed actions	4 (26.7%)	12 (44.4%)	-	-

Note: Significant results ($p < 0.05$) are identified with a bold font. Since participants presented with various levels of posttraumatic, depressive and insomnia symptoms, some of them did not use some parts of the intervention which did not apply to them.

Chi-square tests of independence revealed that age, marital status, ethnicity, level of education, and membership in a First Nation were not associated with these variables (strategy perceived as useful, intention to continue, perceived strong efforts; all *ps* < 0.05), but some Chi-square tests were inconclusive because of insufficient number of observations per cell.

4. Discussion

The goal of our study was to explore and describe gender differences in the usage data and subjective appreciation of an online cognitive behavioral treatment for natural disaster evacuees with posttraumatic, depression and insomnia symptoms. Results showed that the usage of the treatment platform seemed mostly similar for men and women (e.g., objective indicators such as number of logins and number of completed sessions), but gender differences emerged in the number of words written in the platform, and in the subjective appreciation and perceived level of efforts put in applying some treatment strategies. To our knowledge, such gender differences have not been previously reported in clinical studies of online cognitive behavioral treatments. It is therefore challenging to tie our findings to the specific literature on gender differences in the use of online treatments. In the next section, we expand on the observed differences by generating tentative explanations and relating our findings to the broader literature on gender differences in mental health and cognition. We also provide suggestions for further research.

Women wrote a greater number of words than men in sessions 7 and 10. Session 7 included self-assessment of symptoms and progress and consolidation of skills. Participants were invited to write down their experiences for five main treatment domains: posttraumatic symptoms, resilience, sleep, stress management and cognitive therapy. They were also invited to write down their goals for the next five sessions (general goal, specific goals and activities to achieve them), to review their exposure hierarchy (satisfaction with results, what helped them and what held them back) and write their plan for the next week regarding exposure. Session 10 included IRT for nightmares, and participants were invited to write their nightmare (if any) in detail, as well as their new dream script. Session 10 also included imaginal exposure to traumatic memories, and participants were invited to write down the narrative of their trauma, including as many vivid elements as possible (e.g., emotions, sensations and thoughts during the fires and evacuation). They were also invited to review their exposure exercises (progress, successes, difficulties, questions, plan for next weeks), the planning of pleasant activities (progress, inclusion of social and physical activities) and their sleep (improvements, compliance with sleep window, difficulties, plan for next weeks). A greater number of words for women than for men in these sessions suggest that women were more engaged in these parts of treatment; they may have felt a greater need to express themselves through writing or a natural tendency to expand and write about their experience in a more detailed manner. It may also suggest that these therapeutic strategies were more challenging for men.

The association between gender and number of words written in an online treatment has not been previously examined, but many gender differences have been reported in the study of language more generally. For instance, women tend to use a language that is more elaborate and affective than men, whose language is typically more direct and instrumental [44]. Gender differences favoring women were also noted in writing fluency tasks, where women told longer stories than men in autobiographic memory styles and recall of affective experiences [45–47]. These characteristics may make the writing about traumatic experience in detail easier or more accessible for women than men. Women are also typically more likely to use emotion-based coping strategies than men, e.g., [48,49] and thus, they might experience a greater ease than men in putting their emotions into words. When examining women and men's subjective appreciation of the strategies from these sessions, they reported in a similar proportion that they perceived them as useful and that they wanted to continue to implement them in their lives. Thus, the length of written text in the platform might not be indicative of the perceived usefulness of the strategy. The impact of writing a greater or lower number of words in an imaginal exposure exercise is difficult to interpret in the context of a multi-strategy online treatment and, to our knowledge, has not been examined in the literature. Based on the rationale for this therapeutic strategy [50], one could suppose, on the one hand, that a lower number of words for men could indicate avoidance of some aspects of the traumatic event, perhaps emotional aspects. On the other hand, one could also make a case that a higher number of words for women reflects avoidance, as they may include unnecessary elements distracting them from the actual trauma narrative. A closer qualitative analysis of content would be necessary to further these questions.

Further, these results should be interpreted in the light of associations that were found between other sociodemographic variables and the number of words. Participants who were immigrants wrote a significantly lower number of words in some sessions, and there were more men than women with an immigration status in our sample. Consequently, immigration status might have been a confounding factor in the assessment of gender differences for this variable. It is plausible that English was not a first language for some immigrants, and that it influenced the length of their written accounts. Unfortunately, data on first language was not collected in this study, and, to our knowledge, the relationship between immigration status, native language and online treatment usage has not yet been examined in the literature. This factor appears important to consider in the development of treatments that require participants to write detailed responses. A Statistics Canada census has shown that in a literary task, a greater proportion of immigrants whose first language was different than the test language scored at the lowest level on a prose literacy scale, compared to immigrants whose first language was the test language and Canadian-born participants [51]. Future research should investigate the impact for a participant to receive an online treatment in a second language, and whether this influences treatment efficacy. Nonetheless, the development of a more inclusive approach to online treatments, offering content that is available in different languages, or offers alternative to written tasks (e.g., graphs, audio), seems of high importance.

Results revealed a significantly greater reported level of efforts put in cognitive restructuring at mid-treatment for men than women. This included the two cognitive restructuring strategies presented to participants: *changing the interpretation of events* and *challenging cognitive distortions*. At the end of treatment, men also reported in a significantly greater proportion than women that they had put strong efforts in the cognitive restructuring (*cognitive distortions*) strategy. Men appeared to be highly engaged in the cognitive restructuring strategy, both at mid-treatment and at the end of treatment, suggesting sustained effort over time, even when it was no longer the emphasis of treatment. These results are consistent with gender differences in the use of strategies to cope with stress. Men's coping strategies are more likely to be based on problem-solving which seems consistent with cognitive restructuring, while women are more likely to use emotion-based coping to deal with stressors, e.g., [48,49].

Gender differences were also noted in the subjective appreciation of some strategies, although no difference was detected in most of them. Interestingly, the strategies perceived as most useful were not necessarily the ones that participants most wanted to continue or the ones in which participants perceived they had put a lot of effort into (e.g., sleep hygiene and self-compassion for men). The results also revealed that a significantly greater proportion of women wanted to continue using the physical exercise strategy. It appears that physical activity as a behavioral activation strategy resonated more with women in this sample, but the reasons for this effect are unclear. One hypothesis lies in the type of work evacuees did before the fires, with men presumably more likely to be involved in physical labor in the Fort McMurray area [52,53].

It is important to acknowledge that, with the exception of number of words in sessions 7 and 10, we did not detect a gender difference in usage data indicators, including number of completed modules and in number of logins, which are common indicators in treatment usage studies [7]. These results echoed the findings of multiple studies with populations suffering from anxiety, depression and insomnia disorders [18,21,24], which found no significant associations between gender and online program attrition, completion or adherence, i.e., number or completed modules. To our knowledge, only two studies targeted PTSD in their online treatment, and neither study detected a gender effect in attrition despite using large sample sizes [2,19]. The finding that suggests men and women used the platform similarly is not surprising, considering our previous finding that the improvement of men and women on most efficacy outcomes (e.g., decrease in posttraumatic and depressive symptoms) was similar [37]. A similar treatment usage and similar improvement in men and women is consistent with the association frequently reported between adherence to online treatments and increased effectiveness [7,8].

The present results should be interpreted with caution given the exploratory nature of the study. Our limited sample size suggests that our analyses may have lacked statistical power to detect differences. Another limitation is the fact that ethnicity and immigration status were not equally distributed among men and women in our sample. However, this reflects the socioeconomic context of the Fort McMurray area, where the oil sands of the region represent an important sector of employment, especially for men, and attracts workers from all over Canada and from outside the country [52,53]. Although our study was focused on the examination of gender differences, our assessment was limited to self-identified gender and did not measure adhesion to gender roles or biological sex. As the study of subjective appreciation variables was intended to be exploratory, the questionnaire used was not a validated measure. We believe, still, that its inclusion in the platform constitutes a methodological strength that allowed for a first step in studying gender differences beyond treatment efficacy.

Despite these limitations, our study is the first to explore how gender can influence usage data and subjective appreciation of an internet-based cognitive behavioral therapy. Our results expanded on the literature on gender differences in online treatments, which has been limited to a small number of objective indicators. Although many of the usage and subjective appreciation variables of our online cognitive–behavioral treatment were revealed to be similar for men and women, some differed significantly (i.e., number of words in some sessions, perceived level of efforts in cognitive restructuring) and are worth investigating further. This research avenue could provide important clinical insight into how existing and future online treatments could be improved to include gender-specific adaptations. Our study suggests that offering a variety of therapeutic strategy choices to men and women allows them to appreciate and use some more than others while reaching similar therapeutic gains, which seems promising. It highlights the relevance of exploring this line of research further, as the availability of online treatments will most definitely keep expanding. The question of how they should be adapted to sociodemographic and cultural factors is a crucial one, especially as our comprehension of sex and gender becomes more refined.

Author Contributions: Conceptualization, É.B., M.-C.O., J.L., V.B., C.M.M. and G.B.; formal analysis, É.B.; funding acquisition, M.-C.O., C.M.M. and G.B.; investigation, G.B.; methodology, É.B., M.-C.O., J.L. and G.B.; project administration, J.L.; resources, G.B.; supervision, V.B. and G.B.; visualization, É.B.; writing—original draft, É.B.; writing—review & editing, É.B., M.-C.O., J.L., V.B., C.M.M. and G.B. All authors have read and agreed to the published version of the manuscript.

Funding: This study was funded by a grant from the Operating Grant: Health Effects of the Alberta Wildfires program, supported by the Canadian Institutes of Health Research, Alberta Innovates, and the Canadian Red Cross (#381288). ÉB holds a doctoral scholarship from Fonds de Recherche Québec–Santé (#272634) and a master-level award from the Canadian Institutes of Health Research (Frederick Banting and Charles Best Canada Graduate Scholarships, #288256).

Institutional Review Board Statement: The study was conducted according to the guidelines of the Declaration of Helsinki and approved by the Research Ethics Committee for Psychology and Education Sciences of Laval University (protocol code 2017-030 Phase II, date of approval: 7 November 2017).

Informed Consent Statement: Informed consent was obtained from all subjects involved in the study.

Data Availability Statement: The data presented in this study are available on request from the corresponding author. The data are not publicly available due to ethical restrictions.

Acknowledgments: The authors would like to thank Clara Deudon for her assistance with data management.

Conflicts of Interest: The authors declare no conflict of interest.

References

1. Benight, C.C.; Ruzek, J.I.; Waldrep, E. Internet interventions for traumatic stress: A review and theoretically based example. *J. Trauma. Stress* **2008**, *21*, 513–520. [CrossRef] [PubMed]
2. Price, M.; Gros, D.F.; McCauley, J.L.; Gros, K.S.; Ruggiero, K.J. Nonuse and Dropout Attrition for a Web-Based Mental Health Intervention Delivered in a Post-Disaster Context. *Psychiatry* **2012**, *75*, 267–284. [CrossRef] [PubMed]
3. Andrews, G.; Cuijpers, P.; Craske, M.G.; McEvoy, P.; Titov, N. Computer Therapy for the Anxiety and Depressive Disorders Is Effective, Acceptable and Practical Health Care: A Meta-Analysis. *PLoS ONE* **2010**, *5*, e13196. [CrossRef] [PubMed]
4. Amstadter, A.B.; Broman-Fulks, J.; Zinzow, H.; Ruggiero, K.J.; Cercone, J. Internet-based interventions for traumatic stress-related mental health problems: A review and suggestion for future research. *Clin. Psychol. Rev.* **2009**, *29*, 410–420. [CrossRef]
5. Barak, A.; Hen, L.; Boniel-Nissim, M.; Shapira, N. A Comprehensive Review and a Meta-Analysis of the Effectiveness of Internet-Based Psychotherapeutic Interventions. *J. Technol. Hum. Serv.* **2008**, *26*, 109–160. [CrossRef]
6. Andersson, G.; Cuijpers, P. Internet-Based and Other Computerized Psychological Treatments for Adult Depression: A Meta-Analysis. *Cogn. Behav. Ther.* **2009**, *38*, 196–205. [CrossRef] [PubMed]

7. Donkin, L.; Christensen, H.; Naismith, S.; Neal, B.; Hickie, I.B.; Glozier, N. A Systematic Review of the Impact of Adherence on the Effectiveness of e-Therapies. *J. Med. Internet Res.* **2011**, *13*, e52. [CrossRef]
8. Wright, J.H.; Owen, J.J.; Richards, D.; Eells, T.D.; Richardson, T.; Brown, G.K.; Barrett, M.; Rasku, M.A.; Polser, G.; Thase, M.E. Computer-Assisted Cognitive-Behavior Therapy for Depression: A Systematic Review and Meta-Analysis. *J. Clin. Psychiatry* **2019**, *80*, 3573. [CrossRef]
9. Hundt, N.E.; Mignogna, J.; Underhill, C.; Cully, J.A. The Relationship Between Use of CBT Skills and Depression Treatment Outcome: A Theoretical and Methodological Review of the Literature. *Behav. Ther.* **2013**, *44*, 12–26. [CrossRef]
10. Beatty, L.; Binnion, C. A Systematic Review of Predictors of, and Reasons for, Adherence to Online Psychological Interventions. *Int. J. Behav. Med.* **2016**, *23*, 776–794. [CrossRef]
11. Batterham, P.J.; Neil, A.L.; Bennett, K.; Griffiths, K.M.; Christensen, H. Predictors of adherence among community users of a cognitive behavior therapy website. *Patient Prefer. Adherence* **2008**, *2*, 97–105. [PubMed]
12. El Alaoui, S.; Ljótsson, B.; Hedman-Lagerlöf, E.; Kaldo, V.; Andersson, E.; Rück, C.; Andersson, G.; Lindefors, N. Predictors of Symptomatic Change and Adherence in Internet-Based Cognitive Behaviour Therapy for Social Anxiety Disorder in Routine Psychiatric Care. *PLoS ONE* **2015**, *10*, e0124258. [CrossRef] [PubMed]
13. Hasson, H.; Brown, C.; Hasson, D. Factors associated with high use of a workplace web-based stress management program in a randomized controlled intervention study. *Health Educ. Res.* **2010**, *25*, 596–607. [CrossRef]
14. Neil, A.L.; Batterham, P.; Christensen, H.; Bennett, K.; Griffiths, K.M.; Danaher, B. Predictors of Adherence by Adolescents to a Cognitive Behavior Therapy Website in School and Community-Based Settings. *J. Med. Internet Res.* **2009**, *11*, e6. [CrossRef] [PubMed]
15. Fuhr, K.; Schröder, J.; Berger, T.; Moritz, S.; Meyer, B.; Lutz, W.; Hohagen, F.; Hautzinger, M.; Klein, J.P. The association between adherence and outcome in an Internet intervention for depression. *J. Affect. Disord.* **2018**, *229*, 443–449. [CrossRef] [PubMed]
16. Donkin, L.; Hickie, I.; Christensen, H.; Naismith, S.; Neal, B.; Cockayne, N.L.; Glozier, N. Rethinking the Dose-Response Relationship Between Usage and Outcome in an Online Intervention for Depression: Randomized Controlled Trial. *J. Med. Internet Res.* **2013**, *15*, e231. [CrossRef]
17. Chen, H.; Rodriguez, M.A.; Qian, M.; Kishimoto, T.; Lin, M.; Berger, T. Predictors of treatment outcomes and adherence in internet-based cognitive behavioral therapy for social anxiety in China. *Behav. Cogn. Psychother.* **2020**, *48*, 291–303. [CrossRef]
18. Hilvert-Bruce, Z.; Rossouw, P.J.; Wong, N.; Sunderland, M.; Andrews, G. Adherence as a determinant of effectiveness of internet cognitive behavioural therapy for anxiety and depressive disorders. *Behav. Res. Ther.* **2012**, *50*, 463–468. [CrossRef]
19. Al-Asadi, A.M.; Klein, B.; Meyer, D. Pretreatment Attrition and Formal Withdrawal During Treatment and Their Predictors: An Exploratory Study of the Anxiety Online Data. *J. Med. Internet Res.* **2014**, *16*, e152. [CrossRef]
20. Boettcher, J.; Renneberg, B.; Berger, T. Patient Expectations in Internet-Based Self-Help for Social Anxiety. *Cogn. Behav. Ther.* **2013**, *42*, 203–214. [CrossRef]
21. Pittaway, S.; Cupitt, C.; Palmer, D.; Arowobusoye, N.; Milne, R.; Holttum, S.; Pezet, R.; Patrick, H. Comparative, clinical feasibility study of three tools for delivery of cognitive be-havioural therapy for mild to moderate depression and anxiety provided on a self-help basis. *Ment. Health Fam. Med.* **2009**, *6*, 145. [PubMed]
22. Berman, M.I.; Buckey, J.C.; Hull, J.G.; Linardatos, E.; Song, S.L.; McLellan, R.; Hegel, M.T. Feasibility Study of an Interactive Multimedia Electronic Problem Solving Treatment Program for Depression: A Preliminary Uncontrolled Trial. *Behav. Ther.* **2014**, *45*, 358–375. [CrossRef] [PubMed]
23. Farrer, L.M.; Griffiths, K.M.; Christensen, H.; Mackinnon, A.; Batterham, P. Predictors of Adherence and Outcome in Internet-Based Cognitive Behavior Therapy Delivered in a Telephone Counseling Setting. *Cogn. Ther. Res.* **2013**, *38*, 358–367. [CrossRef]
24. Hebert, E.A.; Vincent, N.; Lewycky, S.; Walsh, K. Attrition and Adherence in the Online Treatment of Chronic Insomnia. *Behav. Sleep Med.* **2010**, *8*, 141–150. [CrossRef] [PubMed]
25. Richards, D.; Timulak, L. Satisfaction with therapist-delivered vs. self-administered online cognitive behavioural treatments for depression symptoms in college students. *Br. J. Guid. Couns.* **2013**, *41*, 193–207. [CrossRef]
26. Ström, L.; Pettersson, R.; Andersson, G. Internet-Based Treatment for Insomnia: A Controlled Evaluation. *J. Consult. Clin. Psychol.* **2004**, *72*, 113–120. [CrossRef] [PubMed]
27. Topolovec-Vranic, J.; Cullen, N.; Michalak, A.; Ouchterlony, D.; Bhalerao, S.; Masanic, C.; Cusimano, M. Evaluation of an online cognitive behavioural therapy program by patients with traumatic brain injury and depression. *Brain Inj.* **2010**, *24*, 762–772. [CrossRef]
28. Swift, J.K.; Callahan, J.L. The impact of client treatment preferences on outcome: A meta-analysis. *J. Clin. Psychol.* **2009**, *65*, 368–381. [CrossRef]
29. Smith, A.H.; Norton, P.J.; McLean, C.P. Client Perceptions of Therapy Component Helpfulness in Group Cognitive-Behavioral Therapy for Anxiety Disorders. *J. Clin. Psychol.* **2012**, *69*, 229–239. [CrossRef]
30. Knowles, S.E.; Toms, G.; Sanders, C.; Bee, P.; Lovell, K.; Rennick-Egglestone, S.; Coyle, D.; Kennedy, C.; Littlewood, E.; Kessler, D.; et al. Qualitative Meta-Synthesis of User Experience of Computerised Therapy for Depression and Anxiety. *PLoS ONE* **2014**, *9*, e84323. [CrossRef]
31. Doherty, G.; Coyle, D.; Sharry, J. Engagement with online mental health interventions: An exploratory clinical study of a treatment for depression. In Proceedings of the SIGCHI Conference on Human Factors in Computing Systems, Austin, TX, USA, 5–10 May 2012; pp. 1421–1430. [CrossRef]

32. Insurance Bureau of Canada. Northern Alberta Wildfire Costliest Insured Natural Disaster in Canadian History—Estimate of Insured Losses: $3.58 Billion. 2017. Available online: https://www.ibc.ca/bc/resources/media-centre/media-releases/northern-alberta-wildfire-costliest-insured-natural-disaster-in-canadian-history (accessed on 4 June 2022).
33. Agyapong, V.I.O.; Juhas, M.; Omege, J.; Denga, E.; Nwaka, B.; Akinjise, I.; Corbett, S.E.; Brown, M.; Chue, P.; Li, X.-M.; et al. Prevalence Rates and Correlates of Likely Post-Traumatic Stress Disorder in Residents of Fort McMurray 6 Months After a Wildfire. *Int. J. Ment. Health Addict.* **2019**, *19*, 632–650. [CrossRef]
34. Agyapong, V.I.O.; Juhás, M.; Brown, M.R.G.; Omege, J.; Denga, E.; Nwaka, B.; Akinjise, I.; Corbett, S.E.; Hrabok, M.; Li, X.-M.; et al. Prevalence Rates and Correlates of Probable Major Depressive Disorder in Residents of Fort McMurray 6 Months After a Wildfire. *Int. J. Ment. Health Addict.* **2018**, *17*, 120–136. [CrossRef]
35. Belleville, G.; Ouellet, M.-C.; Lebel, J.; Ghosh, S.; Morin, C.M.; Bouchard, S.; Guay, S.; Bergeron, N.; Campbell, T.; MacMaster, F.P. Psychological Symptoms Among Evacuees from the 2016 Fort McMurray Wildfires: A Population-Based Survey One Year Later. *Front. Public Health* **2021**, *9*, 444. [CrossRef] [PubMed]
36. Belleville, G.; Ouellet, M.-C.; Békés, V.; Lebel, J.; Morin, C.M.; Bouchard, S.; Guay, S.; Bergeron, N.; Ghosh, S.; Campbell, T.; et al. Efficacy of a Therapist-Assisted Self-Help Internet-Based Intervention Targeting PTSD, Depression, and Insomnia Symptoms After a Disaster: A Randomized Controlled Trial. *Behav. Ther.* **2022**, in press. [CrossRef]
37. Binet, É.; Ouellet, M.C.; Lebel, J.; Békés, V.; Morin, C.; Bergeron, N.; Campbell, T.; Ghosh, S.; Bouchard, S.; Guay, S.; et al. Gender-Specific Changes Following an Online Cognitive Behavioral Therapy for Wildfire Evacuees. In Proceedings of the 11th Annual Conference of the Canadian Association of Cognitive and Behavioural Therapies, Online Conference, 6–8 May 2021.
38. Békés, V.; Beaulieu-Prévost, D.; Guay, S.; Belleville, G.; Marchand, A. Women with PTSD benefit more from psychotherapy than men. *Psychol. Trauma Theory Res. Pract. Policy* **2016**, *8*, 720–727. [CrossRef]
39. Wade, D.; Varker, T.; Kartal, D.; Hetrick, S.; O'Donnell, M.; Forbes, D. Gender difference in outcomes following trauma-focused interventions for posttraumatic stress disorder: Systematic review and meta-analysis. *Psychol. Trauma Theory Res. Pract. Policy* **2016**, *8*, 356–364. [CrossRef]
40. Watts, B.V.; Schnurr, P.P.; Mayo, L.; Young-Xu, Y.; Weeks, W.B.; Friedman, M.J. Meta-Analysis of the Efficacy of Treatments for Posttraumatic Stress Disorder. *J. Clin. Psychiatry* **2013**, *74*, e541–e550. [CrossRef]
41. Weathers, F.W.; Litz, B.T.; Keane, T.M.; Palmieri, P.A.; Marx, B.P.; Schnurr, P.P. The PTSD Checklist for DSM-5 (PCL-5). National Center for PTSD. 2013. Available online: http://www.ptsd.va.gov (accessed on 1 September 2022).
42. Kroenke, K.; Spitzer, R.L.; Williams, J.B. The PHQ-9: Validity of a brief depression severity measure. *J. Gen. Intern. Med.* **2011**, *16*, 606–613. [CrossRef]
43. Morin, C.M. *Insomnia: Psychological Assessment and Management*; Guilford Press: New York, NY, USA, 1993.
44. Mulac, A.; Bradac, J.; Gibbons, P. Empirical support for the gender-as-culture hypothesis: An Intercultural Analysis of Male/Female Language Differences. *Hum. Commun. Res.* **2006**, *27*, 121–152. [CrossRef]
45. Pillemer, D.B.; Wink, P.; Di Donato, T.E.; Sanborn, R.L. Gender differences in autobiographical memory styles of older adults. *Memory* **2003**, *11*, 525–532. [CrossRef]
46. Seidlitz, L.; Diener, E. Sex differences in the recall of affective experiences. *J. Pers. Soc. Psychol.* **1998**, *74*, 262–271. [CrossRef] [PubMed]
47. Schultheiss, O.C.; Köllner, M.G.; Busch, H.; Hofer, J. Evidence for a robust, estradiol-associated sex difference in narrative-writing fluency. *Neuropsychology* **2021**, *35*, 323–333. [CrossRef] [PubMed]
48. Tamres, L.K.; Janicki, D.; Helgeson, V.S. Sex Differences in Coping Behavior: A Meta-Analytic Review and an Examination of Relative Coping. *Pers. Soc. Psychol. Rev.* **2002**, *6*, 2–30. [CrossRef]
49. Ptacek, J.T.; Smith, R.E.; Dodge, K.L. Gender Differences in Coping with Stress: When Stressor and Appraisals Do Not Differ. *Pers. Soc. Psychol. Bull.* **1994**, *20*, 421–430. [CrossRef]
50. Foa, E.B.; Hembree, E.A.; Rothbaum, B.O.; Rauch, S.A.M. *Prolonged Exposure Therapy for PTSD: Emotional Processing of Traumatic Experiences: Therapist Guide*, 2nd ed.; Oxford University Press: Oxford, UK, 2019. [CrossRef]
51. Statistics Canada. Literacy Skills among Canada's Immigrant Population (Archived). Statistics Canada Articles and Reports: 81-004-X. Government of Canada. Updated 1 December 2008. Available online: https://www150.statcan.gc.ca/n1/pub/81-004-x/2005005/9112-eng.htm (accessed on 30 July 2021).
52. Statistics Canada. Fort McMurray [Population Centre], Alberta and Saskatchewan [Province] (Table). Census Profile. 2016 Census. Government of Canada. 2019. Available online: https://www12.statcan.gc.ca/census-recensement/2016/dp-pd/prof/index.cfm?Lang=E (accessed on 20 May 2021).
53. Stenson, F. Fort McMurray: Understanding a City of Dreams. *MacLean's*. 16 May 2016. Available online: https://www.macleans.ca/news/canada/fort-mcmurray-a-city-of-dreams/ (accessed on 6 January 2020).

Journal of
Clinical Medicine

MDPI

Article

Clients in Simulated Teletherapy via Videoconference Compensate for Altered Eye Contact When Evaluating Therapist Empathy

Frédéric Grondin [1,2,3], Anna M. Lomanowska [4], Vincent Poiré [1] and Philip L. Jackson [1,2,3,*]

1 École de Psychologie, Université Laval, 2325 All. des Bibliothèques, Québec City, QC G1V 0A6, Canada; frederic.grondin.1@ulaval.ca (F.G.); vincent.poire.1@ulaval.ca (V.P.)
2 Center for Interdisciplinary Research in Rehabilitation and Social Integration (Cirris), 525 Wilfrid-Hamel Blvd, Québec City, QC G1M 2S8, Canada
3 CERVO Brain Research Center, 2601 Chem. de la Canardière, Québec City, QC G1J 2G3, Canada
4 Transitional Pain Service, Toronto General Hospital, University Health Network, 200 Elizabeth St., Toronto, ON M5G 2C4, Canada; anna.lomanowska@uhnresearch.ca
* Correspondence: philip.jackson@psy.ulaval.ca

Abstract: Eye contact is frequently associated with an increased perception of empathy and telepresence, but the currently used videoconferencing (VC) technologies diminish the possibility of naturally conveying eye contact. This study compared the empathy, telepresence, and eye gaze patterns of clients in simulated VC teletherapy sessions where eye contact was altered or facilitated. Forty-two would-be clients met with one of four therapists in training for one 20-min simulated teletherapy session taking place via VC. The session either altered or facilitated eye contact perception by manipulating the positioning of the webcams and of the clients in their chair. Eye-tracking data focusing on the eyes, face, and general body regions of interest were obtained for 25 clients. The results show that facilitating eye contact in VC did not increase the clients' perceptions of empathy or telepresence. However, empathy was associated with greater time spent looking at the eyes and faces of the therapists, but only in the sessions facilitating eye contact. We suggest that clients successfully rely on other verbal and nonverbal cues to detect therapist empathy when eye contact is altered in teletherapy sessions.

Keywords: eye contact; empathy; teletherapy; videoconferencing; eye tracking

Citation: Grondin, F.; Lomanowska, A.M.; Poiré, V.; Jackson, P.L. Clients in Simulated Teletherapy via Videoconference Compensate for Altered Eye Contact When Evaluating Therapist Empathy. *J. Clin. Med.* **2022**, *11*, 3461. https://doi.org/10.3390/jcm11123461

Academic Editors: Birgit Derntl and Stéphane Bouchard

Received: 10 March 2022
Accepted: 14 June 2022
Published: 16 June 2022

1. Introduction

Teletherapy refers to the use of technological means such as videoconferencing (VC) to allow for therapists and clients to meet for psychotherapy when they do not share the same physical space. Under the circumstances brought about by the COVID-19 global pandemic, teletherapy has become a widely-used alternative to in-person psychological treatments. A survey of the members of the American Psychological Association (APA) performed in June 2020 shows that 76% of clinicians who took part in the survey had completely transitioned to teletherapy at that time [1]. While it is currently uncertain how much of the recent uptake in teletherapy will persist beyond the global pandemic [2], there is a need to establish the effectiveness of teletherapy treatments and to identify areas where this clinical practice can be enhanced. A number of meta-analyses and systematic reviews support the claim that treatments delivered through VC are as effective as analog in-person interventions [3–6]. Establishing strong therapeutic alliance is also possible in teletherapy compared to in-person treatments according to numerous systematic reviews [7,8]. However, a recent meta-analysis found alliance to be weaker in teletherapy when integrating the results of 12 comparative studies between teletherapy and in-person therapy [5]. This last finding echoes the frequent concerns of therapists and clients that VC could impact the therapeutic relationship due to difficulties in perceiving and attending to nonverbal cues during VC sessions [9]. Technical limitations such as Internet connection instability, transmission delays, or equipment layout can lead to a relative loss of socioemotional cues called the "filtering effect" [10]. Nonverbal cues, more so than verbal content, thus run the risk of being altered or lost during VC-based interactions.

One such nonverbal behavior frequently compromised when interacting in VC is eye contact. Under typical circumstances, VC systems employed on home computers and laptops do not properly convey eye contact between the interactants due to the angle between the visual target on the screen (the other person's eyes) and the webcam usually mounted atop the computer monitor. This gaze angle produces the impression for interlocutors that their counterpart is looking at their chin when intending to make eye contact. Although several adaptations have been proposed to facilitate eye contact in VC (for a review, see [11]), these adaptations are seldom used in clinical practice due to the need for advanced computational algorithms or specialized equipment. One possible solution that has the advantages of being simple and inexpensive for clinicians and clients is the thoughtful positioning of webcams and interlocutors to decrease the gaze angle to roughly 2° [12]. This solution, however, has not yet been implemented systematically and studied in teletherapy sessions.

The importance of facilitating eye contact in teletherapy sessions stems from its positive contribution to the subjective experience of clients during sessions, notably regarding empathy and telepresence. Empathy, by which therapists convey the emotional understanding and attunement integral to successful therapy [13], is rated higher in face-to-face counseling sessions where eye contact is encouraged. One study investigated the perceived empathy of observers within simulated sessions where the therapist either intended or avoided making eye contact [14]. Therapists were also instructed to modify their body posture to be either leaning forward or staying upright. The results showed that the "high eye contact" condition (intending to make eye contact most of the time) was associated with higher ratings of perceived empathy, regardless of body posture. These findings highlight the significance of eye contact for an observer when assessing the level of empathy of a therapist. Eye contact is also thought to play an important role in facilitating telepresence, or the impression of *being there* with the other person during a VC session [15]. One study found that participants who took part in a quiz with a confederate in a VC interaction reported higher telepresence in the quiz round where eye contact was enabled compared to the quiz round with altered eye contact [16]. Telepresence, incidentally, has also been suggested as a potential correlate of empathy, though the exact nature of the relationship is still debated [10]. Facilitating eye contact in teletherapy could, therefore, lead to the perception of both higher empathy and telepresence in VC.

Multiple methods can be employed to measure and quantify eye contact in human interactions [17]. The use of an eye-tracking apparatus offers the advantages of accurately and objectively measuring where and for how long a person is fixating their gaze. Examining gaze fixations toward specific regions of interests can provide valuable information for clinicians since gaze fixation can be indicative of prolonged attention toward specific visual information [18]. For example, the time a client spends fixating on different body parts (e.g., eyes, face, or body) of the therapist can be used as a marker of increased attention to visual cues expressed in these areas of the body (e.g., eye contact, facial expressions, or body movements). It is still unclear whether facilitating eye contact in VC therapy could result in different eye gaze patterns in clients for these regions of interests, for example, by increasing the time spent looking into the therapist's eyes. A final advantage of precise eye tracking data is in the possibility of investigating correlations with self-reported measures such as the clients' perception of empathy and telepresence.

This article presents the first empirical study to investigate the impact of facilitating eye contact in VC teletherapy on the empathy, telepresence, and eye-tracking patterns using simulated clinical sessions. The relationship between empathy, telepresence, and fixation times of the eyes, face, and general body was also investigated. The hypotheses were as follows:

Hypothesis 1 (H1). *Empathy and telepresence reported by clients will be higher in VC teletherapy sessions where eye contact is facilitated.*

Hypothesis 2 (H2). *Clients will spend more time looking into the eyes and the face of the therapist in VC teletherapy sessions where eye contact is facilitated compared to sessions where it is not.*

Hypothesis 3 (H3). *Empathy and telepresence reported by clients will be correlated with the time spent looking into the face and the eyes of the therapists.*

Hypothesis 4 (H4). *Empathy will be significantly correlated to telepresence in VC teletherapy.*

2. Materials and Methods

2.1. Participants

Forty-four students were recruited through posters and university mailing lists between October 2019 and March 2020, thus before the introduction of social distancing measures required by the advent of the COVID-19 pandemic. Participants were enrolled as clients if they were attending university courses at the time of the study and did not report uncorrected visual or auditory impairments. Clients reporting acute distress or suicidal thoughts received a list of resources, were offered to be accompanied through the process of contacting mental health services, and were excluded from the study. Clients were informed that they would be required to talk about a subject of personal nature of their choice with a therapist under training prior to completing the study questionnaires. The clients were randomly assigned to one of two experimental groups, More-EYE (with eye contact; $n = 20$) and Less-EYE (without eye contact, $n = 23$). One participant who completed the More-EYE condition was removed from the analyses because they misunderstood the experimental task, leaving a final total of 19 participants in the More-EYE group and an overall total of 42 participants. Table 1 presents the sociodemographic data of clients by experimental condition. Groups did not significantly differ based on their sociodemographic profile. Clients received CAD 15 for their participation in the study.

2.2. Materials

2.2.1. Therapists

The therapists were four confederates enrolled in a doctoral degree in clinical psychology (aged 21, 24, 25, and 28 years old, three women). Each therapist had completed at least one year of supervised clinical practice. Therapists were informed that they would meet university students acting as clients in simulations of teletherapy sessions prior to the study but were blind regarding the objectives and hypotheses of the study. They each met 5, 9, 14, and 14 clients counterbalanced across the two groups.

2.2.2. List of Discussion Themes

To encourage clients to choose a relevant topic of discussion while also ensuring that sensitive topics would not be discussed during the sessions, a list of potential themes of discussion used in helping skills training was provided to the clients (p. 19, [19]). Themes were classified as *ideal* (e.g., academic issues), *relatively safe* (e.g., minor family issues), or *proscribed topics* (e.g., traumas) for the context of the study. Frequently chosen topics included *Careers and future plans* and *Academic issues*.

Table 1. The sociodemographic data of clients across the experimental conditions.

Variables	More-EYE Condition (n = 19)	Less-EYE Condition (n = 23)	p Value [a]
	Mean (SD)	Mean (SD)	
Age (years)	23.21 (3.84)	24.22 (5.38)	0.50
Sex (female)	15	20	0.49
Years of education	16.42 (2.09)	17.26 (3.41)	0.36
Chronic medication (Yes) [b]	0	3	0.10
History of mental health disorders (Yes) [c]	2	6	0.20
History of clinical consultation as a client (Yes) [d]	11	9	0.35
Computer Use			
Days/week	6.58 (0.84)	6.87 (0.34)	0.28
Hours/day	5.63 (2.63)	6.22 (2.21)	0.43
Videoconferencing use			
Days/week	0.74 (0.93)	1.44 (1.90)	0.36
Hours/week	0.71 (0.99)	1.50 (1.81)	0.19

[a] The reported p values were obtained from independent t-tests for the *Age* and *Years of education* variables. Mann–Whitney U tests were performed on the *Computer Use* and *Videoconferencing Use* variables because of their non normal data distribution. Chi-squared tests were performed for the *Sex, Chronic Medication, History of mental health disorders*, and *History of clinical consultation as a client* variable. These tests used an alpha level of 0.05 for significance. [b] Chronic medication included the use of psychotropic medication only such as antidepressants and painkillers. [c] History of mental health disorders comprised mood disorders, anxiety disorders, or eating disorders, but excluded attention deficit disorder with or without hyperactivity. [d] History of clinical consultation in psychotherapy as a client.

2.2.3. VC Sessions

The VC sessions were initiated using Zoom version 4.6.0 (Zoom Video Communications, Inc., San Jose, CA, USA) on cabled Internet and were displayed on 24-inch high-definition LCD computer monitors. Therapists and clients wore noise-cancelling headsets and sat in comfortable, adjustable chairs located in two separate lab rooms. This setup ensured that the quality of the video feed was as high as possible, with no noticeable video blurring or audio lag during the sessions. The VC sessions were recorded using OBS Studio, an open-source software for video recording. The two lab rooms were in the same building and close by, but the therapists and clients did not meet physically during the experimental task.

2.2.4. Eye-Tracking Data

The Smart Eye Pro 8 (Smart Eye Inc., Gothenburg, Sweden) eye-tracking system was employed to collect gaze coordinates and fixation information at a frequency of 120 hz. This system uses two synchronized monochromatic cameras (Basler acA640−120 gm) equipped with 6 mm lenses, infrared filters, and infrared flashes to register eye positioning and gaze direction. These cameras were placed 70 cm away from the clients, on each side of the desk on top of which the computer monitor was placed. To prepare the eye-tracking data and to compute the gaze ratios for each region of interest, scripts programmed in Python were used. The fixations identified by the eye tracking software were filtered by removing the fixations from the analysis where the duration was shorter than 70 ms or where the gaze signal quality was inferior to 10% using the thresholds suggested by Smart Eye [20]. The remaining fixations were classified as being directed *on-screen* or *off-screen* (Figure 1). The screen coordinate used for the *on-screen* fixations was the median value of the valid screen coordinates (x, y) provided by the eye tracker. The *on-screen* portion of the fixations were then classified into increasingly smaller and more specific areas of interest, beginning with a *general body* area, then a *face* area, and finally an *eyes* area (Figure 2). To extract the changing coordinates of the eyes and face across time, recordings of each session were first analyzed using a facial behavior analysis toolkit, OpenFace [21]. Body coordinates were manually entered for each recording to encompass the trunk of participants and added to the *face* and *eyes* coordinates to form the *general body* area. These parameters were then used to classify the data over time from the Smart Eye Pro system to extract fixation times relating to the three regions of interest. The resulting gaze duration for each area of interest was then compiled as a percentage ratio of the duration of *on-screen* gaze duration. Of the 42 total participants, 28 clients took part in the eye-tracking procedure and three of these 28 sessions were excluded from analysis following calibration failure or poor gaze detection quality. The final eye-tracking analyses comprised 13 clients for the More-EYE group and 12 clients for the Less-EYE group.

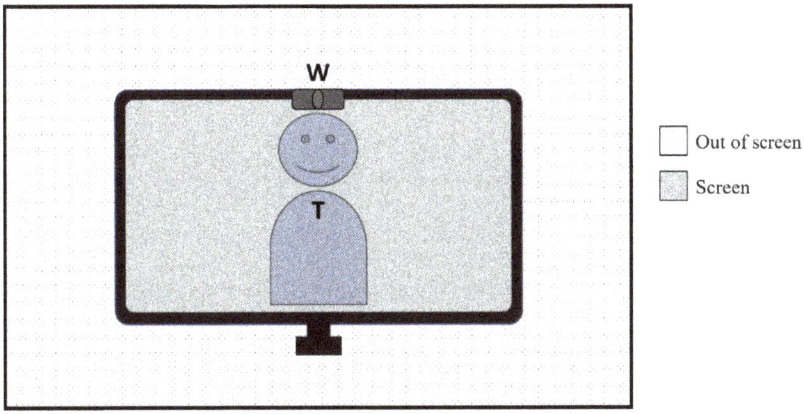

Figure 1. The depiction of *off-screen* versus *on-screen* portions of the visual scene from the client perspective. Legend: T: Therapist. W: Webcam.

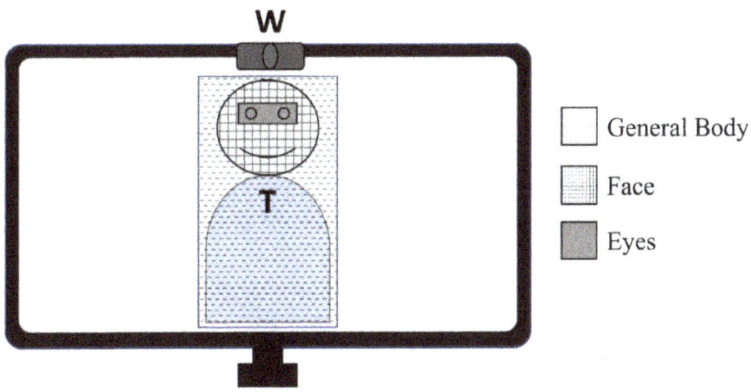

Figure 2. The delineation of the *eyes*, *face*, and *general body* regions of interest included in the *on-screen* portion of the visual scene from the client perspective. Legend: T: Therapist. W: Webcam.

2.2.5. Empathy

A French translation of the Empathic Understanding Subscale (EUS) of the Relationship Inventory was used [22]. The EUS is comprised of 16 items scored on a scale ranging between −3 to +3, with a positive score indicating higher perceived empathy. Upon inspecting the Cronbach alpha of the EUS scores, one item was consistently scored positively by clients when its intended scoring key indicated that the item should be reverse scored. This item ("The therapist understands what I say from an objective, detached point of view") was therefore removed from the analyses. The total scores thus ranged from −45 to +45. The internal consistency analysis showed a Cronbach value of 0.85 for this study. The EUS is frequently used in studies investigating empathy in the context of therapy sessions [14,23].

2.2.6. Telepresence

The French version of the Telepresence in Videoconference Scale (TVS) was used [15]. The scale includes seven items scored from 0 to 100 that are averaged into a total score. Three different subscales are also derived from the TVS: *Physical Presence*, defined as the impression of being in the same room as the therapist; *Social Presence*, defined as the impression of being in an ongoing social interaction with the therapist; and *Absorption*, defined as the impression of feeling immersed in the interaction. The TVS was especially developed to assess the clients' perceptions of telepresence in teletherapy sessions. The TVS showed discriminant validity with associated constructs such as immersive tendencies and the participant's comfort while using a communication medium such as VC [15]. The internal consistency analysis of the TVS revealed a Cronbach value of 0.80 for this study.

2.2.7. Affectivity Changes

The French translation of the Positive Affectivity and Negative Affectivity Scale (PANAS) was used to assess the affectivity changes in clients following the session [24]. The PANAS includes 20 adjectives relating to the positive or negative effects that participants rate according to their level of agreement with each adjective on a 5-point Likert scale. The scores are aggregated on two subscales, *Positivity* and *Negativity*.

2.3. *Procedure*

At the start of the study, therapists took part in an hour-long training course aimed at clarifying their role in the study. Therapists were instructed to explore the discussion theme chosen by the clients with warmth, interest, and openness as they normally would in their clinical practice. They were, however, instructed to refrain from conducting actual therapeutical interventions as the sessions were aimed at simulating teletherapy only. They concluded the training course by completing one 20-min session in VC that served to validate the methodology used for facilitating eye contact in VC (see [12]).

Clients who took part in the study were greeted in a lab room and were reminded that their participation consisted of speaking with a therapist in training about a subject of a personal nature of their choice. Clients such as therapists were not informed that the study examined eye contact, empathy, and telepresence in the VC sessions prior to their completion of the task. Prior to the session, participants completed the consent form, the sociodemographic questionnaire, and the pre-session PANAS. Next, the eye-tracking calibration procedure of the Smart Eye Pro 8 was performed in the 28 sessions where eye-tracking data were registered. Clients then met with the therapists in VC under one of two experimental conditions, the More-EYE and the Less-EYE condition. The More-EYE condition facilitated eye contact perception by diminishing the gaze angle down to approximatively 2°. The More-EYE condition was set up by following a procedure that was developed to minimize the gaze angle by adjusting the positioning of the webcam and of the interactants [12]. This layout ensures that participants looked almost directly into the webcams, which enabled the perception of eye contact in VC. The Less-EYE condition introduced a 10° horizontal gaze angle to ensure that the eye contact perception was altered during the sessions (see Figure 3). Therapists, unlike clients, were always under the More-EYE condition, which was thought to be the 'ideal' experimental condition.

Each VC session lasted 20 min. The experimenters were invited into the Zoom call as an invisible guest to allow for the recording of the session as it unfolded using OBS Studio. Participants received a signal at the 19-min mark to leave some time for the termination of the session. After the session, clients completed the empathy, the telepresence, and the post-session affectivity questionnaires. Participants were then debriefed and received monetary compensation.

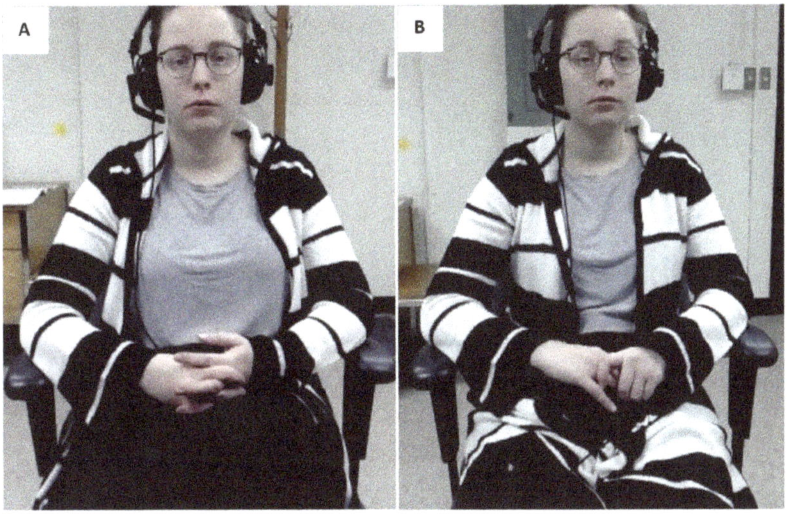

Figure 3. The clients' view of the therapist under the two experimental conditions: (**A**) the More-EYE condition with facilitated eye-contact, and (**B**) the Less-EYE condition with altered eye-contact.

2.4. Analyses

SPSS 22.0.0.0 (IBM Corp., Armonk, NY, USA) was used to perform the statistical tests and the alpha level was set at 0.05. Statistical corrections for multiple comparisons or correlations were not applied to the data as the analyses were hypothesis-driven and the number of tests per analysis was low. Effect sizes of *t*-tests were generated using Cohen's *d* formula [25].

3. Results

To test whether perceived empathy and total telepresence, respectively, increased when eye contact was facilitated in the VC sessions (H1), two one-tailed *t*-tests for independent samples were performed on the empathy and telepresence mean scores (Table 2). Perceived empathy and telepresence did not differ significantly between the More-EYE and Less-EYE conditions. The level of empathy (e.g., [23]) and telepresence (e.g., [26]) reported by clients was high for both conditions in comparison to earlier studies using the same questionnaires. Two-tailed *t*-tests were also performed to compare each of the three subscales of the telepresence questionnaire across conditions and no significant differences were found (Table 2). These results indicate that clients did not report more empathy or telepresence in the sessions where eye contact was facilitated.

Table 2. The comparisons of empathy and telepresence across the experimental conditions.

Variables	More-EYE		Less-EYE		t	p	Cohen's d
	n	Mean (SD)	n	Mean (SD)			
Empathy [a]	19	28.11 (9.31)	23	24.91 (12.63)	0.915	0.18	0.28
Telepresence [b]—total	19	71.28 (14.11)	23	69.13 (10.84)	0.558	0.29	0.17
Telepresence—physical	19	77.63 (19.68)	23	76.30 (15.18)	0.247	0.81	0.08
Telepresence—social	19	89.08 (8.79)	23	85.76 (14.39)	0.878	0.39	0.20
Telepresence—absorption	19	60.79 (21.73)	23	64.57 (26.13)	−0.502	0.62	0.16

[a] Empathy = Empathic Understanding Subscale. [b] Telepresence = Telepresence in Videoconference Scale.

To test whether the clients' gaze distribution differed between the More-EYE and Less-EYE conditions (H2), a Mann–Whitney *U* test was used to compare the *on-screen* time ratios between the More-EYE and the Less-EYE condition (Table 3). These analyses included eye tracking data from the 25 sessions where the Smart Eye Pro 8 was available. The Mann–Whitney U test was selected over parametric tests to account for the non-normal distribution of the eye-tracking data. Regions (*eyes, face, general body*) were not compared between themselves as they were comprised within one another (see Figure 2). This first test showed no significant differences in the time ratios across conditions, indicating that participants spent a similar amount of time looking at the computer screen across conditions. Three Mann–Whitney *U* tests were then performed to compare the mean fixation times for the *eye, face*, and *general body* regions (Table 3). The mean fixation durations for the *eye* and the *face* regions were not significantly different across conditions. The mean *general body* fixation duration was significantly higher in the More-EYE condition, indicating that participants tended to look more at the therapists in the More-EYE condition than in the Less-EYE condition.

Table 3. The comparisons of the fixation durations of the percentage ratios across conditions.

Fixation Duration (%)	n	More-EYE Mean (SD)	n	Less-EYE Mean (SD)	U	p
On-Screen [a]	13	77.20 (14.80)	12	74.97 (8.68)	62.00	0.41
Eye [b]	13	7.37 (11.20)	12	13.99 (19.37)	51.50	0.16
Face [b]	13	69.91 (26.95)	12	66.63 (29.69)	67.00	0.57
General body [b]	13	90.68 (6.49)	12	80.85 (19.90)	38.00	0.03 *

[a] Ratio out of total session duration. [b] Ratio out of on-screen gaze duration. * $p < 0.05$.

To test whether perceived empathy and telepresence were associated with time spent looking at the *eyes, face*, or *general body* of therapists across conditions (H3), the Spearman Rho correlations (r_s) were calculated for each of the two experimental conditions (Table 4). The Spearman Rho correlations were selected based on the non-normality of the eye-tracking data. In the More-EYE condition, empathy marginally correlated ($p = 0.06$) with the time spent looking at the *eyes* of the therapist and significantly correlated with the time spent looking at the *face*. In the Less-EYE condition, these correlations were not statistically significant. These results indicate that the time clients spent looking at the eyes of the therapist was associated with their perceived level of therapist empathy, but only in the More-EYE condition. In both experimental conditions, telepresence did not significantly correlate with the mean gaze duration in any of the three regions of interest.

To test whether empathy ratings were correlated to the telepresence *total scores* as well the *physical presence, social presence*, and *absorption* subscales (H4), Pearson correlations were computed in the More-EYE and Less-EYE conditions (Table 5). The results indicate that empathy correlated significantly with the *social presence* subscale in the Less-EYE condition only.

Manipulations checks were performed using the affectivity changes reported on the affectivity questionnaire. This was conducted to verify whether clients benefitted from the session in the way that they presumably would in an actual teletherapy session. Four two-tailed *t*-tests for paired samples were performed using pre- and post-session levels of positivity and negativity for each of the two conditions. Three clients in the Less-EYE condition encountered technical difficulties with their pre-session affectivity computerized form, bringing the total observation count to 20 for these analyses. The results showed a significant decrease in negativity in the More-EYE condition and a marginally significant ($p = 0.052$) increase in positivity in the Less-EYE condition (Table 6). These results indicate that clients benefitted from the sessions but in different ways between the experimental conditions.

Table 4. The correlations between empathy, telepresence, and time spent looking at the eyes, face, and general body of the therapists.

Fixation Ratios [a]		**Empathy** [b]	**Telepresence** [c]
More-EYE (n = 13)			
Eyes	r_s	0.53	−0.37
	p	0.06	0.21
Face	r_s	0.57	−0.29
	p	0.04 *	0.34
General body	r_s	−0.19	−0.11
	p	0.54	0.71
Less-EYE (n = 12)			
Eyes	r_s	−0.17	0.33
	p	0.60	0.29
Face	r_s	−0.22	0.40
	p	0.49	0.20
General body	r_s	0.10	0.21
	p	0.77	0.52

[a] Ratios out of on-screen gaze duration. [b] Empathy: Empathic Understanding Subscale. [c] Telepresence: Telepresence in Videoconference Scale. * $p < 0.05$.

Table 5. The correlations between empathy and telepresence.

	r with Empathy [a]	p
More-EYE (n = 19)		
Telepresence [b]—total	−0.21	0.39
Telepresence—physical	0.09	0.71
Telepresence—social	0.24	0.33
Telepresence—absorption	−0.18	0.46
Less-EYE (n = 23)		
Telepresence—total	0.31	0.15
Telepresence—physical	0.35	0.10
Telepresence—social	0.81	<0.001 *
Telepresence—absorption	−0.11	0.62

[a] Empathy: Empathic Understanding Subscale. [b] Telepresence: Telepresence in Videoconference Scale. * $p < 0.05$.

Table 6. The client affectivity [a] scores pre- and post-session.

	n	**Pre-Session Mean (SD)**	**Post-Session Mean (SD)**	t	p	**Cohen's d**
More-EYE						
Positivity	19	32.25 (4.24)	33.95 (3.87)	1.624	0.12	0.35
Negativity	19	15.50 (4.29)	12.60 (2.98)	−3.368	0.003 *	0.67
Less-EYE						
Positivity	20	30.20 (5.60)	32.90 (5.48)	2.077	0.052	0.46
Negativity	20	14.15 (4.18)	13.10 (4.00)	−1.437	0.167	0.32

[a] Affectivity: Positive Affectivity and Negative Affectivity Scale. * $p < 0.05$.

Table 7 features the *eyes* and *face* region sizes in pixels for each eye contact condition as well as the *eyes-to-face* ratios between these regions. Mann–Whitney analyses for paired samples were performed to test for differences in the size and ratio between the eye contact conditions. This was carried out to verify whether the manipulation of the camera angle between conditions had an effect on the size of the therapist's *face* and *eyes* regions on the screen that clients looked at during sessions. The Mann–Whitney analyses showed that the *eyes* region was marginally bigger and that the *face* region was significantly bigger in the More-EYE condition compared to the Less-EYE condition. The *eyes-to-face* ratios did not differ significantly. These results indicate that the manipulation of the camera angle resulted in bigger *eyes* and *face* areas for the More-EYE sessions compared to the Less-EYE sessions.

Table 7. The *eyes* and *face* region sizes and *eyes-to-face* ratios [a] between the eye contact conditions.

	n	More-EYE Mean (SD)	*n*	Less-EYE Mean (SD)	*U*	*p*
Eyes region size [b]	13	16,989.69 (5066.59)	12	13,907.35 (2394.85)	43.00	0.060
Face region size	13	29,236.52 (5066.59)	12	24,367.60 (3398.98)	41.00	0.046 *
Eyes-to-face ratio	13	0.580 (0.052)	12	0.573 (0.061)	68.00	0.611

[a] Ratio between the *eyes* region on the total size of the *face* region. See Figure 2 for each region delineation on the screen. [b] Region size in pixels. * $p < 0.05$.

To explore how eye contact unfolded over time, the time spent looking at the therapist's eyes was compared across 5 min segments of the 20 min interaction in the More-EYE and the Less-EYE conditions combined. Table 8 shows the mean and median time spent looking at the eyes of the therapist for each 5 min segment. A Friedman's test (the nonparametric equivalent of a repeated-measures ANOVA) was performed on the time spent looking at the therapist's eyes for all clients across the 5 min segments. The Friedman's test showed no overall significant change in time spent looking at the therapist's eyes, $\chi^2(3) = 5.044$, $p = 0.17$.

Table 8. The time spent looking at the therapist's eyes per 5 min segment of the interaction for all clients.

Segments (min)	*n*	Time Spent Looking at the Eyes of the Therapist (%) Mean (SD)	Median
0–5	25	5.34 (7.26)	1.29
5–10	25	5.98 (10.40)	0.63
10–15	25	8.22 (12.54)	2.72
15–20	25	7.74 (11.07)	2.22

4. Discussion

4.1. Hypothesis 1: Empathy and Telepresence Ratings across Sessions

This study aimed at determining whether facilitating eye contact in VC sessions would lead to heightened impressions of perceived empathy and telepresence compared to sessions where eye contact was altered. Two experimental conditions were compared in this study: one facilitating eye contact (More-EYE) and one altering eye contact (Less-EYE). The results showed that both experimental conditions produced high ratings of empathy and telepresence compared to previous studies (e.g., [14,23]), with no significant influence of eye contact facilitation on reports of empathy and telepresence. This finding is contrary to the initial hypotheses. It appears that solely manipulating the perception of eye contact in VC does not greatly impact the perception of empathy and telepresence. There are multiple possible explanations for the lack of significant differences between the groups. First, although participants could not naturally establish eye contact in the Less-EYE condition, earlier research showed that VC users rapidly learned to interpret the deviated gaze of their interlocutor as intended eye contact [27]. It is therefore possible that this knowledge was sufficient for clients to assess that their therapist was attentive to their subjective experience, a perception that would be conducive to a high rating of empathy regardless of the possibility to actually establish eye contact or not. Another explanation for the lack of significant differences relates to the overall favorable parameters of the sessions. Participants had a reliable, high-quality video feed to support their interaction in both conditions, potentially allowing clients to perceive empathy, even when eye contact is altered. These explanations would need to be tested in contexts where video and audio feeds fluctuate in quality and where the view of the therapist is restricted to assess the impact of these factors on perceived empathy. In terms of telepresence, the results obtained from the *Absorption* subscale showed a high level of variance in both conditions. This suggests that the clients' impression of being absorbed in the interaction varied according to factors outside of the availability of eye contact during sessions, thus affecting the statistical analysis of this variable across experimental conditions.

4.2. Hypothesis 2: Clients' Time Spent Looking at Regions of Interest across Sessions

The study also investigated whether facilitating eye contact influenced the time spent looking at the eyes, face, and general body of therapists compared to sessions where eye contact was not facilitated. The results showed that clients spent more time looking at the body of therapists in the More-EYE condition but, contrary to the hypotheses, they did not significantly look more at the eyes or the face of the therapists than the participants in the Less-EYE condition. In contrast, the data pointed to a nonsignificant increase ($p = 0.16$) in time spent looking at the eyes of the therapist in the Less-EYE condition rather than in the More-EYE condition. One way to reconcile these conflicting results is by reconsidering the assumption that facilitating eye contact would lead clients to look *more* in the eyes of the therapists rather than *less*. In an in-person interaction, prolonged eye contact can cause discomfort, and this effect could be compounded by the experimental task where clients had to open up on a subject of a personal nature to a stranger [28]. However, when eye contact is altered, as it was in the Less-EYE condition, it is possible for clients to fixate more on the eyes of the therapists without feeling discomfort. Therefore, it seems possible that clients in the More-EYE condition tried to avoid eye contact once they had the indication that the therapist was paying attention to them and instead focused on looking elsewhere on the screen, thus leading to the significant increase in time spent looking at the general body of the therapists. It is interesting to note that the exploratory analyses of the time clients spent looking at the therapist's eyes showed no significant change over the course of the 20-min session (Table 8). In future studies, it would be pertinent to examine whether the time spent looking at the therapist's eyes changes over a longer session or across multiple sessions of teletherapy.

4.3. Hypothesis 3: Correlations between Time Spent Looking at Regions of Interest and Empathy and Telepresence across Sessions

The study aimed at identifying whether empathy and telepresence were associated with time spent looking at the eyes, face, and general body of therapists with the hypothesis that more time would be spent looking at the eyes and face in the More-EYE condition. The results showed a marginally significant and a significant correlation between time spent, respectively, looking at the eyes and face of the therapists in the More-EYE condition. These correlations were not observed in the Less-EYE condition. These results lend support to the contention that eye contact is an important indicator of empathy from the perspective of clients, as the clients who experienced facilitated eye contact in VC tended to rate empathy higher as they spent more time making eye contact. However, when considering that no significant difference in empathy was found between the conditions, it seems plausible that clients do not necessarily need proper eye contact to perceive high therapist empathy and that, in the presence of altered eye contact, they adapt by basing their assessment of therapist empathy on other available cues. For example, body posture [14], facial expressions [29], vocal cues [30], and verbal interventions [31] can also influence perceived empathy. These cues were all preserved in the sessions regardless of the experimental condition and thus could have helped clients make a favorable judgement of therapist empathy when eye contact was not facilitated.

4.4. Hypothesis 4: Correlations between Empathy and Telepresence

The results showed that empathy was not significantly correlated with the total telepresence scores in either experimental condition. The investigation of the telepresence subscales revealed that empathy correlated with the social presence subscale in the Less-EYE condition only. Broadly speaking, these results do not support the contention that empathy and telepresence are strongly correlated in VC sessions. However, there seems to be a specific aspect of telepresence related to the impression of being actively participating in an ongoing online interaction with someone (i.e., the ratings on the *social presence* subscale) that is more highly rated in sessions where the clients also report high empathy. The fact that this correlation was found only in the Less-EYE condition also lends more credence to the hypothesis outlined above regarding the possibility that clients rely on factors other than eye contact to rate therapist empathy when eye contact is not facilitated. In other words, when eye contact is altered, clients who feel like they are part of an ongoing interaction with the therapist are likely to also report high empathy. This result, however, needs to be expanded upon with further research to properly identify the aspects of a VC clinical session that are conducive to feeling more *present* in an online interaction.

4.5. Limitations

Some limitations need to be considered along with the findings of this study. The use of a simulated clinical session is useful to bridge the gap between the state of research surrounding empathy in teletherapy and clinical practice, but it is possible that clients undergoing actual treatment in teletherapy would experience the sessions differently than the clients in the experimental sessions. Still, the participants in this study did discuss a personal theme with a therapist in training and they reported benefits in terms of affectivity, lending support to the assumption that the experimental task was a faithful simulation of actual teletherapy.

Another limitation that pertains to the eye-tracking measurements comes from the compromises that were made to manipulate the gaze angle while also making it possible to record the eye-tracking data during the sessions. For instance, participants sat 70 cm away from the eye-tracker, which is in the upper limit of the tolerated distance between the eye-tracker cameras and the participant according to the lenses employed. The computer monitor itself stood 50 cm behind the eye-tracker, thus 1.2 m away from the participants. The uncertainty of measurement of the eye-tracker is typically under 1°, which translates to having an uncertainty of approximatively 2 cm on any given eye-tracking measurement. This uncertainty of measurement could have had a systematic impact on the recorded eye-tracking data, particularly on the eyes' region of interest where the eye-tracking signal could have been miscategorized as being directed toward the face region rather than the eye region. The authors still considered that the validity of the results was sufficient to provide meaningful insights regarding the eye-tracking patterns of the participants since both experimental conditions were impacted in the same way by the uncertainty of measurement. This systematic error could potentially be circumvented with an even more precise eye-tracking setup in future studies. Additionally, the results showing that the *eyes* and *face* regions were significantly bigger in the More-EYE condition (see Table 7) implies that the time spent looking at the eyes and face of the therapist in this experimental condition could have been amplified compared to the Less-EYE condition by the increased size of the *eyes* and *face* regions (see Figure 2 for an illustration of the size of each region). However, these results do not impact the interpretation of other analyses since the *eyes* and *face* regions, albeit bigger in size, were not looked at longer in the More-EYE condition than in the Less-EYE condition (see Table 3). Moreover, the aims of this study regarding the correlations involving the time spent looking at the *eyes* and *face* regions and empathy did not involve comparing the More-EYE correlations to the Less-EYE correlations. The systematic increase in the region size in the More-EYE condition is therefore unlikely to affect the correlational results found in Table 4.

Finally, it should be noted that the participants and therapists in this study were mostly female. Previous studies have shown that female participants are more likely to feel and convey higher levels of empathy than male participants [32]. This sex effect might therefore have inflated the empathy levels in both conditions, though the sex ratios were similar between groups (see Table 1). The therapists also met a similar number of clients in each eye contact condition. Future studies should investigate whether the sex of clients and therapists could influence the levels of empathy found in teletherapy settings.

5. Conclusions

Though eye contact seems to be an important indicator of empathy, this study suggests that participants playing the role of clients were able to perceive a high degree of empathy in a typical VC session where eye contact is altered by the positional offset of the webcam compared to the eyes of the therapist on the screen. Future studies are needed to identify other factors that may contribute to increased perceived empathy in teletherapy as they could be a target of interventions to optimize the clients' experience of teletherapy. These factors include camera framing [33] and the quality of the video feed. Investigating the role of nonverbal behaviors in actual teletherapy sessions could also yield important information on the mechanisms underlying the perception of empathy in teletherapy.

Author Contributions: Conceptualization, F.G., A.M.L. and P.L.J.; Methodology, F.G. and V.P.; Software, V.P.; Validation, F.G.; Formal Analysis, F.G. and V.P.; Investigation, F.G.; Resources, P.L.J.; Data Curation, V.P.; Writing—Original Draft Preparation, F.G.; Writing—Review & Editing, F.G., A.M.L., V.P. and P.L.J.; Visualization, F.G.; Supervision, A.M.L. and P.L.J.; Project Administration, P.L.J.; Funding Acquisition, P.L.J. All authors have read and agreed to the published version of the manuscript.

Funding: This research was funded by the Natural Sciences and Engineering Research Council of Canada (NSERC), grant number RGPIN-2019-06715.

Institutional Review Board Statement: The study was conducted according to the guidelines of the Declaration of Helsinki and approved by the Ethics Committee of Université Laval (protocol code 2017-007 phase II, approved on 30 August 2018).

Informed Consent Statement: Informed consent was obtained from all subjects involved in the study.

Data Availability Statement: A request has been made to make available all data reported in this study through an institutional repository. A reference number will be provided as soon as it is available.

Acknowledgments: F.G. is the recipient of a graduate scholarship from the Social Sciences and Humanities Research Council of Canada (SSHRC) and from the Fonds de recherche du Québec—Nature et technologies (FRQNT). The authors would also like to thank Marc-Antoine Linteau and Laetitia Reduron for their help with the project.

Conflicts of Interest: The authors declare no conflict of interest.

References

1. American Psychological Association. Psychologists Embrace Telehealth to Prevent the Spread of COVID-19 2020. Available online: http://www.apaservices.org/practice/legal/technology/psychologists-embrace-telehealth (accessed on 6 November 2021).
2. Aafjes-van Doorn, K.; Békés, V.; Prout, T.A. Grappling with our therapeutic relationship and professional self-doubt during COVID-19: Will we use video therapy again? *Couns. Psychol. Q.* **2020**, *34*, 473–484. [CrossRef]
3. Berryhill, M.B.; Culmer, N.; Williams, N.; Halli-Tierney, A.; Betancourt, A.; Roberts, H.; King, M. Videoconferencing Psychotherapy and Depression: A Systematic Review. *Telemed. e-Health* **2019**, *25*, 435–446. [CrossRef] [PubMed]
4. Fernandez, E.; Woldgabreal, Y.; Day, A.; Pham, T.; Gleich, B.; Aboujaoude, E. Live psychotherapy by video versus in-person: A meta-analysis of efficacy and its relationship to types and targets of treatment. *Clin. Psychol. Psychother.* **2021**, *28*, 1535–1549. [CrossRef] [PubMed]
5. Norwood, C.; Moghaddam, N.G.; Malins, S.; Sabin-Farrell, R. Working alliance and outcome effectiveness in videoconferencing psychotherapy: A systematic review and noninferiority meta-analysis. *Clin. Psychol. Psychother.* **2018**, *25*, 797–808. [CrossRef]

6. Turgoose, D.; Ashwick, R.; Murphy, D. Systematic review of lessons learned from delivering tele-therapy to veterans with post-traumatic stress disorder. *J. Telemed. Telecare* **2018**, *24*, 575–585. [CrossRef]
7. Simpson, S.G.; Reid, C.L. Therapeutic alliance in videoconferencing psychotherapy: A review. *Aust. J. Rural Health* **2014**, *22*, 280–299. [CrossRef]
8. Watts, S.; Marchand, A.; Bouchard, S.; Bombardier, M. L'alliance thérapeutique lors d'une télépsychothérapie par vidéoconférence pour un trouble du spectre anxieux: Recension systématique des écrits. *Rev. Québécoise Psychol.* **2016**, *37*, 277–302. [CrossRef]
9. Connolly, S.L.; Miller, C.J.; Lindsay, J.A.; Bauer, M.S. A systematic review of providers' attitudes toward telemental health via videoconferencing. *Clin. Psychol. Sci. Pract.* **2020**, *27*, e12311. [CrossRef]
10. Grondin, F.; Lomanowska, A.M.; Jackson, P.L. Empathy in computer-mediated interactions: A conceptual framework for research and clinical practice. *Clin. Psychol. Sci. Pract.* **2019**, *26*, e12298. [CrossRef]
11. Regenbrecht, H.; Langlotz, T. Mutual gaze support in videoconferencing reviewed. *Commun. Assoc. Inf. Syst.* **2015**, *37*, 965–989. [CrossRef]
12. Grondin, F.; Lomanowska, A.M.; Békés, V.; Jackson, P.L. A methodology to improve eye contact in telepsychotherapy via videoconferencing with considerations for psychological distance. *Couns. Psychol. Q.* **2020**, *34*, 586–599. [CrossRef]
13. Elliott, R.; Bohart, A.C.; Watson, J.C.; Murphy, D. Therapist Empathy and Client Outcome: An Updated Meta-Analysis. *Psychotherapy* **2018**, *55*, 399–410. [CrossRef] [PubMed]
14. Dowell, N.M.; Berman, J.S. Therapist nonverbal behavior and perceptions of empathy, alliance, and treatment credibility. *J. Psychother. Integr.* **2013**, *23*, 158–165. [CrossRef]
15. Berthiaume, M.; Bouchard, S.; Brisebois, C.; Robillard, G. The Validation of a Telepresence Scale for Psychotherapy Delivered in Videoconference. In Proceedings of the CYPSY23 23rd Annual CyberPsychology, CyberTherapy & Social Networking Conference, Gatineau, QC, Canada, 26–28 June 2018.
16. Neureiter, K.; Moser, C.; Tscheligi, M. Look into My Eyes & See, What You Mean to Me. Social Presence as Source for Social Capital. *Int. Conf. Soc. Inform.* **2014**, *8851*, 183–198.
17. Jongerius, C.; Hessels, R.S.; Romijn, J.A.; Smets, E.M.A.; Hillen, M.A. The Measurement of Eye Contact in Human Interactions: A Scoping Review. *J. Nonverbal. Behav.* **2020**, *44*, 363–389. [CrossRef]
18. Gwizdka, J.; Dillon, A. Eye-Tracking as a Method for Enhancing Research on Information Search. In *Understanding Search Information and Improving: A Cognitive Approach*; Fu, W.T., van Oostendrop, H., Eds.; Springer: Berlin/Heidelberg, Germany, 2020; pp. 161–181. [CrossRef]
19. Hill, C.E. *Helping Skills: Facilitating Exploration, Insight, and Action*, 4th ed.; American Psychological Association: Washington, DC, USA, 2014.
20. Smart Eye AB (Gothenburg, Sweden). Smart Eye Pro Tech Support. Personal communication, 15 January 2019.
21. Schroff, F.; Kalenichenko, D.; Philbin, J. FaceNet: A unified embedding for face recognition and clustering. In Proceedings of the IEEE Conference on Computer Vision and Pattern Recognition, Boston, MA, USA, 7–12 June 2015; pp. 815–823. [CrossRef]
22. Barrett-Lennard, G.T. Dimensions of therapist response as causal factors in therapeutic change. *Psychol. Monogr. Gen. Appl.* **1962**, *76*, 1–36. [CrossRef]
23. Marci, C.D.; Ham, J.; Moran, E.; Orr, S.P. Physiologic Correlates of Perceived Therapist Empathy and Social-Emotional Process during Psychotherapy. *J. Nerv. Ment. Dis.* **2007**, *195*, 103–111. [CrossRef]
24. Gaudreau, P.; Sanchez, X.; Blondin, J.P. Positive and negative affective states in a performance-related setting testing the factorial structure of the PANAS across two samples of French-Canadian participants. *Eur. J. Psychol. Assess.* **2006**, *22*, 240–249. [CrossRef]
25. Cohen, J. *Statistical Power Analysis for the Behavioral Sciences*, 2nd ed.; Lawrence Erlbaum Associates: Hillsdale, NJ, USA, 1988.
26. Germain, V.; Marchand, G.; Bouchard, S.; Drouin, M.-S.; Guay, S. Effectiveness of Cognitive Behavioural Therapy Administered by Videoconference for Posttraumatic Stress Disorder. *Cogn. Behav. Ther.* **2009**, *38*, 42–53. [CrossRef]
27. Grayson, D.M.; Monk, A.F. Are You Looking at Me? Eye Contact and Desktop Video Conferencing. *ACM Trans. Comput.-Hum. Interact.* **2003**, *10*, 221–243. [CrossRef]
28. Sharpley, C.F.; Sagris, A. Does eye contact increase counsellor-client rapport? *Couns. Psychol. Q.* **1995**, *8*, 145–155. [CrossRef]
29. Sharpley, C.F.; Jeffrey, A.M.; Mcmah, T.; Sharpley, C.F.; Jeffrey, A.M.; Mcmah, T. Counsellor facial expression and client-perceived rapport. *Couns. Psychol. Q.* **2007**, *19*, 343–356. [CrossRef]
30. Imel, Z.E.; Barco, J.S.; Brown, H.J.; Baucom, B.R.; Kircher, J.C.; Baer, J.S.; Kircher, J.C.; Atkins, D.C. The Association of Therapist Empathy and Synchrony in Vocally Encoded Arousal. *J. Couns. Psychol.* **2014**, *61*, 146–153. [CrossRef] [PubMed]
31. Wynn, R.; Wynn, M. Empathy as an interactionally achieved phenomenon in psychotherapy: Characteristics of some conversational resources. *J. Pragmat.* **2006**, *38*, 1385–1397. [CrossRef]
32. Christov-Moore, L.; Simpson, E.A.; Coudé, G.; Grigaityte, K.; Iacoboni, M.; Ferrari, P.F. Empathy: Gender effects in brain and behavior. *Neurosci. Biobehav. Rev.* **2014**, *46*, 604–627. [CrossRef]
33. Nguyen, D.T.; Canny, J. More than face-to-face: Empathy effects of video framing. In Proceedings of the SIGCHI Conference on Human Factors in Computing Systems, Boston MA USA, 4–9 April 2009; ACM: Chicago, IL, USA, 2009.

Journal of
Clinical Medicine

MDPI

Article

Examining Change in the Frequency of Adaptive Actions as a Mediator of Treatment Outcomes in Internet-Delivered Therapy for Depression and Anxiety

Madelyne A. Bisby [1,2,*], Nickolai Titov [2], Blake F. Dear [1], Eyal Karin [1], Andrew Wilhelms [3], Marcie Nugent [3] and Heather D. Hadjistavropoulos [3]

1 eCentreClinic, School of Psychological Sciences, Faculty of Medicine, Health, and Human Sciences, Macquarie University, Sydney 2109, Australia
2 MindSpot Clinic, MQ Health, Macquarie University, Sydney 2109, Australia
3 Department of Psychology, University of Regina, 3737 Wascana Parkway, Regina, SK S4S 0A2, Canada
* Correspondence: madelyne.bisby@mq.edu.au; Tel.: +61-02-9850-8724

Abstract: Adaptive actions, including healthy thinking and meaningful activities, have been associated with emotional wellbeing. The Things You Do Questionnaire—21 item (TYDQ-21) has recently been created to measure the frequency of such actions. A study using the TYDQ-21 found that adaptive actions increased across Internet-delivered therapy for symptoms of depression and anxiety, and higher TYDQ-21 scores were associated with lower psychological distress at post-treatment. The current study examined the relationships between adaptive actions and psychological distress among adults (n = 1114) receiving Internet-delivered therapy as part of routine care in Canada, and explored whether adaptive actions mediated reductions in depression and anxiety. As hypothesised, adaptive actions increased alongside reductions in depression and anxiety symptoms from baseline to post-treatment. Treatment effects were consistent when the intervention was provided with regular weekly therapist support or with optional weekly therapist support, and some (but not all) types of adaptive actions had a mediating effect on change in depressive symptoms. The present findings support further work examining adaptive actions as a mechanism of change in psychotherapy, as well as the utility and scalability of Internet-delivered treatments to target and increase adaptive actions with the aim of improving mental health.

Keywords: anxiety; depression; iCBT; actions; Internet; treatment; guidance

Citation: Bisby, M.A.; Titov, N.; Dear, B.F.; Karin, E.; Wilhelms, A.; Nugent, M.; Hadjistavropoulos, H.D. Examining Change in the Frequency of Adaptive Actions as a Mediator of Treatment Outcomes in Internet-Delivered Therapy for Depression and Anxiety. *J. Clin. Med.* **2022**, *11*, 6001. https://doi.org/10.3390/jcm11206001

Academic Editor: Stéphane Bouchard

Received: 7 September 2022
Accepted: 10 October 2022
Published: 11 October 2022

1. Introduction

An important body of work has previously demonstrated that our thoughts and behaviours, that is, "actions", can have a significant impact on our psychological health [1–3]. More recent work has identified the importance of a broader range of everyday actions such as eating well and sleeping [4,5], as well as those actions which are the target of psychological therapies, like pleasant activities and challenging unhelpful thoughts [6–8]. In a recent Danish study, over 3000 respondents reported the daily actions they took to enhance their mental health. A vast range of actions were reported, from which five main themes emerged: positive mindset (e.g., 'be optimistic'), health behaviours (e.g., 'exercise daily'), social relationships (e.g., 'have a social network'), relaxation (e.g., 'remember to relax'), and use of the brain (e.g., 'solve tasks') [9]. Actively doing something to improve mental health was associated with greater self-reported mental wellbeing in the sample. Moreover, approximately half of respondents reported that they had engaged in something 'to a large extent' to enhance their mental health within the past two weeks [9]. This finding is consistent with other recent research illustrating a strong association between daily actions and psychological health [10], and highlights the clinical potential of increasing the frequency of such actions to facilitate better psychological health.

The Things You Do Questionnaire—21-item (TYDQ-21) was developed to capture adaptive (i.e., helpful) actions most strongly associated with psychological health [10]. Across two surveys, over 6000 Australian respondents from general community samples reported the frequency with which they engaged in a large range of adaptive actions previously identified in the literature as related to psychological health. Using survey methodology [11], responses were ranked and exploratory factor analysis revealed five dominant factors/categories of adaptive actions: Healthy Thinking, Meaningful Activities, Goals and Plans, Healthy Habits, and Social Connections. The results showed that those who engaged in the identified adaptive actions at least half of the days of the week reported lower symptoms of depression and anxiety, and conversely, increased satisfaction with life. The five domains of actions captured by the TYDQ-21 shared some overlap with the five domains identified by Santini et al. [9], including cognitive actions, health behaviours/routines, and social interactions.

In an extension of this work, a subsequent study examined whether the frequency of these actions changed during Internet-delivered psychological treatment and whether these changes were associated with changes in symptoms [12]. Internet-delivered treatments are increasingly available as a form of mental health care [13], and are as effective as face-to-face treatments for a range of mental health conditions [14,15]. Internet-delivered treatments typically include a series of carefully developed modules alongside therapist support over email, private messaging, or telephone [16]. In that study, 409 individuals reported the frequency of adaptive actions on a fortnightly basis during therapist-guided Internet-delivered cognitive behaviour therapy (ICBT) for depression and anxiety [12]. The five categories of actions first identified by Titov et al. [10] were replicated using confirmatory factor analysis, indicating that the five broad domains of action remained consistent across both community and treatment-seeking samples. The frequency of adaptive actions increased across treatment, and increases in adaptive actions mirrored the decreases in depressive and anxiety symptoms over time. At post-treatment, participants who reported engaging in the actions at least half the days of the week reported significantly lower depressive symptoms, lower anxiety symptoms, and this was the case for all five domains of action [12]. Although the study's design did not allow causal conclusions, there was an association between increased frequency of adaptive actions and symptom reductions during Internet-delivered psychological treatment for depression and anxiety.

Notably, all participants in that trial received optional therapist guidance—that is, guidance was provided based on participant preference and clinical need. As previous meta-analyses have identified that psychological treatments with ongoing, regular therapist support are more effective than self-guided treatments [17,18], the increase in adaptive actions across treatment may have been, at least for some participants, driven by contact with the therapist, rather than due to the treatment itself. As a result, there are outstanding questions about the role of therapist guidance in the increased frequency of adaptive actions during treatment. Even within the broad construct of 'therapist guidance', there are differences in how therapist guidance is provided. Whereas optional guidance involves clinical contact at the behest of the participant and identified clinical need, regular guidance is often provided on a structured, weekly basis and can be initiated by the clinician irrespective of patient preference or clinical need [19,20]. When individuals are randomly allocated to one or the other, participants report equivalent and large reductions in anxiety and depression symptoms at post-treatment and 3-month follow-up [20,21], although treatment completion has been lower in participants receiving optional guidance [20]. In contrast, when individuals receive their preferred guidance option, there are no differences in treatment completion and outcomes [22], highlighting the importance of considering individual preferences when providing therapist guidance. It remains unclear how the frequency of daily actions may change differently based on the type of therapist guidance provided alongside Internet-delivered treatment.

The primary aim of the current study was to extend previous psychometric validations of the TYDQ-21 in Australian samples [10,12] to a Canadian sample of individuals seeking treatment at a digital mental health service. We expected the factor structure previously reported with Australian adults would be replicated in a Canadian sample of adults. We also expected that changes in the frequency of adaptive actions would increase during treatment as symptoms of psychological distress decreased, consistent with past work. We explored whether standard or optional therapist support was associated with different magnitude of changes in psychological symptoms and/or adaptive actions, and replicated previous analyses examining whether participants who reported engaging in adaptive actions at least half the days each week, on average, reported lower depressive and anxiety symptoms.

The secondary aim of the current paper was to examine the contribution of increased frequency of adaptive actions to reductions in psychological symptoms across treatment using mediation. Although not to be taken as conclusive evidence of causality, mediation analyses are an important step towards determining whether a particular variable is a mechanism of treatment change [23,24].

2. Materials and Methods

2.1. Design

Observational data were collected as part of routine care at the Online Therapy Unit, funded by the Saskatchewan government to provide transdiagnostic ICBT to Saskatchewan residents. The collection of observational data received ethics approval from the University of Regina, and informed consent was obtained from all participants involved in the study.

2.2. Recruitment

Participants were recruited between 17 December 2020 and 16 December 2021. Interested persons were directed to the study website (www.onlinetherapyuser.ca, accessed on 1 September 2022) and completed an initial assessment via REDCap. Eligibility was then confirmed during a brief telephone screening interview. Participants were considered eligible if they: (1) were 18 or older; (2) endorsed symptoms of depression and/or anxiety; (3) were Saskatchewan residents and would be in the province for at least 8 weeks; (4) reported access to a computer and the Internet; (5) provided a medical contact for emergency purposes; and (6) had interest in and consented to ICBT. Exclusion criteria included: (1) recent hospitalization, high crisis service involvement, or high risk of suicide; (2) severe alcohol or drug problems; (3) concurrent weekly mental health treatment; (4) seeking help for a different mental health condition; or (5) self-reported medical condition which would interfere with participation. Ineligible applicants were referred to community mental health services in their area.

During the recruitment period, 2127 individuals expressed interest and completed an initial assessment, of which 1874 applicants met initial inclusion criteria. The telephone interview was completed by 1660 applicants, and 1435 individuals were accepted into the trial. The current study utilized a subsample of these participants (n = 1114) who reported clinically significant symptoms on the depression or anxiety measure (as defined below), completed pre-treatment questionnaires, and began Lesson 1. Participant flow is provided in Figure 1.

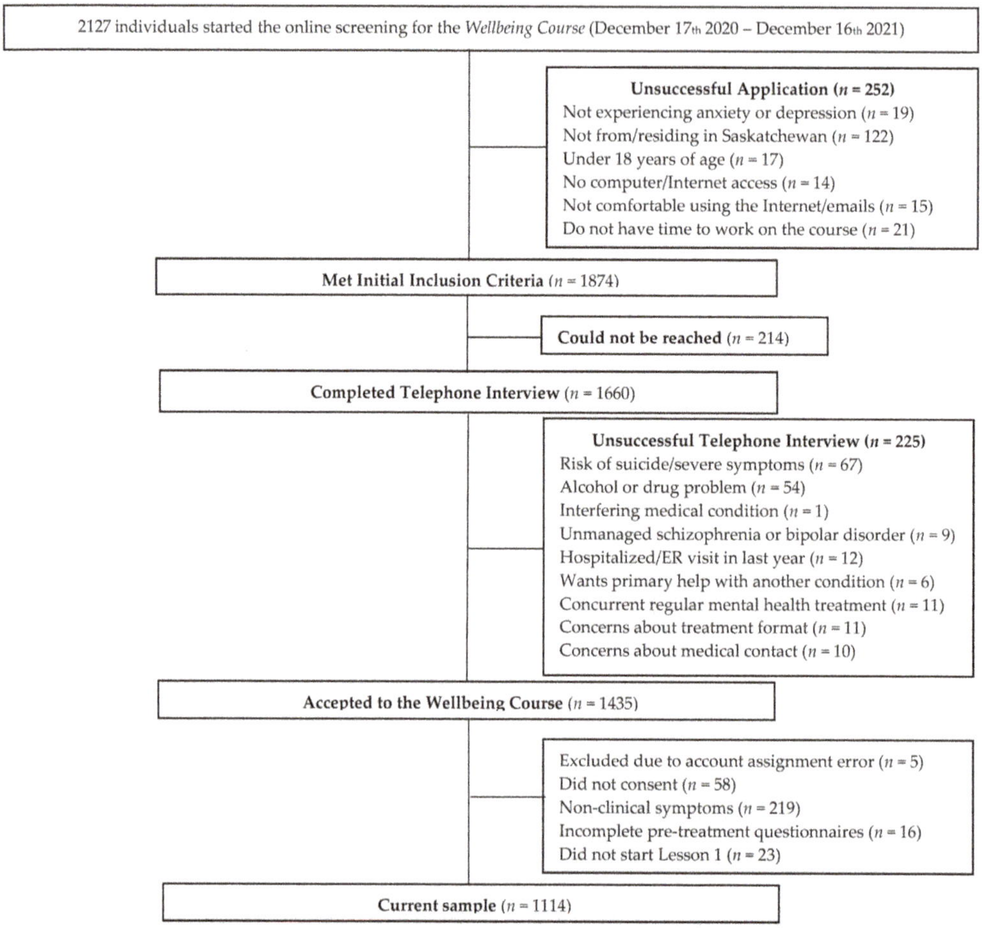

Figure 1. Participant flow chart.

2.3. Intervention

All participants received access to the Wellbeing Course, a transdiagnostic ICBT course developed by the eCentreClinic at Macquarie University (for further detail, see [25]). This 8-week course consists of 5 core lessons gradually released in a sequential order and cover: (1) psychoeducation; (2) thought challenging; (3) controlled breathing and activity scheduling; (4) graded exposure; and (5) relapse prevention planning and goal setting. An optional booster lesson with a review of content was available one month after post-treatment. Each lesson was accompanied by case stories, additional resources, and a downloadable guide, which includes homework tasks and frequently asked questions. Participants were informed that it would take several hours per week to work on the course (e.g., reading materials and practicing skills). The course was delivered on an individual basis (i.e., not in a group format) and participants progressed through the course at their own pace. In line with previous research, however, participants also received weekly automatic emails to facilitate engagement [26]. These emails encouraged them to work through the course at the following pace: 1 week for Lessons 1 and 3, and 2 weeks for Lessons, 2, 4, and 5. Furthermore, therapist support was only available for 8 weeks, which also encouraged participants to complete the course in a timely manner.

2.4. Therapist Guidance

As the current study examined the influence of therapist guidance level on treatment outcome, only those participants with clinical symptoms were included in the current sample to eliminate potential confounds. The level of therapist guidance depended on the participant's preference, whereby participants chose between 'optional support' and 'standard support' (see [20] for further details). Each participant was assigned a single therapist for the duration of the course. In the standard support condition, participants were encouraged to contact therapists as often as they liked during the week via email, and therapists replied once per week with the goal to engage participants, reinforce progress, and highlight lesson material where required. In the optional support condition, therapists only contacted participants if they initiated contact. In both groups, therapists contacted participants in the case of symptom deterioration or an increase in risk of suicide/self-harm. Therapists also provided support over the phone where appropriate. All therapists had training in social work or psychology, and were trained and supervised in ICBT.

2.5. Measures

2.5.1. Primary Outcome

Things You Do Questionnaire 21-item (TYDQ-21). The 21-item version of the TYDQ-21 described in Study 2 of Titov et al. [10] was used in this study. The list included daily actions associated with psychological wellbeing and consisted of five factors—Healthy Thinking (e.g., treating yourself with respect), Meaningful Activities (e.g., doing something enjoyable), Goals and Plans (e.g., setting achievable goals), Healthy Habits (e.g., regular sleep and wake times), and Social Connections (e.g., spending time with family or friends). A 5-point Likert rating scale asked participants how often they performed actions over the past week using the following scoring system: 0 = "Not at all"; 1 = "One or two days"; 2 = "Half the days"; 3 = "Almost every day"; and 4 = "Every day". The TYDQ-21 was administered at pre-treatment and post-treatment, and Cronbach's alpha ranged from 0.91 to 0.94.

2.5.2. Secondary Outcomes

Patient Health Questionnaire 9-item (PHQ-9). The PHQ-9 is a measure of DSM-IV-congruent depressive symptoms over the past two weeks [27,28]. The PHQ-9 has nine items and is scored using a 4-point Likert scale ranging from 0 ("Not at all") to 3 ("Nearly every day"). A PHQ-9 score of $\geq$10 was used to identify those with clinical levels of depression [29], although it was recognised that this threshold may over-estimate cases [30]. Cronbach's alpha in this study ranged from 0.84 to 0.89.

Generalized Anxiety Disorder 7-item (GAD-7). The GAD-7 is a measure of general anxiety symptoms over the past two weeks, designed to detect DSM-IV-congruent generalized anxiety, social anxiety, and panic disorder [31]. The GAD-7 is scored using a 4-point Likert scale ranging from 0 ("Not at all") to 3 ("Nearly every day"), and a score of $\geq$10 was used to identify those with clinical levels of anxiety [31,32]. Cronbach's alpha for this study ranged from 0.87 to 0.91.

2.6. Statistical Analysis

Confirmatory factor analyses were conducted in IBM SPSS Amos version 26 and tested the five-factor structure of the TYDQ-21 identified by Titov et al. [10]. Model fit was determined using the comparative fit index (CFI; $\geq$0.90–0.95), Tucker-Lewis Index (TLI, $\geq$0.90–0.95), and Root Mean Square Error of Approximation (RMSEA; $\leq$0.08) [11,33].

All other analyses were conducted using IBM SPSS version 27. The intent-to-treat sample (n = 1114) was used for treatment outcome and adherence analyses. Missing data at post-treatment were handled using multiple imputation, accounting for baseline symptom severity and lesson completion [34,35]. Generalized estimating equation (GEE) modelling examined changes over time from pre-treatment to post-treatment [36]. Time and therapist support were entered as predictors. A gamma with log link response scale was used to address skewness within the dependent variables [34], and an unstructured working correlation accounted for different rates of change between participants. Cohen's *d* effect sizes and 95% confidence intervals were calculated based on estimated marginal means. One-way ANOVAs were used to compare depression and anxiety symptoms between participants based on the frequency of adaptive actions (i.e., above or below half the days in each week, on average, for each domain).

To examine mediation, the PROCESS v4.0 macro was used [37]. Only complete cases were used for mediation analyses ($n = 751$). Supplementary analyses did not find a significant interaction between time, therapist support level, and TYDQ21 scores for change in depression symptoms ($p = 0.59$) or anxiety symptoms ($p = 0.52$). Given the similarities in the two treatment samples, and given the opportunity to increase statistical power, the two therapist support groups were treated as a single group in mediation analyses. Prior to analysis, all variables were log-transformed to ensure that mediation models reflected the percentage change in the dependent variable which was explained by a one-unit percentage increase in the predictor variable (e.g., log-log regression, [38]). Log-transformed pre-treatment scores (PHQ-9 or GAD-7) were entered as the independent variable (X), post-treatment scores (PHQ-9 or GAD-7) as the dependent variable (Y), and post-treatment TYDQ-21 scores as the mediating variable (M). Pre-treatment TYDQ-21 scores were entered as a covariate, consistent with ANCOVA models of mediation [39]. In the case that a mediating effect was detected (i.e., the indirect effect did not include zero), reverse causality models were then used to test the mediating effect. Specifically, reverse causality models tested whether pre-treatment TYDQ-21 scores also mediated change in the dependent variable (as opposed to post-treatment TYDQ-21 scores in the original model). If reverse mediation was found, we concluded that the original mediating effect was not reliable.

3. Results

3.1. Baseline Demographic and Clinical Characteristics

Participant demographics and symptom severity are presented in Table 1. Participants were mostly female (78.2%), consistent with typical psychotherapy research samples [40–42]. The average age of the sample was 37.14 years (range 18–81 years), and this did not differ between guidance conditions ($p > 0.05$). Approximately half were in paid employment (52.1%), and not currently taking medication for their mental health (57.3%), with no differences between guidance conditions (*p*s > 0.05).

Table 1. Baseline demographic and clinical characteristics.

	Overall	Standard Support	Optional Support
	N = 1114	n = 821	n = 293
Age			
Mean (SD)	37.14 (13.17)	36.95 (13.08)	37.63 (13.38)
Gender			
Male	20.3% (226)	19.9% (164)	21.2% (62)
Female	78.2% (871)	78.6% (645)	77.1% (226)
Other	1.5% (17)	1.5% (12)	1.7% (5)
Employment			
Paid employment	52.1% (580)	51.8% (425)	52.9% (155)
Household	16.5% (184)	16.8% (138)	15.7% (46)
Retired	4.0% (45)	3.7% (30)	5.1% (15)
Student	6.6% (74)	6.6% (54)	6.9% (20)
Unemployed	9.2% (102)	9.1% (75)	9.2% (27)
Health concerns	11.6% (129)	12.1% (99)	10.2% (30)
Current medication			
Yes	476 (42.7%)	42.8% (351)	42.7% (125)
No	638 (57.3%)	57.2% (470)	57.3% (168)

Table 1. *Cont.*

	Overall	Standard Support	Optional Support
	N = 1114	n = 821	n = 293
Depressive Symptoms			
Minimal (0–4)	6.7% (75)	5.6% (46)	9.9% (29)
Mild (5–9)	21.8% (243)	21.0% (172)	24.2% (71)
Moderate (10–14)	34.6% (386)	32.5% (267)	40.6% (119)
Moderately Severe (15–19)	24.6% (274)	27.2% (223)	17.4% (51)
Severe (20+)	12.2% (136)	13.8% (113)	7.8% (23)
Anxiety Symptoms			
Minimal (0–4)	4.7% (52)	3.8% (31)	7.2% (21)
Mild (5–9)	24.2% (270)	23.8% (195)	25.6% (75)
Moderate (10–14)	32.9% (367)	32.8% (269)	33.4% (98)
Severe (15+)	38.2% (425)	39.7% (326)	33.8% (99)

Note. % (n). Chi-square test of significance reported.

In the standard support group, therapists sent an average of 8.35 (SD = 1.61) emails and received an average of 3.01 emails (SD = 2.73) per participant. In the optional support group, therapists sent an average of 4.37 (SD = 2.22) emails and received an average of 2.26 emails (SD = 3.00) per participant.

3.2. *Confirmatory Factor Analysis*

CFAs were used to test the goodness-of-fit of the five-factor model of the TYDQ-21 identified by Titov et al. [10] at pre-treatment and post-treatment. At pre-treatment, the five-factor model showed an acceptable fit to the data: CFI = 0.93, TLI = 0.93, RMSEA = 0.06. Factor loadings ranged from 0.45 to 0.84 (see Supplementary Material, Figure S1). Using complete cases at post-treatment, the five-factor model also showed an appropriate fit: CFI = 0.94, TLI = 0.93, RMSEA = 0.06. Factor loadings at post-treatment ranged from 0.59 to 0.85 (see Supplementary Material, Figure S1).

3.3. *Treatment Engagement*

Participants completed an average of 3.90 (SD = 1.41) lessons in the standard support group and 4.08 (SD = 1.28) lessons in the optional support group, with no significant difference ($p > 0.05$).

3.4. *Change in Adaptive Actions during Treatment*

TYDQ-21 Total Score. Overall, participants reported a 29% increase (95% CI 25%, 33%) in the frequency of adaptive actions measured by the TYDQ-21 from pre- to post-treatment (main effect of time, $p < 0.001$; see Table 2 and Figure 2A). Irrespective of timepoint, those participants who received standard support reported engaging in these adaptive actions to a lesser extent than those who received optional support (main effect of guidance, $p = 0.02$; see Table 3), with similar within-group effect sizes (ds = 0.65). Consistent with this main effect, there were significant differences in TYDQ-21 scores at pre-treatment ($p = 0.021$) and post-treatment ($p = 0.04$) according to guidance. There was no difference in how TYDQ-21 scores changed from pre- to post-treatment based on guidance condition (time x guidance interaction, $p > 0.05$).

TYDQ-21 Factor Scores. Irrespective of guidance condition, participants reported increases in the frequency of adaptive actions on each of the five factors across treatment (main effect of time, ps < 0.001; see Table 2). At the overall level, participants reported increases in Healthy Thinking ($d = 0.60$), Meaningful Activities ($d = 0.50$), and Goals and Plans ($d = 0.48$). Smaller effect sizes were observed for Healthy Habits ($d = 0.27$) and Social Connection ($d = 0.28$). Across timepoints, those participants who received standard support reported lower scores on Healthy Thinking (main effect of guidance, $p = 0.04$), Meaningful Activities ($p = 0.03$), and Goals and Plans ($p = 0.045$), but not Healthy Habits or Social Connections (*ps* > 0.05; see Table 3). No significant time x guidance interactions were observed.

Table 2. Overall treatment outcomes and estimated marginal means (n = 1114).

	Pre	Post	Percentage Change (95% CI)	Within Groups *d* (95% CI)
TYDQ-21 Total Score	34.96 (0.47)	44.95 (0.55)	29 (25, 33)	0.59 (0.50, 0.67)
TYDQ-21 Thoughts Factor	9.68 (0.15)	12.88 (0.17)	33 (28, 38)	0.60 (0.51, 0.68)
TYDQ-21 Activity Factor	6.39 (0.11)	8.39 (0.13)	31 (26, 37)	0.50 (0.41, 0.58)
TYDQ-21 Goals Factor	7.78 (0.15)	10.29 (0.16)	32 (27, 38)	0.48 (0.40, 0.57)
TYDQ-21 Habits Factor	5.16 (0.10)	6.05 (0.10)	17 (12, 23)	0.27 (0.18, 0.35)
TYDQ-21 Social Factor	5.95 (0.11)	6.97 (0.11)	17 (12, 22)	0.28 (0.19, 0.36)
PHQ-9	12.34 (0.19)	8.15 (0.19)	34 (30, 38)	0.66 (0.58, 0.75)
GAD-7	12.32 (0.17)	7.09 (0.17)	42 (39, 46)	0.92 (0.83, 1.01)

Note. Mean and standard error reported. Between-groups effect size at post-treatment reported. CI = Confidence Interval.

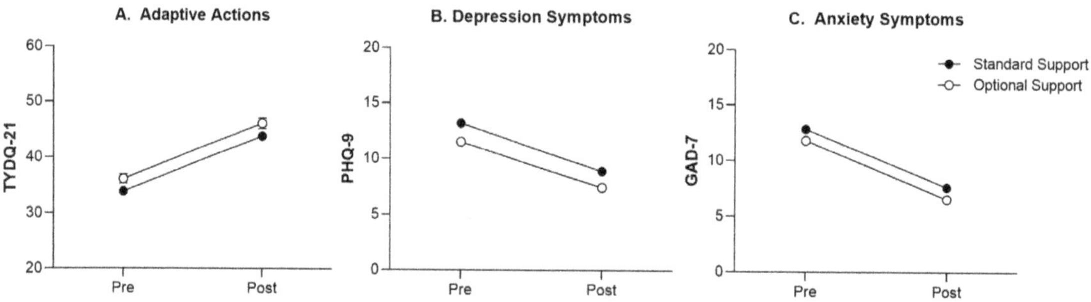

Figure 2. Change in adaptive actions (**A**), depression symptoms (**B**), anxiety symptoms (**C**) from pre-treatment to post-treatment in participants who received standard support and optional support alongside ICBT.

Table 3. Treatment outcomes and estimated marginal means according to guidance condition (n = 1114).

	Standard Support				Optional Support				
	Pre	Post	Percentage Change (95% CI)	Within Groups *d* (95% CI)	Pre	Post	Percentage Change (95% CI)	Within Groups *d* (95% CI)	Between Groups *d* (95% CI)
TYDQ-21 Total	33.87 (0.47)	43.83 (0.59)	29 (25, 34)	0.65 (0.55, 0.75)	36.10 (0.84)	46.10 (0.95)	28 (21, 35)	0.65 (0.48, 0.82)	0.14 (0.00, 0.27)
TYDQ-21 Thoughts	9.39 (0.15)	12.60 (0.19)	34 (29, 39)	0.65 (0.55, 0.75)	9.97 (0.26)	13.16 (0.28)	32 (24, 40)	0.69 (0.52, 0.86)	0.11 (−0.03, 0.24)
TYDQ-21 Activity	6.17 (0.11)	8.15 (0.13)	32 (27, 38)	0.57 (0.47, 0.67)	6.63 (0.11)	8.63 (0.22)	30 (23, 37)	0.67 (0.50, 0.84)	0.13 (−0.01, 0.26)
TYDQ-21 Goals	7.56 (0.15)	9.95 (0.18)	32 (26, 38)	0.50 (0.40, 0.60)	8.01 (0.26)	10.65 (0.29)	33 (23, 43)	0.56 (0.39, 0.72)	0.14 (0.00, 0.27)
TYDQ-21 Habits	4.98 (0.10)	5.93 (0.11)	19 (13, 25)	0.32 (0.22, 0.41)	5.34 (0.17)	6.18 (0.17)	16 (7, 25)	0.29 (0.13, 0.45)	0.08 (−0.05, 0.21)
TYDQ-21 Social	5.77 (0.11)	6.79 (0.11)	18 (12, 23)	0.32 (0.23, 0.42)	6.14 (0.19)	7.16 (0.19)	17 (8, 25)	0.31 (0.15, 0.48)	0.12 (−0.02, 0.25)
PHQ-9	13.21 (0.19)	8.90 (0.20)	33 (29, 37)	0.77 (0.67, 0.87)	11.52 (0.30)	7.46 (0.30)	35 (28, 42)	0.79 (0.62, 0.96)	0.26 (0.12, 0.39)
GAD-7	12.84 (0.17)	7.64 (0.19)	40 (37, 44)	1.01 (0.90, 1.11)	11.82 (0.29)	6.57 (0.28)	44 (38, 51)	1.08 (0.90, 1.25)	0.20 (0.07, 0.34)

Note. Mean and standard error reported. Between-groups effect size at post-treatment reported. CI = Confidence Interval.

3.5. Treatment Outcomes

Depressive Symptoms (PHQ-9). Participants experienced a significant reduction in depressive symptoms from pre- to post-treatment (main effect of time, $p < 0.001$; see Table 3 and Figure 2B). When examined according to guidance condition, depressive symptoms were greater in those who received standard support compared to optional support (main effect of guidance, $p < 0.001$), whereby scores were significantly different between support conditions at pre-treatment ($p < 0.001$) and post-treatment ($p < 0.001$). There was no difference in treatment outcome according to guidance level (time x guidance interaction, $p > 0.05$; see Table 3). Participants in the standard support group reported an average reduction of 33%, while those in the optional support group reported an average reduction of 35%, with similar within-group effect sizes (d range 0.77–0.79).

Those participants who reported engaging in adaptive actions over half the days each week, on average, reported lower depressive symptoms. This was the case for the TYDQ-21 total score and each of the five domains ($ps < 0.001$).

Anxiety Symptoms (GAD-7). Participants reported a significant decrease in anxiety symptoms on the GAD-7 from pre- to post-treatment irrespective of guidance condition (main effect of time, $p < 0.001$; see Table 2 and Figure 2C). Those participants who received standard support reported greater anxiety symptoms than those who received optional support (main effect of guidance, $p < 0.001$; see Table 3), such that anxiety symptoms were significantly different at pre-treatment ($p = 0.003$) and post-treatment ($p = 0.001$). There were no differences in change in anxiety symptoms over the course of treatment based on the level of support received (time x guidance interaction, $p > 0.05$). Participants in the standard support group reported an average reduction of 40%, while those in the optional support group reported an average reduction of 44% in anxiety symptoms, with similar within-group effect sizes (d range 1.01–1.08).

As was observed for depressive symptoms, those participants who reported engaging in adaptive actions over half the days each week, on average, reported lower anxiety symptoms. This was the case for the TYDQ-21 total score and each of the five domains ($ps < 0.001$).

3.6. Mediation of Treatment Outcomes by Adaptive Actions

Change in Depressive Symptoms. As can be seen in Table 4, total scores on the TYDQ-21 did not mediate change in depressive symptoms from pre- to post-treatment. However, three factors of the TYDQ-21 were found to have a small, but significant, mediating effect on change in depressive symptoms: Healthy Thinking (indirect effect = 5%), Meaningful Activities (indirect effect = 4%), and Goals and Plans (indirect effect = 3%).

Change in Anxiety Symptoms. TYDQ-21 scores were not found to have a mediating effect on treatment change in anxiety symptoms when used as a summed total or when examined on a factor level. The mediation models can be seen in Table 4.

Table 4. Mediation of change in symptoms from pre-treatment (X) to post-treatment (Y) using TYDQ-21 post-treatment scores (M; $n = 751$).

Mediator (M)	Path a (X→M)	Path b (M→Y)	Path c (Total Effect X→Y)	Path c′ (Direct Effect X→Y)	Indirect Effect	Reverse Indirect Effect	Conclusion
			PHQ-9 (Depressive Symptoms)				
TYDQ-21 Total	−2 ***	−80 ***	76 ***	74 ***	2 (−3, 6)	-	NS mediation
TYDQ-21 Thoughts	−7 *	−72 ***	78 ***	73 ***	5 (0, 9)	3 (0, 5)	Mediation
TYDQ-21 Activity	−8 *	−57 ***	80 ***	76 ***	4 (1, 8)	0 (−3, 3)	Mediation
TYDQ-21 Goals	−7 *	−49 ***	78 ***	75 ***	3 (0, 6)	2 (0, 5)	Mediation
TYDQ-21 Routine	−4	−51 ***	78 ***	76 ***	2 (−1, 5)	-	NS mediation
TYDQ-21 Social	−4	−42 ***	78 ***	76 ***	2 (0, 4)	-	NS mediation

Table 4. *Cont.*

Mediator (M)	Path a (X→M)	Path b (M→Y)	Path c (Total Effect X→Y)	Path c′ (Direct Effect X→Y)	Indirect Effect	Reverse Indirect Effect	Conclusion
			GAD-7 (Anxiety Symptoms)				
TYDQ-21 Total	0	−87 ***	60 ***	59 ***	0 (−6, 5)	–	NS mediation
TYDQ-21 Thoughts	−4	−89 ***	57 ***	53 ***	4 (−3, 9)	–	NS mediation
TYDQ-21 Activity	−1	−62 ***	62 ***	62 ***	0 (−5, 6)	–	NS mediation
TYDQ-21 Goals	−1	−56 ***	62 ***	61 ***	0 (−5, 6)	–	NS mediation
TYDQ-21 Routine	0	−52 ***	62 ***	63 ***	0 (−5, 4)	–	NS mediation
TYDQ-21 Social	0	−37 ***	62 ***	62 ***	0 (−2, 3)	–	NS mediation

* $p < 0.01$, *** $p < 0.001$. NS = non-significant. Note. All mediation models included pre-treatment scores as a covariate. All paths report the percentage change in the dependent variable caused by a one-unit percentage change in the independent variable.

4. Discussion

The present study sought to further understand the relationship between adaptive actions and symptoms of depression and anxiety during ICBT. The primary aim of the current study was to extend previous psychometric evaluations of the TYDQ-21 to a Canadian sample. The five-factor structure of the measure was replicated in the current study, and the frequency of daily actions increased with Internet-delivered psychological treatment. We compared the change in daily actions across treatment based on whether participants selected to receive standard or optional therapist support. No differences in treatment outcomes were found between guidance conditions, such that both groups demonstrated medium to large reductions (i.e., 33% to 44%) in depressive and anxiety symptoms as well as small to medium increases (i.e., 16% to 34%) in the frequency of adaptive actions. Then, adaptive actions were examined as a mediator of treatment change in depressive and anxiety symptoms—we found that some, but not all, types of daily actions mediated change in depressive symptoms from baseline to post-treatment, but not anxiety symptoms. Taken together, these findings suggest that changes in the frequency of adaptive actions across treatment were related to improvements in psychological distress, and that change in adaptive actions were not related to the amount of therapist support received.

The frequency of adaptive actions captured by the TYDQ-21 increased across treatment, as anticipated. However, a novel finding of the current study was that similar increases in adaptive actions were observed whether participants received regular therapist guidance or only the option of guidance. This was consistent with past work examining the role of therapist guidance in Internet-delivered therapy which report no differences in treatment adherence or outcomes between participants who choose to receive optional or standard guidance [19,21,22]. Notably, over two-thirds (73.7%) of participants chose to receive standard support, and those who selected standard support had more severe depressive and anxiety symptoms and lower TYDQ-21 scores. This finding is similar to previous reports of participants with more severe anxiety symptoms preferring standard support [22], and highlights the importance of considering baseline symptom severity when determining if an individual would benefit from regular, structured therapist guidance. Nevertheless, our findings suggest that therapist guidance may not be essential to support increases in adaptive actions across treatment. However, it should also be noted that all participants in this trial received an interview with a therapist prior to treatment which is likely to increase a participant's motivation and facilitated engagement and outcomes, and thus this finding may not extend to fully automated ICBT interventions.

The current study also found that participants who reported engaging in adaptive actions most of the time (defined as at least half the days in each week) reported lower depressive and anxiety symptoms. This pattern of findings was consistent for the total TYDQ-21 score as well as each of the five domains of actions, potentially suggesting that all domains of adaptive activity (e.g., healthy thinking, meaningful activities, goals and plans, healthy habits, and social connections) are associated with emotional wellbeing. Unexpectedly, the magnitude of change in adaptive actions was smaller than previously seen in a different study which examined changes in the TYDQ-21 during the same ICBT course. For example, Bisby et al. [12] reported a 45% (95% CI 38, 52) increase in the frequency of actions in the Healthy Thinking domain, whereas the current study reports an overall increase of 33% (95% CI 28, 38) in the same domain, and this pattern is consistent across all five domains of the TYDQ-21. However, the magnitude of improvements in depression and anxiety symptoms are consistent across both the current sample and the clinical trial sample (e.g., 34% [95% CI 30, 38] vs. 37% [95% CI 33, 42] in depression), demonstrating consistency in treatment efficacy. The difference in the change in TYDQ-21 scores may be due to the nature of the participant samples used; whereas Bisby et al. [12] used a sample of participants who received treatment through a specialist research clinic in Australia in 2018-2019, the current study used a sample of participants who received treatment as part of government-funded routine care in Canada in 2020-2021. This comparison illustrates the importance of testing the reliability of results across different settings, countries, and timeframes, but also demonstrates the consistency of the overall patterns (i.e., increased frequency of adaptive actions and reduced psychological distress).

A mediating effect of Healthy Thinking, Meaningful Activities, and Goals and Plans were found on the change in depressive symptoms from pre- to post-treatment. This effect was not observed for anxiety symptoms, suggesting that the adaptive actions captured by the TYDQ-21 domains are more relevant for reductions in depressive, rather than anxiety, symptoms during treatment, at least in this sample. An increase in the frequency of the adaptive actions captured by the Healthy Thinking domain is consistent with the use of key strategies taught in cognitive therapies, such as challenging unhelpful/unrealistic thoughts and treating oneself in a fair and reasonable way [43,44]. Similarly, an increase in the actions captured by the Meaningful Activities domain is consistent with strategies taught in behavioural therapies (e.g., doing something enjoyable), which assert that doing more mastery and pleasure activities will result in improved mood [45,46]. Lastly, an increase in how frequently individuals set goals and plan ahead, as captured by an increased frequency of actions in the Goals and Plans domain, is consistent with a change in perspective from past-focus to future-focus, a process which is thought to be dysregulated in depression [47,48]. Future work may examine the variables which drive increased frequency of different adaptive actions during treatment, and compare the release of relevant course material with increases in different domains of actions (e.g., map the increase in Healthy Thinking scores relative to the release of thought challenging material). It is, however, important to note that the mediating effects were relatively small, and therefore future work is needed to further understand the clinical and practical significance of these findings.

The current finding of a mediating effect of increased adaptive actions on treatment-related change in depressive symptoms is supportive of further experimental investigations into this relationship. Several converging lines of evidence are required to determine if a given variable is a mechanism of treatment change, including mediation, experimental manipulation, a dose–response relationship, and temporality [24,49,50]. Future work may compare participants who are prompted to increase the frequency of such actions on a regular basis to those participants who are not—or, on the contrary, compare participants who are prompted to decrease the frequency of such actions to those who are not. In addition, to determine the temporal relationship in change between daily actions and psychological distress, more regular outcome measurements (e.g., weekly/fortnightly) would be required throughout treatment in future studies.

The findings of the current study should be considered in light of several limitations. First, by virtue of being an observational study from a routine care digital mental health service, no control group was included in the current study. As a result, we could not determine whether the increase in frequency of adaptive actions was treatment-related or would have occurred in the absence of treatment. Future research examining change in adaptive actions over time in a no-treatment control group is warranted. Second, mediation analyses were only conducted on the completer sample due to constraints with data analysis. Considering that 33% of post-treatment data were missing (35% standard, 26% optional), and missingness is more likely in participants who do not complete treatment or report high baseline symptoms [34], it is possible that the results may differ if they had been conducted with fewer missing data. It would also be highly beneficial to measure the TYDQ-21 more often during treatment as well as at follow-up. Third, due to the exploratory nature of the current study, we did not correct for multiple comparisons in our analyses. Lastly, there were baseline differences in anxiety and depression symptoms between participants who received optional versus standard therapist support. This is consistent with previous preference trials using the same design, in which participants who chose optional support reported lower distress than those who chose standard support [22]. It would be worthwhile for future research to compare treatment-related change in adaptive actions in different therapist support conditions when participants have been randomly allocated.

Overall, it is important to note that this study used data collected during 2021, and is likely influenced by the ongoing impacts of the COVID-19 pandemic in Canada at that time. As the current study was conducted within a digital mental health service, data collection was not impeded due to the pandemic. However, the data collected during this period do appear to have been somewhat impacted. Indeed, the within-group changes in depression symptoms were smaller in the current sample than previously observed using the same treatment program [12,41,51]. This may be a result of the ongoing impacts of the pandemic on people's lives that are less amenable to change via psychological skills, such as reduced employment (note that fewer individuals were in paid employment in the current sample compared to previous samples from the same setting [51]), social isolation, and medical concerns. Therefore, it would be worthwhile for future research to replicate our analyses using participants who are not experiencing the physical, mental, and emotional impacts of a pandemic.

The present findings speak to the potential for adaptive actions as a mechanism and as a target in psychological treatment. Such actions could form the basis of a brief and self-guided treatments focused on promoting the frequency of these actions to reduce psychological distress, and particularly depression. There is substantial public health potential for developing interventions and treatments with simple, practical messages such as increasing how often individuals perform actions during the week—including doing things they find meaningful and fun, and practicing taking perspective. This approach mirrors that which has been taken by governments worldwide to promote physical health, such as eating fruit and vegetables and participating in regular exercise. Future work which develops and rigorously evaluates such treatments within randomised controlled trials offers both theoretical and pragmatic value.

Supplementary Materials: The following are available online at https://www.mdpi.com/article/10.3390/jcm11206001/s1, Figure S1. Confirmatory factor loadings at assessment (left) and post-treatment (right).

Author Contributions: Conceptualization, M.A.B., H.D.H., N.T.; methodology, M.A.B., E.K., H.D.H.; data curation, A.W., M.N., formal analysis, M.A.B., E.K., writing—original draft preparation, M.A.B., A.W., H.D.H.; writing—review and editing, M.A.B., H.D.H., N.T., B.F.D., E.K., A.W., M.N.; supervision, H.D.H.; project administration, M.N., H.D.H.; funding acquisition, H.D.H., M.N. All authors have read and agreed to the published version of the manuscript.

Funding: This research was funded by the Canadian Institute of Health Research, grant number 152917. The Online Therapy Unit is funded by the Saskatchewan Ministry of Health.

Institutional Review Board Statement: The study was conducted in accordance with the Declaration of Helsinki, and approved by the Institutional Review Board of the University of Regina (REB #2019-197; approved 16 December 2020).

Informed Consent Statement: Informed consent was obtained from all subjects involved in the study.

Data Availability Statement: Not applicable.

Acknowledgments: The authors wish to thank the clients, community advisors, screeners, therapists, research staff, students, and web developers associated with the Online Therapy Unit at the University of Regina, including the therapists from the Saskatchewan Health Authority who also delivered therapy in this trial.

Conflicts of Interest: The authors declare no conflict of interest. The funders had no role in the design of the study; in the collection, analyses, or interpretation of data; in the writing of the manuscript, or in the decision to publish the results.

References

1. Keyes, C.L.M. The Mental Health Continuum: From Languishing to Flourishing in Life. *J. Health Soc. Behav.* **2002**, *43*, 207–222. [CrossRef] [PubMed]
2. Ryff, C.D. Happiness Is Everything, or Is It? Explorations on the Meaning of Psychological Well-Being. *J. Pers. Soc. Psychol.* **1989**, *57*, 1069–1081. [CrossRef]
3. Seligman, M. PERMA and the Building Blocks of Well-Being. *J. Posit. Psychol.* **2018**, *13*, 333–335. [CrossRef]
4. Owen, L.; Corfe, B. The Role of Diet and Nutrition on Mental Health and Wellbeing. *Proc. Nutr. Soc.* **2017**, *76*, 425–426. [CrossRef]
5. Scott, A.J.; Webb, T.L.; Martyn-St James, M.; Rowse, G.; Weich, S. Improving Sleep Quality Leads to Better Mental Health: A Meta-Analysis of Randomised Controlled Trials. *Sleep Med. Rev.* **2021**, *60*, 101556. [CrossRef]
6. Jarrett, R.B.; Vittengl, J.R.; Clark, L.A.; Thase, M.E. Skills of Cognitive Therapy (SoCT): A New Measure of Patients' Comprehension and Use. *Psychol. Assess.* **2011**, *23*, 578–586. [CrossRef]
7. Pilkington, K.; Wieland, L.S. Self-Care for Anxiety and Depression: A Comparison of Evidence from Cochrane Reviews and Practice to Inform Decision-Making and Priority-Setting. *BMC Complement. Med. Ther.* **2020**, *20*, 120. [CrossRef]
8. Terides, M.D.; Dear, B.F.; Fogliati, V.J.; Gandy, M.; Jones, M.P.; Titov, N. Increased Skills Usage Statistically Mediates Symptom Reduction in Self-Guided Internet-Delivered Cognitive–Behavioural Therapy for Depression and Anxiety: A Randomised Controlled Trial. *Cogn. Behav. Ther.* **2018**, *6073*, 43–61. [CrossRef]
9. Santini, Z.I.; Nelausen, M.K.; Kusier, A.O.; Hinrichsen, C.; Schou-Juul, F.; Madsen, K.R.; Meilstrup, C.; Donovan, R.J.; Koushede, V.; Nielsen, L. Impact Evaluation of the "ABCs of Mental Health" in Denmark and the Role of Mental Health-Promoting Beliefs and Actions. *Ment. Health Soc. Incl.* **2022**, *26*, 271–291. [CrossRef]
10. Titov, N.; Dear, B.F.; Bisby, M.A.; Nielssen, O.; Staples, L.G.; Kayrouz, R.; Cross, S.; Karin, E. Measures of Daily Activities Associated With Mental Health (Things You Do Questionnaire): Development of a Preliminary Psychometric Study and Replication Study. *JMIR Form. Res.* **2022**, *16*, e38837. [CrossRef]
11. Boateng, G.O.; Neilands, T.B.; Frongillo, E.A.; Melgar-Quiñonez, H.R.; Young, S.L. Best Practices for Developing and Validating Scales for Health, Social, and Behavioral Research: A Primer. *Front. Public Health* **2018**, *6*, 149. [CrossRef]
12. Bisby, M.A.; Dear, B.F.; Karin, E.; Fogliati, R.; Dudeney, J.; Ryan, K.; Fararoui, A.; Nielssen, O.B.; Staples, L.G.; Kayrouz, R.; et al. An Open Trial of the Things You Do Questionnaire: Changes in Daily Actions during Internet-Delivered Treatment for Depressive and Anxiety Symptoms. 2022, *under review*.
13. Titov, N.; Hadjistavropoulos, H.D.; Nielssen, O.; Mohr, D.C.; Andersson, G.; Dear, B.F. From Research to Practice: Ten Lessons in Delivering Digital Mental Health Services. *J. Clin. Med.* **2019**, *8*, 1239. [CrossRef]
14. Esfandiari, N.; Mazaheri, M.A.; Akbari-Zardkhaneh, S.; Sadeghi-Firoozabadi, V.; Cheraghi, M. Internet-Delivered Versus Face-to-Face Cognitive Behavior Therapy for Anxiety Disorders: Systematic Review and Meta-Analysis. *Int. J. Prev. Med.* **2021**, *12*, 153. [CrossRef]
15. Lundström, L.; Flygare, O.; Andersson, E.; Enander, J.; Bottai, M.; Ivanov, V.Z.; Boberg, J.; Pascal, D.; Mataix-Cols, D.; Rück, C. Effect of Internet-Based vs Face-to-Face Cognitive Behavioral Therapy for Adults With Obsessive-Compulsive Disorder: A Randomized Clinical Trial. *JAMA Netw. Open* **2022**, *5*, e221967. [CrossRef]
16. Andersson, G.; Titov, N.; Dear, B.F.; Rozental, A.; Carlbring, P. Internet-Delivered Psychological Treatments: From Innovation to Implementation. *World Psychiatry* **2019**, *18*, 20–28. [CrossRef]
17. Gandy, M.; Pang, S.T.Y.; Scott, A.J.; Heriseanu, A.I.; Bisby, M.A.; Dudeney, J.; Karin, E.; Titov, N.; Dear, B.F. Internet-Delivered Cognitive and Behavioural Based Interventions for Adults with Chronic Pain: A Systematic Review and Meta-Analysis of Randomized Controlled Trials. *Pain* **2022**, *163*, e1041–e1053. [CrossRef]
18. Karyotaki, E.; Efthimiou, O.; Miguel, C.; Bermpohl, F.M.G.; Furukawa, T.A.; Cuijpers, P.; Riper, H.; Patel, V.; Mira, A.; Gemmil, A.W.; et al. Internet-Based Cognitive Behavioral Therapy for Depression: A Systematic Review and Individual Patient Data Network Meta-Analysis. *JAMA Psychiatry* **2021**, *78*, 361–371. [CrossRef]
19. Dear, B.F.; Gandy, M.; Karin, E.; Fogliati, R.; Fogliati, V.J.; Staples, L.G.; Wootton, B.M.; Sharpe, L.; Titov, N. The Pain Course: A Randomised Controlled Trial Examining an Internet-Delivered Pain Management Program When Provided with Different Levels of Clinician Support. *J. Pain* **2015**, *156*, 1920–1935. [CrossRef]
20. Hadjistavropoulos, H.D.; Schneider, L.H.; Edmonds, M.; Karin, E.; Nugent, M.N.; Dirkse, D.; Dear, B.F.; Titov, N. Randomized Controlled Trial of Internet-Delivered Cognitive Behaviour Therapy Comparing Standard Weekly versus Optional Weekly Therapist Support. *J. Anxiety Disord.* **2017**, *52*, 15–24. [CrossRef]

21. Berger, T.; Caspar, F.; Richardson, R.; Kneubühler, B.; Sutter, D.; Andersson, G. Internet-Based Treatment of Social Phobia: A Randomized Controlled Trial Comparing Unguided with Two Types of Guided Self-Help. *Behav. Res. Ther.* **2011**, *49*, 158–169. [CrossRef]
22. Hadjistavropoulos, H.D.; Schneider, L.H.; Mehta, S.; Karin, E.; Dear, B.F.; Titov, N. Preference Trial of Internet-Delivered Cognitive Behaviour Therapy Comparing Standard Weekly versus Optional Weekly Therapist Support. *J. Anxiety Disord.* **2019**, *63*, 51–60. [CrossRef]
23. Kazdin, A.E. Understanding How and Why Psychotherapy Leads to Change. *Psychother. Res. J. Soc. Psychother. Res.* **2009**, *19*, 418–428. [CrossRef]
24. Lemmens, L.H.J.M.; Müller, V.N.L.S.; Arntz, A.; Huibers, M.J.H. Mechanisms of Change in Psychotherapy for Depression: An Empirical Update and Evaluation of Research Aimed at Identifying Psychological Mediators. *Clin. Psychol. Rev.* **2016**, *50*, 95–107. [CrossRef]
25. Titov, N.; Dear, B.F.; Staples, L.G.; Terides, M.D.; Karin, E.; Sheehan, J.; Johnston, L.; Gandy, M.; Fogliati, V.J.; Wootton, B.M.; et al. Disorder-Specific versus Transdiagnostic and Clinician-Guided versus Self-Guided Treatment for Major Depressive Disorder and Comorbid Anxiety Disorders: A Randomized Controlled Trial. *J. Anxiety Disord.* **2015**, *35*, 88–102. [CrossRef]
26. Titov, N.; Dear, B.F.; Johnston, L.; Lorian, C.; Zou, J.; Wootton, B.; Spence, J.; McEvoy, P.M.; Rapee, R.M. Improving Adherence and Clinical Outcomes in Self-Guided Internet Treatment for Anxiety and Depression: Randomised Controlled Trial. *PLoS ONE* **2013**, *8*, e62873. [CrossRef]
27. Kroenke, K.; Spitzer, R.L.; Williams, J.B.W. The PHQ-9: Validity of a Brief Depression Severity Measure. *J. Gen. Intern. Med.* **2001**, *16*, 606–613. [CrossRef]
28. Kroenke, K.; Spitzer, R.L.; Williams, J.B.W.; Löwe, B. The Patient Health Questionnaire Somatic, Anxiety, and Depressive Symptom Scales: A Systematic Review. *Gen. Hosp. Psychiatry* **2010**, *32*, 345–359. [CrossRef] [PubMed]
29. Manea, L.; Gilbody, S.; McMillan, D. Optimal Cut-off Score for Diagnosing Depression with the Patient Health Questionnaire (PHQ-9): A Meta-Analysis. *Cmaj* **2012**, *184*, 281–282. [CrossRef] [PubMed]
30. Titov, N.; Andersson, G. Using Brief Measures to Identify Depression and Other Mental Disorders: A Challenge for Research and Clinical Practice. *Internet Interv.* **2022**, *28*, 100450. [CrossRef]
31. Spitzer, R.L.; Kroenke, K.; Williams, J.B.W.; Löwe, B. A Brief Measure for Assessing Generalized Anxiety Disorder: The GAD-7. *Arch. Intern. Med.* **2006**, *166*, 1092–1097. [CrossRef] [PubMed]
32. Plummer, F.; Manea, L.; Trepel, D.; McMillan, D. Screening for Anxiety Disorders with the GAD-7 and GAD-2: A Systematic Review and Diagnostic Metaanalysis. *Gen. Hosp. Psychiatry* **2016**, *39*, 24–31. [CrossRef]
33. Hu, L.; Bentler, P.M. Cutoff Criteria for Fit Indexes in Covariance Structure Analysis: Conventional Criteria versus New Alternatives. *Struct. Equ. Model.* **1999**, *6*, 1–55. [CrossRef]
34. Karin, E.; Dear, B.F.; Heller, G.Z.; Crane, M.F.; Titov, N. "Wish You Were Here": Examining Characteristics, Outcomes, and Statistical Solutions for Missing Cases in Web-Based Psychotherapeutic Trials. *J. Med. Internet Res.* **2018**, *5*, e22. [CrossRef]
35. Karin, E.; Crane, M.F.; Dear, B.F.; Nielssen, O.; Heller, G.Z.; Kayrouz, R.; Titov, N. Predictors, Outcomes, and Statistical Solutions of Missing Cases in Web-Based Psychotherapy: Methodological Replication and Elaboration Study. *JMIR Ment. Health* **2021**, *8*, e22700. [CrossRef]
36. Liang, K.Y.; Zeger, S.L. Longitudinal Data Analysis Using Generalized Linear Models. *Biometrika* **1986**, *73*, 13–22. [CrossRef]
37. Hayes, A. Introduction to Mediation, Moderation, and Conditional Process Analysis. In *A Regression-Based Approach*, 3rd ed.; Guilford Press: New York, NY, USA, 2021.
38. Wang, K. Direct Effect and Indirect Effect on an Outcome under Nonlinear Modeling. *Int. J. Biostat.* **2020**, *16*, 2. [CrossRef]
39. Valente, M.J.; MacKinnon, D.P. Comparing Models of Change to Estimate the Mediated Effect in the Pretest–Posttest Control Group Design. *Struct. Equ. Model.* **2017**, *24*, 428–450. [CrossRef]
40. Newby, J.M.; Mewton, L.; Andrews, G. Transdiagnostic versus Disorder-Specific Internet-Delivered Cognitive Behaviour Therapy for Anxiety and Depression in Primary Care. *J. Anxiety Disord.* **2017**, *46*, 25–34. [CrossRef]
41. Titov, N.; Dear, B.F.; Nielssen, O.; Wootton, B.; Kayrouz, R.; Karin, E.; Genest, B.; Bennett-Levy, J.; Purtell, C.; Bezuidenhout, G.; et al. User Characteristics and Outcomes from a National Digital Mental Health Service: An Observational Study of Registrants of the Australian MindSpot Clinic. *Lancet Digit. Health* **2020**, *2*, e582–e593. [CrossRef]
42. Andersson, G.; Paxling, B.; Roch-Norlund, P.; Ostman, G.; Norgren, A.; Almlov, J.; Georen, L.; Breitholtz, E.; Dahlin, M.; Cuijpers, P.; et al. Internet-Based Psychodynamic versus Cognitive Behavioral Guided Self-Help for Generalized Anxiety Disorder: A Randomized Controlled Trial. *Psychother. Psychosom.* **2012**, *81*, 344–355. [CrossRef]
43. Clark, D.A.; Beck, A.T. *Cognitive Therapy of Anxiety Disorders: Science and Practice*; Guilford Press: New York, NY, USA, 2010; Volume 51, pp. 282–283, ISBN 978-1-60623-434-1.
44. Garratt, G.; Ingram, R.E.; Rand, K.L.; Sawalani, G. Cognitive Processes in Cognitive Therapy: Evaluation of the Mechanisms of Change in the Treatment of Depression. *Clin. Psychol. Sci. Pract.* **2007**, *14*, 224–239. [CrossRef]
45. Janssen, N.P.; Hendriks, G.-J.; Baranelli, C.T.; Lucassen, P.; Oude Voshaar, R.; Spijker, J.; Huibers, M.J.H. How Does Behavioural Activation Work? A Systematic Review of the Evidence on Potential Mediators. *Psychother. Psychosom.* **2021**, *90*, 85–93. [CrossRef]
46. Lewinsohn, P.M. A Behavioral Approach to Depression. In *The Psychology of Depression: Contemporary Theory and Research*; Katz, R.J., Ed.; Winston-Wiley: Washington, DC, USA, 1974; pp. 150–172.

47. Dickson, J.M.; Moberly, N.J.; O'Dea, C.; Field, M. Goal Fluency, Pessimism and Disengagement in Depression. *PLoS ONE* **2016**, *11*, e0166259. [CrossRef]
48. Dickson, J.M.; Moberly, N.J. Reduced Specificity of Personal Goals and Explanations for Goal Attainment in Major Depression. *PLoS ONE* **2013**, *8*, e64512. [CrossRef]
49. Holmes, E.A.; Ghaderi, A.; Harmer, C.J.; Ramchandani, P.G.; Cuijpers, P.; Morrison, A.P.; Roiser, J.P.; Bockting, C.L.H.; O'Connor, R.C.; Shafran, R.; et al. The Lancet Psychiatry Commission on Psychological Treatments Research in Tomorrow's Science. *Lancet Psychiatry* **2018**, *5*, 237–286. [CrossRef]
50. Kazdin, A.E. Mediators and Mechanisms of Change in Psychotherapy Research. *Annu. Rev. Clin. Psychol.* **2007**, *3*, 375–406. [CrossRef]
51. Hadjistavropoulos, H.D.; Peynenburg, V.; Thiessen, D.L.; Nugent, M.; Karin, E.; Staples, L.; Dear, B.F.; Titov, N. Utilization, Patient Characteristics, and Longitudinal Improvements among Patients from a Provincially Funded Transdiagnostic Internet-Delivered Cognitive Behavioural Therapy Program: Observational Study of Trends over 6 Years. *Can. J. Psychiatry* **2022**, *67*, 192–206. [CrossRef]

Journal of
Clinical Medicine

MDPI

Article

Understanding Client Difficulties in Transdiagnostic Internet-Delivered Cognitive Behaviour Therapy: A Qualitative Analysis of Homework Reflections

Vanessa Peynenburg [1], Andrew Wilhelms [1], Ram Sapkota [1], Marcie Nugent [1], Katherine Owens [2], Nick Titov [3], Blake Dear [4] and Heather Hadjisatvropoulos [1,*]

[1] Department of Psychology, University of Regina, 3737 Wascana Parkway, Regina, SK S4S 0A2, Canada; vanessa.peynenburg@uregina.ca (V.P.); andrew.wilhelms@uregina.ca (A.W.); ram.sapkota@uregina.ca (R.S.); marcie.nugent@uregina.ca (M.N.)
[2] Online Therapy Team, Regina Adult Mental Health Clinic, Saskatchewan Health Authority, 2110 Hamilton Street, Regina, SK S4P 2E3, Canada; katherine.owens@saskhealthauthority.ca
[3] MindSpot Clinic, MQ Health, Macquarie University, Sydney, NSW 2109, Australia; nick.titov@mq.edu.au
[4] eCentreClinic, School of Psychological Sciences, Macquarie University, Sydney, NSW 2109, Australia; blake.dear@mq.edu.au
* Correspondence: hadjista@uregina.ca

Abstract: Internet-delivered cognitive behaviour therapy (ICBT) is helpful for many clients, but less is known about the challenges clients face during ICBT, such as difficulties with skill practice, development, or maintenance. Understanding client difficulties can help therapists support clients with skill development and prevent treatment drop-out, but has not been systematically studied. This study included a conventional content analysis of clients' responses to a homework reflection question about difficulties with lessons and skills. Data was drawn from a previously published trial of 301 clients who were randomly assigned to receive homework reflection questions during ICBT. A decreasing number of clients responded to the question about skill difficulties with each lesson. Clients who answered the question about difficulties were more engaged with ICBT (i.e., more lessons completed, logins, days enrolled in ICBT, and messages sent to therapists). Clients shared skill-specific challenges (including initial challenges and more advanced challenges), generic challenges (content or skills being cognitively draining or emotionally draining, contextual challenges, forgetfulness, limited time, and lack of familiarity with the skill), or no challenges. Thought challenging (59.6%) and graded exposure (57.5%) were associated with the greatest number of skill-specific challenges. Findings can help therapists anticipate and address common client challenges during ICBT.

Keywords: internet-delivered therapy; cognitive behaviour therapy; online therapy; digital mental health; homework; therapist support; e-health

Citation: Peynenburg, V.; Wilhelms, A.; Sapkota, R.; Nugent, M.; Owens, K.; Titov, N.; Dear, B.; Hadjisatvropoulos, H. Understanding Client Difficulties in Transdiagnostic Internet-Delivered Cognitive Behaviour Therapy: A Qualitative Analysis of Homework Reflections. *J. Clin. Med.* **2022**, *11*, 4226. https://doi.org/10.3390/jcm11144226

Academic Editor: Stéphane Bouchard

Received: 25 May 2022
Accepted: 20 July 2022
Published: 21 July 2022

1. Introduction

Cognitive behaviour therapy (CBT) is an effective psychotherapy that focuses on the development of cognitive and behavioural skills and is commonly used to treat anxiety disorders and depression [1]. Prospective clients face a variety of challenges related to stigma, location, and time that can act as a barrier to receiving face-to-face CBT [2]. Internet-delivered cognitive behaviour therapy (ICBT) is an alternative treatment option that can increase clients' ability to access services, but some clients experience challenges with skill development during treatment. ICBT includes similar skills and content as clients would receive in face-to-face cognitive behaviour therapy (CBT), with all content delivered online typically in the form of lessons often combined with therapist support [3]. Meta-analyses of ICBT in routine care have identified Hedge's g effects of 1.18 for reduced depression (95% CI 1.06–1.29) and 0.94 (95% CI 0.83–1.06) for reduced anxiety [2]. In general, deterioration side effects in ICBT appear to be low, with one review suggesting less than 3%

of clients report deterioration [2]. Despite these promising findings, less is known about clients' difficulties with skill development or behavioural change during ICBT. It may be beneficial to systematically monitor clients' experiences throughout treatment so that therapists can attempt to facilitate skill acquisition with the aims of optimizing symptom improvement and sustaining engagement.

In traditional face-to-face cognitive behaviour therapy (CBT), therapists often assign and review homework exercises [4]. Homework reviews serve several purposes, including the following: reinforcing the importance of skills practiced outside of sessions, clarifying the objectives of assigned homework, problem-solving barriers to skill implementation, and offering feedback or positive reinforcement for clients' efforts [5]. Additionally, homework review increases the likelihood of clients completing future homework exercises [6]. Clients in ICBT also typically receive homework assignments [3], although the nature of the review by the therapist varies widely among ICBT programs [7].

In therapist-assisted ICBT programs, one way that clients and therapists review homework assignments is by email. Soucy et al. [8] coded emails that clients sent to their therapists during ICBT and found that most clients asked fewer than two questions throughout the eight-week treatment. The most common questions were related to enhancing clients' understanding of the materials and applying the skills from the lessons (46.72%). Of note, these questions were spontaneously reported by clients in their emails. Another approach to reviewing homework is to systematically ask clients to answer questions about their completion of homework in the form of homework reflection questionnaires (HWRQs) before clients proceed to the next ICBT lesson. Information gathered from these HWRQs can help therapists understand what challenges their clients are encountering during each lesson. It may be particularly helpful in cases when clients do not spontaneously share difficulties they are having in their emails. The role of including HWRQs on client engagement and client outcomes (regarding depression and anxiety) was recently examined in a factorial trial of ICBT [7]. Clients were randomly assigned to complete HWRQs or not and to receive either once-weekly or twice-weekly therapist support. Contrary to what was hypothesised, clients who were asked to complete HWRQs logged into the website fewer times and spent fewer days in the program overall. A possible explanation for this finding is that some clients felt the additional questions were too demanding, which acted as a deterrent to logging into the program. No benefits were found for the inclusion of HWRQs on improvements in depression or anxiety, so it was concluded that the inclusion of HWRQs may not be beneficial for improving either client engagement or outcomes.

While the inclusion of HWRQs did not alter outcomes, there is a strong tradition in CBT of clients reflecting on homework. Further, therapists involved in the trial [7] reported several benefits to including HWRQs, such as increased knowledge about their clients and improved efficiency when conducting weekly check-ins with clients. Clients provided ratings on how much of the content they reviewed, level of effort in practicing the skills, difficulty practicing the skill, understanding of the lesson, and the helpfulness of the skill. As the course progressed, clients reported being less engaged with the content and putting in less effort over time. The content on de-arousal strategies was rated as the easiest to understand, and clients had the most difficulty practicing thought challenging exercises. These ratings provide information about what skills clients find the most challenging, but to date, there has been no exploration of the specific challenges faced by clients as they worked on lessons in ICBT.

The current study therefore included an evaluation of client responses to questions regarding difficulties with practicing CBT skills as they completed the five lesson transdiagnostic ICBT course. The primary objective of this study was to identify difficulties that clients encountered when completing ICBT, to provide an enhanced understanding of client response to ICBT, and to ultimately inform therapists' practices for addressing clients' challenges to learning and implementing CBT strategies. In this study, we aimed to answer four exploratory questions: (1) What percentage of clients will share difficulties in response to the five core lessons of the ICBT course? (2) Do clients who share difficulties differ from those who do not on measures of demographics, symptom severity, or treatment engagement? (3) What general difficulties do clients identify across all lessons? and (4) What specific difficulties do clients identify related to each lesson and accompanying skill? Understanding the characteristics of clients who share difficulties with homework in ICBT and the nature of those difficulties can help therapists be aware of what challenges their clients are likely to encounter during ICBT and how they can best support them.

2. Materials and Methods

2.1. Participants and Recruitment

This qualitative study was approved by the institutional research ethics board at the University of Regina. Data were obtained from a previously published randomized factorial trial (ClinicalTrials.gov NCT03957330 [7]) conducted between 2 May 2019 and 5 November 2019 investigating the inclusion of HWRQs (yes/no) and different levels of therapist support (once-/twice-weekly email contact). In this trial, ICBT resulted in moderate symptom improvement for depression (Cohen's *d*: 0.69–0.78) and large improvement for anxiety (Cohen's *d*: 0.82–0.91), that were maintained at the 24-week follow-up regardless of treatment condition. The current study specifically focussed on 301 clients who were assigned to the HWRQ condition and subsequently completed consent and started treatment. In this study, we were interested in how clients responded to an optional open-ended question about difficulties they experienced practicing the skill/skills from the previous lesson that was administered at five time points during the ICBT course (i.e., at the beginning of lessons 2–5 and at the beginning of the 8-week post-treatment questionnaires).

Of the 301 clients, 154 (51.2%) completed the question about difficulties they experienced in lesson 1 (CBT model), 151 (50.2%) completed the question for lesson 2 (thought challenging), 114 (37.9%) for lesson 3 (controlled breathing and activity planning), 87 (28.9%) for lesson 4 (graded exposure), and 57 (18.9%) for lesson 5 (goal setting and relapse prevention).

2.2. Intervention

All eligible clients were given access to the 8-week five lesson transdiagnostic ICBT program (the Wellbeing Course), developed by the eCentreClinic at Macquarie University [9] and licensed by the Online Therapy Unit. The course consists of five core lessons, each focusing on a different skill or strategy within CBT. Each lesson consists of 50 to 60 presentational slides and a downloadable guide that includes recommended homework assignments related to skills that correspond with concepts from the lesson slideshows. Case stories based on previous clients' experiences are included in the lessons. The five lessons are made available to clients on a fixed schedule (lesson 1 opens immediately, lesson 2 opens at start of week 2, lesson 3 at start of week 4, lesson 4 at start of week 5, lesson 5 at start of week 7), pending completion of all previous lessons and any active survey. Automated emails are sent to notify clients when a lesson becomes available.

2.3. Measures

The HWRQs were administered at the beginning of lessons 2, 3, 4, and 5 and at post-treatment. Primary outcome measures included the Patient Health Questionnaire 9-item (PHQ-9 [10]) and Generalized Anxiety Disorder–7 (GAD-7 [11]) and are only reported on at pre-treatment in this study. The treatment website tracked client engagement, including the number of logins, days between first and last login, lessons accessed, messages client sent, messages therapist sent, and phone calls with the client. For a full list of the primary and secondary measures included in the factorial trial, see [7].

Homework Reflection Questionnaire (HWRQ)

Starting in the second lesson, clients in the HWRQ condition were asked at the beginning of each lesson to reflect on their experiences with the previous lesson's homework activities. Clients provided ratings on how much of the previous lesson they were able to review, how much effort they put into working on the main skill from the previous lesson, the level of difficulty they had with working on the skills, how understandable the skills were, how helpful they found the skills, and to what extent they had continued to use the skills from previous lessons (see [6] for a summary of the ratings). Clients were also given an optional open-ended question (i.e., "Please share any difficulties you had with [skill]") where they could share difficulties they had with the cycle of symptoms (lesson 1), thought challenging (lesson 2), controlled breathing and activity planning (lesson 3), graded exposure (lesson 4), and goal setting relapse prevention (lesson 5). The open-ended question about clients' difficulties with the skills was the focus of our analyses in this paper.

2.4. *Therapist Support*

Clients were assigned to a therapist from either an ICBT clinic or a community mental health clinic. In both settings, the primary caseload of therapists was ICBT and all therapists received training and supervision in ICBT. As described in Hadjistavropoulos et al. [7], clients were randomized to receive either once-weekly or twice-weekly therapist support. Therapists contacted clients on a predetermined day each week in the once-weekly condition and on two predetermined days in the twice-weekly condition. Emails were composed based on reviewing client progress on the completion of lessons, any completed questionnaires (i.e., symptom questionnaires, HWRQ) and emails from clients. Therapists were expected to take 15 min per email although they had the flexibility to increase the amount of time spent when clinically indicated. Therapists were instructed to call the client by telephone when clinically indicated (i.e., increase in symptom scores of five points or more, endorsed suicidal ideation, client had not logged on in a week, or client requested phone contact).

2.5. *Analyses*

2.5.1. Quantitative Analyses

Analyses related to symptom changes over time are reported in Hadjistavropoulos et al. [7]. A combination of Chi-square analyses and one-way ANOVAs were conducted using SPSS Version 25 to examine any pre-treatment differences in demographic and clinical characteristics between clients who completed the HWRQ question on difficulties for at least one lesson and those who did not (see Table 1). To partially account for multiple comparisons, a p-value of 0.01 was considered statistically significant. Completion of the HWRQ question on difficulties was also compared between those who received once-weekly versus twice-weekly support. As no differences were found on this variable ($\chi^2_{(1, 301)} = 1.85, p = 0.17$), no further analysis of this variable was undertaken.

Table 1. Pre-treatment patient characteristics by group.

Variable	All HWRQ Clients (*n* = 301)		Responded to HW Difficulties Question (*n* = 225)		Did Not Respond to HW Difficulties Question (*n* = 76)		Significance
	n	%	*n*	%	*n*	%	
Age							
Mean (*SD*)	36.06 (12.82)	-	36.90 (13.34)	-	33.58 (10.81)	-	$t(299) = -1.96$, $p = 0.05$
Range	18–88	-	18–88	-	18–65	-	

Table 1. *Cont.*

Variable	All HWRQ Clients (n = 301)		Responded to HW Difficulties Question (n = 225)		Did Not Respond to HW Difficulties Question (n = 76)		Significance
	n	%	n	%	n	%	
Gender							
Male	71	23.6	50	22.2	21	27.6	$\chi^2_{(1, 295)} = 0.85$, $p = 0.36$
Female	224	74.4	170	75.6	54	71.1	
Two spirit	3	1.0	3	1.3	-	-	
Non-binary	1	0.3	1	0.4	-	-	
Not listed	1	0.3	-	-	1	1.3	
Prefers not to disclose	1	0.3	1	0.4	-	-	
Marital status							
Single/never married	77	25.6	56	24.9	21	27.6	$\chi^2_{(1, 301)} = 0.31$, $p = 0.86$
Married/common-law	198	65.8	150	66.7	48	63.2	
Separated/divorced/widowed	26	8.6	19	8.4	7	9.2	
Education							
Less than high school	3	1.0	2	0.9	1	1.3	$\chi^2_{(1, 301)} = 0.88$, $p = 0.83$
High school diploma	65	21.6	46	20.4	19	25.0	
Post high school certificate/diploma	82	27.2	63	28.0	19	25.0	
University education	151	50.2	114	50.7	37	48.7	
Employment status							
Employed part-time/full-time	211	70.1	157	69.8	54	71.1	$\chi^2_{(1, 301)} = 7.40$, $p = 0.19$
Unemployed	18	6.0	13	5.8	5	6.6	
Homemaker	27	9.0	21	9.3	6	7.9	
Student	19	6.3	17	7.6	2	2.6	
Disability	14	4.7	7	3.1	7	9.2	
Retired	12	4.0	10	4.4	2	2.6	
Ethnicity							
White	276	91.7	203	90.2	73	96.1	$\chi^2_{(1, 301)} = 4.03$, $p = 0.13$
Indigenous	14	4.7	11	4.9	3	3.9	
Other	11	3.6	11	4.9	-	-	
Location							
Large city (over 200,000)	138	45.8	105	46.7	33	43.4	$\chi^2_{(1, 301)} = 0.41$, $p = 0.81$
Small to medium city	64	21.3	46	20.4	18	23.7	
Small rural location (under 10,000)	99	32.9	74	32.8	25	32.9	
Mental health characteristics							
Taking psychotropic medications	170	56.5	120	53.3	50	65.8	$\chi^2_{(1, 301)} = 36$, $p = 0.05$
Pre-treatment GAD-7 ≧ 10	189	62.8	143	63.6	46	60.5	$\chi^2_{(1, 301)} = 0.22$, $p = 0.64$
Pre-treatment PHQ-9 ≧ 10	203	67.4	152	67.6	51	67.1	$\chi^2_{(1, 301)} = 0.01$, $p = 0.94$
Non clinical PHQ-9 and GAD-7 scores	35	11.6	27	12.0	8	10.5	$\chi^2_{(1, 301)} = 0.12$, $p = 0.73$
Pre-treatment credibility Mean (*SD*)	21.16 (4.41)	-	21.14 (4.41)	-	21.20 (4.44)	-	$t(299) = 0.09$, $p = 0.93$

Table 1. *Cont.*

Variable	All HWRQ Clients (n = 301)		Responded to HW Difficulties Question (n = 225)		Did Not Respond to HW Difficulties Question (n = 76)		Significance
	n	%	n	%	n	%	
Treatment Engagement							
Accessed Lesson 4	233	77.4	199	88.4	34	44.7	$\chi^2_{(1, 301)} = 62.06$, $p < 0.001$
Accessed Lesson 5	207	68.8	178	79.1	29	38.2	$\chi^2_{(1, 301)} = 44.37$, $p < 0.001$
# of log-ins Mean (*SD*)	20.5 (13.2)	-	23.0 (13.3)	-	13.2 (9.8)	-	$t(299) = -5.88$, $p < 0.001$
Days in program until last access, Mean (*SD*)	67.4 (38.6)	-	74.2 (36.4)	-	47.3 (38.4)	-	$t(299) = -5.49$, $p < 0.001$
# of messages sent by client, Mean (*SD*)	4.3 (3.8)	-	5.1 (3.8)	-	2.1 (2.7)	-	$t(299) = -6.33$, $p < 0.001$
# of phone conversations with client, Mean (*SD*)	1.0 (1.1)	-	1.0 (1.1)	-	1.2 (1.3)	-	$t(299) = 1.80$, $p = 0.07$

Note. HWRQ = homework reflection questionnaires; HW = homework; GAD-7 = Generalized Anxiety Disorder-7; PHQ-9 = Patient Health Questionnaire-9.

2.5.2. Qualitative Analyses

Prior to reviewing the HWRQs, all responses to open-ended questions on treatment satisfaction were also examined to determine whether clients volunteered their opinions about the HWRQs. Clients did not make any explicit references to the HWRQs in their responses.

Conventional content analysis has been recommended when existing literature on a topic is limited [12]. Analysis of the HWRQ was conducted using NVivo 12, a qualitative analysis software by QSR International. The first author began by reviewing approximately 25% of the responses to the HWRQ question about client difficulties for each lesson to generate initial themes and form a codebook. After approximately 25% of the responses had been reviewed, no new themes were emerging in client responses. Two research associates then independently coded all responses to the HWRQ questions using the preliminary codebook. The reviewers could propose new themes if they felt the existing themes did not capture the clients' responses. Proposed themes were discussed in a group meeting with the primary author and reviewers, a revised codebook was formed, and responses were recoded using the new themes. Once all the responses were coded, a report was generated in Nvivo 12 that included the percentage of responses for each code, as well as a list of all the responses that were assigned to a given code. The first author reviewed the report and identified any instances of disagreement. A third reviewer (R.S.) resolved any discrepancies.

3. Results

3.1. Client Characteristics

Pre-treatment characteristics of clients who were randomized to one of the HWRQ conditions (n = 301) are included in Table 1 (see [6] for a description of the full sample). The mean age of clients was 36.06 years (SD = 12.82) and the majority of clients were female (n = 224/301, 74.4%), married or common-law (n = 198/301, 65.8%), had at least some university education (n = 151/301, 50.2%), were employed (n = 211/301, 70.1%), and White (n = 276/301, 91.7%). At intake, 56.5% (n = 170/301) of clients were taking psychotropic medications and only 11.6% (n = 35/301) of clients did not have any scores in the clinical range on measures of generalized anxiety or depression. No significant differences were found on any demographic or clinical characteristics between clients who completed HWRQs and those who did not (p range: 0.05–93).

3.2. Treatment Engagement

Treatment engagement is summarized in Table 1. Overall, clients who completed the HWRQ questions on difficulties were more engaged during the ICBT course in terms of being more likely to access lesson 4 (88.4% vs. 44.7%; $\chi^2_{(1, 301)} = 62.06$, $p < 0.001$) and lesson 5 (79.1% vs. 38.2%; $\chi^2_{(1, 301)} = 44.37$, $p < 0.001$), logging in more times ($t(299) = -5.88$, $p < 0.001$), having more days in the program between their first and last access ($t(299) = -5.49$, $p < 0.001$), and sending a greater number of messages to their therapists ($t(299) = -6.33$, $p < 0.001$) compared to clients who did not answer the HWRQ questions on difficulties.

3.3. Qualitative Domains

The qualitative analysis revealed that clients' responses to the HWRQ item about difficulties with skills were found to fall under two main domains: challenges that were specific to the skill described in that lesson ("specific challenges") and challenges that were experienced by clients across all five lessons ("generic challenges"). A third domain was the absence of challenges with the specific skill from that lesson ("no challenges"). Table 2 summarizes the proportion of responses that fell under each domain for each of the lessons. In general, skill-specific challenges were the most common type of challenge for lesson 1 (cycle of symptoms), 2 (thought challenging) and 4 (graded exposure). In the case of lesson 3 (controlled breathing and activity planning), it was most common for clients to report having no challenges. For lesson 5 on goal setting and relapse prevention, generic challenges were most commonly reported.

Table 2. Frequency of skill-specific challenges, generic challenges and no challenges per skill.

Skills	Total Respondents (*n*)	Skill-Specific Challenges *n* (%)	Generic Challenges Across Skills *n* (%)	No Challenges *n* (%)
Cycle of symptoms L1	154	79 (51.3)	41 (26.6)	37 (24.0)
Thought challenging L2	151	90 (59.6)	37 (24.5)	24 (15.9)
Managing physical symptoms L3	114	27 (23.7)	61 (53.5)	66 (57.9)
Activity planning [1]	114	15 (13.2)	31 (27.2)	24 (21.2)
Controlled breathing [1]	114	12 (10.5)	30 (26.3)	42 (36.8)
Graded exposure L4	87	50 (57.5)	26 (29.9)	12 (13.8)
Relapse prevention/goal setting L5	57	17 (29.8)	21 (36.8)	18 (31.6)

Note. Each response could be coded into more than one theme, resulting in a larger number of coded units than total responses. L1 = Lesson 1; L2 = Lesson 2; L3 = Lesson 3; L4 = Lesson 4; L5 = Lesson 5. [1] Clients were asked about activity planning and controlled breathing in the same reflection questionnaire.

3.3.1. Specific Challenges

In reviewing clients' difficulties with each of the five lessons, clients' comments were coded as initial challenges versus intermediate challenges with the skills taught in the course, which were the following: cycle of symptoms (lesson 1), thought challenging (lesson 2), controlled breathing and activity planning (lesson 3), graded exposure (lesson 4), and relapse prevention (lesson 5). Initial challenges were defined as difficulties with getting started on a particular skill or troubles with seeing how the skill was relevant to their experience. Intermediate challenges were defined as difficulties with mastering the skill or generalizing it to different situations or environments. Table 3 includes example quotes of specific challenges for each of the five lessons, as well as the proportion of responses for each type of challenge.

Table 3. Skill-specific challenges.

Domain/Theme	Example Quote	Total Respondents n (%)
Skill: Cycle of Symptoms		
Specific Challenges		n = 79
Initial challenges	"I find it hard to find cycles within my anxiety since it's been feeling constant lately. The only time I get some relief is my finishing everything I need to do, and sitting down and reading until I start falling asleep." #13947	63 (79.7)
Intermediate challenges	"I've identified my cycle of symptoms. But it's very hard to change it. Lol I've been thinking a lot of realizing my symptoms and finding a way to change my thought process." #12872	16 (20.3)
Skill: Thought Challenging		
Specific Challenges		n = 90
Initial challenges	"Finding the confidence to challenge thoughts was difficult. Often the thoughts we are supposed to be challenging have almost become familiar and comforting to wallow in, so standing up to them feels uncomfortable." #13808	52 (57.8)
Intermediate challenges	"I found it hard because I think my unrealistic thoughts are realistic! I just find it difficult to change my thoughts into better ones." #14124	38 (42.2)
Managing Physical Symptoms		
Skill: Activity Planning		
Specific Challenges		n = 15
Initial challenges	"I just have difficulty setting up a schedule and following it. Again, I try to plan for it but want it to be perfect and then feel that it won't be." #14172	7 (46.7)
Intermediate challenges	"Because I worry a lot about timing and not having enough to get done what I want to, activity planning was a little bit of a struggle for me because I'd feel defeated if I wasn't able to do what I set out to do" #13248	8 (53.3)
Skill: Controlled Breathing		n = 12
Initial challenges	"just calming down enough to breath slower" #13125	4 (33.3)
Intermediate challenges	"Controlled breathing is good for preparation when I'm going into a stressful situation but if I am caught in an unexpected situation it is difficult because I'm scared people will notice it and that will make me feel more nervous." #12886	8 (66.6)
Skill: Graded Exposure		

Table 3. Cont.

Domain/Theme	Example Quote	Total Respondents n (%)
Specific Challenges		n = 50
Initial challenges	"I found I had a hard time coming up with a stepladder approach to my goals at first, and it took a lot of time thinking and reflecting to be able to come up with something I felt was practical." #13952	41 (82.0)
Intermediate challenges	"The hardest part of graded exposure was to move up the ladder. I find excuses to put things off once I get to the medium, hard, very hard." #14096	9 (18.0)
Skill: Relapse Prevention		
Specific Challenges		n = 17
Initial challenges	"It was tough to plan for possible lapses. I had never really thought about being prepared beforehand for something like that and always took a reactionary approach instead of being proactive." #14102	15 (88.2)
Intermediate challenges	"It is easy to plan and think about, but probably harder to enact and notice the signs, especially the ones that are simply thoughts." #12450	2 (11.8)

Cycle of Symptoms

When reflecting on the cycle of symptoms among thoughts, behaviours and physical sensations, clients' initial challenges (79.7%, 63/79) included difficulties with identifying their symptoms, triggers, or knowing where their cycle of symptoms started (e.g., "It took me some time to figure out what exactly my cycle of symptoms were" [#13289]). For intermediate difficulties (20.3%, 16/79), clients commented on challenges with making connections between different types of symptoms or with what steps to take to address their symptoms after they gained an understanding of how they were connected (e.g., "It was fairly easy to identify what my unhelpful thoughts, physical symptoms, and unhelpful behaviours are but a bit difficult to figure out which of one category led to another category" [#12815]).

Thought Challenging

Initial challenges related to thought challenging (57.8%, 52/90) included difficulties with identifying specific thoughts or finding it hard to recognize that the thought was unhelpful (e.g., "The biggest challenge I have at this point is clearly identifying the negative thought" [#12539]). Intermediate challenges (42.2%, 38/90) included difficulties coming up with alternative thoughts, believing the alternative thoughts, or taking action in response to the thought (e.g., "I had trouble coming up with figuring out how to do something helpful as doing any of these things didn't lessen the negative thoughts I had." [#13087]).

Activity Planning

Clients who had initial challenges (46.7%, 7/15) with activity planning described difficulties with identifying activities that they enjoy or challenges related to creating an activity schedule (e.g., "I have been thinking a lot about activity planning but I haven't brought myself to fill in the schedule. I think I have anxiety around writing plans down." [#13914]). Intermediate challenges (53.3%, 8/15) included barriers to engaging in the activities, creating schedules with too many activities, or difficulties with implementing the schedules they had created (e.g., "Trying to do too much and then feeling bad I could not do it all." [#14045]).

Controlled Breathing

Initial challenges for controlled breathing (33.3%, 4/12) included clients feeling uncomfortable about trying the breathing strategy or thinking that controlled breathing will not be helpful for them (e.g., "I'm unsure it will be very helpful for me." [#13312]). Among clients who experienced intermediate challenges (66.6%, 8/12) with controlled breathing, they described having difficulty applying controlled breathing to different situations, experiencing physiological symptoms as a result of controlled breathing (e.g., light-headedness), concerns about others noticing that they were using the strategy, or with the pace of the breathing.

Graded Exposure

Clients' initial challenges (82.0%, 41/50) with graded exposure included difficulties with identifying a target goal or behaviour that they would like to include in their exposure hierarchy or difficulty with breaking down their target goal or behaviour into smaller steps (e.g., "Coming up with something to work on." [#12563]). For clients who started working on graded exposure, intermediate challenges (18.0%, 9/50) included emotional difficulties (e.g., fear, anxiety) with progressing to the next step of their exposure stepladder, moving too quickly from one step to the next, being uncertain about when they should progress from one step to the next, or avoidance of the more challenging activities in their stepladder (e.g., "The hardest part of graded exposure is to move up the ladder. I find excuses to put things off once I get to the medium, hard, very hard." [#14096]).

Relapse Prevention

Clients who reported initial challenges (88.2%, 15/17) with relapse prevention described difficulties with identifying what their triggers or stressors were (e.g., "I have a hard time pinpointing what makes my symptoms flare up so find it challenging to know all that I'll do to keep from relapsing" [#13545]) or reported having difficulties getting started on their relapse prevention plan. Only two responses were identified as intermediate challenges (11.8%), with clients describing difficulties with recognizing a lapse once it had happened and knowing how to implement their relapse prevention plan (e.g., "It is easy to plan and think about, but probably harder to enact and notice the signs, especially the ones that are simply thoughts" [#12450]).

3.3.2. Generic Challenges across Lessons

Clients also described generic challenges that were similar across the five lessons that were unrelated to the specific skills described in each lesson, which accounted for between 24.5% (n = 37/151 for thought challenging) and 53.5% (n = 61/114 for managing physical symptoms) of clients' responses as to what they were experiencing related to each lesson. The following themes were generated based on clients' comments: finding the content/skills cognitively draining, finding the content/skills emotionally draining (e.g., client experienced an increase in symptoms or negative emotions when trying the skill), contextual challenges (e.g., challenges related to work, their health, relationships, or school), forgetting to use the skills when needed, limited time, and the client not being sufficiently familiar with the skill in order to use it (e.g., feeling like they need to review the content or practice more to understand the skill). Table 4 includes example quotes of generic quotes across the five lessons, as well as the proportion of responses for each type of challenge.

When reflecting on the lesson on the cycle of symptoms, the most common generic challenge was that it was emotionally draining (61.0%, 25/41). Clients noted how difficult it was to spend time paying attention to their symptoms and to recognise the impact their symptoms were having on their lives. For the lesson on thought challenging, the most common generic challenge was that the client forgot to use the skill (24.3%, 9/37) when experiencing unhelpful thoughts. Limited time (41.9%, 13/31) was the most common challenge for activity planning and clients described how they felt like they did not have sufficient time to add pleasant activities to their schedules. For controlled breathing, the most common generic challenge was forgetting to use the skill (60.0%, 18/30), with most clients recognizing in hindsight that controlled breathing would have been beneficial, but that they did not use it when they experienced symptoms of over-arousal. Similar to activity planning, clients commented on how limited time was a barrier to practicing graded exposure (30.8%, 8/26). Finally, contextual challenges or challenges related to stressors (e.g., illness, being on holidays, school) were identified as the most common generic challenge related to relapse prevention.

Table 4. Generic challenges per skill and no challenges.

Domain/theme	Example Quote	Cycle of Symptoms n (%)	Thought Challenging n (%)	Managing Physical Symptoms n (%)		Graded Exposure n (%)	Relapse Prevention n (%)	Across Lessons n (%)
				Activity Planning	Controlled Breathing			
Generic Challenges		n = 41	n = 37	n = 31	n = 30	n = 26	n = 21	n = 186
Cognitively Draining	"I feel my concentration is so poor that even concentrating on making the connections between my cycles of symptoms presents a challenge." #12886	5 (12.2)	3 (8.1)	6 (19.4)	4 (13.3)	4 (15.4)	4 (19.0)	26 (14.0)
Emotionally Draining	"It was difficult because it made me feel bad, like I was a bad person. It made me feel like, wow, I can see that I'm thinking unhelpful thoughts a lot but I don't know how to stop because I believe that they are true." #12431	25 (61.0)	6 (16.2)	1 (3.2)	0 (0)	3 (11.5)	0 (0)	35 (18.8)
Contextual challenges or challenges related to stressors	"I have been sick with a kidney infection the last two weeks and hospitalized." #13063	3 (7.3)	7 (18.9)	8 (25.8)	1 (3.3)	7 (26.9)	8 (38.1)	34 (18.3)
Forgot to use skills	"Just remembering to do it when having a difficult time" #13545	1 (2.4)	9 (24.3)	3 (9.7)	18 (60.0)	2 (7.7)	0 (0)	33 (17.7)
Limited Time	"Busy schedule lately has made some things difficult to keep up with." #13261	5 (12.2)	5 (13.5)	13 (41.9)	0 (0)	8 (30.8)	7 (33.3)	38 (20.4)
Not familiar with skill	"I just started the controlled breathing today so need to keep practicing it." #12539	2 (4.9)	7 (18.9)	0 (0)	7 (23.3)	2 (7.7)	2 (9.5)	20 (10.8)
No Challenges	"I didnt really have any difficulty. It just surprised me that all of the symptoms that i have, all connect in some way." #12773	n = 37	n = 24	n = 24	n = 42	n = 12	n = 18	n = 157

3.3.3. No Challenges

A subset of clients reported that they did not experience any difficulties with practicing the skills from the different lessons. This type of comment was more common for participants to make about controlled breathing (36.8%, 42/114), relapse prevention (31.6%, 18/57), the cycle of symptoms (24.0%, 37/154), and activity planning (21.1%, 24/114). It was less frequently made with reference to thought challenging (15.9%, 24/151), and graded exposure (13.8%, 12/57). Of note, clients who made a positive or neutral comment about the skills were also included within this category.

4. Discussion

In face-to-face CBT, homework exercises play an important role in facilitating skill acquisition with therapists encouraged to review homework with clients to reinforce the importance of these skills [4,5]. In ICBT, where therapist contact is often asynchronous, it can be more challenging to engage in homework review with clients. One solution is to encourage clients to complete HWRQs on a weekly basis to elicit feedback about any difficulties clients have with practicing CBT skills [7]. From both a clinical and training perspective, it is helpful to gain an understanding of the challenges clients experience as they learn about and implement different skills during ICBT. The main objectives of the current study were the following: to identify whether clients who reported difficulties in the HWRQ differed from those who did not on any demographic or clinical variables or measures of engagement, and to identify the frequency and nature of skill-specific, as well as generic, challenges that clients experienced.

4.1. Client Difficulties

Only 51.2% (154/301) of clients described difficulties they had with skills in the first HWRQ and the percentage of clients who completed this question decreased with each lesson (Lesson 2: 50.2%; Lesson 3: 37.9%; Lesson 4: 28.9%; Lesson 5: 18.9%). Clients who reported difficulties on the HWRQs were not significantly different from those who did not in terms of demographic characteristics or symptom severity at pre-treatment. However, clients who reported difficulties did appear to be more engaged with ICBT, based on lesson completion, number of logins, days spent in the course, and number of messages sent to therapists. A possible explanation for this finding is that clients who were open about their difficulties with skill development were able to receive tailored support from their therapists to help them overcome their initial, intermediate, or generic challenges. It appeared that completion of the question and sharing difficulties might be a good sign. In guided ICBT for depression, it has been found that clients who took responsibility for their treatment and were "doers" (i.e., provided specific examples of how they applied the content to their lives and addressed barriers during treatment) were more successful in ICBT [13]. A further conclusion might be that clients who withheld sharing difficulties and did not complete the question were less engaged with treatment overall and might need more direct prompting from their therapists to reveal any challenges they were experiencing.

Skill-specific challenges were most common for thought challenging (59.6%, 90/151), followed by graded exposure (57.5%, 50/87), and the cycle of symptoms (51.3%, 79/154). On the other hand, skill-specific challenges were less common for activity planning and controlled breathing exercises (13.2% and 10.5%, respectively), which might be due to clients' familiarity with these skills prior to ICBT (e.g., "Activity planning was something I do but without remembering why it was important" [#14032]). Challenges that clients shared were generally classified as being initial basic rudimentary challenges rather than more complex challenges. In general, it seems therapists need to be prepared to help clients most often with initial challenges related to the skills, rather than more complex challenges. Although a high percentage of respondents noted specific challenges with later lesson skills, such as graded exposure (87.5%, 50/87) and relapse prevention (29.8%, 17/57), the overall number of clients who responded to the question about difficulties with the skills decreased from lesson to lesson. This trend may be explained by lower engagement with the HWRQ over time or lower engagement with ICBT generally over time, since the decrease in number of responses to the question about difficulties seemed to parallel lesson completion.

In addition to skill-specific challenges, clients described generic challenges consistently across skill areas (i.e., cycle of symptoms: 26.6%, thought challenging: 24.4%, activity planning: 27.2%, graded exposure: 29.9%, and relapse prevention: 36.8%). Generic challenges included difficulties with limited time, finding the content/skill emotionally draining, contextual challenges or challenges related to stressors, forgetting to use the skill, finding the content/skill cognitively draining, and lack of familiarity with the skill. Therapists should be mindful that based on the findings of this study, approximately one-quarter of clients would experience at least one of these generic challenges in any given lesson. The most common generic reasons did appear to change over time (cycle of symptoms: emotionally draining; thought challenging and controlled breathing: forgetting to use skill; activity planning, graded exposure, and relapse prevention: limited time), which could be helpful for therapists to know. Of note, limited time was the most common difficulty across lessons and was included in 20.4% ($n = 38$) of responses that were categorized as generic challenges. In other online psychological interventions, clients have shared similar concerns about limited time and external factors competing for their time [14]. While the reasons for treatment non-adherence in ICBT are not well understood, it is possible that clients' difficulties with specific skills contributed to their likelihood of dropping out, especially in cases where therapist contact was asynchronous. By regularly including statements to normalize clients' emotional difficulties with the skills, as well as offering encouragement for skills practice, therapists may help clients manage many of these emotional and practical challenges. Further, the challenges articulated by clients provided suggestions for how the intervention lessons, the automated communications around the lessons, and the support provided alongside them could be improved. For example, in the first lesson, more content may be needed to help clients understand their own cycle of symptoms and triggers, as well as information to normalise that this task could be emotionally draining. For the lesson on thought challenging, more prompts could be provided to help clients identify their thoughts, as well as reminders of the importance of utilizing thought challenging when they noticed an unhelpful thought. Comments about limited time were common for activity planning, graded exposure, and relapse prevention, so it might be helpful to bolster the rationale for these skills in the lesson content so that clients can recognize the importance of integrating the skills in their schedules.

In general, it was interesting to note that the challenges that clients reported in ICBT were the same types of challenges that were described in face-to-face CBT [15], although description of challenges in face-to-face CBT were also not commonly systematically studied [16,17]. In a study of clients experiencing psychosis, common homework challenges included low motivation, poor memory, difficulties understanding worksheets, and perceived relevance and benefits of completing the homework [16]. In another study, clients with depression were interviewed about their experiences with CBT in general and completing homework was the main aspect of treatment that clients described negatively, due to both emotional and practical reasons [15]. Clients described a fear of failure when completing homework, worry about doing it incorrectly, and difficulties completing worksheets on the cycle of symptoms and thought monitoring/challenging. These difficulties aligned with the initial difficulties described by clients for the cycle of symptoms and thought challenging in the current study.

Within the current study, 61.0% (25/41) of clients who reported generic difficulties with the cycle of symptoms found that creating a personal formulation of their symptoms was emotionally draining. This finding appeared consistent with how some clients experience case formulation in face-to-face CBT [18], which typically involves the client and therapist working collaboratively to identify interrelationships between symptom types [19]. In one study, clients were interviewed about their experiences with case formulation after completing CBT and four themes emerged: formulation led to greater understanding of problems, formulation helped clients feel understood and accepted, formulation led to an emotional shift, and formulation helped clients move forward [18]. A subtheme emerged within the theme of an emotional shift, whereby some clients noted that the formulation process resulted in distress because of increased awareness of their problems. One recommendation that followed from our study was that therapists should most likely forewarn clients that they might experience a temporary increase in distress or symptoms after working through their personal formulation, as normalization of clients' feelings plays an important role in the formulation [20].

A promising finding from our study was that ICBT clients' difficulties were similar to those reported in face-to-face CBT [15–18]. Clients did not report any difficulties that seemed specific to ICBT, which may suggest that HW engagement and skill development could be managed well within an online setting. When training therapists in ICBT, it is useful for them to know that clients will encounter similar barriers and challenges when completing HW as they do in face-to-face CBT.

4.2. Limitations and Future Directions

While this study provided a summary of clients' experiences learning about and implementing common CBT skills, it did not include information about clients' experiences with completing the HWRQs. Given that there was not any evidence for HWRQs improving symptoms of depression and anxiety [7], it was possible that some clients either did not find them helpful or found them aversive to complete, which may help explain low completion of the HWRQs overall. Future studies of HWRQs should include questions about clients' experiences with completing HWRQs. Another limitation of this study was the low completion rate of the HWRQs, with the percentage of clients completing the question about difficulties with the skills decreasing from lesson to lesson. We were unable to conclude whether the lower response rate to later questions was a result of fewer clients experiencing difficulties in later lessons or if clients had become disengaged with the HWRQ over time. It was also not possible to know whether clients who did not complete HWRQ had similar experiences to those who did in terms of specific and generic challenges. A potential solution is to make the HWRQs mandatory for clients to complete to proceed with the next ICBT lesson, which would help to ensure that, at least for clients who continue with treatment, information is collected from a larger sample of clients.

4.3. Strengths

This study expands on the findings of a published factorial trial examining the impact of HWRQs on symptoms of depression and anxiety [7]. Although it is well documented that HW is an integral component of CBT [5,21], little is known about clients' experiences completing homework during ICBT. The current study provides insight into clients' experiences with each core skill in the ICBT course, and, by systematically asking all clients about their challenges with HW exercises, we were able to include responses from clients who might not have otherwise discussed these concerns in their messages to therapists. While the findings from the current study do not provide a complete picture of client difficulties, this study provides more information on client difficulties than previously available in the literature. Findings about skill-specific and generic challenges can help inform clinical practice, especially when training therapists in ICBT.

5. Conclusions

This qualitative study contributes to the literature by improving our understanding of clients' difficulties with skill acquisition during ICBT. In this study, clients described a combination of skill-specific challenges and generic challenges across skills. Specific challenges were most common when describing experiences with thought challenging and graded exposure and were often associated with the early stages of skills development (i.e., identifying unhelpful thoughts or creating an exposure hierarchy). Activity planning and controlled breathing were associated with the fewest challenges. Generic challenges were fairly consistent across skill areas, with limited time being the most commonly reported challenge across skills. The findings of this study suggest that those who completed the difficulty questions were more engaged with ICBT, so completion of this question may also be a useful measure of engagement. This study helps therapists understand the most common generic challenges that clients encounter, as well as when they occur during treatment. When therapists are aware of the common challenges that clients encounter, they are better prepared to tailor their messages to both normalise client difficulties and offer suggestions for how to overcome barriers clients experience while completing homework exercises.

Author Contributions: Conceptualization, V.P., H.H. and M.N.; methodology, V.P., H.H.; software, A.W., M.N.; validation, V.P., A.W. and R.S.; formal analysis, V.P., A.W.; investigation, V.P., A.W. and M.N.; resources, M.N., H.H.; data curation, A.W.; writing—original draft preparation, V.P., A.W. and H.H.; writing—review and editing, V.P., R.S., K.O., N.T., B.D. and H.H.; visualization, V.P., A.W.; supervision, V.P., M.N. and H.H.; project administration, V.P., M.N. and H.H.; funding acquisition, H.H., M.N. All authors have read and agreed to the published version of the manuscript.

Funding: This research was funded by the Canadian Institute of Health Research, grant number 152917. The Online Therapy Unit's service delivery is funded by the Saskatchewan Ministry of Health.

Institutional Review Board Statement: The study was conducted in accordance with the Declaration of Helsinki, and approved by the Institutional Review Board of the University of Regina (study ID number: 2019-038; approved 4 April 2019).

Informed Consent Statement: Informed consent was obtained from all subjects involved in the study.

Data Availability Statement: Not applicable.

Acknowledgments: The authors wish to thank the clients, community advisors, screeners, therapists, research staff, students, and web developers associated with the Online Therapy Unit at the University of Regina, including the therapists from the Saskatchewan Health Authority who delivered therapy in this trial.

Conflicts of Interest: The authors declare no conflict of interest. The funders had no role in the design of the study; in the collection, analyses, or interpretation of data; in the writing of the manuscript, or in the decision to publish the results.

References

1. Cuijpers, P.; Cristea, I.A.; Karyotaki, E.; Reijnders, M.; Huibers, M.J.H. How effective are cognitive behavior therapies for major depression and anxiety disorders? A meta-analytic update of the evidence. *World Psychiatry* **2016**, *15*, 245–258. [CrossRef]
2. Andersson, G. Internet-delivered psychological treatments. *Annu. Rev. Clin. Psychol.* **2016**, *12*, 157–179. [CrossRef] [PubMed]
3. Etzelmueller, A.; Vis, C.; Karyotaki, E.; Baumeister, H.; Titov, N.; Berking, M.; Cuijpers, P.; Riper, H.; Ebert, D.D. Effects of Internet-based cognitive behavioral therapy for depression and anxiety: Systematic review and meta-analysis. *J. Med. Internet Res.* **2020**, *22*, e18100. [CrossRef] [PubMed]
4. Kazantzis, N.; Arntz, A.R.; Borkovec, T.; Holmes, E.A.; Wade, T. Unresolved issues regarding homework assignments in cognitive and behavioural therapies: An expert panel discussion at AACBT. *Behav. Change* **2010**, *27*, 119–129. [CrossRef]
5. Kazantzis, N.; Whittington, C.; Zelencich, L.; Kyrios, M.; Norton, P.J.; Hofmann, S.G. Quantity and quality of homework compliance: A meta-analysis of relations with outcome in cognitive behavior therapy. *Behav. Ther.* **2016**, *47*, 755–772. [CrossRef] [PubMed]
6. Bryant, M.J.; Simons, A.D.; Thase, M.E. Therapist skill and patient variables in homework compliance: Controlling an uncontrolled variable in cognitive therapy outcome research. *Cogn. Ther. Res.* **1999**, *23*, 381–389. [CrossRef]
7. Hadjistavropoulos, H.D.; Peynenburg, V.; Thiessen, D.L.; Nugent, M.; Adlam, K.; Owens, K.M.B.; Karin, E.; Dear, B.F.; Titov, N. A pragmatic factorial randomized controlled trial of transdiagnostic internet-delivered cognitive behavioral therapy: Exploring benefits of homework reflection questionnaires and twice-weekly therapist support. *Internet Interv.* **2020**, *22*, 100357. [CrossRef] [PubMed]
8. Soucy, J.; Hadjistavropoulos, H.; Pugh, N.; Dear, B.; Titov, N. What are clients asking their therapist during therapist-assisted Internet-delivered cognitive behaviour therapy? A content analysis of client questions. *Behav. Cogn. Psychother.* **2019**, *47*, 407–420. [CrossRef]
9. Titov, N.; Dear, B.F.; Staples, L.G.; Terides, M.D.; Karine, E.; Sheehan, J.; McEvoy, P.M. Disorder-specific versus transdiagnostic and clinician-guided versus self-guided treatment for major depressive disorder and comorbid anxiety disorders: A randomized controlled trial. *J. Anxiety Disord.* **2015**, *35*, 88–102. [CrossRef]
10. Kroenke, K.; Spitzer, R.L.; Williams, J.B. The PHQ-9: Validity of a brief depression severity measure. *J. Gen. Intern. Med.* **2001**, *16*, 606–613. [CrossRef]
11. Spitzer, R.L.; Kroenke, K.; Williams, J.B.; Lowe, B. A brief measure for assessing generalized anxiety disorder: The GAD-7. *Arch. Intern. Med.* **2006**, *166*, 1092–1097. [CrossRef] [PubMed]
12. Hsieh, H.; Shannon, S.E. Three approaches to qualitative content analysis. *Qual. Health Res.* **2005**, *15*, 1277–1288. [CrossRef] [PubMed]
13. Bendelin, N.; Hesser, H.; Dahl, J.; Carlbring, P.; Nelson, K.Z.; Andersson, G. Experiences of guided Internet-based cognitive-behavioural treatment for depression: A qualitative study. *BMC Psychiatry* **2011**, *11*, 107. [CrossRef] [PubMed]
14. Donkin, L.; Glozier, N. Motivators and motivations to persist with online psychological interventions: A qualitative study of treatment completers. *J. Med. Internet Res.* **2012**, *14*, e91. [CrossRef] [PubMed]
15. Barnes, M.; Sherlock, S.; Thomas, L.; Kessler, D.; Kuyken, W.; Owen-Smith, A.; Lewis, G.; Wiles, N.; Turner, K. No pain, no gain: Depressed clients' experiences of cognitive behavioural therapy. *Br. J. Clin. Psychol.* **2013**, *52*, 347–364. [CrossRef] [PubMed]
16. Dunn, H.; Morrison, A.; Bentall, R. Participants' experiences of homework tasks in cognitive behavioural therapy for psychosis: A qualitative analysis. *Clin. Psychol. Psychother.* **2002**, *9*, 361–369. [CrossRef]
17. Messari, S.; Hallam, R. CBT for psychosis: A qualitative analysis of clients' experiences. *Br. J. Clin. Psychol.* **2003**, *42*, 171–188. [CrossRef]

18. Redhead, S.; Johnstone, L.; Nightingale, J. Clients' experiences of formulation in cognitive behaviour therapy. *Psychol. Psychother.* **2015**, *88*, 453–467. [CrossRef]
19. Kuyken, W.; Padesky, C.A.; Dudley, R. *Collaborative Case Conceptualization*; The Guilford Press: New York, NY, USA, 2009.
20. Leeming, D.; Boyle, M.; MacDonald, J. Accountin? for psychological problems: How user-friendly is formulation? *Clin. Psychol. Forum* **2009**, *200*, 12–15.
21. Kazantzis, N.; Brownfield, N.R.; Mosely, L.; Usatoff, A.S.; Flighty, A.J. Homework in cognitive behavioral therapy: A systematic review of adherence assessment in anxiety and depression (2011–2016). *Psychiatr. Clin. North Am.* **2017**, *40*, 625–639. [CrossRef] [PubMed]

Journal of
Clinical Medicine

MDPI

Systematic Review

The Effects of Virtual Reality in Targeting Transdiagnostic Factors for Mental Health: A Systematic Review of the Literature

Valentina Gardini [1], Giorgia Gamberini [1], Sophia Müller [2], Silvana Grandi [1] and Elena Tomba [1,*]

[1] Department of Psychology, University of Bologna, 40127 Bologna, Italy
[2] Institute for Psychology, Department of Clinical Psychology, University of Bern, 3012 Bern, Switzerland
* Correspondence: elena.tomba@unibo.it

Abstract: Virtual reality (VR) was found to be effective in the treatment of several specific psychopathologies. However, the effects of VR-based interventions beyond the disorder-specific approach and their ability to improve transdiagnostic factors of mental disorders are unknown. This PRISMA systematic review was conducted using databases PubMed and PsycINFO, searching articles published between 2010 and September 2022. Keywords "emotion regulation", "cognitive reappraisal", "avoidance", "impulsivity", "aggression", and "disinhibition" were combined with "virtual reality" to retrieve studies showing the effects of VR-based interventions on these transdiagnostic factors. 29 experimental studies and seven case-studies were selected. A total of 23 considered avoidance, eight dealt with emotion regulation, three concerned aggression, two addressed impulsivity, two dealt with cognitive reappraisal, and none examined disinhibition. Most of the studies included anxiety disorder patients (n = 15), especially with specific phobias (n = 8) and social anxiety disorder (n = 4). VR managed to improve all transdiagnostic factors, with results often maintained at follow-ups (n = 21 studies; range: 1–12 months) and similar to traditional interventions (e.g., cognitive-behavioral therapy). Exploring the transdiagnostic potential of VR may help to reduce costs and improve applicability in clinical psychology. While results were promising, further studies are needed for aggression, impulsivity and cognitive reappraisal, especially including follow-ups, comparisons with first-line treatments, and understudied clinical populations.

Keywords: virtual reality; transdiagnostic factors; avoidance; emotion regulation; cognitive reappraisal; aggression; impulsivity

Citation: Gardini, V.; Gamberini, G.; Müller, S.; Grandi, S.; Tomba, E. The Effects of Virtual Reality in Targeting Transdiagnostic Factors for Mental Health: A Systematic Review of the Literature. *J. Clin. Med.* **2022**, *11*, 6463. https://doi.org/10.3390/jcm11216463

Academic Editor: Stéphane Bouchard

Received: 23 September 2022
Accepted: 29 October 2022
Published: 31 October 2022

1. Introduction

In recent years, virtual reality (VR) has emerged as a new tool to assist clinicians in the treatment of several psychiatric disorders, especially in anxiety, psychotic, substance-related, and eating disorders [1,2] because of its ability to provide a systematic and controlled exposure therapy without the complications of in vivo exposure [3]. Moreover, VR can also be used in association with cognitive-behavioral treatments (CBT) and other psychotherapeutic interventions such as mindfulness-based cognitive therapy [4] and dialectical behavioral therapy [5] that are designed to improve existing treatment protocols for several psychiatric disorders (e.g., anxiety disorders, eating disorders, substance-use disorders, psychosis, etc.) [1].

Nonetheless, several downsides in relation to VR have also been reported that make its application difficult in the clinical setting, such as its high cost [6] and the need to have different software for specifically tackling different psychiatric disorders. Indeed, the disorder-specific approach that has been predominantly used to design VR software and interventions is also the approach that is most widely used for traditional CBT. CBT interventions, in fact, are usually designed for the treatment of one single disorder at a time [7–9], since they are based on assumptions coming from the conventional nosological systems, such as the DSM-5 and the ICD-10 [10,11]. These diagnostic systems view psychopathologies as distinct, independent, and categorical constructs, with patients either meeting or not the diagnostic criteria for a specific psychiatric disorder [12].

Things, however, are much more complicated than this in the clinical experience, where often a person can present more than one psychiatric disorder in comorbidity.

Recently, clinical research in fact turned to the transdiagnostic model to explore mental disorders and overcome the limits of a disorder-specific approach [13]. The transdiagnostic framework emphasizes in particular that mental health disorders share common underlying psychological factors, or transdiagnostic factors [14], which when targeted simultaneously may allow for the treatment of both the main disorder and its comorbidities [9,15]. Thus far, while the literature has no accordance about a shared list of transdiagnostic factors that can cause and maintain several psychological disorders, the internalizing-externalizing model of psychopathology is one of the most widely accepted transdiagnostic models [16]. In the model, transdiagnostic factors are divided into two main categories: internalizing factors, which include several over-inhibited or internally-focused symptoms (e.g., avoidance, negative emotions, social withdrawal, somatic complaints, etc.), and externalizing factors, which in turn include disinhibited or externally-focused behavioral symptoms (e.g., aggression, impulsivity, disinhibition, conduct problems, delinquent behavior, oppositionality, hyperactivity, attention problems, etc.). Subsequently, transdiagnostic interventions based on CBT therapy have been developed to target these specific internalizing and externalizing transdiagnostic factors such as the unified protocol, the shared mechanisms treatments, and transdiagnostic cognitive-behavioral therapy [17]. More specifically, the Unified Protocol for Transdiagnostic Treatment of Emotional Disorders [18] is the most widely studied evidence-based protocol [19], which proved to be effective for the treatment of anxiety and mood disorders [20,21], with results similar to disorder-specific treatments [22,23].

Since many authors agree that transdiagnostic treatments would be more advantageous than disorder-specific treatments for their ability to increase cost efficiency [9,24], if transposed to the development of VR software the transdiagnostic approach might be able to also overcome the limits (in terms of costs and training) of this technology in the field of clinical psychology.

In order to understand the transdiagnostic potential of VR, this systematic review of the literature aims to explore whether some of the main internalizing and externalizing transdiagnostic factors for mental health disorders [12,14] can be improved by VR-based treatments.

2. Materials and Methods

2.1. Protocol and Search Strategy

This systematic review has been conducted accordingly to the Preferred Reporting Items for Systematic Reviews (PRISMA) criteria guidelines [25] and was not registered on a public repository. Two databases (PubMed and PsycINFO) were used to retrieve articles for the present review: authors selected six keywords to identify some of the main internalizing and externalizing transdiagnostic factors for mental health disorders [12,14]: "avoidance", "aggression", "disinhibition", "emotion regulation", "reappraisal", and "impulsivity". In particular, due to the lack of a set list of transdiagnostic factors in the literature, the authors decided to select clinically relevant transdiagnostic factors that have been found to be present and play a role in many psychopathologies. For example, different types of avoidance (e.g., avoidance behaviors, social avoidance, experiential avoidance, cognitive avoidance, etc.) characterize a wide variety of mental health disorders, such as mood and anxiety disorders, post-traumatic stress disorders (PTSD), psychotic disorders, and obsessive-compulsive disorders [26–29]. Similarly, difficulties in using emotion regulation strategies and cognitive reappraisal are linked to the maintenance and development of several psychopathologies and represent some of the main targets of transdiagnostic CBT-based treatments [15,30–32]. Finally, aggressive behaviors, impulsivity, and disinhibition can also be found in diagnostic criteria and clinical presentations of different psychiatric diagnoses and especially externalizing disorders (e.g., substance-use disorders, antisocial personality disorder, attention-deficit-hyperactivity disorder, etc.) [10–12,33–36].

All of the keywords identifying these transdiagnostic factors were combined with the keyword "virtual reality" using the Boolean operator "AND".

During the database search, results were filtered for English and Italian language, journal articles, clinical trials (PubMed), and academic journals (PsycINFO). With regard to publication dates, the authors selected a range between 2010 and September 2022. Duplicate articles generated across databases were identified and excluded.

Titles and abstracts were screened by two authors (G.G., S.M.) in order to asses which ones would fulfill the aforementioned aims of the review. Articles that appeared potentially eligible for the review were retrieved and reviewed by two authors (V.G., G.G.), who independently assessed each of the full reports, arriving at a consensus regarding eligibility. When disagreements between the two authors arose, multiple rounds of full-text revision and discussions were undertaken until consensus was reached, with the involvement of a third author (E.T.) when needed.

A visual representation of the article selection process is presented in the PRISMA flow diagram (Figure 1) below.

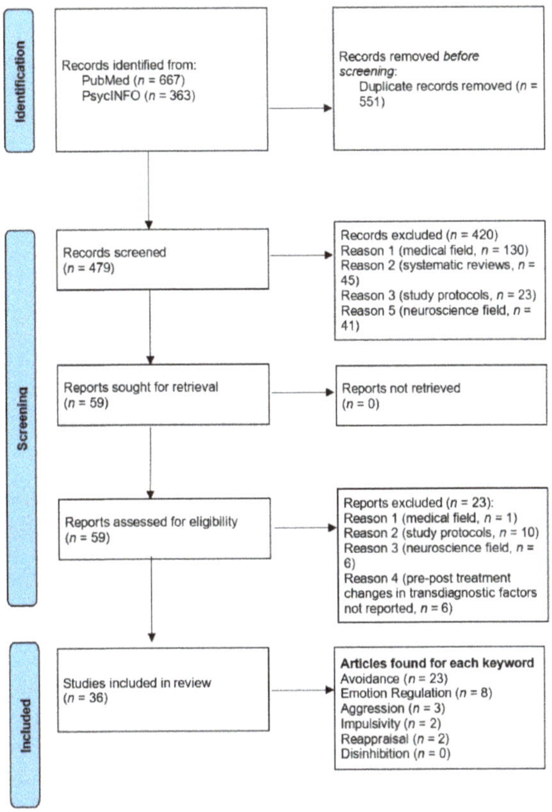

Figure 1. PRISMA flow diagram summarizing the article selection process [25].

2.2. Eligibility Criteria

Articles were considered eligible for the review if they were randomized controlled trials (RCTs), longitudinal studies, or case studies evaluating changes in patients' levels of the considered transdiagnostic factors between pre- and post- VR-based intervention. Study protocols, dissertations, systematic and non-systematic reviews, meta-analyses, medical or neuroscience studies and books (or book chapters) were excluded from the research. More information about inclusion and exclusion criteria for articles selection are summarized in the Population, Intervention, Comparison, Outcomes and Study (PICOS) table below (Table 1) [37].

Table 1. Population, Intervention, Comparison, Outcomes and Study (PICOS) table for inclusion and exclusion criteria [37].

PICOS	Inclusion Criteria	Exclusion Criteria
Patients	• Patients with mental health disorders • Individuals from the general population	• Individuals with physical diseases, hospitalized due to physical conditions or presenting brain damage
Intervention	Any intervention that included the use of Virtual Reality technologies	• Interventions that did not include the use of Virtual Reality • Neuroscience studies
Control Group	Any control group or absence of a control group	None
Outcome	Any type of change in patients' levels of emotion regulation, avoidance, impulsivity, aggression, reappraisal, and disinhibition.	None
Study Design	• Longitudinal studies (pre-post intervention) • Randomized and non-randomized controlled trials • Case studies	• Study protocols • Systematic and non-systematic reviews • Meta-analyses • Medical or neuroscience studies • Books (or book chapters)

2.3. Data Extraction

Following the database search, duplicate articles generated across the two databases (PubMed and PsycINFO) were selected and removed. The authors then proceeded to screen titles and abstracts of the articles and excluded those which did not seem relevant to the keywords and aims listed above. All of the remaining articles were subsequently read thoroughly in order to examine whether changes in the aforementioned transdiagnostic factors following a VR-based intervention were assessed between pre- and post- treatment. When present, data regarding follow-ups were also collected. Data extraction was performed independently by two of the authors (G.G. and V.G.). The authors followed the PICOS pre-set extraction criteria (see Table 1) and systematically summarized the relevant data of each article in a separate table (Table S1).

2.4. Quality and Risk of Bias Assessment

Quality and risk of bias assessment was conducted using a customized checklist retrieved from the National Institutes of Mental Health's tool (2021) [38] on experimental articles only, while this assessment was not conducted on case studies. See Table S2 for criteria.

3. Results

3.1. Results of Literature Search

A total of 1030 articles were retrieved from PubMed and PsycINFO. After the removal of 551 duplicates (53.50%) and the exclusion of 420 articles (40.78%) (see Figure 1), a total of 59 articles (5.73%) were considered potentially eligible for the review. After full-text screening of the articles, 36 articles (3.50%; *n* = 29 experimental studies and *n* = 7 case studies) were finally included in the review.

The number of studies taken into consideration for each transdiagnostic factor varied. Avoidance was the most studied transdiagnostic factor found in 23 articles (63.89%) (*n* = 19 experimental studies and *n* = 4 case studies) [39–61], followed by emotion regulation, which was found in eight articles (22.22%; *n* = 7 experimental studies and *n* = 1 case study) [62–69]; aggression, which was found in three experimental studies (8.33%) [70–72]; impulsivity, which was found in two studies (5.56%; *n* = 1 experimental study and *n* = 1 case study) [71,73]; and cognitive reappraisal, which was found in two studies (5.56%; *n* = 1 experimental study and *n* = 1 case study) [63,74]. No studies were found for the transdiagnostic factor of disinhibition. Moreover, two studies took into consideration two transdiagnostic factors simultaneously: emotion regulation and reappraisal [63], and aggression and impulsivity [71].

3.2. Characteristics of the Studies

Among the 36 articles that were selected for the review, different sample sizes were used. Sixteen experimental studies (44.44%) had less than 50 participants [40,44,45,47,48,50,51,54,58,60,62,63,66–68,72], nine (25%) included between 50 and 100 participants [39,46,49,53,55,59,64,69,70], and only a few (*n* = 4, 11.11%) had a sample size larger than 100 participants [43,52,56,71]. Finally, seven (19.44%) articles were multiple or single case studies including between one and eight participants [41,42,57,61,65,73,74].

In terms of research design, only 23 out of 36 studies (63.89%) were controlled studies, of which 19 were randomized controlled trials (RCTs) (82.61%) [39,43,45,46,48–51,53–56,59,60,63,64,66,68,71] and four (17.39%) were non-randomized controlled studies [47,67,69,70]. Six studies out of 36 (16.67%) were uncontrolled clinical trials [40,44,52,58,62,72], and seven (19.44%) were case studies [41,42,57,61,65,73,74]. A total of 21 studies (58.33%) also included a follow-up (ranging from 1 to 12 months) [39,42–47,49,51,54–56,58–61,63,64,71–73].

Regarding sociodemographic characteristics of the samples in the reviewed studies, the age range went from young children to adults (around 8 to 51 years of age). However, the great majority of the studies were carried out on adult samples between ~19 and 51 years of age (*n* = 31, 86.11%), with only two studies (5.56%) carried out on children between ~8 and 10 years of age [42,69], and three (8.33%) on adolescents between ~12 and 15 [64,68,74] Moreover, mixed gender was predominant in the studies (*n* = 23; 36.11%), with some exceptions: four studies (11.11%) had an all-male sample [41,70,72,74], and four (11.11%) had an all-female sample [57,61,65,73]. Moreover, five studies (13.89%) did not clearly state the participants' gender [44,49,53,60,71].

Lastly, regarding the kind of VR technology that was used among all 36 studies, 28 (77.78%) used immersive VR [39–46,48–52,54–56,58–62,64–68,70,71], 3 (8.33%) Cave Automatic Virtual Environment (CAVE) [53,69,73], and only five (13.89%) used non-immersive VR technology [47,57,63,72,74]. See Table S1 for characteristics of the studies and the specific contents, data and results of the selected papers.

3.3. Clinical and Non-Clinical Populations Included in the Studies

The majority of the studies (*n* = 17; 47.22%) carried out on adults focused on clinical populations. Patients with anxiety disorders were the most frequent population involved in the studies (*n* = 15, 41.67%), of which eight (22.22%) included patients with specific phobia [41,44,45,47,54,55,60,61], four (11.11%) included patients with social anxiety disorder (SAD) [39,46,49,59], and three (8.33%) included patients with panic disorder and agoraphobia [50,51,53]. Patients with PTSD [40,52,72] and psychotic disorders [43,56,58] were the second most found clinical populations, appearing in three (8.33%) studies each. Other less studied clinical populations included eating disorders (*n* = 1, 2.78%) [57], borderline personality disorders (*n* = 1, 2.78%) [54], OCD (*n* = 1, 2.78%) [73] and forensic patients (*n* = 1, 2.78%) [71]. Four (11.11%) studies, instead, were carried out on the general population or on healthy adults [62,63,67,70].

In the studies carried out on children (n = 2, 5.56%), one (2.78%) was carried out on children with specific phobias (dogs) [42] and one (2.78%) on children with autism spectrum disorder [69]. Adolescent samples in the studies, instead, were taken from the general population (n = 2, 5.56%) [64,68] or involved teens with acute anxiety, suicidal thoughts and low mood [74] (see Table S1 for additional details of each study).

3.4. Quality and Risk of Bias Assessment

Quality and risk of bias assessment was performed only on experimental studies. As shown in Table S3, the quality of the selected 29 experimental studies widely differed. In particular, 15 (51.72%) were ranked as having a strong quality [39,43,45,46,51,53–56,58–60,64,71,72], eight (27.59%) were ranked as having moderate quality [44,47–49,52,66,68,70], and six (20.69%) were ranked as weak [40,50,62,63,67,69]. A methodological issue often found throughout the reviewed studies was the absence of a follow-up: 11 (37.93%) out of the 29 experimental studies did not include follow-up for the selected outcomes [40,48,50,52,53,62,66–70].

3.5. Results about the Effects of Virtual Reality-Based Interventions on Transdiagnostic Factors

3.5.1. Avoidance

The first result that emerged from the 23 studies (63.89%) (n = 19 experimental studies and n = 4 case studies) [39–61] taking into consideration the transdiagnostic factor of "avoidance" was the heterogeneity of the different types of avoidance considered. More specifically, in the majority of the studies (n = 13; 56.52%) [41,42,44–47,50–52,54,55,60,61], VR was used to decrease the levels of behavioral avoidance (that is, the individual act of not entering or prematurely leaving a fear-evoking or distressing situation or stimulus) [25] in a wide variety of clinical and non-clinical populations.

Virtual reality exposure treatment (VRET) in particular appeared to be a useful form of intervention to reduce behavioral avoidance in adults with specific phobias (such as flying, driving, going to the dentist, spiders) [41,44,45,54,55,60,61], social anxiety disorder [46], panic disorder with agoraphobia [50,51], and PTSD [52], with results always maintained or even improved [55] over time when a follow-up was present [46,47,51,54,60]. The duration of follow-ups considered spanned between one month and a year. This same technique was also effective in reducing behavioral avoidance in children with a phobia of dogs, with results maintained at a one month follow-up [42]. When compared to other forms of treatment or control conditions, VRET turned out to be more effective than providing informative pamphlets to patients with dental phobia [45] and equally as effective as in-vivo exposure for patients with social anxiety disorder [46] or specific phobias [54]. When traditional forms of psychological therapy were added to VR, such as cognitive therapy [50,51], no additional improvement was found compared to using VR alone. Only in one study were greater changes in behavioral avoidance found in a group of patients with specific phobias (spiders) undergoing one-session treatment (a form of gradated and repeated systematic exposures to the feared stimuli) compared to VRET [55].

Promising results also came from the application of VR-based treatments for the improvement of social avoidance, which is another type of avoidance similar to behavioral avoidance but specific to social situations. This transdiagnostic factor was taken into consideration in six (26.09%) studies, where it was effectively reduced by VR-based treatments in patients with social anxiety disorder [39,46,49,59] and with psychosis [58,59]. Once again, results were maintained over time for both populations (follow-ups range: 3-weeks to 12 months). The combination of VR with cognitive-behavioral therapy (VR-CBT) was also effective in reducing social avoidance more than a waiting list condition in patients with psychosis, with results maintained at six months follow-up [56] and with no differences when compared to traditional CBT in patients with fear of public speaking [59]. Regarding comparisons between VRET and in-vivo exposure, VRET was more effective than the latter in reducing social avoidance in SAD patients and more practical according to therapists in one study [40], but less effective in another [46].

Finally, fewer but promising results were found for the ability of VR-based treatment to improve other types of avoidance, such as agoraphobic avoidance in patients with psychosis [43] or panic disorder with agoraphobia [53], cognitive avoidance in city violence crime victims with PTSD or acute stress disorder [40], alcohol-approach avoidance in patients with substance-use disorder [48], and food avoidance in a patient with bulimia nervosa [57] (see Table S1 for additional details of each study).

3.5.2. Emotion Regulation

Similarly to avoidance, emotion regulation was another transdiagnostic factor that was operationalized in several different ways in the studies. Across the eight articles ($n = 7$ experimental studies and $n = 1$ case study) [62–69] that took into consideration this factor, different dimensions of emotion regulation and emotion regulation strategies were considered.

Three studies [62,66,68] focused on the ability of VR to help regulating emotions by inducing relaxation both in the general population adults [62,66] and adolescents [68]. Interestingly, the characteristics of the VR scenarios seemed to increase this effect. For example, natural VR scenes were shown to increase relaxation more than to control (empty indoor classrooms) VR scenes [62]. The same was seen for VR scenarios where an avatar resembling the participant helped adolescents to regulate their emotions and achieve relaxation more than neutral avatars [68]. VR also produced improvements in relaxation for patients with generalized anxiety disorder when combined with a mindfulness-based intervention [66]. Unfortunately, these studies did not include a control group or a follow-up.

A promising effect of VR in improving emotion expression and regulation was also found in children with autism spectrum disorders undergoing VR training [69], with results better than the waiting list condition although no follow up was included. Healthy adults going through reappraisal-based training in a VR environment also managed to lower the emotional ratings they associated with negative images, showing that VR training can indeed have an impact on emotion regulation. This has been proved also by a case report finding that mindfulness exercises performed in VR reduced negative emotions in a patient with borderline personality disorder and substance use disorder [65].

Moreover, when compared or combined with more traditional forms of psychological interventions, VR also produced some promising results in improving emotion regulation and emotion regulation strategies. The combination of emotion regulation training with risk reduction interventions in VR managed to reduce general population adolescents' levels of emotional awareness, emotional self-efficacy, emotion regulation strategies and affect regulation, with results often comparable or even better than those obtained by a group using role-playing instead of VR training, and maintained at three-months follow-up [64]. Although VR in combination with a mindfulness-based intervention (MBI + VR) resulted in being as effective as the mindfulness-based intervention alone (MBI) in improving several emotion regulation strategies (i.e., the ability to act with awareness, to control impulses, to self-regulate, to listen to their own body, to describe internal experiences and levels of emotional clarity) in adults with general anxiety disorder [66], MBI + VR even achieved additional improvements in teaching patients to not judge their inner experiences (e.g., thoughts, emotions) and to concentrate even when experiencing negative emotions. Similarly, a VR cognitive-bias modification of interpretations (VR-CBM-I) managed to reduce the emotional response to a stressor more and the resulting sadness more than the standard protocol (CBM-I) [67] (see Table S1 for additional details of each study).

3.5.3. Aggression

Regarding the transdiagnostic factor of aggression, different results were found in three experimental studies carried out in both clinical and general population samples.

The first result showed that VR reduced aggressive behaviors while driving in a sample of war veterans with PTSD, driving anxiety and/or aggression problems, and also helped them to increase their skill training. Even if they rated the virtual experience as not very realistic, the results were maintained at a one-month follow-up [72].

In the second article, using a VR Anger Exposure Training, patients' levels of anger and aggression after experiencing conflict situations with a friend or a stranger in the virtual environment decreased. In particular, anger scores decreased, especially after anger management exercises when compared to anger expression exercises, regardless if the other person was a stranger or a friend [70].

In the final article, a specific form of VR therapy called Virtual Reality Aggression Prevention Therapy (VRAPT) was able to reduce levels of aggression in forensic patients, even though there was no significant difference with the waiting-list condition. This reduction was also maintained at the three months follow-up [71] (see Table S1 for additional details of each study).

3.5.4. Impulsivity

Impulsivity was a transdiagnostic factor that only produced two articles, out of which one was a multiple case study [73] and one was an experimental study [71], both of which were carried out on clinical populations.

Starting from the experimental study, impulsivity was a secondary outcome taken into consideration in a RCT mainly focusing on aggression, showing results about how this factor decreased after VRAPT treatment was administered on forensic patients. In particular, following treatment, levels of non-planning impulsiveness improved more than in the waiting list condition, with maintenance of results at three months follow-up [71].

In the multiple case study, VR was able to reduce obsessive-compulsive symptoms (such as impulsive thoughts and compulsive behaviors) in three OCD patients, with results maintained at an eight months follow-up [73] (see Table S1 for additional details of each study).

3.5.5. Cognitive Reappraisal

Only two of the articles included in this review [63,74] observed the transdiagnostic factor of cognitive reappraisal ($n = 1$ experimental study and $n = 1$ case study).

The first study was an RCT comparing two different VR training groups (a reappraisal training group and a choice reaction task training group) on their ability to influence the emotional rating participants gave to pictures [63]. Although the main results on the study regarded emotional regulation, this article is relevant in showing that VR technologies can be useful in teaching cognitive reappraisal to healthy adults.

The second study, instead, was a double case study that showed that, following a VR treatment, two children (one with acute anxiety and posttraumatic flashbacks due to past medical treatments and another with suicidal thoughts and low mood) were able to achieve a better expression of their emotions and to reappraise their experience thanks to VR therapy, especially through the perspective-taking feature given by the VR software (ProReal) that was used during treatment [74] (see Table S1 for additional details of each study).

4. Discussion

VR has emerged in the literature as a new frontier for the treatment of several psychiatric disorders, with several types of software being developed across the years to tackle a variety of mental disorders [1,2]. However, the disorder-specific approach that has been adopted so far for the development of VR increases the costs needed to apply this technology in the field of clinical psychology [6]. Therefore, the aim of this review was to explore the transdiagnostic potential of VR by searching the literature to investigate the effects of VR-based treatments on a set of six internalizing and externalizing transdiagnostic factors that have been selected for being linked to multiple psychopathologies. Despite these keywords representing only some of the most clinically relevant transdiagnostic factors for mental health, the combination of these keywords with the term "virtual reality" led to a heterogeneous selection of studies carried out on very different clinical and non-clinical populations, further proving the transdiagnostic potential of these factors. While several promising results emerged about the ability of VR to improve these factors in different populations, the review also underlined some differences in the methodological quality of the studies found and in the number of studies carried out on each transdiagnostic factor. Generally, the majority of the results focused on avoidance (especially behavioral and social avoidance) and emotion regulation, while the other transdiagnostic factors (i.e., aggression, impulsivity, cognitive reappraisal and disinhibition) turned out to be understudied. Similarly, patients with anxiety disorders represented the most studied clinical population, but interesting applications of VR on other clinical and non-clinical populations (e.g., PTSD, psychotic disorders, eating disorders, OCD, etc.) were also found. Moreover, although more than half of the studies were controlled (with a prevalence of RCTs and a few non-randomized controlled trials), only a small proportion compared VR-based interventions with traditional psychotherapies (e.g., CBT, Mindfulness, DBT, etc.) and a waiting-list control condition was often preferred. The absence of studies using VR in combination with drug therapy to improve these transdiagnostic factors also did not make it possible to collect information about the potential of VR to improve the results of pharmacotherapy or promote adherence to drug therapy for different mental health patients. Follow-ups were also included in more than half of the studies, but maintenance of results over time was never investigated beyond one year. These differences in methodologies across the articles explains the fact that only half of them reached a strong quality score.

More specifically, the transdiagnostic factors that were the focus of most of the selected studies were behavioral and social avoidance, which are largely associated with anxiety disorders [75–77]. This was not surprising, considering that the very first applications of VR in clinical psychology consisted in using this technology to provide an alternative to in-vivo exposure [78,79]. In particular, through the use of VR, patients can improve their conditions by being exposed virtually to situations or objects that elicit the same sense of discomfort as the ones in real life [79,80], thus reducing avoidance of these stimuli.

The results of the review further underline how this is still the way VR is most frequently implemented in psychological treatments, with very positive results. Indeed, in all the studies found, VR was able to reduce behavioral and social avoidance between pre- and post-treatment, confirming how this technology may represent a promising psychological tool that was also as effective as traditional in vivo exposure in some studies [39,46,54]. However, various studies compared VR or used VR in combination with first-line treatments tackling behavioral and social avoidance, such as CBT. While these studies showed that VR combined with cognitive-behavioral therapy (VR-CBT) was effective in reducing social avoidance long-term [56] and with no differences when compared to traditional CBT [59], further studies are definitely needed in order to confirm these promising results.

Similarly, while VR was found to improve other types of avoidance (e.g., agoraphobic avoidance, cognitive avoidance, food avoidance, and alcohol-approach avoidance) that are linked to disorders outside of the anxiety category (e.g., psychosis, PTSD, substance-use disorders, and eating disorders, respectively) [40,43,48,53,57], our review of the literature was not able to find more than a few studies for these factors and clinical populations. Indeed, since the literature showed that different kinds of avoidance can be involved in the maintenance or development of different kinds of pathologies [81–83], investing in a VR software capable of tackling this factor transdiagnostically would be of clinical relevance.

Another transdiagnostic factor that plays a role in several psychopathologies is emotion regulation, which was also the second most found factor in the review. VR interventions were capable of increasing relaxation and diminishing negative emotions, particularly fear and anger, in several studies carried out in the general population [62,65,68], as well as of teaching emotion regulation strategies in clinical and non-clinical participants [63,66,69]. Also successful was the combination of VR with other traditional interventions meant to improve emotion regulation, such as Mindfulness-Based Interventions [65,66]. However, once again, studies comparing or combining VR with other forms of interventions were few, and further research is needed to test these results. The ability of VR to improve emotion regulation would hold clinical utility not only for the treatment of psychological disorders, but also for their prevention, as several authors underline how difficulties in emotion regulation are strictly linked to the development of several psychopathologies (e.g., anxiety and mood disorders, eating disorders, substance-related disorders, and more) [84,85]. Moreover, many of the types of software that tackle emotion regulation can already be considered transdiagnostic in nature because they can be used in many different populations, although there are no studies about the same software being applied to improve this transdiagnostic factor across clinical samples with different psychiatric diagnoses.

On the other hand, not many studies appeared for the transdiagnostic factors of impulsivity, aggression, and cognitive reappraisal. Nonetheless, the up-to-date literature showed promising results about VR software lowering levels of impulsivity and impulsive behaviors in specific populations, more specifically patients with OCD [73] and in forensic patients [71]. In this latter population, VR was also capable of lowering levels of aggression [71] through Virtual Reality Aggression Prevention Therapy. By using VR, aggressive behaviors were also reduced in veterans with PTSD when driving [72] and in people of the general population [70], further proving that a single transdiagnostic VR software would have the potential to be applied on multiple clinical and non-clinical populations.

Finally, VR also emerged as a tool to teach cognitive reappraisal in children, highlighting the intergenerational potential of VR interventions to help clinicians to create a better alliance with children during treatment [74]. VR cognitive reappraisal training could also be used alongside emotion regulation training in VR, since it has been seen that participants rated negative images less severely after undergoing this kind of virtual training [63]. Tackling more than one transdiagnostic factor with a single piece of software would further decrease the costs linked to VR technologies. This would lead to a more frequent implementation of VR in the clinical field, which in turn might help to engage more people towards seeking psychological treatment, especially treatments that target cognitive reappraisal, such as CBT. Indeed, the resemblance between VR and technology used in everyday life could help to lower the stigma associated with traditional psychotherapy.

5. Conclusions

Results of this review further supported the use of VR in clinical psychology, in particular for improving transdiagnostic factors. Moreover, VR has also shown similar results compared to CBT, especially when treating behavioral avoidance [40,51,59], which suggests that it might be a valid alternative to traditional psychotherapies for anxiety disorders. Third-wave cognitive-behavioral therapies, such as mindfulness-based intervention, might also benefit from the addition of a technological VR tool [65,66]. However, additional studies are needed to prove the transdiagnostic potential of VR (in particular or what concerns its ability to improve aggression, impulsivity, and cognitive reappraisal, as well as understudied forms of avoidance), and clinicians still need to work on developing VR software that are truly transdiagnostic in nature and on testing them on more varied clinical and non-clinical populations. Moreover, while promising, the results of the present review need to be considered in light of its methodological limitations.

The main limitation of this review was the choice of a limited and arbitrary number of keywords representing transdiagnostic factors for the literature search. Indeed, we were not able to find a shared, set list of transdiagnostic factors to consider for our keywords. Although an attempt was made to choose the main internalizing and externalizing factors for mental disorders that are also linked to a wide number of psychopathologies [10–12,15,26–36], this arbitrary selection might also have led to the neglect other important keywords. Future reviews might help with investigating the effects of VR-based interventions on other important transdiagnostic factors. Similarly, conducting the bibliographic research using only two databases (PubMed and PsycINFO) and only choosing articles published after 2010 might have led to the exclusion of other relevant studies. While not mandatory, not registering the systematic review protocol on any public repository (e.g., PROSPERO) might be another limitation of the review. However, although a PROSPERO registration has become a widely recommended practice for systematic reviews over the past few years, no differences in quality of research has been found in the literature between registered and non-registered systematic reviews [86], and the use of PRISMA and PICOS criteria encourages and allows replicability of results.

Other limitations were also related to the quality and methodologies of the studies found. Indeed, future research should focus on carrying out studies with a stronger quality and less risk of bias, especially by including follow-ups and RCTs comparing VR to other more traditional psychotherapies (e.g., CBT, mindfulness, DBT, etc.), at least for what concerns the effects of VR-based interventions on transdiagnostic factors. Future studies may also try to investigate the transdiagnostic potential of VR when used in combination with drug therapy and whether VR may help with increasing adherence to treatment.

Ultimately, since the great majority of the articles had adult samples (with only very few studies carried out on adolescents or children), future studies should also consider testing the application of VR-based interventions for the improvement of transdiagnostic factors in people of different ages. Similarly, VR research on transdiagnostic factors should try to expand more outside the field of anxiety disorders and to explore the use of VR in other understudied clinical and non-clinical populations, including the general population at risk for the development of psychopathologies.

Supplementary Materials: The following supporting information can be downloaded at: https://www.mdpi.com/article/10.3390/jcm11216463/s1, Table S1: Characteristics, transdiagnostic factors considered and relevant outcomes of selected studies; Table S2: Quality assessment and risk of bias criteria for observational cohort, case–control, and controlled intervention studies; Table S3: Assessment of quality and risk of bias of selected experimental studies.

Author Contributions: Conceptualization, V.G. and E.T.; Methodology, G.G.; Software, G.G.; Validation, V.G., G.G. and E.T.; Formal Analysis, S.M.; Investigation, G.G. and V.G.; Resources, V.G.; Data Curation, G.G.; Writing—Original Draft Preparation, G.G.; Writing—Review & Editing, V.G.; Visualization, S.G.; Supervision, E.T.; Project Administration, E.T. All authors have read and agreed to the published version of the manuscript.

Funding: This research received no external funding.

Institutional Review Board Statement: Not applicable.

Informed Consent Statement: Not applicable.

Acknowledgments: The authors would like to thank the collaborators from the virtual reality research team of the Department of Psychology, University of Bologna, in particular Chiara Ruini, and Eliana Tossani.

Conflicts of Interest: The authors declare that they have no conflict of interest.

References

1. Emmelkamp, P.; Meyerbröker, K. Virtual Reality Therapy in Mental Health. *Ann. Rev. Clin. Psychol.* **2021**, *17*, 495–519. [CrossRef] [PubMed]
2. Freeman, D.; Reeve, S.; Robinson, A.; Ehlers, A.; Clark, D.; Spanlang, B.; Slater, M. Virtual Reality in the Assessment, Understanding, and Treatment of Mental Health Disorders. *Psychol. Med.* **2017**, *47*, 2393–2400. [CrossRef] [PubMed]
3. Wiederhold, B.K.; Wiederhold, M.D. *Virtul Reality Therapy for Anxiety Disorders: Advances in Evaluation and Treatment*; American Psychological Association: Washington, DC, USA, 2005.
4. Damen, K.H.B.; van der Spek, E.D. Virtual Reality as E-Mental Health to Support Starting with Mindfulness-Based Cognitive Therapy. *Entertainment Comput.—ICEC* **2018**, *2018*, 241–247. [CrossRef]
5. Lamb, R.; Crowe, A.; Stone, J.; Annetta, L.; Zambone, A.; Owens, T. Virtual reality enhanced Dialectical behavioural therapy. *Br. J. Guid. Couns.* **2022**. [CrossRef]
6. Lindner, P.; Dagöö, J.; Hamilton, W.; Miloff, A.; Andersson, G.; Schill, A.; Carlbring, P. Virtual Reality Exposure Therapy for Public Speaking Anxiety in Routine Care: A Single-Subject Effectiveness Trial. *Cogn. Behav. Ther.* **2020**, *50*, 1–21. [CrossRef] [PubMed]
7. McEvoy, P.M.; Nathan, P.; Norton, P.J. Efficacy of Transdiagnostic Treatments: A Review of Published Outcome Studies and Future Research Directions. *J. Cogn. Psychother.* **2009**, *23*, 20–33. [CrossRef]
8. McManus, F.; Shafran, R.; Cooper, Z. What Does a Transdiagnostic Approach Have to Offer the Treatment of Anxiety Disorders? *Br. J. Clin. Psychol.* **2010**, *49*, 491–505. [CrossRef]

9. Titov, N.; Dear, B.F.; Schwencke, G.; Andrews, G.; Johnston, L.; Craske, M.G.; McEvoy, P. Transdiagnostic internet treatment for anxiety and depression: A randomised controlled trial. *Behav. Res. Ther.* **2011**, *49*, 441–452. [CrossRef]
10. American Psychiatric Association. *The Diagnostic and Statistical Manual of Mental Disorders*, 5th ed.; American Psychiatric Association: Washington, DC, USA, 2013.
11. World Health Organization (WHO). *The ICD-10 Classification of Mental and Behavioural Disorders*; World Health Organization: Washington, DC, USA, 2010.
12. Krueger, R.F.; Eaton, N.R. Transdiagnostic factors of mental disorders. *World Psychiatry Off. J. World Psychiatr. Assoc. (WPA)* **2015**, *14*, 27–29. [CrossRef]
13. Dalgleish, T.; Black, M.; Johnston, D.; Bevan, A. Transdiagnostic approaches to mental health problems: Current status and future directions. *J. Consult. Clin. Psychol.* **2020**, *88*, 179–195. [CrossRef]
14. Eaton, N.R.; Rodriguez-Seijas, C.; Carragher, N.; Krueger, R.F. Transdiagnostic factors of psychopathology and substance use disorders: A review. *Soc. Psychiatry Psychiatr. Epidemiol.* **2015**, *50*, 171–182. [CrossRef] [PubMed]
15. Barlow, D.H.; Allen, L.B.; Choate, M.L. Toward a Unified Treatment for Emotional Disorders—Republished Article. *Behav. Ther.* **2016**, *47*, 838–853. [CrossRef] [PubMed]
16. Carragher, N.; Krueger, R.F.; Eaton, N.R.; Slade, T. Disorders without borders: Current and future directions in the meta-structure of mental disorders. *Soc. Psychiatry Psychiatr. Epidemiol.* **2015**, *50*, 339–350. [CrossRef] [PubMed]
17. Norton, P.J.; Roberge, P. Transdiagnostic Therapy. *Psychiatr. Clin. N. Am.* **2017**, *40*, 675–687. [CrossRef]
18. Ellard, K.K.; Bernstein, E.E.; Hearing, C.; Baek, J.H.; Sylvia, L.G.; Nierenberg, A.A.; Barlow, D.H.; Deckersbach, T. Transdiagnostic treatment of bipolar disorder and comorbid anxiety using the Unified Protocol for Emotional Disorders: A pilot feasibility and acceptability trial. *J. Affect. Disord.* **2017**, *219*, 209–221. [CrossRef]
19. Sakiris, N.; Berle, D. A systematic review and meta-analysis of the Unified Protocol as a transdiagnostic emotion regulation based intervention. *Clin. Psychol. Rev.* **2019**, *72*, 101751. [CrossRef]
20. Ellard, K.K.; Fairholme, C.P.; Boisseau, C.L.; Farchione, T.J.; Barlow, D.H. Unified Protocol for the Transdiagnostic Treatment of Emotional Disorders: Protocol Development and Initial Outcome Data. *Cogn. Behav. Pract.* **2010**, *17*, 88–101. [CrossRef]
21. Farchione, T.J.; Fairholme, C.P.; Ellard, K.K.; Boisseau, C.L.; Thompson-Hollands, J.; Carl, J.R.; Gallagher, M.W.; Barlow, D.H. Unified Protocol for Transdiagnostic Treatment of Emotional Disorders: A randomized controlled trial. *Behav. Ther.* **2013**, *43*, 666–678. [CrossRef]
22. Steele, S.J.; Farchione, T.J.; Cassiello-Robbins, C.; Ametaj, A.; Sbi, S.; Sauer-Zavala, S.; Barlow, D.H. Efficacy of the Unified Protocol for transdiagnostic treatment of comorbid psychopathology accompanying emotional disorders compared to treatments targeting single disorders. *J. Psychiatr.* **2018**, *104*, 211–216. [CrossRef]
23. Barlow, D.H.; Farchione, T.J.; Bullis, J.R.; Gallagher, M.W.; Murray-Latin, H.; Sauer-Zavala, S.; Bentley, K.H.; Thompson-Hollands, J.; Conklin, L.R.; Boswell, J.F.; et al. The Unified Protocol for Transdiagnostic Treatment of Emotional Disorders Compared With Diagnosis-Specific Protocols for Anxiety Disorders: A Randomized Clinical Trial. *JAMA Psychiatry* **2017**, *74*, 875–884. [CrossRef]
24. McHugh, R.K.; Murray, H.W.; Barlow, D.H. Balancing fidelity and adaptation in the dissemination of empirically-supported treatments: The promise of transdiagnostic interventions. *Behav. Res. Ther.* **2009**, *47*, 946–953. [CrossRef] [PubMed]
25. Page, M.J.; McKenzie, J.E.; Bossuyt, P.M.; Boutron, I.; Hoffmann, T.C.; Mulrow, C.D.; Shamseer, L.; Tetzlaff, J.M.; Akl, E.A.; Brennan, S.E.; et al. The PRISMA 2020 statement: An updated guideline for reporting systematic reviews. *BMJ* **2021**, *372*, 71. [CrossRef] [PubMed]
26. Harvey, A.G.; Watkins, E.; Mansell, W.; Shafran, R. *Cognitive Behavioural Processes across Psychological Disorders: A Transdiagnostic Approach to Research and Treatment*; Oxford University Press: Oxford, UK, 2004.
27. Besharat, M.A.; Atari, M.; Mirjalili, R.S. Transdiagnostic Processes in Generalized Anxiety Disorder and Obsessive-Compulsive Disorder: Worry, Cognitive Avoidance, Intolerance of Uncertainty, and Metacognitive Beliefs. *PCP* **2019**, *7*, 281–290. [CrossRef]
28. Im, S.; Kahler, J. Evaluating the empirical evidence for three transdiagnostic mechanisms in anxiety and mood disorders. *J. Gen. Psychol.* **2022**, *149*, 232–257. [CrossRef]
29. Bach, B.; Eikenæs, I.U. Transdiagnostic conceptualization of social avoidance through the lens of personality functioning and traits. *J. Clin. Psychol.* **2021**, *77*, 1249–1258. [CrossRef]
30. Sloan, E.; Hall, K.; Moulding, R.; Bryce, S.; Mildred, H.; Staiger, P.K. Emotion regulation as a transdiagnostic treatment construct across anxiety, depression, substance, eating and borderline personality disorders: A systematic review. *Clin. Psychol. Rev.* **2017**, *57*, 141–163. [CrossRef]
31. Sheppes, G.; Suri, G.; Gross, J.J. Emotion regulation and psychopathology. *Annu. Rev. Clin. Psychol.* **2015**, *11*, 379–405. [CrossRef]
32. Riepenhausen, A.; Wackerhagen, C.; Reppmann, Z.C.; Deter, H.-C.; Kalisch, R.; Veer, I.M.; Walter, H. Positive Cognitive Reappraisal in Stress Resilience, Mental Health, and Well-Being: A Comprehensive Systematic Review. *Emot. Rev.* **2022**, *14*, 310–331. [CrossRef]
33. Ten Have, M.; De Graaf, R.; Van Weeghel, J.; Van Dorsselaer, S. The association between com-mon mental disorders and violence: To what extent is it influenced by prior victimization, negative life events and low levels of social support? *Psychol. Med.* **2014**, *44*, 1485–1498. [CrossRef]
34. Johnson, S.; Carver, C.; Joormann, J. Impulsive responses to emotion as a transdiagnostic vulnerability to internalizing and externalizing symptoms. *J. Affect. Disord.* **2013**, *150*, 872–878. [CrossRef]

35. Young, S.E.; Friedman, N.P.; Miyake, A.; Willcutt, E.G.; Corley, R.P.; Haberstick, B.C.; Hewitt, J.K. Behavioral disinhibition: Liability for externalizing spectrum disorders and its genetic and environmental relation to response inhibition across adolescence. *J. Abnorm. Psychol.* **2009**, *118*, 117–130. [CrossRef] [PubMed]
36. Nelson, L.D.; Strickland, C.; Krueger, R.F.; Arbisi, P.A.; Patrick, C.J. Neurobehavioral Traits as Transdiagnostic Predictors of Clinical Problems. *Assessment* **2016**, *23*, 75–85. [CrossRef] [PubMed]
37. Counsell, C. Formulating questions and locating primary studies for inclusion in systematic reviews. *Ann. Intern. Med.* **1997**, *127*, 380–387. [CrossRef] [PubMed]
38. National Institute of Mental Health. *The National Institute of Mental Health Strategic Plan;* National Institute of Mental Health (NIH Publication 08-6368): Bethesda, MD, USA, 2008.
39. Bouchard, S.; Dumoulin, S.; Robillard, G.; Guitard, T.; Klinger, É.; Forget, H.; Loranger, C.; Roucaut, F.X. Virtual reality compared with in vivo exposure in the treatment of social anxiety disorder: A three-arm randomised controlled trial. *Br. J. Psychiatry J. Ment. Sci.* **2017**, *210*, 276–283. [CrossRef] [PubMed]
40. Cárdenas-López, G.; de la Rosa, A.; Durón, R.; Durán, X. Virtual reality exposure for trauma and stress-related disorders for city violence crime victims. *Int. J. Child Health Hum. Dev.* **2016**, *9*, 315–322.
41. Czerniak, E.; Caspi, A.; Litvin, M.; Amiaz, R.; Bahat, Y.; Baransi, H.; Sharon, H.; Noy, S.; Plotnik, M. A Novel Treatment of Fear of Flying Using a Large Virtual Reality System. *Aerosp. Med. Hum. Perform.* **2016**, *87*, 411–416. [CrossRef]
42. Farrell, L.J.; Miyamoto, T.; Donovan, C.L.; Waters, A.M.; Krisch, K.A.; Ollendick, T.H. Virtual Reality One-Session Treatment of Child-Specific Phobia of Dogs: A Controlled, Multiple Baseline Case Series. *Behav. Ther.* **2020**, *52*, 478–491. [CrossRef]
43. Freeman, D.; Lambe, S.; Kabir, T.; Petit, A.; Rosebrock, L.; Yu, L.M.; Dudley, R.; Chapman, K.; Morrison, A.; O'Regan, E.; et al. Automated virtual reality therapy to treat agoraphobic avoidance and distress in patients with psychosis (gameChange): A multicentre, parallel-group, single-blind, randomised, controlled trial in England with mediation and moderation analyses. *Lancet Psychiatry* **2022**, *9*, 375–388. [CrossRef]
44. Gujjar, K.R.; van Wijk, A.; Sharma, R.; de Jongh, A. Virtual Reality Exposure Therapy for the Treatment of Dental Phobia: A Controlled Feasibility Study. *Behav. Cogn. Psychother.* **2018**, *46*, 367–373. [CrossRef]
45. Gujjar, K.R.; van Wijk, A.; Kumar, R.; de Jongh, A. Efficacy of virtual reality exposure therapy for the treatment of dental phobia in adults: A randomized controlled trial. *J. Anxiety Disord.* **2019**, *62*, 100–108. [CrossRef]
46. Kampmann, I.L.; Emmelkamp, P.M.; Hartanto, D.; Brinkman, W.P.; Zijlstra, B.J.; Morina, N. Exposure to virtual social interactions in the treatment of social anxiety disorder: A randomized controlled trial. *Behav. Res. Ther.* **2016**, *77*, 147–156. [CrossRef] [PubMed]
47. Kaussner, Y.; Kuraszkiewicz, A.M.; Schoch, S.; Markel, P.; Hoffmann, S.; Baur-Streubel, R.; Kenntner-Mabiala, R.; Pauli, P. Treating patients with driving phobia by virtual reality exposure therapy—A pilot study. *PLoS ONE* **2020**, *15*, e0226937. [CrossRef] [PubMed]
48. Kim, D.Y.; Lee, J.H. The Effects of Training to Reduce Automatic Action Tendencies Toward Alcohol Using the Virtual Alcohol Approach-Avoidance Task in Heavy Social Drinkers. *Cyberpsychol. Behav. Soc. Netw.* **2019**, *22*, 794–798. [CrossRef] [PubMed]
49. Kim, M.K.; Eom, H.; Kwon, J.H.; Kyeong, S.; Kim, J.J. Neural effects of a short-term virtual reality self-training program to reduce social anxiety. *Psychol. Med.* **2020**, *52*, 1296–1305. [CrossRef]
50. Malbos, E.; Rapee, R.M.; Kavakli, M. Isolating the effect of Virtual Reality Based Exposure Therapy for agoraphobia: A comparative trial. *Stud. Health Technol. Inform.* **2011**, *167*, 45–50.
51. Malbos, E.; Rapee, R.M.; Kavakli, M. A controlled study of agoraphobia and the independent effect of virtual reality exposure therapy. *Aust. N. Z. J. Psychiatry* **2013**, *47*, 160–168. [CrossRef]
52. Maples-Keller, J.L.; Price, M.; Rauch, S.; Gerardi, M.; Rothbaum, B.O. Investigating Relationships Between PTSD Symptom Clusters Within Virtual Reality Exposure Therapy for OEF/OIF Veterans. *Behav. Ther.* **2017**, *48*, 147–155. [CrossRef]
53. Meyerbroeker, K.; Morina, N.; Kerkhof, G.A.; Emmelkamp, P.M. Virtual reality exposure therapy does not provide any additional value in agoraphobic patients: A randomized controlled trial. *Psychother. Psychosom.* **2013**, *82*, 170–176. [CrossRef]
54. Michaliszyn, D.; Marchand, A.; Bouchard, S.; Martel, M.O.; Poirier-Bisson, J. A randomized, controlled clinical trial of in virtuo and in vivo exposure for spider phobia. *Cyberpsychol. Behav. Soc. Netw.* **2010**, *13*, 689–695. [CrossRef]
55. Miloff, A.; Lindner, P.; Dafgård, P.; Deak, S.; Garke, M.; Hamilton, W.; Heinsoo, J.; Kristoffersson, G.; Rafi, J.; Sindemark, K.; et al. Automated virtual reality exposure therapy for spider phobia vs. in-vivo one-session treatment: A randomized non-inferiority trial. *Behav. Res. Ther.* **2019**, *118*, 130–140. [CrossRef]
56. Pot-Kolder, R.; Geraets, C.; Veling, W.; van Beilen, M.; Staring, A.; Gijsman, H.J.; Delespaul, P.; van der Gaag, M. Virtual-reality-based cognitive behavioural therapy versus waiting list control for paranoid ideation and social avoidance in patients with psychotic disorders: A single-blind randomised controlled trial. *Lancet Psychiatry* **2018**, *5*, 217–226. [CrossRef]
57. Roncero, M.; Perpiñá, C. Normalizing the eating pattern with virtual reality for bulimia nervosa: A case report. *Rev. Mex. De Trastor. Aliment.* **2015**, *6*, 152–159. [CrossRef]
58. Rus-Calafell, M.; Gutiérrez-Maldonado, J.; Ribas-Sabaté, J. A virtual reality-integrated program for improving social skills in patients with schizophrenia: A pilot study. *J. Behav. Ther. Exp. Psychiatry* **2014**, *45*, 81–89. [CrossRef] [PubMed]
59. Safir, M.P.; Wallach, H.S.; Bar-Zvi, M. Virtual reality cognitive-behavior therapy for public speaking anxiety: One-year follow-up. *Behav. Modif.* **2012**, *36*, 235–246. [CrossRef] [PubMed]
60. Shiban, Y.; Brütting, J.; Pauli, P.; Mühlberger, A. Fear reactivation prior to exposure therapy: Does it facilitate the effects of VR exposure in a randomized clinical sample? *J. Behav. Ther. Exp. Psychiatry* **2015**, *46*, 133–140. [CrossRef]

61. Wrzesien, M.; Botella, C.; Bretón-López, J.; González, E.D.; Burkhardt, J.; Raya, M.A.; Pérez-Ara, M. Treating small animal phobias using a projective-augmented reality system: A single-case study. *Comput. Hum. Behav.* **2015**, *49*, 343–353. [CrossRef]
62. Anderson, A.P.; Mayer, M.D.; Fellows, A.M.; Cowan, D.R.; Hegel, M.T.; Buckey, J.C. Relaxation with Immersive Natural Scenes Presented Using Virtual Reality. *Aerosp. Med. Hum. Perform.* **2017**, *88*, 520–526. [CrossRef]
63. Bosse, T.; Gerritsen, C.; de Man, J.; Treur, J. Towards virtual training of emotion regulation. *Brain Inform.* **2014**, *1*, 27–37. [CrossRef]
64. Hadley, W.; Houck, C.; Brown, L.K.; Spitalnick, J.S.; Ferrer, M.; Barker, D. Moving Beyond Role-Play: Evaluating the Use of Virtual Reality to Teach Emotion Regulation for the Prevention of Adolescent Risk Behavior Within a Randomized Pilot Trial. *J. Pediatr. Psychol.* **2019**, *44*, 425–435. [CrossRef]
65. Navarro-Haro, M.V.; Hoffman, H.G.; Garcia-Palacios, A.; Sampaio, M.; Alhalabi, W.; Hall, K.; Linehan, M. The Use of Virtual Reality to Facilitate Mindfulness Skills Training in Dialectical Behavioral Therapy for Borderline Personality Disorder: A Case Study. *Front. Psychol.* **2016**, *72*, 1573.
66. Navarro-Haro, M.V.; Modrego-Alarcón, M.; Hoffman, H.G.; López-Montoyo, A.; Navarro-Gil, M.; Montero-Marin, J.; García-Palacios, A.; Borao, L.; García-Campayo, J. Evaluation of a Mindfulness-Based Intervention With and Without Virtual Reality Dialectical Behavior Therapy® Mindfulness Skills Training for the Treatment of Generalized Anxiety Disorder in Primary Care: A Pilot Study. *Front. Psychol.* **2019**, *10*, 55. [CrossRef] [PubMed]
67. Otkhmezuri, B.; Boffo, M.; Siriaraya, P.; Matsangidou, M.; Wiers, R.W.; Mackintosh, B.; Ang, C.S.; Salemink, E. Believing Is Seeing: A Proof-of-Concept Semiexperimental Study on Using Mobile Virtual Reality to Boost the Effects of Interpretation Bias Modification for Anxiety. *JMIR Ment. Health* **2019**, *6*, e11517. [CrossRef] [PubMed]
68. Wrzesien, M.; Rodríguez, A.; Rey, B.; Raya, M.A.; Baños, R.; Vara, M.D. How the physical similarity of avatars can influence the learning of emotion regulation strategies in teenagers. *Comput. Hum. Behav.* **2015**, *43*, 101–111. [CrossRef]
69. Yuan, S.; Ip, H. Using virtual reality to train emotional and social skills in children with autism spectrum disorder. *Lond. J. Prim. Care* **2018**, *10*, 110–112. [CrossRef]
70. Jo, H.J.; Jung, Y.H.; Hong, Y.J.; Shin, Y.B.; Baek, K.D.; Kim, E.; Kim, J.J. The Applicability of Virtual Reality-Based Training for Controlling Anger in Aggressive Individuals. *Cyberpsychol. Behav. Soc. Netw.* **2022**, *25*, 278–286. [CrossRef]
71. Klein Tuente, S.; Bogaerts, S.; Bulten, E.; Keulen-de Vos, M.; Vos, M.; Bokern, H.; IJzendoorn, S.V.; Geraets, C.; Veling, W. Virtual Reality Aggression Prevention Therapy (VRAPT) versus Waiting List Control for Forensic Psychiatric Inpatients: A Multicenter Randomized Controlled Trial. *J. Clin. Med.* **2020**, *9*, 2258. [CrossRef]
72. Zinzow, H.M.; Brooks, J.O.; Rosopa, P.J.; Jeffirs, S.; Jenkins, C.; Seeanner, J.; Hodges, L.F. Virtual reality and cognitive-behavioral therapy for driving anxiety and aggression in veterans: A pilot study. *Cogn. Behav. Pract.* **2018**, *25*, 296–309. [CrossRef]
73. Laforest, M.; Bouchard, S.; Bossé, J.; Mesly, O. Effectiveness of In Virtuo Exposure and Response Prevention Treatment Using Cognitive-Behavioral Therapy for Obsessive-Compulsive Disorder: A Study Based on a Single-Case Study Protocol. *Front. Psychiatry* **2016**, *7*, 99. [CrossRef]
74. Falconer, C.J.; Davies, E.B.; Grist, R.; Stallard, P. Innovations in Practice: Avatar-based virtual reality in CAMHS talking therapy: Two exploratory case studies. *Child Adolesc. Ment. Health* **2019**, *24*, 283–287. [CrossRef]
75. Parsons, T.D.; Rizzo, A.A. Affective outcomes of virtual reality exposure therapy for anxiety and specific phobias: A meta-analysis. *J. Behav. Ther. Exp. Psychiatry* **2008**, *39*, 250–261. [CrossRef]
76. Opriş, D.; Pintea, S.; García-Palacios, A.; Botella, C.; Szamosközi, Ş.; David, D. Virtual reality exposure therapy in anxiety disorders: A quantitative meta-analysis. *Depress. Anxiety* **2012**, *29*, 85–93. [CrossRef] [PubMed]
77. Maples-Keller, J.L.; Bunnell, B.E.; Kim, S.J.; Rothbaum, B.O. The Use of Virtual Reality Technology in the Treatment of Anxiety and Other Psychiatric Disorders. *Harv. Rev. Psychiatry* **2017**, *25*, 103–113. [CrossRef] [PubMed]
78. Vincelli, F. From imagination to virtual reality: The future of clinical psychology. *Cyberpsychol. Behav. Impact Internet Multimed. Virtual Real. Behav. Soc.* **1999**, *2*, 241–248. [CrossRef]
79. Gorini, A.; Griez, E.; Petrova, A.; Riva, G. Assessment of the emotional responses produced by exposure to real food, virtual food and photographs of food in patients affected by eating disorders. *Ann. Gen. Psychiatry* **2010**, *9*, 30. [CrossRef] [PubMed]
80. Gutiérrez-Maldonado, J.; Wiederhold, B.K.; Riva, G. Future Directions: How Virtual Reality Can Further Improve the Assessment and Treatment of Eating Disorders and Obesity. *Cyberpsychol. Behav. Soc. Netw.* **2016**, *19*, 148–153. [CrossRef]
81. Griffith, J.W.; Zinbarg, R.E.; Craske, M.G.; Mineka, S.; Rose, R.D.; Waters, A.M.; Sutton, J.M. Neuroticism as a common dimension in the internalizing disorders. *Psychol. Med.* **2010**, *40*, 1125–1136. [CrossRef]
82. Rodriguez-Seijas, C.; Eaton, N.R.; Krueger, R.F. How Transdiagnostic Factors of Personality and Psychopathology Can Inform Clinical Assessment and Intervention. *J. Personal. Assess.* **2015**, *97*, 425–435. [CrossRef]
83. Yarger, H.A.; Redcay, E. A conceptual model of risk and protective factors associated with internalizing symptoms in autism spectrum disorder: A scoping review, synthesis, and call for more research. *Dev. Psychopathol.* **2020**, *32*, 1254–1272. [CrossRef]
84. Aldao, A.; Nolen-Hoeksema, S.; Schweizer, S. Emotion-regulation strategies across psychopathology: A meta-analytic review. *Clin. Psychol. Rev.* **2010**, *30*, 217–237. [CrossRef]
85. Cludius, B.; Mennin, D.; Ehring, T. Emotion regulation as a transdiagnostic process. *Emotion* **2020**, *20*, 37–42. [CrossRef]
86. Rombey, T.; Doni, K.; Hoffmann, F.; Pieper, D.; Allers, K. More Systematic Reviews Were Registered in PROSPERO Each Year, but Few Records' Status Was up-to-Date. *J. Clin. Epidemiol.* **2020**, *117*, 60–67. [CrossRef] [PubMed]

Journal of
Clinical Medicine

MDPI

Systematic Review

From Virtual Reality to Regenerative Virtual Therapy: Some Insights from a Systematic Review Exploring Inner Body Perception in Anorexia and Bulimia Nervosa

Clelia Malighetti [1], Maria Sansoni [1,*], Santino Gaudio [2,3], Marta Matamala-Gomez [4], Daniele Di Lernia [1], Silvia Serino [1] and Giuseppe Riva [5,6]

1 Department of Psychology, Università Cattolica del Sacro Cuore, Largo Gemelli 1, 20100 Milan, Italy
2 Department of Neuroscience, Functional Pharmacology, Uppsala University, Husargatan 3, 75237 Uppsala, Sweden
3 Department of Biomedicine and Prevention, University of Rome Tor Vergata, Viale Montpellier 1, 00133 Rome, Italy
4 Department of Psychology, Mind and Behavior Technological Center, University of Milano-Bicocca, Piazza dell'Ateneo Nuovo 1, 20126 Milan, Italy
5 Applied Technology for Neuro-Psychology Lab, IRCCS Istituto Auxologico Italiano, Via Magnasco 2, 20149 Milan, Italy
6 Humane Technology Lab, Università Cattolica del Sacro Cuore, Largo Gemelli 1, 20100 Milan, Italy
* Correspondence: maria.sansoni@unicatt.it; Tel.: +39-02-72-343-863

Abstract: Despite advances in our understanding of the behavioral and molecular factors that underlie the onset and maintenance of Eating Disorders (EDs), it is still necessary to optimize treatment strategies and establish their efficacy. In this context, over the past 25 years, Virtual Reality (VR) has provided creative treatments for a variety of ED symptoms, including body dissatisfaction, craving, and negative emotions. Recently, different researchers suggested that EDs may reflect a broader impairment in multisensory body integration, and a particular VR technique—VR body swapping—has been used to repair it, but with limited clinical results. In this paper, we use the results of a systematic review employing PRISMA guidelines that explore inner body perception in EDs (21 studies included), with the ultimate goal to analyze the features of multisensory impairment associated with this clinical condition and provide possible solutions. Deficits in interoception, proprioception, and vestibular signals were observed across Anorexia and Bulimia Nervosa, suggesting that: (a) alteration of inner body perception might be a crucial feature of EDs, even if further research is needed and; (b) VR, to be effective with these patients, has to simulate/modify both the external and the internal body. Following this outcome, we introduce a new therapeutic approach—Regenerative Virtual Therapy—that integrates VR with different technologies and clinical strategies to regenerate a faulty bodily experience by stimulating the multisensory brain mechanisms and promoting self-regenerative processes within the brain itself.

Keywords: regenerative medicine; inner body perception; anorexia nervosa; bulimia nervosa; proprioception; interoception; vestibular system

Citation: Malighetti, C.; Sansoni, M.; Gaudio, S.; Matamala-Gomez, M.; Di Lernia, D.; Serino, S.; Riva, G. From Virtual Reality to Regenerative Virtual Therapy: Some Insights from a Systematic Review Exploring Inner Body Perception in Anorexia and Bulimia Nervosa. *J. Clin. Med.* **2022**, *11*, 7134. https://doi.org/10.3390/jcm11237134

Academic Editor: Stéphane Bouchard

Received: 9 September 2022
Accepted: 20 November 2022
Published: 30 November 2022

1. Introduction

Despite advances in our understanding of the behavioral and molecular factors that underlie the onset and maintenance of eating disorders (EDs), it is still necessary to optimize treatment strategies and establish their efficacy. In this context, over the past 25 years, Virtual Reality (VR) has provided creative treatments for a variety of ED symptoms, including body dissatisfaction, craving, and negative emotions [1–4]. VR represents indeed an advanced imaginal system, able to generate emotions as if people were undergoing the same situations in real life [5,6]. Thanks to VR, clinicians may provide controlled exposure therapy (i.e., VR exposure) to their patients [7–9], offering a safe space in which to undergo experiences [10] or stimuli that are critical for the improvement of patients' clinical conditions [8,9,11–13]. This characteristic enables patients to feel present in the virtual environment as if coping with the stimuli in real life [14], demonstrating to be particularly effective for exposure treatments [2]. In comparison to in vivo exposure (e.g., implemented through Cognitive Behavioral Therapy—CBT, guided imagery, etc.), VR offers a higher level of control and safety, permits the inclusion of contextual and proximal cues, prevents unforeseen events during exposure and helps to customize exposure to the needs of each patient, thereby lowering any treatment resistance and boosting motivation. Occasionally in vivo exposure can indeed be complex (e.g., it may be hard to uphold the required standards of safety and confidentiality when exposure is undertaken in a real-world setting, the time to travel to the exposure location may be long, there could be poor control over the stimuli, etc.) [10]. These restrictions can be somewhat circumvented by exposure in the clinic, although this method only permits exposure to proximate signals (e.g., meals), not to contextual cues (e.g., kitchen). Imagery is a second in vivo exposure option that is often carried out when facing EDs. However, if on the one hand imagery exposure addresses some of the aforementioned drawbacks, on the other hand, it also requires a significant amount of cognitive effort and may exhaust patients. As a result, there is a higher chance that patients will use avoidance tactics: clinicians, in fact, cannot fully control the scenario that patients are imagining [10]. When compared to imagery exposure, VR stimulates a variety of sensory modalities (e.g., auditory and visual), making it easier for participants who have trouble picturing scenes to participate. Additionally, since clinicians can see what the patient is seeing at any given time, VR aids in the identification of the stimuli that trigger a given emotional response [10]. VR-based cue exposure therapy (i.e., VR-CET) has proven greater effectiveness than CBT in decreasing binge and purge episodes in individuals with bulimia nervosa (BN) and binge-eating disorder (BED), showing a higher reduction in overeating episodes and a decrease in binge abstinence rates [15]. These findings are confirmed by other studies [16,17] which support the greater effectiveness of VR exposure for EDs when compared to in vivo one.

Recently, different researchers have suggested that EDs may reflect a broader impairment in multisensory body integration [18–21]. According to the Allocentric Lock Theory [22–25], patients suffering from Anorexia Nervosa (AN) are trapped in an outdated and negative memory of the body that cannot be changed even after a rigorous diet or significant weight loss: these patients are therefore prevented from updating their stored representation of the body (third-person perspective—offline) with new information coming from real-time perception-driven inputs (first-person perspective—online) [9,26–29]. Following this theory, a new VR technique called body swapping illusion [26,28,29] has been preliminary used as a clinical tool for EDs [29,30]. Using synchronous multisensory stimulation, body swapping induces the illusory experience of owning a virtual body: the perception of viewing an entire virtual body from a first-person perspective enables the participants to perceive the virtual body as their real one [31]. This methodology helps to reduce body-size overestimation in patients suffering from EDs, particularly AN [9,26,28,29]. However, differently from other clinical contexts (i.e., pain treatment) where the body swapping illusion is clinically effective [32], the existing results in EDs are disappointing: the effects of the VR experience are only temporary and tend to disappear in just a few hours after the treatment [33].

In this paper, we use the results of a systematic review that employs PRISMA guidelines and aims at exploring inner body perception in EDs, on the one hand, to understand the role played by deficits of inner body perception in the etiology of Eds; on the other, to use the results of this analysis to enhance the effects of VR-induced body modifications and propose a new approach to treat EDs.

Inner Body Perception in Eating Disorders

Inner body perception is an umbrella term that encompasses primarily interoception, proprioception, and the vestibular system [34].

Interoception is "the sense of the physiological condition of the body" [35] and it is involved in a wide range of subjective experiences and fundamental aspects of bodily experience, such as body ownership [36] and self-awareness [37]. Particularly, Garfinkel et al. [38,39] distinguished and operationalized three different aspects of interoception: Interoceptive Accuracy (IAc), Interoceptive Sensitivity (IAs), and Interoceptive metacognitive Awareness (IAw). Specifically, IAc represents the ability to perceive inner bodily sensations, such as heartbeat; IAs represents the cognitive beliefs regarding the perception of the body, measured through self-report instruments; and IAw assesses the extent to which confidence predicts accuracy [38]. Proprioception is the sense of body position and movement [40,41], while the vestibular sense is intimately related to the inner experience of having a body [42], maintaining its orientation in the surrounding space thanks to the ability to provide continuous information about the body position [43,44].

There is evidence that multisensory integration may be disturbed in EDs e.g., [45,46], causing a mismatch between how the body is perceived and what the body is physically like [47]. Specifically, an impaired capacity to accurately sense, process, and integrate body signals has been observed in individuals with EDs [48], manifesting as a disturbance in bodily experience [34]. Poor ability to correctly perceive sensation from the inner body—a core element of multisensory impairments [34]—could be connected with observed deficits in coherently integrating input arising from within the body with the metacognitive perceptions of the body itself. Some studies have postulated that aberrant interoception—or the perception and integration of signals relating to body homeostasis (e.g., hunger, heartbeat, respiration)—might contribute to AN symptoms, including body image distortion, extreme restriction despite starvation and alexithymia [49–52]. In support of this notion, several lines of evidence have reported alterations in neural responses to taste stimuli, in individuals both with active symptomatology and in remission [53]. This deficit might be interpreted as dysfunctional integration of bodily information supporting a recent framework proposed by Riva and Dakanalis [20]. This model suggests that patients with AN are characterized by multisensory integration deficits that could affect the ability to properly relate the internal bodily signals with their positive or negative implications [20].

Along with this, numerous studies have now reported variations in the right parietal lobe function in EDs [54–58], suggesting altered proprioceptive perception related to body image representation. For example, Grunwald et al. [59] showed deficits in haptic perception and tactile-visual transformation in patients with AN, as well as diminished parietal activation during a task, suggesting proprioceptive integrative deficits in the parietal lobes. Similarly, Mohr et al. [60] conducted an fMRI study of body size estimation in AN patients and found evidence that body size overestimation may be related to issues with the retrieval of a multimodal body schema stored in the precuneus/posterior parietal cortex. This evidence suggests that parietal dysfunctions could be connected to body schema disturbances and that these kinds of alterations can also induce deficits in spatial orientation processes [61,62]. Several authors suggest the use of neurofeedback [63], invasive [64] and non-invasive brain stimulation techniques [64,65] to target the altered inner body perception of individuals with EDs. However, to date, no trials employing such methodologies have been implemented in this clinical population. The only technique that has been tested on patients with EDs is the cold-water caloric vestibular stimulation (CVS) [66]. CVS activates key nodes of the anterior cingulo-insular network (aCIN), altered in a wide variety of psychiatric and neurological conditions (e.g., EDs) [67], promoting vestibular neuromodulation. CVS works by performing a cold-water caloric vestibular stimulation of the ears. Specifically, external auditory canals are warmed or cooled using air or water irrigators. Temperature changes that are both warming and cooling cause the endolymphatic fluid in the semicircular canals to change in density, which in turn causes convection currents that cause cupular deflection, alter the tonic firing rate of the vestibular nerves and cause vestibulo-ocular reflex or horizontal nystagmus [68]. Schonherr and colleagues [66], revealed that after CVS (on the left and right ears), patients with AN reported a significantly smaller estimation of thigh width than before, closer to the real measurement. According to these authors, the Body-Perception-Index (BPI) reduced dramatically, too. Nevertheless, although these results are promising, they referred to only a few patients and no further trials have been implemented to replicate these findings on a bigger sample. For this reason, understanding how inner body perception is altered in EDs is an essential step to appropriately support patients, developing adequate interventions able to target not only their cognitive and emotional processes but also their bodily correlates. This systematic review represents, therefore, the first step to achieving this goal: before developing such interventions it is, indeed, essential to collect information to clearly define and fully understand if and how alterations in inner body perception are related. To reach this goal, the authors investigated the domains connected to inner body perception (i.e., interoception, proprioception, and vestibular systems) focusing on the tasks used for assessing such dimensions, as well as on the primary outcomes, in order to explore possible alterations in the two main ED clinical clusters: AN and BN.

2. Methods

A systematic review of scientific literature was performed to identify studies that reported assessment of inner body perception in individuals with AN and BN. To offer a broad panoramic of the current state of the art on the topic, we did not define a beginning year of publication for the articles to be included. A review protocol following the Preferred Reporting Items for Systematic Reviews and Meta-Analysis (PRISMA) guidelines [69] was compiled.

2.1. Data Sources and Search Strategy

Data sources of relevant publications on experimental studies were collected on the 5th of August 2022 through a computer-based search in three high-profile databases: PubMed, Web of Science (Web of Knowledge), and PsycINFO. Each database was searched independently according to three specific iteration research strings: (Eating Disorder) OR (Anorexia) OR (Bulimia) AND ("Internal Body" OR "Body Sensation" OR "Proprioception" OR "Interoception" OR "Interoceptive" OR "Vestibular" OR "Autonomic system" OR "Visceral" OR "Internal Perception" OR "Body experience"). To make this study repeatable in the future, detailed results of the search strategy are available in the Supplementary Materials. The selection of these strings was made in an attempt to capture a broad range of features regarding bodily perception and EDs. Citations were retrieved independently for each iterative search crossing all databases. The complete list was exported and aggregated to remove duplicates and then imported into Rayyan [70] for the title and abstract screening. The list of studies selected for inclusion was also sent to leading experts in the field for suggestions and identification of any missing studies. As a result, one study [71] was screened and included in the review.

2.2. Study Selection and Inclusion Criteria

Inner body perception is considered to be composed of different sensory inputs: proprioceptive, interoceptive, and vestibular e.g., [34,72]. To be included in the review, studies were required to:

(a) Investigate a sample of individuals that meet a current diagnosis of AN and BN, according to the Diagnostic and Statistical Manual of mental disorders (DSM) or International Classification of Diseases (ICD). In other words, studies in which the participants self-reported the diagnosis, used self-reported measures to identify participants' diagnosis, or in which the diagnosis was not provided by a professional (e.g., a clinical psychologist) were not included in the systematic review. Both adults and adolescents with a current diagnosis of AN or BN were considered eligible. Studies that considered the participants' sample as aggregated (e.g., reporting under the same category of EDs multiple diagnoses) were also not included in the systematic review;
(b) Include a healthy control group (HC) or a population of normative values to compare the clinical group with;

(c) Use tasks or instruments to evaluate interoception according to Craig's definition [35,38]; or proprioception according to Blanke's definition [40]; or vestibular perception according to Lopez's definition [73]. Studies that employed self-reported questionnaires to assess such dimensions were excluded;
(d) Use tasks that directly evaluate one or more sensory domains. Interoceptive input was considered present when the task tested sensitivity to visceral activity [35]. Proprioceptive input was considered present when the task was based on a sensory judgment about limb and body position [40]. Vestibular input was considered present when the task tested the sensation of any change in balance, position, direction, or movement of the eyes, head, or body [73].
(e) Use behavioral and cognitive tasks. Studies involving manipulation of the variable of interest (e.g., through medications or psychological interventions) were not included in the systematic review;
(f) Be original articles: reviews, meeting abstracts, conference proceedings, notes, letters to the editor, research protocols, patents, editorials, books or chapters, and other editorial materials were not considered eligible for this systematic review;
(g) Be quantitative studies: qualitative studies were not included;
(h) Be in English, enroll humans (i.e., studies that use animals were excluded) and have an available full text.

A flow chart of the search strategy according to the PRISMA Flow Diagram is available in Figure 1.

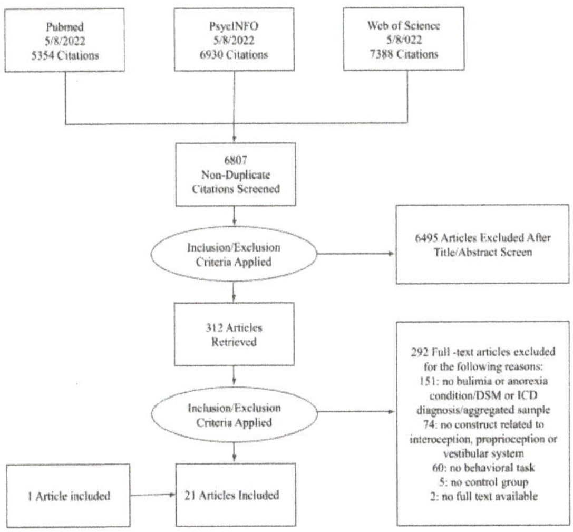

Figure 1. Flow chart of the systematic review. The figure illustrates the search strategy of the systematic review conducted under PRISMA guidelines.

2.3. Study Inclusion

Two reviewers (C.M. and M.S.) independently screened all non-duplicate titles and abstracts, searching for eligible articles. The same reviewers retrieved and analyzed the full text for all relevant articles, resolving discrepancies in opinions by consensus. D.D.L. was designated as the third reviewer to arbitrate potential differences in agreement.

2.4. Data Extraction

Two reviewers (C.M. and M.S.) independently extracted the following data: group sample, composition and gender; specific diagnosis; interoceptive, proprioceptive and vestibular task or instrument used for the assessment; construct measured; and primary outcomes. Data are available in Table 1.

Table 1. Studies characteristics according to extraction parameters.

Authors and Year	Sample	Gender	Diagnosis	Task/Instrument	Constructs Measured	Primary Outcomes
(Ambrosecchia et al., 2017 [74])	AN: 24 HC: 25	F	AN	Heartbeat perception task	Interoception	Results showed no differences between AN and HCs in heartbeat perception task.
(Aschenbrenner et al., 2009 [75])	AN:16 BN: 24 HC: 23	F	AN BN	"Sniffin' Sticks" Test Battery and "Taste Strip" Test Kit	Interoception	Compared to HC and BN, individuals with AN showed lowered olfactory and gustatory sensitivities.
(Bär et al., 2006 [76])	AN: 15 HC: 15	F	AN	Heat Pain Thresholds	Interoception	The heat pain thresholds were significantly increased in the acute state of AN and decreased after weight had been regained for 6 months.
(Bellard et al., 2022 [77])	AN: 27 RAN: 29 HC: 35	F	AN	Affective touch	Interoception	AN and RAN did not differ in their pleasantness ratings to touch for another compared to HC, but when evaluating touch for self, both AN and RAN rated CT-optimal touch as less pleasant than HCs.
(Brown et al., 2022 [78])	AN: 10 HC: 10	F	AN	Behavioral Water Load Task	Interoception	Participants with AN drank significantly less water than HC, but reported greater increases in negative affects pre-to-post-Water Load Task.
(Case et al., 2011 [79])	AN:10 HC: 10	F	AN	Size Weight Illusion	Proprioception	Results showed a reduction in size weight illusion in individuals with AN compared to controls.
(Crucianelli et al. 2016 [80])	AN: 25 HC: 30	F	AN	Affective touch	Interoception	Results showed less pleasure in people with AN regarding affective touch compared to HCs.
(Crucianelli et al., 2020 [81])	AN: 27 RAN: 24 HC: 27	F	AN	Affective Touch	Interoception	Both AN and RAN anticipated tactile experiences and rated delivered tactile stimuli as less pleasant than HCs.

Table 1. *Cont.*

Authors and Year	Sample	Gender	Diagnosis	Task/Instrument	Constructs Measured	Primary Outcomes
(Demartini et al., 2017 [82])	AN: 20 FMS: 20 HC: 20	F	AN; FMCS (Functional Motor Symptoms)	Heartbeat Perception Task	Interoception	Results showed no differences between people with AN and HC in interoceptive sensitivity and interoceptive awareness.
(Di Lernia et al., 2019 [83])	AN: 1 (single case) HC: 4	F	AN	Heartbeat Perception Task; Metacognitive Confidence in Heartbeat Task Perception; Interoceptive Buffer Saturation Index	Interoception	The patient with AN showed a dissociation of interceptive axes with widespread perceptional deficits.
(Epstein et al., 2001 [84])	AN:20 HC: 20	F	AN	"Proprioception Test" and "Right-Left Orientation Test"	Proprioception	People with AN showed significantly lower scores in the "right-left orientation test" at pre-treatment assessment as compared to HCs.
(Fontana et al., 2009 [85])	AN: 15 BN: 15 HC: 11	F	AN BN	Kinematics (or segmental) Method	Vestibular Signals	Patients with BN were more unstable than HCs, showing significant differences in anteroposterior center of mass (CoM) excursions and length of the path, while individuals with AN showed no significant differences from HCs.
(Goldzak-Kunik et al., 2012 [71])	AN: 15 HC: 15	F	AN	Interoception: Cold Pain, VAS for Cold, Unpleasantness, and Pain. Proprioception: Kinesthesia task	Interoception and Proprioception	Patients with AN and HCs did not differ in cold pain responses and at the kinaesthesia task.
(Kinnaird et al., 2020 [86])	AN: 37 HC: 37	F	AN	Heartbeat Perception Task; Metacognitive Confidence in Heartbeat Task Perception	Interoception	Heartbeat perception performance was not found to be altered in the AN group compared to the HC group. However, confidence ratings in task performance in the AN group were lower compared to the HC group.
(Lutz et al., 2019 [87])	AN: 20 HC: 20	F	AN AN	Heartbeat Perception Task; Interoceptive Sensibility Task	Interoception	Results showed that people with AN and HCs did not differ significantly in interoceptive accuracy or interoceptive sensibility.

Table 1. *Cont.*

Authors and Year	Sample	Gender	Diagnosis	Task/Instrument	Constructs Measured	Primary Outcomes
(Mergen et al., 2018 [88])	AN: 27 HC: 40	F	AN	One-Point-Localization Task	Proprioception	Results showed no difference between AN and HC in their performance since both groups showed alterations in the localization task.
(Pollatos et al., 2016 [89])	AN: 15 HC: 15	F	AN	Heartbeat Perception Task	Interoception	During the self-focus, individuals with AN showed lower Interoception accuracy compared to HCs.
(Richard et al., 2019 [90])	AN: 37 HC: 39	F	AN	Heartbeat Perception Task	Interoception	Results showed no evidence of lower heartbeat perception in people with AN compared to HCs.
(Wollast et al., 2022 [91])	AN: 25 HC: 25	F	AN	Heartbeat Perception Task	Interoception	A deficit in interoceptive accuracy was observed for the individuals suffering from AN at rest as well as when an emotional context was induced, compared to HCs.
(Yamamotova et al., 2009 [92])	BN:21 HC: 21	F	BN	Heat Pain Threshold using Analgesia Meterradiant Heat applied to 1 cm^2	Interoception	BN had a higher pain threshold than HCs in all six conditions. BN also had shorter tolerance latency of cold pressor than HCs.
(Zopf et al., 2016 [93])	AN: 23 HC: 23	F	AN	Rubber Hand Illusion; Proprioception Drift	Proprioception	Results showed the reduced influence of proprioceptive signals on hand location estimates in AN compared to HCs.

AN = Anorexia Nervosa; BN = Bulimia Nervosa; HCs = Healthy Controls; RAN = Recovered from AN; FMS = Functional Motor Symptoms.

3. Results

Of 19,672 studies retrieved from PubMed, PsycINFO, and Web of Science, 6807 were non-duplicates. After screening all non-duplicate titles and abstracts, 6495 did not fit the preliminary inclusion criteria. Subsequently, the full text of 312 articles was retrieved and the studies were analyzed for the specific inclusion criteria. Of these 312 studies, 292 were excluded. Reasons for exclusion were lack of appropriateness of the study sample (e.g., no AN or BN diagnosis according to DSM or ICD, employment of an aggregated sample of EDs, etc.), no pertinence of the construct analyzed in the study (i.e., no proprioception, interoception or vestibular system examined), or no appropriate task involved (e.g., manipulation of the construct through medications, assessment implemented using self-reported questionnaires instead of tasks, etc.). Other reasons for exclusion were the absence of a control group, or of an available full text. Please see Figure 1 for more details about the inclusion/exclusion process. Therefore, only 20 articles met the inclusion criteria and were identified as suitable for our review. One additional paper [71] was also included upon suggestion by leading experts in the field, leading to a total of 21 papers included in the review.

In the following paragraphs, study characteristics and results will be presented. The Section 3 will focus on the assessment of proprioceptive, interoceptive, and vestibular perception, as well as on the primary outcomes of the studies. Detailed information about study characteristics, including sample, gender, diagnosis, task or instrument employed, assessed construct, and primary outcomes measured are presented in Table 1.

3.1. Study Characteristics

Table 1 shows study characteristics according to extraction parameters. Sixteen studies explored interoception in AN or BN [71,74–78,80–83,86,87,89–92], five investigated proprioception [71,79,84,88,93] and one vestibular signals [85]. Among these studies, one [71] assessed interoception and proprioception within the same work.

In terms of the sample, most studies compared patients with AN and an HC group [71,74,76,78–80,84,86–91,93]. One study [83] was a single case study on a patient with AN who was compared with a group of four HCs. Two studies [75,85] compared patients with AN, BN, and a group of HCs, one study [92] compared patients with BN with HCs and other two studies compared the clinical sample (i.e., AN) both with HCs and with recovered patients [77,81]. Lastly, one study compared patients with AN, HCs, and patients reporting functional motor symptoms [82]. In general, the clinical samples of included studies ranged from one participant [83] to a maximum of 37 individuals [86,90], and all studies included female participants.

3.2. Tasks Employed to Assess Interoception, Proprioception, and Vestibular Processes

3.2.1. Interoception

Eight studies [74,82,83,86,87,89–91] investigated cardiac IAc [94] by using the heartbeat perception task [95]. This technique consists of silently counting heartbeats in a defined time frame (25 s, 35 s, 45 s, 100 s) without any external heartbeat information and focusing only on inner body perception. The heartbeats reported by patients are compared to the real heartbeats measured through an ECG or other appropriate medical equipment (e.g., pulse oximeter). Wollast et al. [91] repeated the task twice: while at rest and after listening to a song. This second task was used for emotional induction and was modeled after that used by Mayer et al. [96], who employed a sad piece of music to induce negative emotions, thus simulating, in this way, physiological reactions and modifications in the heart rate. Three studies [83,86,87] added measures for a comprehensive interoception assessment. Indeed, besides IAc, these authors also assessed IAw, asking the participant to provide a degree of confidence regarding their performance on the heartbeat perception task. To assess this, confidence ratings were used. In particular, following the heartbeat perception task, participants were asked to rate the level of confidence in their performance on a scale from 1 (least confident) to 100 (most confident), mostly using a Visual Analog Scale. Di Lernia et al. [83] also assessed the interoceptive buffer saturation index (IBs). This task, based on a verbal estimation of interoceptive tactile stimuli led with a specific device [83], aims to reversely evaluate the amount of interoceptive processing through distortions in the time perception of the stimuli [97].

Three studies [77,80,81] assessed interoception using Affective Touch [98–101]. In Bellard et al. [77] the Affective Touch consisted of Self and Other-directed Affective Touch video clips. Specifically, touch was delivered across five different body regions: non-C Tactile (CT)-innervated body site (i.e., palm) vs. CT-innervated body sites (i.e., ventral forearm, upper arm, cheek, and back) with three different speeds: static (0 cm/s), slow (5 cm/s) and fast (30 cm/s). After watching each video, participants answered two questions using a 100-point VAS scale (i.e., 0 = very unpleasant, 100 = extremely pleasant): "How much would you like to be touched like that?" (Self-directed touch) and "How pleasant do you think that action was for the person being touched?" (3rd person perspective—Other-directed touch). The task was implemented among patients with AN, recovered patients, and HCs to analyze differences in interoception. In their study, Crucianelli et al. [80] measured the perceived pleasantness of stroking touches applied to the forearm of patients with AN and HCs while participants were looking at photos of young women's faces displaying smiling, rejecting, or neutral expressions. Tactile simulations were conducted with CT afferents-optimal (3 cm/s) and non-optimal (18 cm/s) velocities while simultaneously displaying the photos. Participants were guided to leave the stimulated arm inside a box open on two opposite sides: this detail guaranteed adequate delivery of the touch while at the same time preventing the participant from receiving visual feedback of the tactile stimuli. Lastly, in their subsequent work, Crucianelli et al. [81] added to the two stroking touches used in their previous study [80] (3 and 18 cm/s, respectively, CT afferents, optimal and non-optimal) and other tactile stimulations administered at five different speeds: an additional CT-optimal stroking touch (6 cm/s), one borderline touch (9 cm/s) and another not CT-optimal stroking touch (27 cm/s). Due to the high number of stroking touches implemented, stimulation was cycled between the two locations on the participant's forearm to prevent habituation and fatigue of CT fibers. To avoid visual feedback, in this study participants were blindfolded throughout the task. As with Bellard et al. [77], the study by Crucianelli et al. [81] compared persons with AN, recovered patients, and HCs.

Among the studies that focused on interoception, two [75,78] explored gastric interoception [94]. Aschenbrenner et al. [75] utilized the "sniffin' sticks" test battery [102] and the "taste strip" test kit [103] for the assessment of patients with AN, BN, and HCs' olfactory and gustatory functions, respectively. The sniffin' sticks test consists of a felt-tip pen-like odor dispenser that is used for an ortho-nasal examination of olfactory function and comprises three tests of olfactory functions: tests for odor threshold, odor discrimination, and odor identification. The taste strip test [103] consists of the administration of spoon-shaped filter paper strips impregnated with four taste qualities presented with increasing concentrations and placed on the left and right side of the anterior third of the tongue, resulting in a total of 32 trials. Participants in Aschenbrenner's study [75] had to identify the taste from a list of four descriptors. For each correct answer, patients received one point, which accounted for a maximum score of 32. The study by Brown et al. [78] employed the Water Load Task (WLT) to noninvasively assess gastric interoception in patients with AN and HCs. Participants sat in a half-supine position and were asked to drink water until their stomach was "completely full" (i.e., entirely filled with water). In total, 1.5 L of water was available for drinking. The exercise stopped when participants raised their hands to communicate that they had reached complete fullness. The task was halted by personnel after five minutes if the participant had not raised their hand. Researchers registered how long it took participants to reach complete fullness and, at the conclusion of the exercise, participants were asked to estimate how much water they had drunk. Precisely, participants were instructed to use a 1.5 L carafe completely full of water to pour into another empty one the quantity of water they believed they had drunk. Positive numbers indicated an overestimation of water drank since the accuracy of this estimate was computed by deducting the water estimated from the water actually consumed. Individuals were then asked to rate their level of confidence in this estimate using a range of 0 to 100.

Finally, three studies [71,76,92] investigated acute pain, which is a primary interoceptive perception [94]. Bär et al. [76] provided an assessment that included heat pain measures collected from individuals with AN and HCs. The heat pain thresholds were assessed on both arms by an ascending method of limits with a contact thermode attached to the left or right volar wrist. To determine heat pain thresholds, individuals were asked to press the stop button immediately when thermal perception had become painful. Goldzak-Kunik et al. [71] investigated cold pain in patients with AN compared to a control group of healthy people using an ice cube as a pain temperature stimulus. Three trials of 15, 30, and 45 s in duration respectively were administered with 15 min of breaks to separate the trials. Once each trial was concluded, participants rated cold, unpleasantness, and pain using three different VAS scales. Yamamotova et al. [92] assessed the thermal pain threshold latency among patients with BN and HCs using the Analgesia Meter (IITC Life Science USA Model 33), which employs radiant heat of constant intensity to an area of 1 cm^2. The assessment was carried out under six consecutive conditions, three at rest and three under stress: rest I, mental arithmetic task, rest II, eating sweet food, rest III, and cold pressor test.

3.2.2. Proprioception

In our review, we found that five studies investigated proprioceptive perception in individuals with AN and HCs [71,79,84,88,93]. Specifically, Epstein et al. [84] analyzed the proprioceptive aspects of body perception through the "proprioception test" and the "right-left orientation test". The proprioception test assesses the capacity to locate one's body parts in space. The task consists of asking the subject to touch, on verbal command, specific points on the body, without any visual input. In particular, participants in Epstein's study [84] were instructed to use their right index finger to touch ten different points on their bodies. Importantly, participants did not have to move any part of their body other than their right arm and hand. Regarding the second task used by Epstein et al. [84], the right-left orientation test evaluates three features of right-left orientation (i.e., orientation toward one's own body, toward a confronting person, and the combined orientation of the previous two).

Zopf et al. [93] used the Rubber Hand Illusion (RHI) paradigm instead to explore if the body location perception of patients was influenced differently by two types of multisensory conflicts: visual-proprioceptive hand location and visual-tactile touch synchrony. This paradigm involves, in fact, the interaction between touch, vision, and proprioceptive perception of the body in space [104,105]. The RHI paradigm [106] consists of a perceptual illusion of feeling ownership of a fake hand and provides a quantitative measure of embodiment. During the RHI paradigm, participants feel as if a fake hand belongs to them due to synchronous visuo-tactile stimulation of both a fake rubber hand, located within the visual field of the participant, and the participant's real hand, located outside the visual field of the participant. This task provides two outcome measures: proprioceptive drift [107] and the level of ownership illusion [106]. Proprioceptive drift is calculated by asking participants to indicate the position of the tip of their left index finger prior to and following each visuo-tactile stimulation (performed in asynchronous and synchronous conditions). The difference between hand estimates before and after inducing the RHI is the "proprioceptive drift" [107]. The level of ownership illusion over the rubber hand is obtained using self-report questionnaires that provide a subjective measure of the illusion e.g., [106]. Zopf and colleagues [93] measured the effect of the illusion through the reaching responses toward visual targets and the movement endpoints and the extent of the illusion using explicit bodily judgments with a set of evaluations adapted from existing RHI questionnaires [106,108]. Case et al. [79] utilized a size-weight illusion battery to evaluate visual and proprioceptive information, instead. The illusion used in the task consists in leading the subject to underestimate the weight of a larger object when compared to a smaller object of identical shape and weight. Mergen et al. [88] used the One-Point-Localization task to assess the distorted representation in AN through two experiments. This task is an adaptation of the localization paradigm, which consists of asking participants to localize a tactile stimulus placed on their skin on a screen that showed a live image of the touched body part. The aim of experiment 2 was to extend the results from experiment 1 by exploring differences in the task on neutral and sensitive body parts [88]. During both experiments, the investigator touched the participants' back or abdomen with a rubber stick, and participants were asked to click the mouse as soon as they perceived the body stimulation. The click generated a photograph of the back/abdomen which was subsequently presented to participants with the outlines obscured. At this point, participants were asked to indicate the position of the perceived touch on the image and confirm this position with a second mouse click [88]. Lastly, Goldzak-Kunik et al. [71] used a kinesthesia task to examine sensory dimensions relevant to spatial and motion aspects of body size perception. A vertical handle was put in the sloping rails of an apparatus at around chest height and participants were instructed to estimate the relative height of each hand, holding it while wearing blindfolds. As the slope changed in a set pattern of rises and declines, the left hand was lifted or lowered.

3.2.3. Vestibular System

Only one study examined vestibular signals [85]. Precisely, Fontana et al. [85] investigated the postural stability of individuals with AN, BN, and HCs, through the analysis and quantification of their postural strategies under standardized quiet-standing conditions: with eyes open (EO) and closed (EC). The acquisition duration was 60 s and participants were asked to present the feet spread apart at shoulder width. The kinematics (or segmental) method was adopted to quantify the Center of Mass (CoM) position, which in the study by Fontana et al. [85] was conceptual, with no direct measure to locate it in space. A passive marker optoelectronic system (Vicon 460) was employed and the CoM position was estimated using the positions of three-dimensional markers and a biomechanical model.

3.3. *Primary Outcomes in Anorexic and Bulimic Patients*

The included studies showed different results that will be carefully evaluated in the discussion of this review.

3.3.1. Interoception Outcomes

Eight studies [74,82,83,86,87,89–91] used the heartbeat perception task [95] for the assessment of cardiac interoception in patients with AN. Di Lernia et al. [83], Pollatos et al. [89] and Wollast et al. [91] showed deficits in IAc in patients with AN compared to controls. Specifically, Di Lernia et al. [83] performed a complete interoceptive assessment before and after an outpatient rehabilitative hospital program and the results showed severe deficits in accuracy, buffer saturation, and sensitivity in the patient compared to the control group. Pollatos et al. [89] displayed that compared to HCs, people with AN exhibited lower IAc during self-focus. In line with these outcomes, also Wollast et al. [91] found a deficit in IAw in the patients suffering from AN compared to the HCs, both at rest and when an emotional context was induced. Ambrosecchia et al. [74], Demartini et al. [82], Kinnaird et al. [86], Lutz et al. [87] and Richard et al. [90] showed no differences between patients with AN and HCs in IAw, instead.

With regard to interoceptive touch sensitivity, all studies [77,80,81] revealed deficits in interoception borne by patients with AN. Crucianelli et al. [80] showed that individuals with AN perceived affective touch as less pleasant compared to HCs, suggesting that this reduced pleasantness may be at least in part related to a dysfunctional CT afferent system. In agreement with this result, also the study by Crucianelli et al. [81] indicated that both patients with AN and recovered participants anticipated tactile experiences and rated delivered tactile stimuli as less pleasant than HCs. However, this difference was not related to the CT optimality of the stimulation. Instead, variations in top-down beliefs, alexithymia, and interoceptive sensitivity predicted changes in how CT-optimal touch was perceived. As a result, tactile anhedonia in AN may last even after a generally successful recovery and it is associated with a taught, flawed top-down expectation of tactile pleasantness rather than a bottom-up interoceptive deficiency in the CT system. The study by Bellard et al. [77] also evidenced this when evaluating touch for self: women with AN and recovered patients compared to HCs rated CT-optimal touch as less pleasant than HCs, even if they did not differ in pleasantness ratings when evaluating affective touch for another person.

The studies that explored gastric interoception reported similar results. Specifically, Aschenbrenner et al. [75] showed that individuals with BN and AN exhibit lowered olfactory and gustatory sensitivities compared to HCs. These deficits improved with increasing BMI and decreasing eating pathology in the course of treatment. Moreover, Brown et al. [78] displayed that participants with AN tend to overestimate the amount of water consumed and report greater levels of pre and post-Water Load Task fullness compared to HCs. However, regarding this latter result, no group-by-time interaction was found, suggesting that overall, there were no significant differences in change of fullness between groups. Furthermore, individuals with AN also reported greater increases in negative affects pre to post Water Load Task compared to HCs, but confidence regarding consumption estimation was not different between the two groups.

Ultimately, results concerning pain perception are mixed. Bär et al. [76] showed that heat pain thresholds significantly increased in the acute state of AN and decreased after weight had been regained for six months. Yamamotova et al. [92] showed that thermal pain threshold latency is longer in patients with BN than in HCs and that the BN group has a significantly higher pain threshold under all six experimental conditions. Finally, Goldzak-Kunik et al. [71] did not show differences between the AN and the HC group in cold pain responses.

3.3.2. Proprioception Outcomes

Proprioceptive perception has been investigated in patients with AN by five studies [71,79,84,88,93]: three of them point out a difference between proprioception in individuals with AN and healthy women, while the other two indicated no difference between groups. Case et al. [79] found that individuals with AN show a reduced size-weight illusion compared to controls, indicating a decreased capacity to combine visual and proprioceptive information. This alteration could lead to distorted body perception. Epstein et al. [84] demonstrated that patients with AN compared to an HC group reported significantly lower scores in the "right-left orientation test" at pre-treatment assessment and no significant differences at post-treatment. Zopf et al. [93] found a reduced influence of proprioceptive signals on hand location estimates in AN compared to controls. Contrary to these results, Mergen et al. [88] revealed that patients with AN and HCs did not differ in the ability to accurately localize the tactile stimulus onto a visual presentation of the body. Furthermore, no differences were found between the performance at the back and the abdomen. However, both groups showed distorted perceptions in both experiments and for at least one body part. Goldzak-Kunik [71] also found no differences between individuals with AN and controls in the performance obtained in the "kinesthesia" task.

3.3.3. Vestibular Outcomes

Fontana et al. [85] was the only study that assessed vestibular deficits in individuals with an ED. The results proved that women with BN are more unstable than HC individuals, showing significant differences in CoM anteroposterior excursions and length of the road, while patients with AN showed no significant differences from HCs.

4. Discussion

In the manuscript we suggest that it is possible to use technology (i.e., VR) to create simulative bodily experiences and that these experiences can alter the functioning of the body, triggering regenerative processes able to address complex pathologies. The aim of this systematic review was to explore studies that investigated whether inner body perception was altered in AN and BN in order to facilitate the development of clinical interventions targeting such dimensions through technology. Overall, the analyzed studies in this review show that inner body perception seems to be indeed altered in EDs, with different alteration patterns in AN and BN.

4.1. Interoceptive Deficits in Anorexia and Bulimia Nervosa

Results from the systematic review suggest that patients with AN might exhibit interoceptive perception deficits, as reported by lower accuracy scores on the heartbeat counting task compared to HCs. Specifically, individuals with AN showed difficulties in distinguishing actual interoceptive sensations from anticipated ones, particularly at low levels of bodily arousal, compared with HCs. A similar pattern was found in individuals with remitted AN: recovered patients reported altered neural activation during anticipation and receipt of sucrose tastes [109]. Some studies reveal indeed that habituation to fullness is protracted after eating [52], indicating that the return to homeostasis after state changes may also be impaired in people with AN. This alteration might reflect a dysfunctional integration of bodily information since lower IAc is associated with a higher malleability of body representations [36,110]. Along these lines, Berner et al. [109] suggest that a brain-based difficulty predicting and adapting to internal state shifts may contribute to the severity and persistence of AN. Support for this perspective can also be found in theories linking interoceptive prediction error to anxiety [111], associations between perceived sensory sensitivity and emotion dysregulation in AN [112], and the observed relationships among markers of AN severity and prefrontal and striatal hyperactivation after aversive interoception [109]. However, certain studies of this review did not find evidence for altered interoceptive heartbeat perception. Thus, moderating factors might contribute to such heterogeneity. One explanation of this inconsistency may be the variability of the samples included in these studies (inpatients, outpatients, smaller sample size, duration of the pathology, comorbidities, etc.), which results in heterogeneity in weight and treatment progress. Furthermore, individuals were evaluated at different stages of treatment, suggesting that treatment progress may have an impact when investigating interoceptive deficits in AN. In particular, interoceptive deficits might interact with weight gain or recovery periods, which can therefore be confounding factors and should be controlled for in interoceptive experimental studies. Specifically, Richard et al. [90] found that individuals who gained more weight and spent more time hospitalized showed higher IAs. This result indicates that interoceptive processes may be influenced by state-dependent factors and heterogeneity in treatment progress. However, there is evidence that interoception remain reduced in patients with AN at the end of treatment [89], suggesting that this alteration of bodily signals might be an ongoing risk factor for the maintenance of AN. Although heartbeat counting tasks are commonly used to assess interoception, it should be noted that there are methodological limitations to this approach [113]. For example, knowledge of one's resting heart rate influences the accuracy of heartbeat counting tasks [114]. In addition, only around a third of participants can accurately count their own heartbeat at rest, which opens up the possibility that floor effects may explain some null findings [94,115]. Furthermore, in some cases the task might be perceived as difficult, leading patients with AN to a higher level of stress and arousal that affects performance.

The systematic review also identified experimental studies focused on assessing pain in individuals with AN. Because pain represents the first and primary interoceptive input, this specific afferent information maintains its value in disclosing the way the interoceptive system works in AN. In relation to pain processing in individuals with AN, our results showed an increase in pain thresholds in the acute phase of the disease that decreased six months after regaining weight. However, other studies found no differences in cold pain perception among people with AN. Our findings are in line with previous studies suggesting that individuals with AN, BN, or BED have elevated thresholds to thermally [116] and mechanically induced pain, but they do not exhibit similar alterations in their sensitivity to cold [117]. Several psychological and biological mechanisms have been associated with decreased sensitivity to pain in EDs, including impairments in emotional and cognitive processing such as alexithymia and dissociation, nutritional restrictions, decreased skin temperature, blood pressure, and broader dysregulation of the vegetative nervous system [118,119]. Furthermore, the reduced pain sensitivity found in AN might be associated with insular dysfunction [120]. Strigo et al. [121] showed that patients with AN have a reduced capacity to accurately perceive bodily signals [51,112], which seems to persist even after recovery. The observed mismatch between subjective experiences (ratings) and objective responses (brain activation) in AN suggests, therefore, abnormal integration processes and, possibly, a dissociation between reported and actual interoceptive states. Deficits in interoceptive perception might play an important role in the etiology and maintenance of EDs. This decreased pain sensitivity in AN might be due to a reduction in the ability to correctly perceive the inner body dimension. In relation to pain processing, the variability of the results might be explained by a lack of consistency of measures across studies (e.g., the use of heat vs. cold stimuli). Another reason could be a limitation in the methodology used for induction of thermal pain, as well as the lack of pain threshold and tolerance measures. Many studies have repeatedly found increased pain thresholds in individuals with EDs [116,118,122], whereas others have shown no differences in pain thresholds compared to HCs e.g., [123].

One of the modalities in which impairments were consistently associated with EDs was sensitivity in gastric interoception. Individuals with AN exhibit lowered olfactory and gustatory sensitivities. These deficits might be transferred to the perception of bodily signals in general, including the accuracy of bodily signals such as hunger and satiety. Our review, in fact, also showed that participants with AN drank significantly less water than HCs and reported greater increases in negative affects after the task (i.e., Water Load Task). The perception of fullness was greater in AN compared to HCs, but since there was no group-by-time interaction, overall there were no significant differences in change in fullness between groups. At present, it is not known whether these perceptual distortions are a determinant or a result of AN or whether they improve following successful treatment. Furthermore, this lack of satiety aversion is thought to be related to people who overestimate their visual self-image. Garner and Garfinkel [124] reviewed several studies that display how individuals with AN are less accurate in judging interoceptive sensations than HCs. Several lines of experimental inquiry have suggested indeed that patients with AN may misperceive internal experiences, particularly those related to satiety. Further, the more individuals with AN overestimate their body size, the less sucrose aversion they manifest. An analysis of sensations after eating indicates that patients with AN feel fuller before eating than HCs. Individuals with AN also reporte more postprandial bloating, nausea, and thoughts of food. These findings suggest that patients with AN may experience sensations associated with eating differently than HCs do. It is, therefore, possible that people with AN have an altered ability to recognize certain visceral sensations related to hunger, satiety, and pain, suggesting a reduced capacity to accurately perceive inner body signals. In this regard, the reduced pleasantness of tactile stimuli we found in our review among individuals with AN might be read in light of this reduction in the ability to integrate and accurately perceive inner body signals. These findings, however, might also be explained by the possibility that the observed decrease in pleasantness perception is a result of an effort to regulate (i.e., lessen) anxiogenic stimuli. Anxiety is quite common among people with EDs and is accompanied by enhanced activation of cognitive control in an effort to balance out the diminished limbic function (i.e., more strategic choices can compensate for the impaired ability to perceive interoceptive information). Therefore, the decreased physiological pleasure that we noticed could be an effort to cognitively regulate an "unwanted" stimulating experience (i.e., pleasant interpersonal touch) [125].

Regarding BN, our review showes that patients with BN present lower sensitivity to pain, which seems to be a stable phenomenon and persists under various experimental conditions. This result is also consistent with the finding that pain sensitivity remains low in women who are long-term recovered from BN [126]. Supporting this idea, a recent study by Pollatos and Georgiou [127] observed an abnormal integration of different interoceptive signals in patients with BN. It is, therefore, possible to assume that individuals with BN and AN have a reduced ability to correctly elaborate the probabilistic process connecting the different inputs from exteroceptive, proprioceptive, interoceptive, and vestibular sensory systems that are essential for body self-consciousness.

4.2. Proprioception in Anorexia and Bulimia Nervosa

The studies included in this systematic review found several impairments in AN compared to controls with regard to the proprioceptive component of inner body perception. These findings are in line with other researchessuggesting impairments in spatial orientation in AN [61,62,128]. There is evidence that individuals with AN show impaired spatial cognition and that those deficits might be related to poor awareness of interoceptive inputs [129]. Furthermore, AN is characterized by alterations in posterior parietal areas [130] that are also related to the egocentric spatial reference frame directly involved in spatial cognition [131]. In this view, the low capacity of individuals with AN to integrate egocentric and allocentric spatial reference frames related to alterations in posterior parietal areas [34] may explain impaired proprioceptive processing. Moreover, it is known that parietal cortex activity is linked to the processing of proprioceptive sensory information and the integration of multisensory body information to update body size and location information [132–134]. Furthermore, Zopf et al. [93] reported a decrease in proprioceptive signals on hand location in patients with AN compared to HCs, suggesting that individuals with AN are more influenced by external visual information and relatively less by proprioceptive information. This tendency in individuals with AN toward external visual body information could be attributed to differences in the processing of proprioceptive signals. In a haptic task without vision, in which active exploration of objects depends on proprioceptive body position, Grunwald et al. [59] showed impairments in the processing and storage of proprioceptive information in individuals with AN compared to HCs. Typically, where visual information is available, proprioceptive and visual hand location information is integrated to form hand location estimates [135]. However, in individuals with AN, there is a deficit in proprioceptive-visual integration that could result in vision becoming a more dominant source of information. In addition, the study conducted by Zopf et al. [93] revealed that in individuals with AN multisensory body perception changed: the proprioceptive signals decreased and the relative influence of external visual information increased for the perception of a body location. The authors [93] suggested that this tendency of patients with AN toward external visual body information is due to changes in proprioceptive signal processing. The recurrent changes in the physical body could potentially cause modifications in multisensory body perception in AN. In relation to localization, one study showed no differences between AN and HCs in the ability to localize the stimulus or between performances at different body parts [88]. However, in that study, both groups showed systematically distorted perceptions across experiments and for at least one body part. The authors suggested that focusing on localization instead of on body size or distance estimation could minimize the cognitive-affective influences [88]. Furthermore, even if patients with AN reported a significantly worse cognitive-affective body image compared to HCs, this did not affect the One-Point-Localization Task performance. These findings could suggest that body distortion in AN may be related also to the cognitive-affect component besides perceptual alterations [88]. In contrast with Zopf's assumption of visual dominance over body location perception in AN [93], Case et al. [79] displayed that patients with AN have a cross-modal sensory integration deficit with a greater reliance on proprioceptive information, compared to HCs. The study suggests less influence of visual object information on the perception of heaviness in AN. One explanation of this impoverished visual process in AN might be malnutrition, which affects vision or sensory integration as has been shown by Mohr [136], or a preference for proprioceptive information. Altered proprioceptive information about the body could explain the over-evaluation of weight and size in AN and the distorted perception of body image [79]. Furthermore, as suggested by Case and colleagues [79], distortions are likelier to occur in proprioception than in vision since we have a proprioceptive sense primarily of our own bodies and those of others. Since AN primarily affects the sense of one's own body, proprioception would seem a more likely candidate for a sensory disturbance. Hence, the altered multisensory integration could be explained by a different internal model of heaviness in individuals with AN that could generate different expectations based on visual information [79]. Reduced size-weight illusion (SWI) in individuals with AN fits with the emerging picture of interoceptive and proprioceptive impairments in this population and more specifically underlies dysfunctional multisensory integration. This result could be a first step in the explanation of how visual body image distortions can occur even without a visual deficit and could also explain deficits in implicit body image and body schema found in relation to parietal lobe functioning e.g., [55,57,59,137]. However, as this review found, other research (e.g., [88]) displayed no differences between patients with AN and controls in the ability to examine sensory dimensions relevant to spatial and motion aspects of body-size perception: it is, therefore, necessary to implement further studies in order to shed light on the topic of proprioceptive alterations in EDs and clarify these controversial results.

4.3. Vestibular System in Anorexia and Bulimia Nervosa

In this review, the vestibular system appears to be the least investigated dimension of all inner body perceptions in AN and BN. However, vestibular signs play a crucial role in the connection between the spatial description of the inner body and the spatial description of the outside world that allows the development of the allocentric representation of the body [129]. The findings of our review evidence that vestibular signals are impaired in BN but not in patients with AN, suggesting that future studies are needed to deepen the understanding of vestibular signals in EDs. A possible reason behind this is that the reduced postural control could be mostly influenced by musculoskeletal variables. The rapid and significant changes in body weight that are typical of BN may change the proportion of lean-to-fat mass and consequently have an impact on the musculoskeletal system. According to this, body weight variations rather than BMI measurements alone may be responsible for the observed alterations in postural control.

5. Conclusions and Future Direction

Deficits in interoception, proprioception, and vestibular signals were observed across AN and BN, suggesting that: (a) alteration of inner body perception might be a crucial feature of EDs, even if further research is needed and (b) VR, to be effective with these patients, has to simulate/modify both the external and the internal body.

First, these results are in agreement with the vision of Riva and colleagues [20,131] who have linked EDs to increased precision of prior body beliefs and/or decreased precision of sensory data, both internal (interoception) and external (proprioception). Moreover, our review reveals a distinction that needs to be further investigated in AN regarding the reliance on vision and proprioception information related to body location and weight estimation. Additional research is needed to know what underlies changes in the processing of visual and proprioceptive signals in EDs and how these modifications may affect the perception of all aspects that rely on visual and proprioceptive signals, such as the location, shape, size, and weight of the body as well as external objects [79,138]. Moreover, the majority of the reviewed articles focused on the AN population instead of BN: this suggests a lack of studies on proprioception and interoception in this clinical population. More research is, therefore, necessary to better understand this aspect and the other dimensions of interoception (cardiac, gastric, and pain) in BN. In addition, there are few studies investigating vestibular signs in EDs. Due to the importance of this system for body perception and body representation in understanding these clinical conditions, further and more sophisticated studies are necessary. Lastly, all the studies we included in our review focus on female patients. Since EDs are a growing phenomenon also among men [139] and gender differences have been found in interoceptive accuracy [140], future studies should focus on male patients with EDs, in order to clarify the role of interoception, proprioception, and vestibular signals in this population, comparing them not only to HCs but also to female patients with EDs to seek for possible differences.

Second, up to now, existing body swapping illusions simulate the external body only, embodying the user in the avatar generated by VR [141]. However, as demonstrated by previous research [33], this approach is not able to permanently correct an impaired body perception in EDs. Why? Our review provides a possible explanation for this: VR simulates and corrects only the representation of the external body (body image) and not the internal one (inner body/body schema), which also apparently plays a critical role in the etiology of EDs. In fact, our experience of the body is the result of the integration of many bodily signals that have to be controlled and matched [34,142]: from (a) outside (exteroception, the body perceived through the senses), from (b) within (inner body), including interoception, the sense of the physiological conditions of the body, proprioception, the sense of the position of the body/body segments and vestibular input, the sense of motion of the body) and from (c) memory [34]. To overcome this problem, we recently suggested a new clinical approach [143]—Regenerative Virtual Medicine (RVM)—that integrates VR with different technology-based somatic modification techniques which are also able to address and modify our inner body experience.

The core elements of RVM are rooted in the Bayesian model of the mind [144,145], which considers the brain as a predictive system that constantly generates probabilistic permutations of its own states in an attempt to maintain a corrected homeostatic balance. From this point of view, an aberration in these predictions, in the past stored models, or in the sensory afferent input, can lead to pathological states and, ultimately, reflect on the body itself. The proposal of RVM suggests that the aberrant contents of pathological bodily representation can be accessed, rewritten, and ultimately modified through the means of technology able to modulate and alter all the components of our body experience. Specifically, this framework suggests using at the same time different technologies—VR, interoceptive technologies, and brain stimulation technologies (see Figure 2)—targeting a different component of our bodily experience to deliver new unexpected healthy probabilistic multisensory representations. A critical role is played by interoceptive technologies [146] for their ability to modulate the inner body. Interoceptive technologies consist of tools that produce direct modulations of interoceptive signals (such as c-fiber stimulation [147,148]), or sonoception [149,150], as well as tools that create illusions by giving people false feedback about their physiological states [151]. Specifically, RVT is based on the following steps: (a) the creation of a synthetic full-body illusion in VR (external body) that is synchronized with an interoceptive modulation (inner body), which can generate considerable prediction error; (b) the use of brain stimulation techniques to lessen the impact of predictions made from the top-down; (c) the application of conscious awareness to increase the accuracy of the multisensory experience; (d) reconstructing and re-explaining the emotional content of the multisensory experience to increase its level of reward using cognitive reappraisal. This process should lead the brain to activate internal regenerative processes able to rewrite the pathological condition and trigger a healing response [143]. Unfortunately, at the moment RVT is just a new method based on the principles of computational neuroscience and not a validated approach. Future studies and clinical trials are required for considering RVT as a possible alternative to the methods used by psychiatry and psychotherapy in the treatment of EDs. To support the use of RVT, artificial intelligence [142] could be particularly useful to integrate information coming from social network systems (SNS). SNS expose people to social comparison; when people with EDs contact with their ideal bodies or shapes in SNS (e.g., social media), they are more likely to feel negative emotions that hinder their motivations to make a change toward healthier bodies. In this sense, natural language processing [152,153] could be used to monitor patients undergoing RVT to identify those at risk of suicide [154], in need of psychological support [155], as well as to oversee the evolution of symptoms and the severity of the pathology.

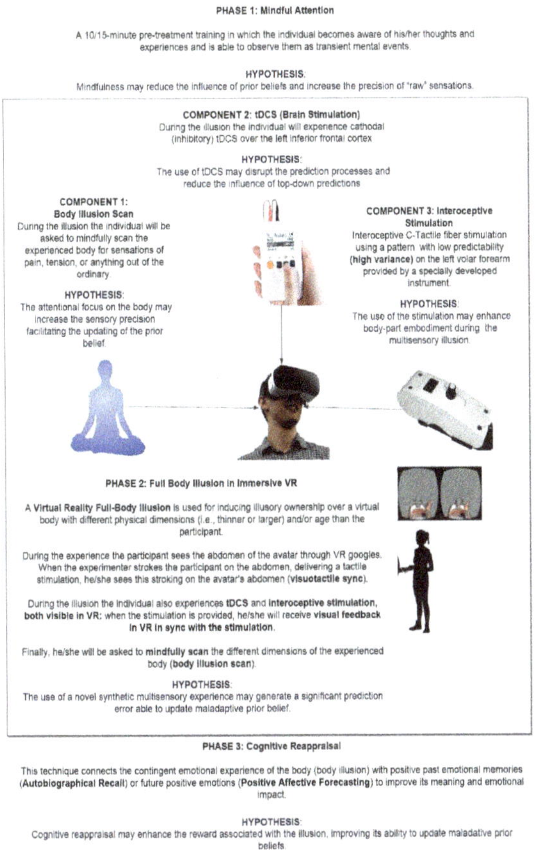

Figure 2. The different tools used in Regenerative Virtual Therapy (Adapted from Riva et al., 2021 [143]). tDCS: transcranial Direct Current Stimulation; VR: Virtual Reality.

Supplementary Materials: The following supporting information can be downloaded at: https://www.mdpi.com/article/10.3390/jcm11237134/s1, Table S1: Detailed search strategy for Eating Disorders; Table S2: Detailed search strategy for Anorexia; Table S3: Detailed search strategy for Bulimia.

Funding: Research partially supported by the Italian Ministry of Health.

Conflicts of Interest: The authors declare no conflict of interest.

References

1. Ciążyńska, J.; Maciaszek, J. Various Types of Virtual Reality-Based Therapy for Eating Disorders: A Systematic Review. *J. Clin. Med.* **2022**, *11*, 4956. [CrossRef]
2. Clus, D.; Larsen, M.E.; Lemey, C.; Berrouiguet, S. The Use of Virtual Reality in Patients with Eating Disorders: Systematic Review. *J. Med. Internet Res.* **2018**, *20*, e157. [CrossRef]
3. Ferrer-Garcia, M.; Gutiérrez-Maldonado, J.; Riva, G. Virtual Reality Based Treatments in Eating Disorders and Obesity: A Review. *J. Contemp. Psychother.* **2013**, *43*, 207–221. [CrossRef]

4. Riva, G.; Bernardelli, L.; Castelnuovo, G.; Di Lernia, D.; Tuena, C.; Clementi, A.; Pedroli, E.; Malighetti, C.; Sforza, F.; Wiederhold, B.; et al. A Virtual Reality-Based Self-Help Intervention for Dealing with the Psychological Distress Associated with the COVID-19 Lockdown: An Effectiveness Study with a Two-Week Follow-Up. *Int. J. Environ. Res. Public Health* **2021**, *18*, 8188. [CrossRef]
5. Riva, G.; Mantovani, F.; Capideville, C.S.; Preziosa, A.; Morganti, F.; Villani, D.; Gaggioli, A.; Botella, C.; Alcañiz, M. Affective Interactions Using Virtual Reality: The Link between Presence and Emotions. *Cyberpsychol. Behav.* **2007**, *10*, 45–56. [CrossRef] [PubMed]
6. Riva, G.; Malighetti, C.; Serino, S. Virtual reality in the treatment of eating disorders. *Clin. Psychol. Psychother.* **2021**, *28*, 477–488. [CrossRef] [PubMed]
7. Brown, T.; Vogel, E.N.; Adler, S.; Bohon, C.; Bullock, K.; Nameth, K.; Riva, G.; Safer, D.L.; Runfola, C.D. Bringing Virtual Reality from Clinical Trials to Clinical Practice for the Treatment of Eating Disorders: An Example Using Virtual Reality Cue Exposure Therapy. *J. Med. Internet Res.* **2020**, *22*, e16386. [CrossRef] [PubMed]
8. Riva, G. Virtual Reality in Psychotherapy: Review. *Cyberpsychol. Behav.* **2005**, *8*, 220–230. [CrossRef] [PubMed]
9. Riva, G. The Key to Unlocking the Virtual Body: Virtual Reality in the Treatment of Obesity and Eating Disorders. *J. Diabetes Sci. Technol.* **2011**, *5*, 283–292. [CrossRef]
10. Ferrer-García, M.; Gutiérrez-Maldonado, J. The use of virtual reality in the study, assessment, and treatment of body image in eating disorders and nonclinical samples: A review of the literature. *Body Image* **2012**, *9*, 1–11. [CrossRef]
11. Sansoni, M.; Malighetti, C.; Riva, G. Psychological and Educational Interventions Among Cancer Patients: A Systematic Review to Analyze the Role of Immersive Virtual Reality for Improving Patients' Well-Being. In *Extended Reality. XR Salento*; De Paolis, L.T., Arpaia, P., Sacco, M., Eds.; Lecture Notes in Computer Science; Springer: Cham, Switzerland, 2022; Volume 13446. [CrossRef]
12. Sansoni, M.; Scarzello, G.; Serino, S.; Groff, E.; Riva, G. Mitigating negative emotions through virtual reality and embodiment. *Front. Hum. Neurosci.* **2022**, *16*, 916227. [CrossRef]
13. Sansoni, M.; Riva, G. 360-VIRTOncology: Virtual Reality to Improve Cancer Patients' Well-Being. *Cyberpsychol. Behav. Soc. Netw.* **2022**, *25*, 620–622. [CrossRef] [PubMed]
14. Gorini, A.; Capideville, C.S.; De Leo, G.; Mantovani, F.; Riva, G. The Role of Immersion and Narrative in Mediated Presence: The Virtual Hospital Experience. *Cyberpsychol. Behav. Soc. Netw.* **2011**, *14*, 99–105. [CrossRef] [PubMed]
15. Ferrer-Garcia, M.; Pla-Sanjuanelo, J.; Dakanalis, A.; Vilalta-Abella, F.; Riva, G.; Fernandez-Aranda, F.; Forcano, L.; Riesco, N.; Sánchez, I.; Clerici, M.; et al. A Randomized Trial of Virtual Reality-Based Cue Exposure Second-Level Therapy and Cognitive Behavior Second-Level Therapy for Bulimia Nervosa and Binge-Eating Disorder: Outcome at Six-Month Followup. *Cyberpsychol. Behav. Soc. Netw.* **2019**, *22*, 60–68. [CrossRef]
16. Ferrer-García, M.; Gutiérrez-Maldonado, J.; Pla-Sanjuanelo, J.; Vilalta-Abella, F.; Riva, G.; Clerici, M.; Ribas-Sabaté, J.; Andreu-Gracia, A.; Fernandez-Aranda, F.; Forcano, L.; et al. A Randomised Controlled Comparison of Second-Level Treatment Approaches for Treatment-Resistant Adults with Bulimia Nervosa and Binge Eating Disorder: Assessing the Benefits of Virtual Reality Cue Exposure Therapy. *Eur. Eat. Disord. Rev.* **2017**, *25*, 479–490. [CrossRef]
17. Marco, J.H.; Perpiñá, C.; Botella, C. Effectiveness of cognitive behavioral therapy supported by virtual reality in the treatment of body image in eating disorders: One year follow-up. *Psychiatry Res.* **2013**, *209*, 619–625. [CrossRef]
18. Chirico, A.; Malighetti, C.; Serino, S.; Cipresso, P.; Pedroli, E.; Tuena, C.; Riva, G. Towards an advancement of multisensory integration deficits in anorexia nervosa: Exploring temporal discrimination processing of visuo-auditory stimuli. *Annu. Rev. Cybertherapy Telemed.* **2020**, *17*, 53–58.
19. Dakanalis, A.; Gaudio, S.; Serino, S.; Clerici, M.; Carrà, G.; Riva, G. Body-image distortion in anorexia nervosa. *Nat. Rev. Dis. Prim.* **2016**, *2*, 16026. [CrossRef]
20. Riva, G.; Dakanalis, A. Altered Processing and Integration of Multisensory Bodily Representations and Signals in Eating Disorders: A Possible Path toward the Understanding of Their Underlying Causes. *Front. Hum. Neurosci.* **2018**, *12*, 49. [CrossRef]
21. Teaford, M.; McMurray, M.S.; Billock, V.; Filipkowski, M.; Smart, L.J. The somatosensory system in anorexia nervosa: A scoping review. *J. Exp. Psychopathol.* **2021**, *12*, 2043808720987346. [CrossRef]
22. Riva, G. Neuroscience and eating disorders: The allocentric lock hypothesis. *Med. Hypotheses* **2012**, *78*, 254–257. [CrossRef] [PubMed]
23. Riva, G.; Gaudio, S. Allocentric lock in anorexia nervosa: New evidences from neuroimaging studies. *Med. Hypotheses* **2012**, *79*, 113–117. [CrossRef] [PubMed]
24. Riva, G.; Gaudio, S.; Dakanalis, A. I'm in a virtual body: A locked allocentric memory may impair the experience of the body in both obesity and anorexia nervosa. *Eat. Weight Disord. Stud. Anorex. Bulim. Obes.* **2013**, *19*, 133–134. [CrossRef] [PubMed]
25. Riva, G. Out of my real body: Cognitive neuroscience meets eating disorders. *Front. Hum. Neurosci.* **2014**, *8*, 234. [CrossRef]
26. Serino, S.; Pedroli, E.; Keizer, A.; Triberti, S.; Dakanalis, A.; Pallavicini, F.; Chirico, A.; Riva, G. Virtual Reality Body Swapping: A Tool for Modifying the Allocentric Memory of the Body. *Cyberpsychol. Behav. Soc. Netw.* **2016**, *19*, 127–133. [CrossRef] [PubMed]
27. Serino, S.; Chirico, A.; Pedroli, E.; Polli, N.; Cacciatore, C.; Riva, G. Two-phases innovative treatment for anorexia nervosa: The potential of virtual reality body-swap. *Ann. Rev. Cyber Ther. Telemed.* **2017**, *15*, 111–115.
28. Serino, S.; Dakanalis, A. Bodily illusions and weight-related disorders: Clinical insights from experimental research. *Ann. Phys. Rehabil. Med.* **2017**, *60*, 217–219. [CrossRef]
29. Serino, S.; Polli, N.; Riva, G. From avatars to body swapping: The use of virtual reality for assessing and treating body-size distortion in individuals with anorexia. *J. Clin. Psychol.* **2018**, *75*, 313–322. [CrossRef]

30. Keizer, A.; Van Elburg, A.; Helms, R.; Dijkerman, H.C. A Virtual Reality Full Body Illusion Improves Body Image Disturbance in Anorexia Nervosa. *PLoS ONE* **2016**, *11*, e0163921. [CrossRef] [PubMed]
31. Petkova, V.I.; Ehrsson, H.H. If I Were You: Perceptual Illusion of Body Swapping. *PLoS ONE* **2008**, *3*, e3832. [CrossRef]
32. Matamala-Gomez, M.; Maselli, A.; Malighetti, C.; Realdon, O.; Mantovani, F.; Riva, G. Virtual Body Ownership Illusions for Mental Health: A Narrative Review. *J. Clin. Med.* **2021**, *10*, 139. [CrossRef]
33. Riva, G. Letter to the Editor: Virtual reality in the treatment of eating and weight disorders. *Psychol. Med.* **2017**, *47*, 2567–2568. [CrossRef] [PubMed]
34. Riva, G. The neuroscience of body memory: From the self through the space to the others. *Cortex* **2018**, *104*, 241–260. [PubMed]
35. Craig, A.D. How do you feel? Interoception: The sense of the physiological condition of the body. *Nat. Rev. Neurosci.* **2002**, *3*, 655–666. [CrossRef] [PubMed]
36. Tsakiris, M.; Jiménez, A.T.; Costantini, M. Just a heartbeat away from one's body: Interoceptive sensitivity predicts malleability of body-representations. *Proc. R. Soc. B Biol. Sci.* **2011**, *278*, 2470–2476. [CrossRef] [PubMed]
37. Babo-Rebelo, M.; Wolpert, N.; Adam, C.; Hasboun, D.; Tallon-Baudry, C. Is the cardiac monitoring function related to the self in both the default network and right anterior insula? *Philos. Trans. R. Soc. B Biol. Sci.* **2016**, *371*, 20160004. [CrossRef] [PubMed]
38. Garfinkel, S.N.; Seth, A.K.; Barrett, A.B.; Suzuki, K.; Critchley, H.D. Knowing your own heart: Distinguishing interoceptive accuracy from interoceptive awareness. *Biol. Psychol.* **2015**, *104*, 65–74. [CrossRef] [PubMed]
39. Garfinkel, S.N.; Critchley, H.D. Interoception, emotion and brain: New insights link internal physiology to social behaviour. Commentary on: "Anterior insular cortex mediates bodily sensibility and social anxiety" by Terasawa et al. (2012). *Soc. Cogn. Affect. Neurosci.* **2013**, *8*, 231–234. [CrossRef] [PubMed]
40. Blanke, O. Multisensory brain mechanisms of bodily self-consciousness. *Nat. Rev. Neurosci.* **2012**, *13*, 556–571. [CrossRef] [PubMed]
41. Proske, U. The role of muscle proprioceptors in human limb position sense: A hypothesis. *J. Anat.* **2015**, *227*, 178–183. [CrossRef] [PubMed]
42. Azañón, E.; Tamè, L.; Maravita, A.; Linkenauger, S.A.; Ferrè, E.R.; Tajadura-Jiménez, A.; Longo, M.R. Multimodal contributions to body representation. *Multisens. Res.* **2016**, *29*, 635–661. [CrossRef]
43. Berthoz, A. How does the cerebral cortex process and utilize vestibular signals. In *Disorders of the Vestibular System*; Oxford University Press: New York, NY, USA, 1996.
44. Ferrè, E.R.; Haggard, P. The vestibular body: Vestibular contributions to bodily representations. *Cogn. Neuropsychol.* **2016**, *33*, 67–81. [CrossRef] [PubMed]
45. Cabanac, M.; Duclaux, R. Obesity: Absence of Satiety Aversion to Sucrose. *Science* **1970**, *168*, 496–497. [CrossRef] [PubMed]
46. Chieffi, S.; Iavarone, A.; La Marra, M.; Messina, G.; Villano, I.; Ranucci, S.; Messina, A.; Piombino, L.; Dalia, C.; Monda, M. Memory for proprioceptive targets in bulimia nervosa. *J. Psychiatry* **2015**, *18*, 2.
47. Gaudio, S.; Brooks, S.; Riva, G. Nonvisual Multisensory Impairment of Body Perception in Anorexia Nervosa: A Systematic Review of Neuropsychological Studies. *PLoS ONE* **2014**, *9*, e110087. [CrossRef] [PubMed]
48. Natenshon, A.H. Eating Disorders: A Treatment Apart. The Unique Use of the Therapist's Self in the Treatment of Eating Disorders. In *Eating Disorders: A Paradigm of the Biopsychosocial Model of Illness*; Intech: Vienna, Austria, 2017; pp. 159–192.
49. Kerr, K.L.; Moseman, S.E.; Avery, J.A.; Bodurka, J.; Zucker, N.L.; Simmons, W.K. Altered Insula Activity during Visceral Interoception in Weight-Restored Patients with Anorexia Nervosa. *Neuropsychopharmacology* **2015**, *41*, 521–528. [CrossRef] [PubMed]
50. Nunn, K.; Frampton, I.; Fuglset, T.S.; Törzsök-Sonnevend, M.; Lask, B. Anorexia nervosa and the insula. *Med. Hypotheses* **2011**, *76*, 353–357. [CrossRef] [PubMed]
51. Pollatos, O.; Kurz, A.-L.; Albrecht, J.; Schreder, T.; Kleemann, A.M.; Schöpf, V.; Kopietz, R.; Wiesmann, M.; Schandry, R. Reduced perception of bodily signals in anorexia nervosa. *Eat. Behav.* **2008**, *9*, 381–388. [CrossRef]
52. Zucker, N.L.; Merwin, R.M.; Bulik, C.M.; Moskovich, A.; Wildes, J.E.; Groh, J. Subjective experience of sensation in anorexia nervosa. *Behav. Res. Ther.* **2013**, *51*, 256–265. [CrossRef]
53. Oberndorfer, T.A.; Frank, G.; Simmons, A.N.; Wagner, A.; McCurdy, D.; Fudge, J.L.; Yang, T.T.; Paulus, M.P.; Kaye, W.H. Altered Insula Response to Sweet Taste Processing After Recovery from Anorexia and Bulimia Nervosa. *Am. J. Psychiatry* **2013**, *170*, 1143–1151. [CrossRef]
54. Blechert, J.; Ansorge, U.; Tuschen-Caffier, B. A body-related dot-probe task reveals distinct attentional patterns for bulimia nervosa and anorexia nervosa. *J. Abnorm. Psychol.* **2010**, *119*, 575–585. [CrossRef] [PubMed]
55. Guardia, D.; Lafargue, G.; Thomas, P.; Dodin, V.; Cottencin, O.; Luyat, M. Anticipation of body-scaled action is modified in anorexia nervosa. *Neuropsychologia* **2010**, *48*, 3961–3966. [CrossRef] [PubMed]
56. Komatsu, H.; Nagamitsu, S.; Ozono, S.; Yamashita, Y.; Ishibashi, M.; Matsuishi, T. Regional cerebral blood flow changes in early-onset anorexia nervosa before and after weight gain. *Brain Dev.* **2010**, *32*, 625–630. [CrossRef] [PubMed]
57. Nico, D.; Daprati, E.; Nighoghossian, N.; Carrier, E.; Duhamel, J.-R.; Sirigu, A. The role of the right parietal lobe in anorexia nervosa. *Psychol. Med.* **2009**, *40*, 1531–1539. [CrossRef]
58. Sachdev, P.; Mondraty, N.; Wen, W.; Gulliford, K. Brains of anorexia nervosa patients process self-images differently from non-self-images: An fMRI study. *Neuropsychologia* **2008**, *46*, 2161–2168. [CrossRef]

59. Grunwald, M.; Ettrich, C.; Assmann, B.; Dähne, A.; Krause, W.; Busse, F.; Gertz, H.-J. Deficits in haptic perception and right parietal theta power changes in patients with anorexia nervosa before and after weight gain. *Int. J. Eat. Disord.* **2001**, *29*, 417–428. [CrossRef]
60. Mohr, H.M.; Zimmermann, J.; Röder, C.; Lenz, C.; Overbeck, G.; Grabhorn, R. Separating two components of body image in anorexia nervosa using fMRI. *Psychol. Med.* **2009**, *40*, 1519–1529. [CrossRef]
61. Cipolletta, S.; Malighetti, C.; Serino, S.; Riva, G.; Winter, D. Intrapersonal, interpersonal, and physical space in anorexia nervosa: A virtual reality and repertory grid investigation. *Psychiatry Res.* **2017**, *252*, 87–93. [CrossRef]
62. Malighetti, C.; Serino, S.; Riva, G.; Cipolletta, S. Inside and outside the self. Virtual reality and repertory grids in the spatial analysis of anorexic patients' meanings. *Annu. Rev. Cybertherapy Telemed.* **2016**, *14*, 78–81.
63. Bartholdy, S.; Musiat, P.; Campbell, I.C.; Schmidt, U. The Potential of Neurofeedback in the Treatment of Eating Disorders: A Review of the Literature. *Eur. Eat. Disord. Rev.* **2013**, *21*, 456–463. [CrossRef]
64. Duriez, P.; Khalil, R.B.; Chamoun, Y.; Maatoug, R.; Strumila, R.; Seneque, M.; Gorwood, P.; Courtet, P.; Guillaume, S. Brain Stimulation in Eating Disorders: State of the Art and Future Perspectives. *J. Clin. Med.* **2020**, *9*, 2358. [CrossRef]
65. Dunlop, K.A.; Ewoodside, B.; Edownar, J. Targeting Neural Endophenotypes of Eating Disorders with Non-invasive Brain Stimulation. *Front. Neurosci.* **2016**, *10*, 30. [CrossRef] [PubMed]
66. Schonherr, A.; Albrecht May, C. Influence of Caloric Vestibular Stimulation on Body Experience of Anorectic Patients. *Case Stud. J.* **2015**, *4*, 2886236.
67. Miller, S.M. Vestibular neuromodulation: Stimulating the neural crossroads of psychiatric illness. *Bipolar Disord.* **2016**, *18*, 539–543. [CrossRef]
68. Been, G.; Ngo, T.T.; Miller, S.M.; Fitzgerald, P.B. The use of tDCS and CVS as methods of non-invasive brain stimulation. *Brain Res. Rev.* **2007**, *56*, 346–361. [CrossRef] [PubMed]
69. Moher, D.; Liberati, A.; Tetzlaff, J.; Altman, D.G.; PRISMA Group. Preferred Reporting Items for Systematic Reviews and Meta-Analyses: The PRISMA Statement. *Ann. Intern. Med.* **2009**, *151*, 264–269. [CrossRef]
70. Elmagarmid, A.; Fedorowicz, Z.; Hammady, H.; Ilyas, I.; Khabsa, M.; Ouzzani, M. Rayyan: A systematic reviews web app for exploring and filtering searches for eligible studies for Cochrane Reviews. In *Evidence-Informed Public Health: Opportunities and Challenges*; Abstracts of the 22nd Cochrane Colloquium; John Wiley & Sons: Hyderabad, India, 2014; pp. 21–26.
71. Goldzak-Kunik, G.; Friedman, R.; Spitz, M.; Sandler, L.; Leshem, M. Intact sensory function in anorexia nervosa. *Am. J. Clin. Nutr.* **2012**, *95*, 272–282. [CrossRef] [PubMed]
72. Berlucchi, G.; Aglioti, S.M. The body in the brain revisited. *Exp. Brain Res.* **2010**, *200*, 25. [CrossRef]
73. Lopez, C. Making Sense of the Body: The Role of Vestibular Signals. *Multisens. Res.* **2015**, *28*, 525–557. [CrossRef]
74. Ambrosecchia, M.; Ardizzi, M.; Russo, E.; Ditaranto, F.; Speciale, M.; Vinai, P.; Todisco, P.; Maestro, S.; Gallese, V. Interoception and Autonomic Correlates during Social Interactions. Implications for Anorexia. *Front. Hum. Neurosci.* **2017**, *11*, 219. [CrossRef]
75. Aschenbrenner, K.; Scholze, N.; Joraschky, P.; Hummel, T. Gustatory and olfactory sensitivity in patients with anorexia and bulimia in the course of treatment. *J. Psychiatr. Res.* **2008**, *43*, 129–137. [CrossRef] [PubMed]
76. Bär, K.J.; Boettger, S.; Wagner, G.; Wilsdorf, C.; Gerhard, U.J.; Boettger, M.K.; Blanz, B.; Sauer, H. Changes of pain perception, autonomic function, and endocrine parameters during treatment of anorectic adolescents. *J. Am. Acad. Child Adolesc. Psychiatry* **2006**, *45*, 1068–1076. [CrossRef] [PubMed]
77. Bellard, A.; Trotter, P.; McGlone, F.; Cazzato, V. Vicarious ratings of self vs. other-directed social touch in women with and recovered from Anorexia Nervosa. *Sci. Rep.* **2022**, *12*, 13429. [CrossRef] [PubMed]
78. Brown, T.A.; Perry, T.R.; Kaye, W.H.; Wierenga, C.E. Pilot study of a water load test as a measure of gastric interoception in anorexia nervosa. *Eat. Weight. Disord. Stud. Anorex. Bulim. Obes.* **2022**, *27*, 2223–2228. [CrossRef] [PubMed]
79. Case, L.K.; Wilson, R.C.; Ramachandran, V.S. Diminished size–weight illusion in anorexia nervosa: Evidence for visuo-proprioceptive integration deficit. *Exp. Brain Res.* **2011**, *217*, 79–87. [CrossRef] [PubMed]
80. Crucianelli, L.; Cardi, V.; Treasure, J.; Jenkinson, P.M.; Fotopoulou, A. The perception of affective touch in anorexia nervosa. *Psychiatry Res.* **2016**, *239*, 72–78. [CrossRef]
81. Crucianelli, L.; Demartini, B.; Goeta, D.; Nisticò, V.; Saramandi, A.; Bertelli, S.; Todisco, P.; Gambini, O.; Fotopoulou, A. The Anticipation and Perception of Affective Touch in Women with and Recovered from Anorexia Nervosa. *Neuroscience* **2020**, *464*, 143–155. [CrossRef]
82. Demartini, B.; Goeta, D.; Romito, L.; Anselmetti, S.; Bertelli, S.; D'Agostino, A.; Gambini, O. Anorexia nervosa and functional motor symptoms: Two faces of the same coin? *J. Neuropsychiatry Clin. Neurosci.* **2017**, *29*, 383–390. [CrossRef]
83. Di Lernia, D.; Serino, S.; Polli, N.; Cacciatore, C.; Persani, L.; Riva, G. Interoceptive Axes Dissociation in Anorexia Nervosa: A Single Case Study with Follow Up Post-recovery Assessment. *Front. Psychol.* **2019**, *9*, 2488. [CrossRef]
84. Epstein, J.; Wiseman, C.V.; Sunday, S.R.; Klapper, F.; Alkalay, L.; Halmi, K.A. Neurocognitive evidence favors "top down" over "bottom up" mechanisms in the pathogenesis of body size distortions in anorexia nervosa. *Eat. Weight. Disord.-Stud. Anorex. Bulim. Obes.* **2001**, *6*, 140–147. [CrossRef]
85. Fontana, M.P.; Menegoni, F.; Vismara, L.; Galli, M.; Romei, M.; Bergamini, E.; Petroni, M.L.; Capodaglio, P. Balance in patients with anorexia and bulimia nervosa. *Eur. J. Phys. Rehabil. Med.* **2009**, *45*, 335–340. [PubMed]
86. Kinnaird, E.; Stewart, C.; Tchanturia, K. Interoception in Anorexia Nervosa: Exploring Associations with Alexithymia and Autistic Traits. *Front. Psychiatry* **2020**, *11*, 64. [CrossRef] [PubMed]

87. Lutz, A.P.; Schulz, A.; Voderholzer, U.; Koch, S.; van Dyck, Z.; Vögele, C.V. Enhanced cortical processing of cardio-afferent signals in anorexia nervosa. *Clin. Neurophysiol.* **2019**, *130*, 1620–1627. [CrossRef] [PubMed]
88. Mergen, J.; Keizer, A.; Koelkebeck, K.; Heuvel, M.R.V.D.; Wagner, H. Women with Anorexia Nervosa do not show altered tactile localization compared to healthy controls. *Psychiatry Res.* **2018**, *267*, 446–454. [CrossRef] [PubMed]
89. Pollatos, O.; Herbert, B.M.; Berberich, G.; Zaudig, M.; Krauseneck, T.; Tsakiris, M. Atypical self-focus effect on interoceptive accuracy in anorexia nervosa. *Front. Hum. Neurosci.* **2016**, *10*, 484. [CrossRef]
90. Richard, A.; Meule, A.; Georgii, C.; Voderholzer, U.; Cuntz, U.; Wilhelm, F.H.; Blechert, J. Associations between interoceptive sensitivity, intuitive eating, and body mass index in patients with anorexia nervosa and normal-weight controls. *Eur. Eat. Disord. Rev.* **2019**, *27*, 571–577. [CrossRef]
91. Wollast, R.; Fossion, P.; Kotsou, I.; Rebrassé, A.; Leys, C. Interoceptive Awareness and Anorexia Nervosa: When Emotions Influence the Perception of Physiological Sensations. *J. Nerv. Ment. Dis.* **2022**, *210*, 390–393. [CrossRef]
92. Yamamotova, A.; Papezova, H.; Uher, R. Modulation of thermal pain perception by stress and sweet taste in women with bulimia nervosa. *Neuro Endocrinol. Lett.* **2009**, *30*, 237–244.
93. Zopf, R.; Contini, E.; Fowler, C.; Mondraty, N.; Williams, M.A. Body distortions in Anorexia Nervosa: Evidence for changed processing of multisensory bodily signals. *Psychiatry Res.* **2016**, *245*, 473–481. [CrossRef]
94. Martin, E.; Dourish, C.; Rotshtein, P.; Spetter, M.; Higgs, S. Interoception and disordered eating: A systematic review. *Neurosci. Biobehav. Rev.* **2019**, *107*, 166–191. [CrossRef]
95. Schandry, R. Heart Beat Perception and Emotional Experience. *Psychophysiology* **1981**, *18*, 483–488. [CrossRef]
96. Mayer, J.D.; Allen, J.P.; Beauregard, K. Mood inductions for four specific moods: A procedure employing guided imagery vignettes with music. *J. Ment. Imag.* **1995**, *19*, 151–159.
97. Craig, A.D. How do you feel—Now? The anterior insula and human awareness. *Nat. Rev. Neurosci.* **2009**, *10*, 59–70. [CrossRef]
98. Case, L.K.; Laubacher, C.M.; Olausson, H.; Wang, B.; Spagnolo, P.A.; Bushnell, M.C. Encoding of touch intensity but not pleasantness in human primary somatosensory cortex. *J. Neurosci.* **2016**, *36*, 5850–5860. [CrossRef] [PubMed]
99. Gordon, I.; Voos, A.C.; Bennett, R.H.; Bolling, D.Z.; Pelphrey, K.A.; Kaiser, M.D. Brain mechanisms for processing affective touch. *Hum. Brain Mapp.* **2011**, *34*, 914–922. [CrossRef]
100. McGlone, F.; Wessberg, J.; Olausson, H. Discriminative and Affective Touch: Sensing and Feeling. *Neuron* **2014**, *82*, 737–755. [CrossRef] [PubMed]
101. McGlone, F.; Vallbo, A.B.; Olausson, H.; Loken, L.; Wessberg, J. Discriminative touch and emotional touch. *Can. J. Exp. Psychol.* **2007**, *61*, 173–183. [CrossRef]
102. Hummel, T.; Sekinger, B.; Wolf, S.R.; Pauli, E.; Kobal, G. 'Sniffin'sticks': Olfactory performance assessed by the combined testing of odor identification, odor discrimination and olfactory threshold. *Chem. Senses* **1997**, *22*, 39–52. [CrossRef] [PubMed]
103. Mueller, C.; Kallert, S.; Renner, B.; Stiassny, K.; Temmel, A.F.P.; Hummel, T.; Kobal, G. Quantitative assessment of gustatory function in a clinical context using impregnated "taste strips". *Rhinol. J.* **2003**, *41*, 2–6.
104. Cardini, F.; Haggard, P.; Ladavas, E. Seeing and feeling for self and other: Proprioceptive spatial location determines multisensory enhancement of touch. *Cognition* **2013**, *127*, 84–92. [CrossRef]
105. Pavani, F.; Spence, C.; Driver, J. Visual Capture of Touch: Out-of-the-Body Experiences with Rubber Gloves. *Psychol. Sci.* **2000**, *11*, 353–359. [CrossRef]
106. Botvinick, M.; Cohen, J. Rubber hands 'feel' touch that eyes see. *Nature* **1998**, *391*, 756. [CrossRef] [PubMed]
107. Tsakiris, M.; Haggard, P. The Rubber Hand Illusion Revisited: Visuotactile Integration and Self-Attribution. *J. Exp. Psychol. Hum. Percept. Perform.* **2005**, *31*, 80–91. [CrossRef] [PubMed]
108. Longo, M.R.; Schüür, F.; Kammers, M.P.; Tsakiris, M.; Haggard, P. What is embodiment? A psychometric approach. *Cognition* **2008**, *107*, 978–998. [CrossRef] [PubMed]
109. Berner, L.A.; Simmons, A.N.; Wierenga, C.E.; Bischoff-Grethe, A.; Paulus, M.P.; Bailer, U.F.; Ely, A.V.; Kaye, W.H. Altered interoceptive activation before, during, and after aversive breathing load in women remitted from anorexia nervosa. *Psychol. Med.* **2017**, *48*, 142–154. [CrossRef]
110. Keizer, A.; Smeets, M.A.; Postma, A.; van Elburg, A.; Dijkerman, H.C. Does the experience of ownership over a rubber hand change body size perception in anorexia nervosa patients? *Neuropsychologia* **2014**, *62*, 26–37. [CrossRef]
111. Paulus, M.P.; Stein, M.B. Interoception in anxiety and depression. *Brain Struct. Funct.* **2010**, *214*, 451–463. [CrossRef]
112. Merwin, R.M.; Moskovich, A.A.; Wagner, H.R.; Ritschel, L.A.; Craighead, L.W.; Zucker, N.L. Emotion regulation difficulties in anorexia nervosa: Relationship to self-perceived sensory sensitivity. *Cogn. Emot.* **2013**, *27*, 441–452. [CrossRef]
113. Brener, J.; Ring, C. Towards a psychophysics of interoceptive processes: The measurement of heartbeat detection. *Philos. Trans. R. Soc. B Biol. Sci.* **2016**, *371*, 20160015. [CrossRef]
114. Murphy, J.; Brewer, R.; Hobson, H.; Catmur, C.; Bird, G. Is alexithymia characterised by impaired interoception? Further evidence, the importance of control variables, and the problems with the Heartbeat Counting Task. *Biol. Psychol.* **2018**, *136*, 189–197. [CrossRef]
115. Khalsa, S.S.; Lapidus, R.C. Can Interoception Improve the Pragmatic Search for Biomarkers in Psychiatry? *Front. Psychiatry* **2016**, *7*, 121. [CrossRef] [PubMed]
116. Lautenbacher, S.; Pauls, A.M.; Strian, F.; Pirke, K.-M.; Krieg, J.-C. Pain sensitivity in anorexia nervosa and bulimia nervosa. *Biol. Psychiatry* **1991**, *29*, 1073–1078. [CrossRef] [PubMed]

117. de Zwaan, M.; Biener, D.; Bach, M.; Wiesnagrotzki, S.; Stacher, G. Pain sensitivity, alexithymia, and depression in patients with eating disorders: Are they related? *J. Psychosom. Res.* **1996**, *41*, 65–70. [CrossRef] [PubMed]
118. Papezová, H.; Yamamotová, A.; Nedvídková, J. Pain modulation role of melatonin in eating disorders. *Eur. Psychiatry* **2001**, *16*, 68–70. [CrossRef]
119. Yamamotová, A.; Papezova, H. Does the pain perception depend on the type of vegetative reactivity? Comparison of healthy women with eating disorders patients. *Homeost. Praha* **2000**, *40*, 134–136.
120. Scharner, S.; Stengel, A. Alterations of brain structure and functions in anorexia nervosa. *Clin. Nutr. Exp.* **2019**, *28*, 22–32. [CrossRef]
121. Strigo, I.A.; Matthews, S.C.; Simmons, A.N.; Oberndorfer, T.; Klabunde, M.; Bsc, L.E.R.; Kaye, W.H. Altered insula activation during pain anticipation in individuals recovered from anorexia nervosa: Evidence of interoceptive dysregulation. *Int. J. Eat. Disord.* **2012**, *46*, 23–33. [CrossRef]
122. Yamamotova, A.; Bulant, J.; Bocek, V.; Papezova, H. Dissatisfaction with own body makes patients with eating disorders more sensitive to pain. *J. Pain Res.* **2017**, *10*, 1667–1675. [CrossRef]
123. Schmahl, C.; Meinzer, M.; Zeuch, A.; Fichter, M.; Cebulla, M.; Kleindienst, N.; Ludäscher, P.; Steil, R.; Bohus, M. Pain sensitivity is reduced in borderline personality disorder, but not in posttraumatic stress disorder and bulimia nervosa. *World J. Biol. Psychiatry* **2010**, *11*, 364–371. [CrossRef]
124. Garner, D.M.; Garfinkel, P.E. Body image in anorexia nervosa: Measurement, theory and clinical implications. *Int. J. Psychiatry Med.* **1982**, *11*, 263–284. [CrossRef] [PubMed]
125. Connan, F.; Campbell, I.C.; Katzman, M.; Lightman, S.L.; Treasure, J. A neurodevelopmental model for anorexia nervosa. *Physiol. Behav.* **2003**, *79*, 13–24. [CrossRef] [PubMed]
126. Stein, D.; Kaye, W.H.; Matsunaga, H.; Myers, D.; Orbach, I.; Har-Even, D.; Frank, G.; Rao, R. Pain perception in recovered bulimia nervosa patients. *Int. J. Eat. Disord.* **2003**, *34*, 331–336. [CrossRef]
127. Pollatos, O.; Georgiou, E. Normal interoceptive accuracy in women with bulimia nervosa. *Psychiatry Res.* **2016**, *240*, 328–332. [CrossRef] [PubMed]
128. Serino, S.; Dakanalis, A.; Gaudio, S.; Carrà, G.; Cipresso, P.; Clerici, M.; Riva, G. Out of body, out of space: Impaired reference frame processing in eating disorders. *Psychiatry Res.* **2015**, *230*, 732–734. [CrossRef]
129. Guardia, D.; Carey, A.; Cottencin, O.; Thomas, P.; Luyat, M. Disruption of Spatial Task Performance in Anorexia Nervosa. *PLoS ONE* **2013**, *8*, e54928. [CrossRef] [PubMed]
130. Gaudio, S.; Quattrocchi, C.C. Neural basis of a multidimensional model of body image distortion in anorexia nervosa. *Neurosci. Biobehav. Rev.* **2012**, *36*, 1839–1847. [CrossRef]
131. Riva, G.; Gaudio, S. Locked to a wrong body: Eating disorders as the outcome of a primary disturbance in multisensory body integration. *Conscious. Cogn.* **2018**, *59*, 57–59. [CrossRef]
132. Culham, J.C.; Cavina-Pratesi, C.; Singhal, A. The role of parietal cortex in visuomotor control: What have we learned from neuroimaging? *Neuropsychologia* **2006**, *44*, 2668–2684. [CrossRef]
133. Ehrsson, H.H.; Holmes, N.P.; Passingham, R.E. Touching a Rubber Hand: Feeling of Body Ownership Is Associated with Activity in Multisensory Brain Areas. *J. Neurosci.* **2005**, *25*, 10564–10573. [CrossRef]
134. Ehrsson, H.H.; Spence, C.; Passingham, R.E. That's my hand! Activity in premotor cortex reflects feeling of ownership of a limb. *Science* **2004**, *305*, 875–877. [CrossRef]
135. Holmes, N.P.; Snijders, H.J.; Spence, C. Reaching with alien limbs: Visual exposure to prosthetic hands in a mirror biases proprioception without accompanying illusions of ownership. *Percept. Psychophys.* **2006**, *68*, 685–701. [CrossRef] [PubMed]
136. Mohr, C.; Porter, G.; Benton, C. Psychophysics reveals a right hemispheric contribution to body image distortions in women but not men. *Neuropsychologia* **2007**, *45*, 2942–2950. [CrossRef]
137. Grunwald, M.; Weiss, T.; Krause, W.; Beyer, L.; Rost, R.; Gutberlet, I.; Gertz, H.-J. Theta power in the EEG of humans during ongoing processing in a haptic object recognition task. *Cogn. Brain Res.* **2001**, *11*, 33–37. [CrossRef]
138. Spitoni, G.F.; Serino, A.; Cotugno, A.; Mancini, F.; Antonucci, G.; Pizzamiglio, L. The two dimensions of the body representation in women suffering from Anorexia Nervosa. *Psychiatry Res.* **2015**, *230*, 181–188. [CrossRef] [PubMed]
139. Dakanalis, A.; Riva, G. Current considerations for eating and body-related disorders among men. In *Handbook on Body Image: Gender Differences, Sociocultural Influences and Health Implications*; Nova Publishers: New York, NY, USA, 2013; pp. 195–216.
140. Prentice, F.; Hobson, H.; Spooner, R.; Murphy, J. Gender differences in interoceptive accuracy and emotional ability: An explanation for incompatible findings. *Neurosci. Biobehav. Rev.* **2022**, *141*, 104808. [CrossRef] [PubMed]
141. Riva, G.; Wiederhold, B.K.; Chirico, A.; di Lernia, D.; Mantovani, F.; Gaggioli, A. Brain and Virtual Reality: What Do They Have in Common and How to Exploit Their Potential. *Annu. Rev. Cybertherapy Telemed.* **2018**, *2018*, 3–8.
142. Riva, G.; Wiederhold, B.K.; di Lernia, D.; Chirico, A.; Riva, E.F.M.; Mantovani, F.; Cipresso, P.; Gaggioli, A. Virtual Reality Meets Artificial Intelligence: The Emergence of Advanced Digital Therapeutics and Digital Biomarkers. *Annu. Rev. Cybertherapy Telemed.* **2019**, *17*, 3–7.
143. Riva, G.; Serino, S.; Di Lernia, D.; Pagnini, F. Regenerative Virtual Therapy: The Use of Multisensory Technologies and Mindful Attention for Updating the Altered Representations of the Bodily Self. *Front. Syst. Neurosci.* **2021**, *15*, 749268. [CrossRef]
144. De Ridder, D.; Vanneste, S.; Freeman, W. The Bayesian brain: Phantom percepts resolve sensory uncertainty. *Neurosci. Biobehav. Rev.* **2014**, *44*, 4–15. [CrossRef]

145. Friston, K. The freeenergy principle: A unified brain theory? *Nat. Rev. Neurosci.* **2010**, *11*, 127–138. [CrossRef]
146. Schoeller, F.; Haar, A.; Jain, A.; Maes, P. Enhancing human emotions with interoceptive technologies. *Phys. Life Rev.* **2019**, *31*, 310–319. [CrossRef] [PubMed]
147. Björnsdotter, M.; Morrison, I.; Olausson, H. Feeling good: On the role of C fiber mediated touch in interoception. *Exp. Brain Res.* **2010**, *207*, 149–155. [CrossRef] [PubMed]
148. Di Lernia, D.; Lacerenza, M.; Ainley, V.; Riva, G. Altered Interoceptive Perception and the Effects of Interoceptive Analgesia in Musculoskeletal, Primary, and Neuropathic Chronic Pain Conditions. *J. Pers. Med.* **2020**, *10*, 201. [CrossRef] [PubMed]
149. Riva, G.; Serino, S.; Di Lernia, D.; Pavone, E.F.; Dakanalis, A. Embodied Medicine: Mens Sana in Corpore Virtuale Sano. *Front. Hum. Neurosci.* **2017**, *11*, 120. [CrossRef] [PubMed]
150. Wiederhold, B.K.; Riva, G. Virtual Reality Therapy: Emerging Topics and Future Challenges. *Cyberpsychol. Behav. Soc. Netw.* **2019**, *22*, 3–6. [CrossRef] [PubMed]
151. Iodice, P.; Porciello, G.; Bufalari, I.; Barca, L.; Pezzulo, G. An interoceptive illusion of effort induced by false heart-rate feedback. *Proc. Natl. Acad. Sci. USA* **2019**, *116*, 13897–13902. [CrossRef]
152. Barańska, K.; Różańska, A.; Maćkowska, S.; Rojewska, K.; Spinczyk, D. Determining the Intensity of Basic Emotions among People Suffering from Anorexia Nervosa Based on Free Statements about Their Body. *Electronics* **2022**, *11*, 138. [CrossRef]
153. Rojewska, K.; Maćkowska, S.; Maćkowski, M.; Różańska, A.; Barańska, K.; Dzieciątko, M.; Spinczyk, D. Natural Language Processing and Machine Learning Supporting the Work of a Psychologist and Its Evaluation on the Example of Support for Psychological Diagnosis of Anorexia. *Appl. Sci.* **2022**, *12*, 4702. [CrossRef]
154. Coppersmith, G.; Leary, R.; Crutchley, P.; Fine, A. Natural language processing of social media as screening for suicide risk. *Biomed. Inform. Insights* **2018**, *10*, 1–11. [CrossRef]
155. Yan, H.; Fitzsimmons-Craft, E.E.; Goodman, M.; Krauss, M.; Das, S.; Cavazos-Rehg, P. Automatic detection of eating disorder-related social media posts that could benefit from a mental health intervention. *Int. J. Eat. Disord.* **2019**, *52*, 1150–1156. [CrossRef]

Journal of
Clinical Medicine

MDPI

Article

*e*LoriCorps Immersive Body Rating Scale and *e*LoriCorps Mobile Versions: Validation to Assess Body Image Disturbances from Allocentric and Egocentric Perspectives in a Nonclinical Sample of Adolescents

Johana Monthuy-Blanc [1,2], Giulia Corno [1,3,*], Marilou Ouellet [1], Fadel Touré [1], Francisca Bourbeau [1], Michel Rousseau [1], Audrey Charette [1], Nicolas Moreau [1,4], Normand Roy [1,5], Vicky Drapeau [6], Marie-Eve Mathieu [7] and Stéphane Bouchard [1,3,8]

1 GR2TCA-Loricorps-Groupe de Recherche Transdisciplinaire des Troubles du Comportement Alimentaire, Université du Québec à Trois-Rivières, 3351, Boulevard des Forges, Trois-Rivières, QC G8Z 4M3, Canada; johana.monthuy-blanc@uqtr.ca (J.M.-B.); marilou.ouellet@uqtr.ca (M.O.); fadel.toure@uqtr.ca (F.T.); francisca.bourbeau@uqtr.ca (F.B.); michel.rousseau@uqtr.ca (M.R.); audrey.charette@uqtr.ca (A.C.); nicolas.moreau@uottawa.ca (N.M.); normand.roy@umontreal.ca (N.R.); stephane.bouchard@uqo.ca (S.B.)

2 Centre de Recherche de l'Institut Universitaire en Santé Mentale de Montréal, 7401 Rue Hochelaga, Montreal, QC H1N 3M5, Canada

3 Chaire de Recherche du Canada en Cyberpsychologie Clinique, Université du Québec en Outaouais, 283, Boul Alexandre-Taché, Gatineau, QC J8X 3X7, Canada

4 School of Social Work, University of Ottawa, 120 University, Office 12035, Ottawa, ON K1N 6N5, Canada

5 Groupe de Recherche Interuniversitaire sur l'Intégration Pédagogique des Technologies de l'Information et de la Communication, Université de Montréal, 90, Avenue Vincent-d'Indy, Montreal, QC H2V 2S9, Canada

6 Département D'éducation Physique, Faculté des Sciences de L'éducation, Université Laval, Pavillon de l'Éducation Physique et des Sports, Local 2214, 2320, Rue des Bibliothèques, Quebec, QC G1V 0A6, Canada; vicky.drapeau@fse.ulaval.ca

7 Chaire de Recherche du Canada en Activité Physique et Obésité Juvénile, Université de Montréal, Boulevard Édouard-Montpetit, Montreal, QC H3T 1J4, Canada; me.mathieu@umontreal.ca

8 Centre de Recherche du Centre Intégré de Santé et de Services Sociaux de l'Outaouais, 20 Rue Pharand, Gatineau, QC J9Y 6H9, Canada

* Correspondence: giulia.me.corno@gmail.com

Abstract: A growing number of studies have used virtual reality (VR) for the assessment and treatment of body image disturbances (BIDs). This study, conducted in a community sample of adolescents, documents the convergent and discriminant validity between (a) the traditional paper-based Figure Rating Scale (paper-based FRS), (b) the VR-based Body Rating Scale (*e*LoriCorps-IBRS 1.1), and (c) the mobile app-based Body Rating Scale (*e*LoriCorps-IBRS 1.1-Mobile). A total of 93 adolescents (14 to 18 years old) participated in the study. Body dissatisfaction and body distortion were assessed through the paper-based FRS, the *e*LoriCorps-IBRS 1.1 and the *e*LoriCorps-IBRS 1.1-Mobile. Eating disorder symptoms, body image avoidance, and social physique anxiety were also measured. Correlation analyses were performed. Overall, the results showed a good and statistically significant convergence between allocentric perspectives as measured by the paper-based FRS, the *e*LoriCorps-IBRS 1.1 and the *e*LoriCorps-IBRS 1.1-Mobile. As expected, the egocentric perspective measured in VR produced different results from the allocentric perspective, and from cognitive–attitudinal–affective dimensions of BIDs, with the exception of body distortion. These differences support the discriminant validity of the egocentric perspective of *e*LoriCorps-IBRS 1.1 and are consistent with emerging evidence, highlighting a difference between experiencing the body from an egocentric (i.e., the body as a subject) and allocentric (i.e., the body as an object) perspective. The egocentric perspective could reflect a perceptual–sensory–affective construction of BIDs, whereas allocentric measures seem to be more related to a cognitive–affective–attitudinal construction of BIDs. Moreover, the results support the validity of the *e*LoriCorps-IBRS 1.1-Mobile with promising perspectives of implementation among young populations.

Citation: Monthuy-Blanc, J.; Corno, G.; Ouellet, M.; Touré, F.; Bourbeau, F.; Rousseau, M.; Charette, A.; Moreau, N.; Roy, N.; Drapeau, V.; et al. *e*LoriCorps Immersive Body Rating Scale and *e*LoriCorps Mobile Versions: Validation to Assess Body Image Disturbances from Allocentric and Egocentric Perspectives in a Nonclinical Sample of Adolescents. *J. Clin. Med.* **2022**, *11*, 1156. https://doi.org/10.3390/jcm11051156

Academic Editor: Michele Roccella

Received: 23 December 2021
Accepted: 19 February 2022
Published: 22 February 2022

Keywords: body dissatisfaction; body distortion; virtual reality; mobile application; convergent and discriminant validity; egocentric perceptual-sensory-affective dimension of body image

1. Introduction

1.1. Body Image Disturbances

Adolescence is marked by physical changes due to puberty and to the development of identity, which can be challenging in social contexts where standards of beauty are related to thinness and muscularity [1]. Body dissatisfaction is dramatically widespread among adolescents: studies have reported that 24% to 46% of adolescent females are dissatisfied with their bodies. The percentages for adolescent males were lower, 12–26%, but still alarming [2–5]. Body image-related issues are associated with a very strong desire to lose weight and change body shape [6]. Indeed, according to Cazale, Paquette and Bernèche [7], 41% of adolescent females report being dissatisfied with their body and wanting to be thinner, while 8% report wanting to be heavier. For males, the study revealed 24% want to be thinner, and 24% want to be heavier. Body image disturbances (BIDs, mainly body dissatisfaction and body distortion) are particularly relevant among youth, and especially during adolescence. During this period, BIDs present major risk factors for the development, maintenance and relapse of eating disorders (EDs) [8,9], such as anorexia nervosa, bulimia nervosa and binge eating disorder [10–15]. Some studies suggest that the level of body dissatisfaction can vary across different age groups [16,17]. However, other studies have found that body dissatisfaction seemed largely stable during a lifetime [5,18–20] and, considering the possible major consequences associated with BIDs, it is of paramount importance to identify and prevent BIDs, to promptly intervene before they become chronic, and to improve our understanding of the underlying factors that maintain BIDs.

Despite countless studies on body image, the definition of this concept is still not unanimous e.g., [21–23]. In this paper, body image is considered to be a multidimensional construct, indicating a personal and mental representation of one's physical appearance, which encompasses body-related cognitions, emotions, behaviors, and perceptions [24–26]. Body image dissatisfaction (which reflects the cognitive–affective dimension of BIDs) and body distortion (which reflects the perceptual dimension of BIDs) are two of the most-studied manifestations of BIDs [27–30]. Body image dissatisfaction refers to the extent people like or dislike the shape and/or size of their own body and whether they accept and value it [27]. Body distortion refers to a disturbance in accurately estimating one's own body size [27], and is observed when there is a difference between actual and perceived body size. The relation between these two dimensions remains an object of scientific debate [21]. Indeed, Cash and Deagle [27], and more recently Cornelissen et al. [31], suggested that attitudinal and perceptual components might represent two distinct phenomena. Nevertheless, several studies have proposed that BIDs may be driven by distorted attitudes toward a person's own body (i.e., body dissatisfaction), indicating that perceptual distortions could be explained solely in terms of changes in attitudinal body image [21,32,33].

1.2. Measures of BIDs

To prevent BIDs in adolescence, it is important to be able to assess and promptly identify these disturbances. In the last few decades, several different tools were used to measure body image [21,23,27]. BIDs have usually been assessed through self-report questionnaires, such as the "Drive for Thinness" and "Body Dissatisfaction" subscales of the Eating Disorder Inventory 2 (EDI-2) [34], the Body Shape Questionnaire (BSQ) [35], the Body Image Avoidance Questionnaire (BIAQ) [36], and the Social and Physique Anxiety Scale [37]. In clinical and research settings, it is quite common to use body size estimation tasks (from the calculation of height and weight) to evaluate body distortion and body dissatisfaction using depictive or metric methods [21]. In depictive methods, participants are asked to estimate their perceived and ideal body size using figure rating scales (traditional paper-based FRS, 3D FRS) e.g., [38] or [39], deforming mirrors [40], and by deforming the entire body using photographs or videos [21,41–43]. With FRS, body size dissatisfaction is calculated by subtracting the ideal body size from the perceived body size, whereas body distortion corresponds to the participant's actual BMI minus the BMI of the perceived body size. In metric methods, participants are asked to indicate the size of different body parts (e.g., shoulders, hips, waist), for instance, with a rod, a caliper, or movable markers on a wall [44,45]. These distances of different body parts are then measured, for example, in centimeters. Thus, by depictive methods participants are asked to express their judgement on a global body appearance, whereas by metric methods participants are asked to focus on single and specific body parts [21]. Self-report questionnaires have been criticized as they often yield inconsistent and inconclusive results [23,46,47]. The alternative paper-based FRS has received criticism for employing figures that display unrealistic representations of a person's body, the lack of ecological validity due to the exclusive use of frontal displays (i.e., allocentric perspective), and the absence of figures that represent obesity [48]. To counter these limitations, a growing number of studies have recently explored the potential of virtual reality (VR) technologies by presenting scenarios through allocentric and egocentric (i.e., first person) perspectives [47,49,50]. The real-time rendering and exploration of the 3D images led to referring to virtual bodies, as opposed to only body figures, when describing the stimuli. VR allows assessment of BIDs from the same perspective as the paper-based FRS, which entails looking at bodies perceived as being presented in front of the person the allocentric perspective—(i.e., third-person point of view), and from a novel point of view, which involves looking at the body through one's eyes as if it is experienced as the person's own body—the egocentric perspective—(i.e., first-person point of view). Recently, researchers and clinicians started to investigate the nature and role of egocentric and allocentric body image perspectives. Indeed, Riva and Gaudio [51] proposed the Allocentric Lock Theory, which claims that: (a) the spatial allocentric perspective involves somatorepresentations (representations of the memory of the body and knowledge, beliefs, and attitudes about one's own body); (b) the spatial egocentric perspective involves somatoperceptions (perceptions of the actual state of the body and tactile stimuli from sensory inputs); and (c) individuals with—or at risk of developing—eating disorders are "locked" into a negative allocentric memory of their own body that is not adequately corrected by the information originating from the egocentric perspective [51–56]. Concretely, this manifests itself in an individual as a disruption in the way the body is experienced and remembered, and all the sensory information stored in short-term memory that could negate this disruption (e.g., significant weight loss) cannot change the allocentric (long-term memory) body perception that remains ingrained with rigidity. As a result, the maintenance of this misperception of the body is the result of the inability to update perceptual data in long-term memory [57].

1.3. *eLoriCorps-IBRS a VR-Based BIDs Assessment Tool*

In 1998, Riva and colleagues recreated, for the first time, a traditional paper-based FRS in VR. They developed the body image virtual reality scale (BIVRS) [58], which consisted of seven, and later nine, female and male virtual bodies ranging from underweight to overweight, displayed in an allocentric perspective. Since then, researchers have developed more realistic and inclusive versions of VR-based FRS—e.g., [46]. Traditionally, participants are asked to observe a line-up of 3D virtual bodies presented in an allocentric perspective and to select the body that corresponds to their perceived body size and their ideal body size. Recently, Monthuy-Blanc et al. [47] developed and documented the validity of the *e*LoriCorps Immersive Body Rating Scale version 1.0 (*e*LoriCorps-IBRS 1.0). In this first version, users could observe seven virtual bodies matching their self-reported sex, ranging from underweight to overweight (i.e., BMI from 15.00 to 33.00 kg/m^2), presented both in an allocentric and egocentric perspective. As depicted in the article, *e*LoriCorps-IBRS 1.0 replicated the exact same position as the paper-based FRS: virtual bodies have shoulders, arms and legs slightly rotated sideways. For each perspective, participants were asked to select their ideal and perceived body. The authors found a convergent validity of the allocentric ratings of the *e*LoriCorps-IBRS 1.0 with the paper-based FRS. Results from the egocentric perspective revealed novel reflections about the nature of body image. Indeed, ideal body size and body dissatisfaction in the egocentric perspective differed when assessed by the allocentric VR-based versus paper-based FRS. However, the validity of the allocentric ratings from *e*LoriCorps-IBRS 1.0 was investigated among the adult population. Moreover, the egocentric perspective has not yet been studied in adolescents.

Displaying the virtual bodies in the same position as the body figures in the paper-based FRS represented an attempt to limit the differences between the stimuli presented on paper and in VR. However, issues arose when experiencing the virtual bodies in the egocentric perspective. When immersed in VR looking down, participants saw their body as slightly turned to the right, with a prominent left shoulder and a body position that did not match their proprioception. The attempt to keep paper and VR versions similar for measuring body image may be impractical, as there are also other small differences, such as skin textures, details of the body and so forth. With the advent of future VR applications that could provide more body sizes than the seven original paper-based FRS, the possibility to select skin tone and texture as well as hair features that match those of the users, and tailor selected features of portions of the virtual bodies to patients' needs, the *e*LoriCorps-IBRS 1.0 was slightly revised—*e*LoriCorps-IBRS version 1.1 (*e*LoriCorps-IBRS 1.1) —to position the virtual bodies as fully facing the users in the standard anatomical position with no body rotation. Given the growing need to assess adolescents' BIDs outside of the experimental research laboratory (e.g., ecological momentary assessment) with portable smartphone apps, an allocentric version of the virtual bodies was developed, the *e*LoriCorps mobile application (*e*LoriCorps-IBRS 1.1-Mobile) to be validated specifically with adolescents.

1.4. Objectives

The current study bears two objectives. The first objective (O.1) is to assess the convergent validity between the allocentric perspective of BIDs measured with the paper-based FRS and *e*LoriCorps (-IBRS 1.1 and -IBRS 1.1-Mobile) in an adolescent sample. The convergent validity was expected to be high between the allocentric (paper, VR, mobile application) assessments of body dissatisfaction and body distortion. The second objective (O.2) is to test the discriminant validity between the egocentric perspective of BIDs measured with the VR-based *e*LoriCorps-IBRS 1.1 and the allocentric perspective measured with paper-based FRS and *e*LoriCorps (-IBRS 1.1 and -IBRS 1.1-Mobile) in an adolescent sample. Consistently, with the adult validation study, it was expected that the egocentric VR perspective would yield results that were not strongly correlated with the allocentric (paper, VR, mobile application) measures of body dissatisfaction and perceptual body distortion [47]. Moreover, we explored the relationships between dimensions of BIDs in egocentric and allocentric perspectives and other constructs associated with BIDs, such as eating disorder symptoms (EDI-A), body image avoidance (BIAQ-A), and social physique anxiety (SPAS-12).

2. Materials and Methods

2.1. Sample

During recruitment, 84 females (80.77%) and 20 males (19.23%), all Caucasians and Canadian residents, expressed an interest in the study. Among these 84 females, 11 presented a prior or current presence of EDs. Adolescents with missing data were removed from the database, forming a a final sample of 93 participants (72% female and 28% male). Ages ranged from 14 to 18 years (m = 15.4 s.d. 1.01). The average height, weight and BMI of the participants were, respectively, 1.66 m (s.d. 0.82), 61.1 kg (s.d. 10.85), and 22.3 kg/m^2 (s.d. 3.94). They were recruited at schools and community organizations which hold a partnership with the research group and had previously expressed an interest in *e*LoriCorps-IBRS 1.0. Inclusion criteria required that participants were French-speaking, self-identified as female or male, and aged between 14 and 18 years.

2.2. Equipment and Material

The study was conducted using the *e*LoriCorps-IBRS 1.1 (see [47] for a detailed description of the first version of the VR-base scale). The virtual environment ran on an HP wx4600 PC computer (3 GHz, 3.48 GB RAM, ASUS GeForce 8800GTX graphics card; Hewlett-Packard, Montréal, QC, Canada), combined with Vuzix VR920 HMD (Vuzix, Rochester, New York, NY, USA), an InterSense Cube3 motion tracker (InterSense LLC, Billerica, MA, USA), and a hand-controlled joystick from a Wii RVL-003 (Nintendo Canada, Vancouver, BC, Canada). The VR is based on Daydream Google technology. The *e*LoriCorps mobile app runs on the Google Pixel 2 phone, Android 11 version (Octa-core 4 × 2.35 GHz Kryo and 4 × 1.9 GHz Kryo, 64 GB RAM, display AMOLED, 5.0 inches, 1080 × 1920 pixels) with a Google Daydream View headset and its Bluetooth controller. The *e*LoriCorps mobile application requires the Google View VR headset and controller. All designed by Google, MountainView, CA, USA.

2.3. Assessment Measures

The sociodemographic questionnaire included height, weight (to obtain body mass index, BMI), nationality, assigned sex at birth, and age. These variables were assessed to describe the sample (see the Sample section for the statistics).

*e*LoriCorps Immersive Body Rating Scale version 1.1 (*e*LoriCorps-IBRS 1.1). This instrument employed virtual bodies holding a standard anatomical pause see Figures 1 and 2 that show screenshots from the VR-based, mobile app-based and paper-based perspective are slightly distorted compared to reality (e.g., fisheye distortion in the allocentric illustration, and variations in viewpoints in the egocentric perspective). This instrument contains two environments for assessing the allocentric and egocentric perspectives (administered in a random sequence) and a female and male version of each to be used, depending on the sex at birth of the user. A neutral VR environment was also implemented to familiarize participants with the use of the *e*LoriCorps-IBRS 1.1. In the allocentric perspective environment, participants were immersed in VR facing a line-up of seven virtual bodies and walked around each of them. After examining each virtual body for 40 to 60 seconds (see [47] for a detailed description of the procedure), the participants walked to face the virtual body that best represented their own body (Perceived Body Size—Allo. VR), and then to the virtual body they wanted to look like (Ideal Body Size—Allo. VR). In the egocentric perspective virtual environment, participants looked down at their feet and experienced each of the seven bodies for 40 to 60 seconds (see [47] for a detailed description of the procedure). Participants then transitioned to the virtual body they estimated as best representing their body size (Perceived Body Size—Ego. VR) and to the virtual body they wanted to look like (Ideal Body Size—Ego. VR).

Body Dissatisfaction scores, for the allocentric perspective (i.e., Body Dissatisfaction. VR) and the egocentric perspective (i.e., Body Dissatisfaction-Ego. VR), were calculated from the perceived body size minus the ideal body size. A positive score indicated that the participant desired a thinner body than their perceived body size, and a negative score indicated that the participant desired a larger body than their perceived body size. Scores can range from −6 (i.e., no dissatisfaction) to ± 6 (i.e., extreme dissatisfaction).

Body Distortion scores were calculated from the actual body size of the participant minus the perceived body size for the allocentric perspective (i.e., Body Distortion-Allo. VR) and the egocentric perspective (i.e., Body Distortion-Ego. VR). A positive score indicated that the participant perceived their body as thinner than their actual BMI, while a negative score meant that the participant perceived their body as bigger than their actual BMI. Scores can range from 0 (i.e., no distortion) to ± 6 (i.e., extreme distortion).

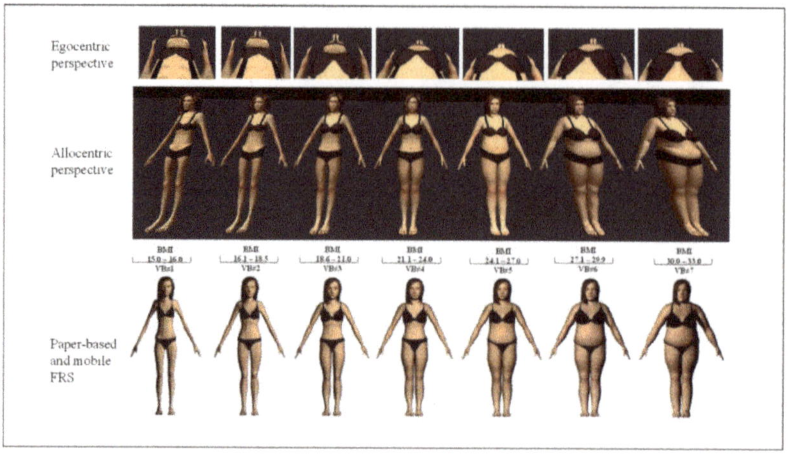

Figure 1. Representation of the allocentric and egocentric perspectives of *e*LoriCorps-IBRS 1.1 used with female participants.

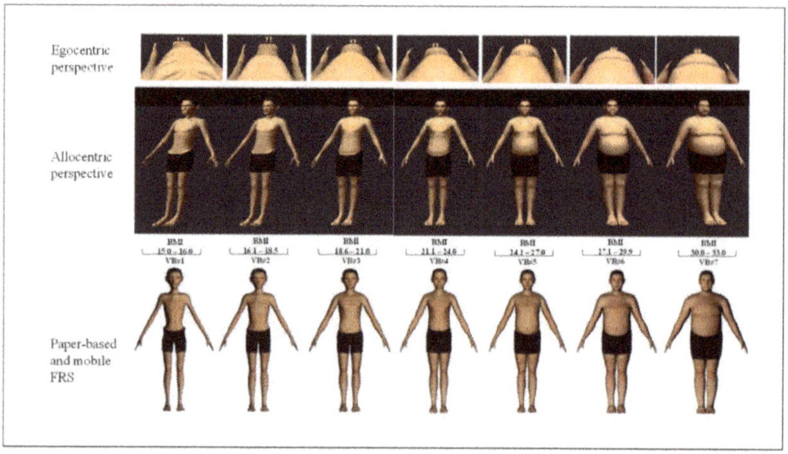

Figure 2. Representation of the allocentric and egocentric perspectives of *e*LoriCorps-IBRS 1.1 used with male participants.

*e*LoriCorps mobile app based Body Rating Scale (*e*LoriCorps-IBRS 1.1-Mobile; developed by Loricorps' team, at Université du Québec à Trois-Rivières, Quebec, CANADA). This instrument employed an app-based FRS with seven virtual bodies on a visual analog scale, showing a female or male version of each depending on the sex at birth of the user. A cell phone with the mobile app already open was given to the participant. Then, they were asked to observe the virtual bodies and select the one best representing their body size (Perceived Body Size—Allo. mobile) and the one they wanted to look like (Ideal Body Size—Allo. mobile). All scores range from 0 to ±6. Body Dissatisfaction scores for the mobile app (i.e., Body Dissatisfaction—Allo. mobile) were calculated from the perceived body size minus the ideal body size. Body Distortion scores were calculated for the mobile app (i.e., Body Distortion—Allo. mobile) from the actual BMI of the participant minus the BMI of the perceived body size. Scores can range from 0 (i.e., not dissatisfied) to ±6 (i.e., extremely dissatisfied).

Figure rating scale. The FRS [59] is a paper-based questionnaire consisting of seven body figures, presented in an allocentric perspective, that increase in size from thinnest to largest, numbered from 1 to 7. Participants were asked to circle their Perceived Body size and their Ideal Body size. Body Dissatisfaction (i.e., Body Dissatisfaction—Paper-based FRS) and Body Distortion (i.e., Perceptual Body Distortion—Paper-based FRS) scores were calculated as recommended by the authors [59], which is similar to the procedures employed for the *e*LoriCorps-IBRS 1.1.

Eating Disorder Inventory. The French very short version of the Eating Disorder Inventory-Adolescent version (EDI-A) represents a 16-item multidimensional self-report questionnaire that assesses symptoms of eating disorders in adolescent populations [60]. This instrument was validated among a community sample of female and male adolescents [60]. The questionnaire comprises eight subscales (i.e., Drive for Thinness, Bulimia, Body Dissatisfaction corresponding to the ED-Symptom Index as well as Ineffectiveness, Perfectionism, Interpersonal Distrust, Interoceptive Awareness and Maturity Fears corresponding to the ED-Personality-Trait Index) and is based on a Likert scale from 0 "not at all" to 5 "extremely". The EDI total score, index score and each subscale total scores were reported. In our sample, Cronbach's alpha was 0.78, showing excellent internal consistency [61].

Social Physique Anxiety Scale. The Social Physique Anxiety Scale (SPAS-12) [37], validated in French by Maïano et al. [62], is a 12-item self-report scale developed to assess the degree to which people become anxious when others observe or evaluate their physiques. This questionnaire was validated among a community sample of male and female adolescents [62]. The instrument is based on a Likert scale from 1 "not at all" to 5 "extremely". In our sample, Cronbach's alpha was 0.92, illustrating excellent internal consistency [61].

Body Image Avoidance Questionnaire. The Body Image Avoidance Questionnaire (BIAQ-A) [36], Adolescents French version of Maïano et al. [63], is a 19-item self-report measure of behavioral avoidance of situations and experiences that could provoke concerns about one's own physical appearance, such as social activities that involve eating or wearing tight-fitting clothes. The questionnaire was validated among a community sample of female and male adolescents [63] and is characterized by four subscales: clothing (i.e., wearing clothes that hide one's own body), social activities (i.e., avoiding social activities that imply eating or that draw attention to one's own body), eating restraint, and grooming/weighing (i.e., checking behaviors such as weighing or scrutinizing one's own body in the mirror). Items can score from 0 "never" to 5 "always". The questionnaire's internal consistency reliability (in the present study: Cronbach $\alpha = 0.63$) is consistent with what was reported in other studies (e.g., Cronbach α ranged between 0.64 and 0.89 [64]).

Simulator Sickness Questionnaire. The French version of the Simulator Sickness Questionnaire [65] measures cybersickness or the presence of physiological discomfort during VR immersion. The 16-item questionnaire employs a Likert scale from 0 "none" to 3 "severe". In our sample, Cronbach's alpha was 0.84, indicating excellent internal consistency [61]. SSQ total raw scores were calculated, as recommended by Bouchard et al. [66].

2.4. Procedure

The study protocol was approved beforehand by the ethics committees of the Université du Québec à Trois-Rivières (UQTR; CER-21-280-08-02.24). Parents were informed of the study but their consent was not required. In Quebec, the participation of teenagers aged 14 and over does not require parental consent. The study did not include any compensation since it was integrated into the community's regular activities. Participants were recruited from 285 schools in Quebec. Students aged 14 and older were informed about the study directly in their classes, by the teacher, or during FitSpirit physical activity (visit the website www.fitspirit.ca for further information; Leduc et al. [67]). They were free to participate or not and were required to speak with the project contact representative of their school or FitSpirit-referent-person if they expressed interest in participating. The research assistants responsible for collecting the data in schools were Ph.D. students. The height and weight of the participants were measured without shoes. Then, all participants completed the paper-based questionnaires (EDI-A, BIAQ, SPAS) and the paper-based FRS. Next, the *e*LoriCorps-IBRS 1.1 and *e*LoriCorps-IBRS 1.1-Mobile versions were administered, randomly, by the experimenter. Before administering the test, the experimenter explained the procedure to participants and provided them with bottled water (in case they felt ill). Participants were informed that some cybersickness could occur and were encouraged to mention it if it happened. After the experiment with the *e*LoriCorps-IBRS 1.1, the Simulator Sickness Questionnaire was administered to all participants. Finally, the participants were invited to document their immersive experience through four open questions related to their impressions and feelings towards the immersions.

2.5. Statistical Analysis

In comprehensive and comparative perspectives, the data analysis is based on virtual body score for (i) actual body size and (ii) perceived and ideal body size measures. For the actual body size measure, see Figures 1 and 2 for the correspondence between VB and BMI. For perceived and ideal body size measures, virtual body-VB#1 corresponds to visual analog scale (VAS) less than or equal to 14%; virtual body VB#2 corresponds to VAS between over 14% and equal to or less than 29%; virtual body VB#3 corresponds to VAS between over 29% and equal to or less than 43%; virtual body VB#4 corresponds to VAS between over 43% and equal to or less than 57%: virtual body VB#5 corresponds to VAS over 57% and equal to or less than 71%; virtual body VB#6 corresponds to VAS over 71% and equal to or less than 86%; virtual body VB#7 corresponds to VAS over 86%. To document the potential impact of the participant's sex at birth on the results, all statistical analyses were also performed separately for females and males. The results did not differ when analyzed separately for each sex (i.e., significant differences remained significant, and non-significant differences remained non-significant). Therefore, to maximize statistical power, results for the aggregated sample were reported (results analyzed by sex are available upon request). Parametric variables were represented as mean ± standard deviation (SD). The statistical analysis was performed using Stata 16.1 software. Pearson correlation was performed to analyze the relationship between questionnaires and body dissatisfaction and body distortion. Since multiple analyses were performed in this study, a correction for the inflation of Type 1 error was applied to the alpha level to consider results of objectives 1 (O.1) and 2 (O.2) as statistically significant. A Bonferroni correction was applied familywise for each component of BIDs (i.e., for Perceived Body Size score, Ideal Body Size score, Body Dissatisfaction score, and Body Distortion score), resulting in a p-value lower than 0.008 (0.05/6) for Pearson correlations. Regarding BMI, two outliers were found in the data. Since raw BMI data were not used in the analysis (only used to calculate the body distortion), the potential effect of the two outliers on the results became neutralized. Other data were normally distributed. An a priori power analysis was conducted using G*Power3 using a two-tailed test, a medium effect size (d= 0.50), and an alpha of 0.05. Result showed that a total sample of 29 participants was required to achieve a power of 0.80 [68].

3. Results

Descriptive statistics on the main measures are reported in Table 1.

Analyses for the convergent and discriminant validity are reported in Table 2. Results revealed almost all correlations were statistically significant, and the application of a strict Bonferroni correction did not strongly influence the findings. The significance level must also be interpreted in the context of a large sample, hence focusing more on the strength of the correlations than on the significance levels.

Table 1. Descriptive statistics.

		M	SD	Min–Max
Actual Body Size-adj		3.84	1.34	1–7
Perceived Body Size score				
	Paper-based FRS	4.12	0.87	2–6
	Allo. VR	3.83	0.79	2–6
	Ego. VR	3.77	0.74	2–6
	Allo. Mobile	3.64	0.95	1–6
Ideal Body Size score				
	Paper-based FRS	3.89	0.68	2–6
	Allo. VR	3.45	0.65	1–5
	Ego. VR	3.51	0.73	1–6
	Allo. Mobile	3.44	0.95	1–6
Body Dissatisfaction				
	Paper-based FRS	0.23	0.90	−2–+3
	Allo. VR	0.38	0.75	−1–+2
	Ego. VR	0.27	0.61	−1–+2
	Allo. Mobile	0.17	0.85	−2–+2
Body Distortion				
	Paper-based FRS	−0.28	1.07	−3–+3
	Allo. VR	0.38	1.42	−3–+4
	Ego. VR	0.06	1.31	−3–+4
	Allo. Mobile	0.17	1.05	−2–+4
EDI-A	Total	27.30	10.53	0–60
	Symptoms Index	9.27	5.02	0–25
	Personality Trait Index	20.09	7.92	0–45
	Body Dissatisfaction	4.81	1.82	1–10
	Drive for Thinness	3.26	3.20	0–10
	Bulimia	2.05	1.98	0–9
	Ineffectiveness	4.21	1.43	2–10
	Perfectionism	4.57	2.35	0–10
	Interpersonal Distrust	5.51	2.28	0–10
	Interoceptive Awareness	5.21	1.65	0–10
	Maturity Fears	2.22	2.28	0–10
SPAS-12	Total	34.38	5.94	24–50
BIAQ-A	Total	23.61	7.98	7–43
	Clothing	11.25	4.78	2–24
	Social Activities	1.61	2.94	0–12
	Eating Restraint	3.36	2.49	0–15
	Grooming and Weighing	7.38	2.76	0–13
SSQ	Total raw score	18.88	4.13	16–38

Note. BMI: Body Mass Index; Paper-based FRS: allocentric paper-based Figure Rating Scale; Allo. VR: Allocentric perspective from the *e*LoriCorps-IBRS 1.1; Ego VR: Egocentric perspective from the *e*LoriCorps-IBRS 1.1; Allo. Mobile: Allocentric perspective from the *e*LoriCorps-IBRS 1.1-Mobile; EDI-A: Eating Disorder Inventory-Adolescent version; SPAS-12: Social Physique Anxiety Scale; BIAQ-A: Body Image Avoidance Questionnaire-Adolescent version; SSQ: Simulator Sickness Questionnaire.

The convergent validity of the *e*LoriCorps-IBRS 1.1-Mobile and the FRS allocentric perspective assessments of body image (O.1) was good (mean $r = 0.71$, $ps < 0.000$) for perceived body size and body distortion. Correlations were still significant, but lower (mean $r = 0.53$, $ps < 0.000$) for ideal body size and for body dissatisfaction. Correlations between the allocentric VR and mobile versions of the *e*LoriCorps-IBRS 1.1 were strong for perceived body size estimation and body distortion (mean $r = 0.73$, $ps < 0.000$), and lower for ideal body size estimation and body dissatisfaction (mean $r = 0.49$, $ps < 0.000$), and thus consistent with patterns observed with the FRS.

Table 2. Convergent and discriminant validity in adolescents, assessed by Pearson correlations for each component of BIDs between the allocentric perspective (paper, virtual reality, mobile application) and egocentric perspective (virtual reality by the *e*LoriCorps-IBRS 1.1) assessments.

	Pearson Correlation	*p*-Value
Perceived Body Size score		
Paper-based FRS vs. Allo. VR	0.73	<0.008 *
Paper-based vs. Ego. VR	0.45	<0.008 *
Allo. VR vs. Ego. VR	0.49	<0.008 *
Paper-based FRS vs. Allo. Mobile	0.66	<0.008 *
Allo Mobile vs. Allo. VR	0.72	<0.008 *
Allo Mobile vs. Ego. VR	0.32	0.003 *
Ideal Body Size score		
Paper-based FRS vs. Allo. VR	0.53	<0.008 *
Paper-based vs. Ego. VR	0.20	0.06
Allo. VR vs. Ego. VR	0.29	<0.008 *
Paper-based FRS vs. Allo. Mobile	0.48	<0.008 *
Allo. Mobile vs. Allo. VR	0.40	<0.008 *
Allo. Mobile vs. Ego. VR	0.08	0.44
Body Dissatisfaction score		
Paper-based FRS vs. Allo. VR	0.68	<0.008 *
Paper-based vs. Ego. VR	0.46	<0.008 *
Allo. VR vs. Ego. VR	0.47	<0.008 *
Paper-based FRS vs. Allo. Mobile	0.58	<0.008 *
Allo. Mobile vs. Allo. VR	0.58	<0.008 *
Allo. Mobile vs. Ego. VR	0.24	0.025
Body Distortion score		
Paper-based FRS vs. Allo. VR	0.74	<0.008 *
Paper-based vs. Ego. VR	0.76	<0.008 *
Allo. VR vs. Ego. VR	0.82	<0.008 *
Paper-based FRS vs. Allo. Mobile	0.75	<0.008 *
Allo. Mobile vs. Allo. VR	0.73	<0.008 *
Allo. Mobile vs. Ego. VR	0.67	<0.008 *

Note. Paper-based FRS: allocentric paper-based Figure Rating Scale; Allo. VR: Allocentric perspective from the *e*LoriCorps-IBRS 1.1; Ego VR: Egocentric perspective from the *e*LoriCorps-IBRS 1.1; Allo. Mobile: Allocentric perspective from *e*LoriCorps-IBRS 1.1-Mobile. * $p < 0.008$.

The discriminant validity of the egocentric perspective from the *e*LoriCorps-IBRS 1.1 (O.2) in this adolescent sample was supported by low correlations between assessments from the allocentric perspective of the paper based-FRS vs. the egocentric perspective of the *e*LoriCorps-IBRS 1.1 for perceived body size ($r = 0.45$, $p < 0.008$), and body dissatisfaction ($r = 0.46$, $p < 0.008$), and by a non-significant correlation regarding the assessment of ideal body size ($p = 0.06$). Contrary to expectations, a higher correlation was identified for the assessment of body distortion ($r = 0.76$, $p < 0.008$). The same pattern of results was discovered for the correlations between the allocentric assessments vs. the egocentric ones of the *e*LoriCorps-IBRS 1.1, except for body distortion ($r = 0.82$, $p < 0.008$). Concerning the allocentric perspective of *e*LoriCorps-IBRS 1.1-Mobile, results showed lowest correlations with the egocentric perspective of the *e*LoriCorps-IBRS 1.1 for perceived body size ($r = 0.31$, $p = 0.003$), and by a non-significant correlation regarding the assessment of ideal body size ($p = 0.44$), and body dissatisfaction ($p = 0.025$). As previously mentioned, a higher correlation was identified for the assessment of body distortion ($r = 0.67$, $p < 0.008$). To show that correlations in favor of discriminant validity are indeed different from those in favor of convergent validity, correlation coefficients were compared with document statistical differences (Field, 2018). Correlations between the egocentric VR-based perspective and the allocentric VR-based perspective were significantly lower than the correlations between the allocentric-VR based perspective and the allocentric paper-based perspective for perceived body size ($p < 0.01$), ideal body size ($0.02 < p < 0.05$) and body dissatisfaction ($p < 0.01$). Regarding body distortion, the correlation between the egocentric VR-based perspective and the allocentric VR-based perspective was significantly higher than the correlation between the allocentric-VR based perspective and the allocentric paper-based perspective ($0.02 < p < 0.05$). Correlations between the egocentric VR-based perspective and the allocentric paper-based FRS were significantly lower ($ps < 0.01$) than correlations between the allocentric VR-based perspective and the allocentric paper-based FRS for perceived body size, ideal body size and body dissatisfaction. The correlation between the egocentric VR-based perspective and the allocentric paper-based FRS was not significantly different ($p > 0.20$) from the correlation between the allocentric VR-based and the allocentric paper-based FRS for body distortion. Correlations between the egocentric VR-based and the allocentric mobile-based perspectives were significantly lower ($ps < 0.01$) than correlations between the allocentric VR-based and the allocentric mobile-based perspectives for perceived body size, ideal body size and body dissatisfaction. The correlation between the egocentric VR-based perspective and the allocentric mobile-based perspective was not significantly different ($0.10 < p < 0.20$) from the correlation between the allocentric VR-based perspective and the allocentric mobile-based perspective for body distortion. In summary, the discriminant validity of the egocentric perspective from the *e*LoriCorps-IBRS 1.1 is particularly confirmed with the allocentric perspective of the technology-based method (*e*LoriCorps-IBRS 1.1 and *e*LoriCorps-IBRS 1.1-Mobile) to measure ideal body size.

Exploratory discriminant validity analyses display significant correlations between body dissatisfaction and body distortion scores and external variables (see Tables 3 and 4). The allocentric *e*LoriCorps-IBRS 1.1 and *e*LoriCorps-IBRS 1.1-Mobile assessments of body dissatisfaction were significantly related to the total score of the BIAQ. Furthermore, both the mobile- and VR-based allocentric body distortion assessments were significantly correlated with the total score of the EDI-A, the Personality Index and Symptoms Index, whereas the total score of the BIAQ was significantly associated only with the VR-based allocentric body distortion assessment. The SPAS-12 was not significantly associated with body dissatisfaction or with body distortion. Body dissatisfaction and body distortion measured in the allocentric paper-based FRS were not significantly associated with any attitudinal–affective–cognitive variables associated with BIDs.

Table 3. Pearson correlations (with exact *p* values in brackets) for the total of questionnaires measuring components of BID and three rating scales administered to adolescents: a paper-based FRS, the *e*LoriCorps-IBRS 1.1 allocentric and egocentric perspectives, and the *e*LoriCorps-IBRS 1.1-Mobile allocentric perspective.

	EDI-A	EDI-A-S-Index	EDI-A-P-Index	SPAS-12	BIAQ-A
Body Dissatisfaction score					
Paper-based FRS	0.12 (0.25)	0.11 (0.30)	0.15 (0.16)	0.19 (0.07)	0.15 (0.15)
Allo. VR	0.09 (0.38)	0.10 (0.31)	0.13 (0.21)	0.15 (0.17)	0.23 (0.03 *)
Ego. VR	0.03 (0.79)	0.001 (0.99)	0.04 (0.67)	0.10 (0.371)	0.05 (0.63)
Allo. Mobile	−0.01 (0.93)	0.05 (0.66)	0.02 (0.82)	0.08 (0.45)	0.25 (0.02 *)
Body Distortion score					
Paper-based FRS	0.10 (0.36)	0.16 (0.12)	0.10 (0.34)	−0.03 (0.79)	0.16 (0.14)
Allo. VR	0.22 (0.04 *)	0.23 (0.03 *)	0.24 (0.02 *)	0.05 (0.66)	0.23 (0.03 *)
Ego. VR	0.06 (0.59)	0.07 (0.47)	0.15 (0.16)	−0.008 (0.94)	0.19 (0.08)
Allo. Mobile	0.28 (0.01 **)	0.30 (0.005 **)	0.13 (0.21)	−0.014 (0.90)	0.157 (0.16)

Note. EDI-A: Eating Disorder Inventory Scale; S-Index: Symptoms Index; P-Index: Personality; Trait Index SPAS-12: Social and Physique Anxiety Scale; BIAQ-A: Body Image Avoidance Questionnaire; Paper-based FRS: paper Figure Rating Scale; Allo. VR: Allocentric perspective from the *e*LoriCorps-IBRS 1.1; Ego VR: Egocentric perspective from the *e*LoriCorps-IBRS 1.1; Allo. Mobile: Allocentric perspective from the *e*LoriCorps-IBRS 1.1-Mobile. * $p < 0.05$; ** $p < 0.01$.

Regarding the specific correlations between the EDI-A and BIAQ subscales and body dissatisfaction and body distortion, the allocentric *e*LoriCorps-IBRS 1.1 body dissatisfaction assessment was significantly correlated to maturity fear and eating restraint, whereas the allocentric *e*LoriCorps-IBRS 1.1-Mobile body dissatisfaction assessment was significantly associated with maturity fear, covering up the body with clothes that hide one's own body, and avoidance of social activities that could provoke concerns about one's own physical appearance. Body dissatisfaction measured in the egocentric VR-based perspective was negatively associated with interoceptive awareness. Eating restraint significantly correlated with all measures of body distortion, whereas avoidance of social activities was significantly related to body distortion measured in the allocentric VR-based perspective. Finally, maturity fear was significantly related to body distortion, measured in the allocentric paper-based and VR-based condition and in the egocentric VR-based condition. The relationships were medium with correlations ranging from 0.21 to 0.29 [69]. These effect sizes appear to be generally lower for body distortion than for the body dissatisfaction scores.

Table 4. Pearson's correlations (with exact p values in brackets) for the subscales of questionnaires measuring components of BIDs and three rating scales administered to adolescents: a paper-based FRS, the *e*LoriCorps-IBRS 1.1 allocentric and egocentric perspectives, and the *e*LoriCorps-IBRS 1.1-Mobile allocentric perspective.

	Body Dissatisfaction				Body Distortion			
	Paper-FRS	Allo. VR	Ego. VR	Allo. M.	Paper-FRS	Allo. VR	Ego. VR	Allo. M.
EDI-A-BD	0.03 (0.82)	0.09 (0.39)	0.02 (0.89)	−0.05 (0.64)	0.11 (0.30)	0.22 (0.04 *)	0.09 (0.40)	0.21 (0.07)
EDI-A-DT	0.12 (0.26)	0.18 (0.09)	−0.02 (0.86)	0.13 (0.26)	0.18 (0.01)	0.23 (0.04 *)	0.09 (0.44)	0.17 (0.13)
EDI-A-BU	−0.17 (0.12)	−0.14 (0.21)	−0.09 (0.43)	0.11 (0.34)	0.01 (0.91)	−0.11 (0.32)	−0.001 (0.99)	−0.03 (0.77)
EDI-A-IN	−0.008 (0.94)	0.02 (0.84)	−0.08 (0.47)	0.03 (0.79)	0.16 (0.14)	0.19 (0.07)	0.18 (0.10)	0.24 (0.03 *)
EDI-A-PE	−0.02 (0.82)	0.001 (0.99)	0.003 (0.98)	0.07 (0.51)	0.08 (0.45)	0.11 (0.33)	0.10 (0.35)	−0.06 (0.62)
EDI-A-ID	0.001 (0.99)	0.11 (0.29)	0.19 (0.07)	−0.006 (0.96)	−0.03 (0.77)	0.06 (0.57)	0.002 (0.99)	−0.02 (0.85)
EDI-A-IA	−0.05 (0.65)	−0.02 (0.87)	−0.22 (0.04 *)	−0.05 (0.68)	−0.09 (0.42)	−0.02 (0.82)	−0.10 (0.35)	−0.04 (0.70)
EDI-A-MF	0.17 0.10	0.27 (0.01 *)	0.01 (0.90)	0.28 (0.01 *)	0.27 (0.01 *)	0.35 (0.001 **)	0.27 (0.01 *)	0.20 (0.08)
BIAQ-C	0.150 (0.17)	0.11 (0.30)	0.12 (0.25)	0.24 (0.03 *)	0.009 (0.93)	0.05 (0.64)	0.009 (0.93)	−0.04 (0.73)
BIAQ-S	0.11 (0.31)	0.20 (0.06)	−0.04 (0.69)	0.24 (0.03 *)	0.14 (0.21)	0.24 (0.02 *)	0.18 (0.09)	0.12 (0.28)
BIAQ-E	0.15 (0.16)	0.31 (0.003 **)	0.09 (0.36)	0.13 (0.25)	0.29 (0.007 **)	0.36 (0.001 **)	0.26 (0.01 *)	0.25 (0.02 *)
BIAQ-G	−0.03 (0.81)	−0.02 (0.82)	−0.11 (0.32)	−0.07 (0.52)	0.02 (0.84)	0.004 (0.97)	0.07 (0.55)	0.17 (0.12)

Note. EDI-A: Eating Disorder Inventory Scale; BD: Body Dissatisfaction Subscale; DT: Drive for Thinness Subscale; BU: Bulimia Subscale; IN: Infectiveness Subscale; PE: Perfectionism Subscale; ID: Interpersonal Distrust Subscale; IA: Interoceptive Awareness Subscale; MF: Maturity Fear Subscale; BIAQ-A: Body Image Avoidance Questionnaire; C: Clothing Subscale; S: Social Activity Subscale; E: Eating Restraint Subscale; G: Grooming and Weighing Subscale; Paper-FRS: paper Figure Rating Scale; Allo. VR: Allocentric perspective from the *e*LoriCorps-IBRS 1.1; Ego VR: Egocentric perspective from the *e*LoriCorps-IBRS 1.1; Allo. Mobile: Allocentric perspective from the *e*LoriCorps-IBRS 1.1-Mobile. * $p < 0.05$; ** $p < 0.01$.

4. Discussion

The current study examined (O.1) the convergent validity between the allocentric-based assessments (paper-based FRS, *e*LoriCorps-IBRS 1.1 and *e*LoriCorps-IBRS 1.1-Mobile) of BIDs and (O.2) the discriminant validity of the egocentric perspective (measured with the VR-based *e*LoriCorps-IBRS 1.1) versus the allocentric-based assessments (paper-based FRS, *e*LoriCorps-IBRS 1.1 and *e*LoriCorps-IBRS 1.1-Mobile) of BIDs in a community sample of adolescents. Moderate convergent validity was discovered between the allocentric (paper, VR, mobile application) assessments of body dissatisfaction and body distortion. As expected, the egocentric VR perspective yielded results that were not strongly correlated with the allocentric (paper, VR), and not significantly correlated with the allocentric mobile-based measures of body dissatisfaction. However, correlations did not significantly differ regarding body distortion. Concerning the exploratory discriminant analyses, the different strengths of relationships between dimensions of BIDs in egocentric and allocentric perspectives and other attitudinal–affective–cognitive variables associated with BIDs, such as eating disorders symptoms (EDI-A), body image avoidance (BIAQ-A), and social physique anxiety (SPAS-12), are further discussed in the following paragraphs. Adolescents who participated in this study reported marginal dissatisfaction about their body size. Participants tended to slightly overestimate their body size when using traditional paper-based FRS, and to slightly underestimate it when using *e*LoriCorps-IBRS 1.1-Mobile. Participants tended to select an ideal body closer to their actual body size when using the paper-based FRS than when using a technology-based instrument. The overall results of convergent and discriminant validity tended to reveal two main observations. First, it must be noted that for all body distortion measures, participants' means were close to zero and standard deviations represented the highest of all measures. This observation is consistent with findings from other authors who stated that body distortion appears primarily in clinical populations rather than in the general population [21,70].

4.1. Allocentric Convergent and Egocentric Discriminant Validity of the eLoriCorps-IBRS 1.1 in Adolescents

Convergent validity (O.1) between the allocentric perspective of the *e*LoriCorps-IBRS 1.1 and the paper-based FRS was confirmed when assessing perceived body size, ideal body size, body dissatisfaction, and body distortion. These results obtained from a community sample of adolescents mirror the results that the authors found when validating the first version of the *e*LoriCorps (i.e., *e*LoriCorps-IBRS 1.0) among a community sample of adults [47], and were in line with results from Fisher et al. [71], who did not observe a significant difference in assessing body distortion between a paper-based FRS and a VR-based FRS. Convergent validity was found between the *e*LoriCorps-IBRS 1.1-Mobile and both the allocentric perspective of the *e*LoriCorps-IBRS 1.1 and of the paper-based FRS for all body image-related variables (i.e., perceived body size assessment, ideal body size assessment, body dissatisfaction, body distortion). These results are quite encouraging when researchers and clinicians work with adolescents. The use of the mobile application *e*LoriCorps-IBRS 1.1-Mobile can offer a more portable and acceptable way to assess the allocentric perspective of body image-related variables among youth populations. These mobile-based methods might be more appealing for teenagers, who already integrate cell phone usage in their daily routine to accomplish different tasks (e.g., searching for information, interacting with peers, watching videos and playing games), and particularly when implementing the cognitive (allocentric) and perceptual (egocentric) training of BIDs.

Discriminant validity (O.2) between the egocentric- and allocentric-based assessments was confirmed for all body image-related variables with the exception of body distortion. More precisely, results seem to indicate that assessing ideal body size, perceived body size and body size dissatisfaction in an egocentric perspective is somewhat different than assessing the same phenomena in an allocentric perspective, both in VR-based and mobile-based assessments and by using paper-based FRS. Similar results were obtained by the authors among a community sample of adults [47].

4.2. Egocentric-Perceptual-Sensory-Affective Construction: The Hidden and Deepest Part of the "BIDs Iceberg"?

Experiencing the body in an egocentric perspective might be quite different than experiencing the body from a "third-person" point of view. Indeed, the body is experienced both as an object (i.e., third-person allocentric perspective) in the physical world, and as a subject (i.e., first-person egocentric perspective), on a daily basis. This is particularly true during the "famous storming-adolescent-period" which constitutes a real challenge due to both the physical and psychological upheaval [72]. The "object-body", theorized by Foucault (1975) as "Body-machine", is experienced, judged, and observed by others only in an allocentric perspective, and vice versa. The allocentric representation of one's own body is constantly compared with the allocentric perspective of others' bodies. The internalization of an observer's point of view on one's own body is called "self-objectification" [73], which implies the internalization of an objectified cultural ideal of beauty. In Canadian society, the youth population (as our sample) is vulnerable to the widespread societal messaging prevalent in Western cultures, which favors thin, muscular bodies [74]. The fear to change one's own body was highlighted by our results on the correlation between BIDs and maturity fears. A mechanism of constant body surveillance or systematic monitoring of one's own body is triggered. The discrepancy between one's body-as-an-object and this ideal-cultural-prescription, can provoke body dissatisfaction, body shame, social physique anxiety, body checking, and body avoidance, which are all recognized predictors for the development of eating disorders [55,75–79]. While the body as-an-object could be more exposed to inter-individual comparison in a (Western) cultural context, the egocentric construction of the body-as-a-subject, could be exposed to intra-individual comparison in one's own ecological daily context (mood, physiological hunger, and satiety sensations, etc.). Indeed, as theorized by the Allocentric Lock Theory, the egocentric perspective involves somatoperceptions, more precisely interoceptive percepts about the nature and state of the body [51–56]. Thus, the perception of the body from a first-person point of view could be influenced by one's own interoceptive awareness, which refers to the ability to identify, access, understand and respond appropriately to internal bodily signals [80]. More precisely, this subjective perception of sensations arising from inside the body encompasses the proprioceptive experience of body state, the perception of hunger/satiety signals, cardiovascular, respiratory, colorectal and urinary sensations. The results of the present study appear to point in this direction, as a significant negative correlation was identified between the egocentric assessment of body dissatisfaction and interoceptive awareness. However, future studies are required to shed light on this association. An increasing number of studies have been investigating impaired interoceptive awareness in eating disorders (composing the famous EDI measurement) [81], especially among anorexia and bulimia nervosa patients [82]. This suggests that interoceptive awareness disturbances are both a vulnerability and a reinforcing factor of a pathological drive for thinness leading to restrictive eating [34,83–87]. Furthermore, exploring bodily sensations from an egocentric perspective can increase one's own ability to reconnect with internal bodily signals, especially food-related signals (hunger and satiety cues). This echoes two different intervention approaches: (i) yoga allows to bridge the gap between the mind–body experience and enhances the experience of embodiment [88], and (ii) an adaptative nutritional approach—intuitive eating [89]—to decrease the negative impacts of restrained eating [47,87,90,91]. The intuitive movement (yoga) and eating are employed in the recent prevention and treatment of eating disorders, including binge-eating disorder [92,93]. In conclusion, the egocentric perspective could reflect a perceptual–sensory–affective construction of the body, whereas an allocentric representation could reflect a cognitive–affective–attitudinal construction of the body. Therefore, egocentric- vs allocentric-based body image disturbances become two sides of the same coin.

4.3. Implications for Innovative Integrative Intervention

Traditionally, BIDs were assessed through different methods, such as self-reported questionnaires, depictive and metric body size estimation tasks. While body image distortion can be measured only by body size estimation tasks, body dissatisfaction can be measured by either self-reported questionnaires or body size estimation tasks. But, when we are implementing these two evaluative methods, are we sure that we are measuring the same phenomenon? In short, we do not believe so. Body dissatisfaction as measured by well-established self-reported questionnaires was not associated with the same construct assessed by any of the depictive methods used in this study. We could hypothesize that these two methods are assessing different shadows of body dissatisfaction. The self-reported questionnaire could be assessing cognitive–attitudinal–affective dimensions of body dissatisfaction [81], whereas through depictive methods it is also possible to reach and explore perceptual–sensory–affective dimensions of body dissatisfaction (i.e., the lived body) [94], and particularly the sensory dimension, owing to embodiment-egocentric perspectives, as they require judgement and evaluation of the physical dimensions of the body.

In preventive and therapeutic implications, this study supports the hypothesis of the self-objectification of the allocentric perspective of the body, which may be more related to phenomena such as avoidance of situations that could trigger concerns about one's own physical appearance, and dysfunctional eating attitudes such as body checking and the drive to achieve thinness. Indeed, in this developmental period and social context, the adolescents' object–body should represent the target content of an eating disorder preventive program [95]. On the other hand, the egocentric body representation could tap into something different from the allocentric perspectives via the perceptual–sensory–affective construction of the body. In the preventive view, the change from allocentric–object–body to egocentric–subject–body could be akin to the change from cultural beauty to inner beauty through the acceptance process. In this case, since the virtual bodies represent the adult body, it may be possible that adolescents of the current study can project themselves more easily in the allocentric perspective, as the representation of their body in mind is related to an interpersonal comparison, which is driven by the internalization of the ideal body. In the egocentric perspective, it may be harder for adolescents to embody the bodies of adults as the egocentric perspective is an intraindividual experience. Targeting BIDs is one of the most difficult preventive and therapeutic goals to achieve, and yet body image remains to be fully understood. Knowing that BIDs are not only related to the cognitive representation of the body in memory, but also to the body perception-driven input from multiple sensory modalities, may allow the development of innovative treatments based on cognitive and perceptual training. These integrated treatments based on holistic body experiences should include multidimensional modalities of BIDs, targeting the body-as-an-object/subject. An increasing number of VR-based interventions focus on targeting different facets of BIDs. However, to the author's knowledge, only one study protocol [96] and a pilot study [97] proposed an intervention targeting both egocentric and allocentric BIDs. In line with recent studies focused on a comprehensive integrated model [98,99], the promising VR-based integrated interventions could address the perceptual-dual-disorders (e.g., eating disorders, body dysmorphic disorder, obsessive-compulsive disorder [100]) by taking into account the current gender-inclusive society [101].

4.4. Strengths and Limitations in this Current Study Inspiring Further Studies

There were several strengths to this study combining BIDs among an adolescent sample, in an egocentric–immersive–virtual perspective and an ecological non-immersive mobile application. To our knowledge, the current study constitutes the first validation of a VR-based assessment of BIDs (*e*LoriCorps-IBRS 1.1) in a community sample of adolescents with a larger sample than previous VR-based studies [102]. Consistent with the recent VR-based validation in a community sample of adults [47], the present study highlights the contribution of an egocentric–immersive–virtual perspective to understand the perceptual–sensory–affective construction of the body image (vs. allocentric–cognitive-affective–attitudinal construction). The validation of the mobile application version (*e*LoriCorps-IBRS 1.1-Mobile) implies favoring the use of mobile-based assessment methods in self-regulation (preventive intervention) and self-management (therapeutic intervention). The main limitation of this study is the lack of "gold-standard" psychometric instruments to compare with the egocentric VR perspective, which is a novel tool. Another important limitation is that the virtual bodies were more representative of adult bodies than adolescent ones. In order to maintain a certain consistency between the instruments, the adult version of the paper-based FRS was preferred to the adolescent version [103]. This limitation did not seem to have impeded participants from identifying a perceived body size that was close to their actual body size. Results of the exploratory analyses should be taken with caution as multiple correlations were performed. Finally, another limitation was the small number of male adolescents participants compared with the number of female adolescents participants. Future studies should include the same proportion of female and male adolescents in order to explore possible gender-based differences.

Future studies should examine the validity of *e*Loricorps-IBRS 1.1 in an eating disorder sample. More precisely, people with a high BMI may perceive themselves to be larger than the response scale allows, which may lead to a significant response bias, especially in clinical eating disorder populations, including all body weights and shapes. Consequently, it is possible to note that the number of available virtual bodies in the *e*Loricorps-IBRS continuum might restrict people in their choices. Moving toward a nine virtual body continuum could help limit this bias. In line with this limitation, it could prove necessary to develop and assess virtual bodies that better represent the morphological characteristics of adolescents' bodies. Furthermore, the promising perspectives of self-management interventions that focus on cognitive and perceptual training of BIDs include the development and assessment of a mobile egocentric-based version of the *e*Loricorps-IBRS 1.1. Indeed, an allocentric and egocentric mobile assessment instrument could be particularly suitable for addressing evaluation and prevention programs within a youth population who develop object-body and subject-body simultaneously. In comprehensive research on self-objectification of the allocentric perspective of the body, the question of whether there are differences when employing adolescent and adult versions of the body continuum should be explored. Indeed, bodily experience, more precisely self-objectification, may play an important role in the development and maintenance of eating disorders [8].

5. Conclusions

In conclusion, this validation study provides evidence that the allocentric perspective of *e*LoriCorps-IBRS 1.1 is a valid tool to assess perceptual–sensory–affective dimensions (egocentric perspective) and cognitive–affective–attitudinal (allocentric perspective) dimensions of BIDs in adolescents. As expected, when comparing it with the validation of the *e*LoriCorps-IRBS 1.0 in a community sample of adults, the egocentric perspective measured in VR produced different results compared to all measures from the allocentric perspective [paper-based FRS, *e*LoriCorps (-IBRS 1.1 and -IBRS 1.1-Mobile)] and from cognitive–attitudinal–affective dimensions of BIDs (EDI-A, BIAQ-A and SPAS-12). These differences support the discriminant validity of the egocentric perspective of *e*LoriCorps-IBRS 1.1 and are consistent with emerging evidence that the egocentric perceptive could reflect a perceptual–sensory–affective construction of BIDs. Allocentric measures appear to be more related to a cognitive–affective–attitudinal construction of BIDs. Moreover, the results support the validity of rating virtual bodies using the *e*LoriCorps-IBRS 1.1-Mobile, with the potential to be more enticing and to enable ecological momentary assessment. Furthermore, it could be suitable to develop a specific-fitting adolescent virtual body continuum integrated into a mobile egocentric-based version of the *e*Loricorps-IBRS 1.1 in order to detect, prevent and treat eating disorders.

Author Contributions: Conceptualization, J.M.-B. and S.B.; methodology, J.M.-B. and M.R.; software VR, J.M.-B.; software mobile App, J.M.-B. and F.T.; data collection, J.M.-B., A.C. and F.B.; formal analysis, J.M.-B., S.B., M.R. and G.C.; writing—original draft preparation, J.M.-B., S.B., G.C. and M.O.; writing—review and editing, J.M.-B., G.C., M.O., F.T., F.B., M.R., A.C., N.M., N.R., V.D., M.-E.M. and S.B.; supervision, J.M.-B.; project administration, J.M.-B.; funding acquisition, J.M.-B. All authors have read and agreed to the published version of the manuscript.

Funding: This research was funded by RBC Royal Bank, the Lemaire family, Fond. UQTR-RBC Banque Royale-PI-Loricorps, 2017–2021 (0288007), by the Social Sciences and Humanities Research Council of Canada, 2018-2023 (CRSH-SAVOIR-430-2018-00970–PIE-IC), by the Canada Research Chair in Clinical Cyberpsychology (950-210762), and the Fond de Recherche du Québec—Santé (FRQS; 289006).

Institutional Review Board Statement: This study was conducted in accordance with the Declaration of Helsinki, and approved by the Ethics Committee of the Université du Québec à Trois-Rivières (UQTR; CER-21-280-08-02.24).

Informed Consent Statement: Informed consent was obtained from all subjects involved in the study.

Data Availability Statement: The data presented in this study are available on request from the corresponding author. The data are not publicly available due to ethical restrictions.

Acknowledgments: Special thanks go to RBC Royal Bank, the Lemaire family, Fondation of Université du Québec à Trois-Rivières, Social Sciences, Humanities Research Council of Canada, Canada Research Chair in Clinical Cyberpsychology, Centre de Recherche de l'Institut Universitaire en Santé Mentale de Montréal, and Fond de Recherche du Québec—Santé whose patronage helped finance the completion of this study. Special thanks to Edouard Blanc for the infographic development of the virtual body constituting the *e*LoriCorps-IBRS 1.1. Special thanks to Fillactive organization and Chavigny High School for their community support. Thanks to Marlene Menzies comments and revisions on the text and Francisca Bourbeau, Vincent Lemieux and Lola Tournayre for helping with data collection.

Conflicts of Interest: Stéphane Bouchard is president of, and owns shares in, Cliniques et Dveloppement In Virtuo, a company that distributes virtual environments, and any conflict of interest is managed under UQO's conflict of interest policy. The other authors declare no conflict of interest.

References

1. Markey, C.N. Invited commentary: Why body image is important to adolescent development. *J. Youth Adolesc.* **2010**, *39*, 1387–1391. [CrossRef] [PubMed]
2. Bucchianeri, M.M.; Arikian, A.J.; Hannan, P.J.; Eisenberg, M.E.; Neumark-Sztainer, D. Body dissatisfaction from adolescence to young adulthood: Findings from a 10-year longitudinal study. *Body Image* **2013**, *10*, 1–7. [CrossRef] [PubMed]
3. Neumark-Sztainer, D.; Goeden, C.; Story, M.; Wall, M. Associations between Body Satisfaction and Physical Activity in Adolescents: Implications for Programs Aimed at Preventing a Broad Spectrum of Weight-Related Disorders. *Eat. Disord.* **2004**, *12*, 125–137. [CrossRef] [PubMed]
4. Presnell, K.; Bearman, S.K.; Stice, E. Risk factors for body dissatisfaction in adolescent boys and girls: A prospective study. *JMIR Form. Res.* **2004**, *36*, 389–401. [CrossRef] [PubMed]
5. Wang, S.B.; Haynos, A.F.; Wall, M.M.; Chen, C.; Eisenberg, M.E.; Neumark-Sztainer, D. Fifteen-Year Prevalence, Trajectories, and Predictors of Body Dissatisfaction from Adolescence to Middle Adulthood. *Clin. Psychol. Sci.* **2019**, *7*, 1403–1415. [CrossRef] [PubMed]
6. Dakanalis, A.; Pla-Sanjuanelo, J.; Caslini, M.; Volpato, C.; Riva, G.; Clerici, M.; Carrà, G. Predicting onset and maintenance of men's eating disorders. *Int. J. Clin. Health Psychol.* **2016**, *16*, 247–255. [CrossRef] [PubMed]
7. Cazale, L.; Paquette, M.; Bernèche, F. Poids, apparence corporelle et actions à l'égard du poids. *L'Enquête Québécoise Sur La St. Des Jeunes Du Second.* **2012**, *1*, 121–148.
8. Dakanalis, A.; Clerici, M.; Bartoli, F.; Caslini, M.; Crocamo, C.; Riva, G.; Carrà, G. Risk and maintenance factors for young women's DSM-5 eating disorders. *Arch. Womens Ment. Health* **2017**, *20*, 721–731. [CrossRef]
9. Gardner, R.M. Assessment of body image disturbance in children and adolescents. In *Body Image, Eating Disorders, and Obesity in Youth: Assessment, Prevention, and Treatment*; American Psychological Association: Washington, DC, US, 2001; pp. 193–213.
10. American Psychological Association (APA). *Diagnostic and Statistical Manual of Mental Disorders DSM-5*, 5th ed.; American Psychiatric Publishing: Arlington, VA, USA, 2013.
11. Artoni, P.; Chierici, M.L.; Arnone, F.; Cigarini, C.; De Bernardis, E.; Galeazzi, G.M.; Minneci, D.G.; Scita, F.; Turrini, G.; De Bernardis, M.; et al. Body perception treatment, a possible way to treat body image disturbance in eating disorders: A case–control efficacy study. *Eat. Weight Disord.* **2021**, *26*, 499–514. [CrossRef]
12. Lewer, M.; Bauer, A.; Hartmann, A.S.; Vocks, S. Different Facets of Body Image Disturbance in Binge Eating Disorder: A Review. *Nutrients* **2017**, *9*, 1294. [CrossRef]
13. Ricciardelli, L.A.; McCabe, M.P. Children's body image concerns and eating disturbance: A review of the literature. *Clin. Psychol. Rev.* **2001**, *21*, 325–344. [CrossRef]
14. Rohde, P.; Stice, E.; Marti, C.N. Development and predictive effects of eating disorder risk factors during adolescence: Implications for prevention efforts. *Int. J. Eat. Disord.* **2015**, *48*, 187–198. [CrossRef] [PubMed]
15. Smolak, L. Body image in children and adolescents: Where do we go from here? *Body Image* **2004**, *1*, 15–28. [CrossRef]
16. Esnaola, I.; Rodríguez, A.; Goñi, A. Body dissatisfaction and perceived sociocultural pressures: Gender and age differences. *Salud Ment.* **2010**, *33*, 21–29.
17. Baker, L.; Gringart, E. Body image and self-esteem in older adulthood. *Ageing Soc.* **2009**, *29*, 977–995. [CrossRef]

18. Runfola, C.D.; Von Holle, A.; Trace, S.E.; Brownley, K.A.; Hofmeier, S.M.; Gagne, D.A.; Bulik, C.M. Body dissatisfaction in women across the lifespan: Results of the UNC-SELF and Gender and Body Image (GABI) studies. *Eur. Eat. Disord Rev.* **2013**, *21*, 52–59. [CrossRef]
19. Tiggemann, M.; McCourt, A. Body appreciation in adult women: Relationships with age and body satisfaction. *Body Image* **2013**, *10*, 624–627. [CrossRef]
20. Quittkat, H.L.; Hartmann, A.S.; Düsing, R.; Buhlmann, U.; Vocks, S. Body Dissatisfaction, Importance of Appearance, and Body Appreciation in Men and Women Over the Lifespan. *Front. Psychiatry* **2019**, *10*. [CrossRef]
21. Mölbert, S.C.; Thaler, A.; Mohler, B.J.; Streuber, S.; Romero, J.; Black, M.J.; Zipfel, S.; Karnath, H.O.; Giel, K.E. Assessing body image in anorexia nervosa using biometric self-avatars in virtual reality: Attitudinal components rather than visual body size estimation are distorted. *Psychol. Med.* **2018**, *48*, 642–653. [CrossRef]
22. Grilo, C.M.; Crosby, R.D.; Machado, P.P. Examining the distinctiveness of body image concerns in patients with anorexia nervosa and bulimia nervosa. *Int. J. Eat. Disord.* **2019**, *52*, 1229–1236. [CrossRef]
23. Kling, J.; Kwakkenbos, L.; Diedrichs, P.C.; Rumsey, N.; Frisén, A.; Brandão, M.P.; Silva, A.G.; Dooley, B.; Rodgers, R.F.; Fitzgerald, A. Systematic review of body image measures. *Body Image* **2019**, *30*, 170–211. [CrossRef] [PubMed]
24. Cash, T.F. Cognitive-behavioral perspectives on body image. In *Body Image: A Handbook of Theory, Research, and Clinical Practice*; G. Press: New York, NY, USA, 2002; pp. 38–46.
25. Cash, T.F.; Smolak, L. *Body Image: A Handbook of Science, Practice, and Prevention*; Guilford Press: New York, NY, USA, 2011.
26. Glashouwer, K.A.; van der Veer, R.M.L.; Adipatria, F.; de Jong, P.J.; Vocks, S. The role of body image disturbance in the onset, maintenance, and relapse of anorexia nervosa: A systematic review. *Clin. Psychol. Rev.* **2019**, *74*, 101771. [CrossRef] [PubMed]
27. Cash, T.F.; Deagle III, E.A. The nature and extent of body-image disturbances in anorexia nervosa and bulimia nervosa: A meta-analysis. *Int. J. Eat. Disord.* **1997**, *22*, 107–125. [CrossRef]
28. Grogan, S. *Body Image: Understanding Body Dissatisfaction in Men, Women and Children*, 2nd ed.; Routledge/Taylor & Francis Group: New York, NY, USA, 2008.
29. Hagman, J.; Gardner, R.M.; Brown, D.L.; Gralla, J.; Fier, J.M.; Frank, G.K.W. Body size overestimation and its association with body mass index, body dissatisfaction, and drive for thinness in anorexia nervosa. *Eat. Weight Disord.* **2015**, *20*, 449–455. [CrossRef] [PubMed]
30. Wertheim, E.H.; Paxton, S.J. Body image development in adolescent girls. In *Body Image: A Handbook of Science, Practice, and Prevention*, 2nd ed.; The Guilford Press: New York, NY, USA, 2011; pp. 76–84.
31. Cornelissen, K.K.; Widdrington, H.; McCarty, K.; Pollet, T.V.; Tovée, M.J.; Cornelissen, P.L. Are attitudinal and perceptual body image the same or different? Evidence from high-level adaptation. *Body Image* **2019**, *31*, 35–47. [CrossRef]
32. Mergen, J.; Keizer, A.; Koelkebeck, K.; van den Heuvel, M.R.C.; Wagner, H. Women with Anorexia Nervosa do not show altered tactile localization compared to healthy controls. *Psychiatry Res.* **2018**, *267*, 446–454. [CrossRef]
33. Smeets, M.A.M. The Rise and Fall of Body Size Estimation Research in Anorexia Nervosa: A Review and Reconceptualization. *Eur. Eat. Disord. Rev.* **1997**, *5*, 75–95. [CrossRef]
34. Garner, D.M.; Olmstead, M.P.; Polivy, J. Development and validation of a multidimensional eating disorder inventory for anorexia nervosa and bulimia. *Int. J. Eat. Disord.* **1983**, *2*, 15–34. [CrossRef]
35. Cooper, P.J.; Taylor, M.J.; Cooper, Z.; Fairbum, C.G. The development and validation of the body shape questionnaire. *Int. J. Eat. Disord.* **1987**, *6*, 485–494. [CrossRef]
36. Rosen, J.C.; Srebnik, D.; Saltzberg, E.; Wendt, S. Development of a body image avoidance questionnaire. *J. Consult. Clin. Psychol.* **1991**, *3*, 32–37. [CrossRef]
37. Hart, E.A.; Leary, M.R.; Rejeski, W.J. The Measurement of Social Physique Anxiety. *J. Sport Exerc. Psychol.* **1989**, *11*, 94–104. [CrossRef]
38. Thompson, J.K.; Psaltis, K. Multiple aspects and correlates of body figure ratings: A replication and extension of Fallon and Rozin (1985). *Int. J. Eat. Disord.* **1988**, *7*, 813–817. [CrossRef]
39. Gardner, R.M.; Brown, D.L. Body image assessment: A review of figural drawing scales. *Pers. Individ. Differ.* **2010**, *48*, 107–111. [CrossRef]
40. Traub, A.C.; Orbach, J. Psychophysical Studies of Body-Image: I. The Adjustable Body-Distorting Mirror. *Arch. Gen. Psychiatry* **1964**, *11*, 53–66. [CrossRef] [PubMed]
41. Probst, M.; Vandereycken, W.; Van Coppenolle, H.; Pieters, G. Body size estimation in anorexia nervosa patients: The significance of overestimation. *J. Psychosom. Res.* **1998**, *44*, 451–456. [CrossRef]
42. Probst, M. Eating Disorders and Physical Activity: A Complex Relationship. In *Physical Activity and Mental Health: A Practice-Oriented Approach*; Edi Ermes: Milan, Italy, 2014; pp. 101–113.
43. Tovée, M.J.; Benson, P.J.; Emery, J.L.; Mason, S.M.; Cohen-Tovée, E.M. Measurement of body size and shape perception in eating-disordered and control observers using body-shape software. *Br. J. Psychol.* **2003**, *94*, 501–516. [CrossRef]
44. Serino, S.; Pedroli, E.; Keizer, A.; Triberti, S.; Dakanalis, A.; Pallavicini, F.; Chirico, A.; Riva, G. Virtual Reality Body Swapping: A Tool for Modifying the Allocentric Memory of the Body. *Cyberpsychol. Behav. Soc. Netw.* **2016**, *19*, 127–133. [CrossRef]
45. Slade, P.D.; Russell, G.F. Awareness of body dimensions in anorexia nervosa: Cross-sectional and longitudinal studies. *Psychol. Med.* **1973**, *3*, 188–199. [CrossRef]

46. Fisher, S.; Abdullah, A.; Charvin, I.; Da Fonseca, D.; Bat-Pitault, F. Comparison of body image evaluation by virtual reality and paper-based figure rating scales in adolescents with anorexia nervosa: Retrospective study. *Eat. Weight Disord.* **2020**, *25*, 735–743. [CrossRef]
47. Monthuy-Blanc, J.; Bouchard, S.; Ouellet, M.; Corno, G.; Iceta, S.; Rousseau, M. "eLoriCorps Immersive Body Rating Scale": Exploring the Assessment of Body Image Disturbances from Allocentric and Egocentric Perspectives. *J. Clin. Med.* **2020**, *9*, 2926. [CrossRef]
48. Gardner, R.M.; Boice, R. A computer program for measuring body size distortion and body dissatisfaction. *Behav. Res. Meth. Instrum. Comput.* **2004**, *36*, 89–95. [CrossRef] [PubMed]
49. Corno, G.; Serino, S.; Cipresso, P.; Baños, R.M.; Riva, G. Assessing the Relationship Between Attitudinal and Perceptual Component of Body Image Disturbance Using Virtual Reality. *Cyberpsychol. Behav. Soc. Netw.* **2018**, *21*, 679–686. [CrossRef] [PubMed]
50. Provenzano, L.; Porciello, G.; Ciccarone, S.; Lenggenhager, B.; Tieri, G.; Marucci, M.; Dazzi, F.; Loriedo, C.; Bufalari, I. Characterizing Body Image Distortion and Bodily Self-Plasticity in Anorexia Nervosa via Visuo-Tactile Stimulation in Virtual Reality. *J. Clin. Med.* **2019**, *9*, 98. [CrossRef] [PubMed]
51. Riva, G.; Gaudio, S. Allocentric lock in anorexia nervosa: New evidences from neuroimaging studies. *Med. Hypotheses* **2012**, *79*, 113–117. [CrossRef] [PubMed]
52. Riva, G.; Gaudio, S.; Dakanalis, A. I'm in a virtual body: A locked allocentric memory may impair the experience of the body in both obesity and anorexia nervosa. *Eat. Weight Disord.* **2014**, *19*, 133–134. [CrossRef]
53. Riva, G. Neuroscience and eating disorders: The allocentric lock hypothesis. *Med. Hypotheses* **2012**, *78*, 254–257. [CrossRef]
54. Riva, G. The Key to Unlocking the Virtual Body: Virtual Reality in the Treatment of Obesity and Eating Disorders. *J. Diabetes Sci.* **2011**, *5*, 283–292. [CrossRef]
55. Riva, G. The neuroscience of body memory: From the self through the space to the others. *Cortex* **2018**, *104*, 241–260. [CrossRef]
56. Gaudio, S.; Riva, G. Body Image in Anorexia Nervosa: The Link Between Functional Connectivity Alterations and Spatial Reference Frames. *Biol. Psychiatry* **2013**, *73*, e25–e26. [CrossRef]
57. Riva, G. Neurobiology of Anorexia Nervosa: Serotonin Dysfunctions Link Self-Starvation with Body Image Disturbances through an Impaired Body Memory. *Front. Hum. Neurosci.* **2016**, *10*. [CrossRef]
58. Riva, G. Virtual Reality in Psychological Assessment: The Body Image Virtual Reality Scale. *Cyberpsychol. Behav.* **1998**, *1*, 37–44. [CrossRef]
59. Stunkard, A.J.; Sørensen, T.; Schulsinger, F. Use of the Danish Adoption Register for the study of obesity and thinness. *Res. Publ. Assoc. Res. Nerv. Ment. Dis.* **1983**, *60*, 115–120. [PubMed]
60. Maïano, C.; Morin, A.J.S.; Monthuy-Blanc, J.; Garbarino, J.-M.; Ninot, G. Development and validity of a very short form of the Eating Disorder Inventory. *Compr. Psychiatry* **2016**, *65*, 141–149. [CrossRef] [PubMed]
61. Cicchetti, D.V. Guidelines, criteria, and rules of thumb for evaluating normed and standardized assessment instruments in psychology. *Psychol. Assess.* **1994**, *6*, 284–290. [CrossRef]
62. Maïano, C.; Morin, A.J.S.; Eklund, R.C.; Monthuy-Blanc, J.; Garbarino, J.-M.; Stephan, Y. Construct Validity of the Social Physique Anxiety Scale in a French Adolescent Sample. *J. Pers. Assess.* **2010**, *92*, 53–62. [CrossRef]
63. Maïano, C.; Morin, A.J.S.; Monthuy-Blanc, J.; Garbarino, J.-M. The Body Image Avoidance Questionnaire: Assessment of its construct validity in a community sample of French adolescents. *Int. J. Behav. Med.* **2009**, *16*, 125–135. [CrossRef]
64. Pellizzer, M.L.; Tiggemann, M.; Waller, G.; Wade, T.D. Measures of body image: Confirmatory factor analysis and association with disordered eating. *Psychol Assess.* **2018**, *30*, 143–153. [CrossRef] [PubMed]
65. Bouchard, S.; Robillard, G.; Renaud, P.; Bernier, F. Exploring new dimensions in the assessment of virtual reality induced side effects. *J. Comput. Inf. Technol.* **2011**, *1*, 20–32.
66. Bouchard, S.; Berthiaume, M.; Robillard, G.; Forget, H.; Daudelin-Peltier, C.; Renaud, P.; Blais, C.; Fiset, D. Arguing in Favor of Revising the Simulator Sickness Questionnaire Factor Structure When Assessing Side Effects Induced by Immersions in Virtual Reality. *Front. Psychiatry* **2021**, *12*, 739742. [CrossRef]
67. Leduc, G.; Gilbert, J.-A.; Ayotte, A.; Moreau, N.; Drapeau, V.; Lemoyne, J.; Monthuy-Blanc, J.; Tremblay, J.; Mathieu, M.-E. The FitSpirit approach for increasing physical activity in canadian teenage girls: Protocol of a longitudinal, quasi-experimental study. *BMC Public Health* **2021**, *21*, 229. [CrossRef]
68. Faul, F.; Erdfelder, E.; Lang, A.G.; Buchner, A. G*Power 3: A flexible statistical power analysis program for the social, behavioral, and biomedical sciences. *Behav Res. Methods* **2007**, *39*, 175–191. [CrossRef] [PubMed]
69. Cohen, J. *Statistical Power Analysis for the Behavioral Sciences*, 2nd ed.; 12 Lawrence Erlbaum Associates Inc.: Hillsdale, NJ, USA, 1988; p. 13.
70. Gardner, R.M.; Brown, D.L. Body size estimation in anorexia nervosa: A brief review of findings from 2003 through 2013. *Psychiatry Res.* **2014**, *219*, 407–410. [CrossRef] [PubMed]
71. Fischer, C.; Malycha, C.P.; Schafmann, E. The Influence of Intrinsic Motivation and Synergistic Extrinsic Motivators on Creativity and Innovation. *Front. Psychol.* **2019**, *10*, 137. [CrossRef] [PubMed]
72. Hall, S. Adolescence: Its Psychology and Its Relation to Physiology, Anthropology, Sociology, Sex, Crime, Religion and Education. *Am. J. Psychiatry* **1904**, *61*, 375–381. [CrossRef]

73. Tiggemann, M.; Lynch, J.E. Body image across the life span in adult women: The role of self-objectification. *Dev. Psychol.* **2001**, *37*, 243–253. [CrossRef] [PubMed]
74. Rodgers, R.F.; Damiano, S.R.; Wertheim, E.H.; Paxton, S.J. Media exposure in very young girls: Prospective and cross-sectional relationships with BMIz, self-esteem and body size stereotypes. *Dev. Psychol.* **2017**, *53*, 2356–2363. [CrossRef] [PubMed]
75. Riva, G. Out of my real body: Cognitive neuroscience meets eating disorders. *Front. Hum. Neurosci.* **2014**, 8. [CrossRef]
76. Dakanalis, A.; Timko, A.C.; Clerici, M.; Riva, G.; Carrà, G. Objectified Body Consciousness (OBC) in Eating Psychopathology. *Assessment* **2017**, *24*, 252–274. [CrossRef]
77. Dakanalis, A.; Zanetti, M.A.; Riva, G.; Clerici, M. Psychosocial moderators of the relationship between body dissatisfaction and symptoms of eating disorders: A look at a sample of young Italian women. *Eur. Rev. Appl. Psychol.* **2013**, *63*, 323–334. [CrossRef]
78. Noll, S.M.; Fredrickson, B.L. A mediational model linking self-objectification, body shame and disordered eating. *Psychol. Women Q.* **1998**, *22*, 623–636. [CrossRef]
79. Dakanalis, A.; Riva, G. Mass media, body image and eating disturbances: The underline mechanism through the lens of the objectification theory. In *Body image: Gender Differences, Sociocultural Influences and Health Implication*; Latzer, J., Merrick, J., Stein, D., Eds.; Nova Science: New York, NY, USA, 2013; pp. 217–236.
80. Craig, A.D. How do you feel? Interoception: The sense of the physiological condition of the body. *Nat. Rev. Neurosci.* **2002**, *3*, 655–666. [CrossRef] [PubMed]
81. Garner, D.M.; Olmsted, M.P.; Polivy, J. The Eating Disorder Inventory: A Measure of Cognitive-Behavioral Dimensions of Anorexia. In *Anorexia Nervosa: Recent Developments in Research*; Alan R. Liss, Inc.: New York, NY, USA, 1983; pp. 173–184.
82. Oswald, A.; Chapman, J.; Wilson, C. Do interoceptive awareness and interoceptive responsiveness mediate the relationship between body appreciation and intuitive eating in young women? *Appetite* **2017**, *109*, 66–72. [CrossRef] [PubMed]
83. Clausen, L.; Rosenvinge, J.H.; Friborg, O.; Rokkedal, K. Validating the Eating Disorder Inventory-3 (EDI-3): A Comparison Between 561 Female Eating Disorders Patients and 878 Females from the General Population. *J. Psychopathol. Behav. Assess.* **2011**, *33*, 101–110. [CrossRef] [PubMed]
84. Fassino, S.; Pierò, A.; Gramaglia, C.; Abbate-Daga, G. Clinical, psychopathological and personality correlates of interoceptive awareness in anorexia nervosa, bulimia nervosa and obesity. *Psychopathology* **2004**, *37*, 168–174. [CrossRef]
85. Jacquemot, A.M.M.C.; Park, R. The Role of Interoception in the Pathogenesis and Treatment of Anorexia Nervosa: A Narrative Review. Front. *Psychiatry* **2020**, *11*. [CrossRef]
86. Khalsa, S.S.; Craske, M.G.; Li, W.; Vangala, S.; Strober, M.; Feusner, J.D. Altered interoceptive awareness in anorexia nervosa: Effects of meal anticipation, consumption and bodily arousal. *Int. J. Eat. Disord.* **2015**, *48*, 889–897. [CrossRef]
87. Tribole, E.; Resch, E. *Intuitive Eating: A Revolutionary Anti-Diet Approach*, 4th ed.; St. Martin's Essentials: New York, NY, USA, 2020.
88. Piran, N.; Neumark-Sztainer, D. Yoga and the experience of embodiment: A discussion of possible links. *Eat. Disord* **2020**, *28*, 330–348. [CrossRef]
89. Tribole, E.; Resch, E. *Intuitive Eating: A Recovery Book for the Chronic Dieter: Rediscover the Pleasures of Eating and Rebuild Your Body Image*, 1st. ed.; Diane Pub Co: Collingdale, PA, USA, 1995.
90. Monthuy-Blanc, J.; Lemieux, V.; Thériault, J.; Rousseau, M. Exploratory Study: A Blind Integrated School-Based Prevention Program on Eating Disorders and Obesity. *Can. J. Commun. Ment. Health* **2021**, *39*, 61–84. [CrossRef]
91. Richard, A.; Meule, A.; Friese, M.; Blechert, J. Effects of Chocolate Deprivation on Implicit and Explicit Evaluation of Chocolate in High and Low Trait Chocolate Cravers. *Front. Psychol.* **2017**, *8*. [CrossRef]
92. Smitham, D.L.A. *Evaluating an Intuitive Eating Program. for Binge Eating Disorder: A Benchmarking Study*; University of Notre Dame: Notre Dame, IN, USA, 2008.
93. Diers, L.; Rydell, S.A.; Watts, A.; Neumark-Sztainer, D. A yoga-based therapy program designed to improve body image among an outpatient eating disordered population: Program description and results from a mixed-methods pilot study. *Eat. Disord* **2020**, *28*, 476–493. [CrossRef]
94. Andrieu, B. Sentir sa santé. In *Les Sensations de Santé: Pour une Épistémologie des Pratiques Corporelles du Sujet de Santé*; Presses Universitaires de Nancy: Nancy, France, 2011; pp. 259–282.
95. Jordana Ovejero, O.; Espinoza Guzmán, P.; González González, M.; Subiza Pérez, I.; Becerra Castro, A.; Raich Escursell, R.M.; Mora Giral, M.S. Universal prevention program of eating, weight and body image problems in adolescents: A 12-month follow-up. *Psicothema* **2020**, *32*, 204–213. [PubMed]
96. Fonseca-Baeza, S.; Corno, G.; Baños, R.M. An intervention protocol proposal to modify the body image disturbance using Virtual Reality. *Calid. Vida Salud* **2018**, *11*, 48–61.
97. Malighetti, C.; Chirico, A.; Serino, S.; Cavedoni, S.; Matamala-Gomez, M.; Stramba-Badiale, C.; Mancuso, V.; Corno, G.; Polli, N.; Cacciatore, C.; et al. Manipulating body size distortions and negative body-related memories in patients with Anorexia Nervosa: A virtual reality-based pilot study. *Annu. Rev. Cyber Ther. Telemed.* **2020**, *18*, 177–181.
98. Compte, E.; Sepulveda, A.; Torrente, F. Approximations to an Integrated Model of Eating Disorders and Muscle Dysmorphia among University Male Students in Argentina. *Men Masc.* **2018**, *23*, 288–305. [CrossRef]
99. Malcolm, A.; Pikoos, T.; Castle, D.J.; Labuschagne, I.; Rossell, S.L. Identity and shame in body dysmorphic disorder as compared to obsessive-compulsive disorder. *J. Obs. Compuls. Relat. Disord.* **2021**, *31*, 100686. [CrossRef]
100. Szerman, N.; Peris, L. Precision Psychiatry and Dual Disorders. *J. Dual Diagn.* **2018**, *14*, 237–246. [CrossRef]

101. Tiggemann, M.; Martins, Y.; Churchett, L. Beyond muscles: Unexplored parts of men's body image. *J. Health Psychol.* **2008**, *13*, 1163–1172. [CrossRef]
102. Ferrer-García, M.; Gutiérrez-Maldonado, J. The use of virtual reality in the study, assessment, and treatment of body image in eating disorders and nonclinical samples: A review of the literature. *Body Image* **2012**, *9*, 1–11. [CrossRef]
103. Sherman, D.K.; Iacono, W.G.; Donnelly, J.M. Development and validation of body rating scales for adolescent females. *Int. J. Eat. Disord* **1995**, *18*, 327–333. [CrossRef]

Journal of
Clinical Medicine

MDPI

Protocol

The Virtual "Enfacement Illusion" on Pain Perception in Patients Suffering from Chronic Migraine: A Study Protocol for a Randomized Controlled Trial

Sara Bottiroli [1,2,*], Marta Matamala-Gomez [3], Marta Allena [2], Elena Guaschino [2], Natascia Ghiotto [2], Roberto De Icco [2,4], Grazia Sances [2] and Cristina Tassorelli [2,4]

1 Faculty of Law, Giustino Fortunato University, 82100 Benevento, Italy
2 Headache Science and Neurorehabilitation Center, IRCCS Mondino Foundation, 27100 Pavia, Italy
3 Mind and Behavior Technological Center, Department of Psychology, University of Milano-Bicocca, 20126 Milan, Italy
4 Department of Brain and Behavioral Sciences, University of Pavia, 27100 Pavia, Italy
* Correspondence: sara.bottiroli@mondino.it

Citation: Bottiroli, S.; Matamala-Gomez, M.; Allena, M.; Guaschino, E.; Ghiotto, N.; De Icco, R.; Sances, G.; Tassorelli, C. The Virtual "Enfacement Illusion" on Pain Perception in Patients Suffering from Chronic Migraine: A Study Protocol for a Randomized Controlled Trial. *J. Clin. Med.* **2022**, *11*, 6876. https://doi.org/10.3390/jcm11226876

Academic Editor: Stéphane Bouchard

Received: 25 September 2022
Accepted: 17 November 2022
Published: 21 November 2022

Abstract: Background: given the limited efficacy, tolerability, and accessibility of pharmacological treatments for chronic migraine (CM), new complementary strategies have gained increasing attention. Body ownership illusions have been proposed as a non-pharmacological strategy for pain relief. Here, we illustrate the protocol for evaluating the efficacy in decreasing pain perception of the enfacement illusion of a happy face observed through an immersive virtual reality (VR) system in CM. Method: the study is a double-blind randomized controlled trial with two arms, involving 100 female CM patients assigned to the experimental group or the control group. The experimental group will be exposed to the enfacement illusion, whereas the control group will be exposed to a pleasant immersive virtual environment. Both arms of the trial will consist in three VR sessions (20 min each). At the baseline and at the end of the intervention, the patients will fill in questionnaires based on behavioral measures related to their emotional and psychological state and their body satisfaction. Before and after each VR session, the level of pain, the body image perception, and the affective state will be assessed. Discussion: this study will provide knowledge regarding the relationship between internal body representation and pain perception, supporting the effectiveness of the enfacement illusion as a cognitive behavioral intervention in CM.

Keywords: pain; chronic migraine; virtual reality; embodiment; enfacement illusion; body image

1. Introduction

Migraine is known as one of the most prevalent and disabling neurological disorders worldwide [1]. Usually, it recurs in an episodic pattern (less than 15 days/month—episodic migraine), but in a small, though clinically relevant portion of sufferers, migraine may acquire an aggressive evolution being present on 15 or more days/month. This is so-called chronic migraine (CM) [2]. CM is mainly managed through pharmacological treatment, requiring both the acute drugs taken during attacks and the preventive treatment aimed at reducing the frequency of attacks [3]. Unfortunately, available treatment options have limited efficacy (50% reduction of migraine days in 50% of patients), they may be poorly tolerated, and they can induce clinically relevant side effects [4,5]. In addition, when considering that CM is a complex neurological disorder that may manifest with variable phenotypical profiles and response to treatments, it is important to tailor the treatment approach to patient's characteristics and inter-individual differences. In this regard, it should be noted that CM is often associated with several comorbidities [6], including those of a psychological nature, such as dependence behaviors, anxiety, depression, and personality disorders [7–12], which could affect the course of treatment [7,8]. As consequence, persistent pain associated to CM poses a high socio-economic burden [13,14], including the costs of pharmacological treatments, primary care visits, and hospitalizations, together with the impact on the patient's productivity and everyday life [14,15]. Because of this, recent years have seen a proliferation of new therapeutic strategies to address migraine-related pain, as well as new techniques that offer promising approaches for development that could be integrated into pharmacological options.

Nowadays there is an increasing interest in the integration of new technologies for clinical practices [16]. In particular, virtual reality (VR) has been widely used to promote mental health in populations presenting different clinical conditions [17]. Recently, several investigations showed the effectiveness of a VR-based approach for pain relief in patients suffering from chronic pain [18–20]. Indeed, VR has been shown as being effective as a treatment strategy for burn pain, acute pain, or induced pain [21–26]. VR as an analgesic option that can be used in two modalities: as a distraction therapy through immersiveness, and as a tool for modulating body representation through virtual body ownership illusions (BOI) [18,24,27,28]. Distraction therapy consists in temporally diverting the patient's attention from the pain through the VR experience [29]. In detail, the cognitive mechanisms that mediate VR-based interventions as a distraction therapy for pain relief are attention, concentration, and emotional alteration [30]. Moreover, the immersiveness on such VR environments allows participants to fully interact with the environment increasing the distraction from pain [28,31,32].

The use of virtual body ownership illusions for pain relief relies on inducing the sense of embodiment toward virtual bodies for changing body representation [33,34]. The sense of "embodiment" refers to the sense of having a body [35] and it is the result of a complex interaction between bottom-up and top-down sensory information [36]. According to this, the sense of embodiment consists in three subcomponents: the sense of self-location, the sense of agency, and the sense of body ownership [33]. Once embodiment is successfully induced, the subject feels as though they are inside a body that is moving according to his/her own intentions and interacting with the environment [33]. In the last few years, there has been a proliferation of studies trying to understand how to experimentally manipulate bodily perception and embodiment by using virtual body ownership illusions [37,38]. This is possible because a main feature of the VR system is its capability to induce a sense of 'presence', that is the sense of 'being there' within the virtual environment [39–41]. According to this, a large number of studies have tested virtual body ownership illusions by using synchronous visuo-tactile or visuo-motor correlations for inducing the sense of embodiment in a VR environment where participants could feel fully immersed into and present in the generated virtual world. [42–45]. In this regard, it has been demonstrated that watching the face of another person while that face and one's own face are stroked synchronously induces the illusion of self-recognition toward the other face, the so-called "enfacement illusion" [46,47].

The enfacement illusion is the result of the plasticity of the self-face representation, which can be temporarily modified to include another person's facial features [46,47]. Hence, the enfacement illusion has resulted as a good strategy for changing self-representation, with important implications for all those subjects who have distorted body representations, including patients suffering from chronic pain [48–50]. Indeed, a recent study showed that it is possible to induce the enfacement illusion by using VR systems [51]. The enfacement illusion is associated with improved emotional contagion and emotional recognition. It has indeed demonstrated that there is a sort of "mood migration" from the virtual face to another person's face in case of synchronicity between them [52]. In line with this point, a recent study [53] has shown that by applying synchronous visuo–tactile stimulation observed through videos, it is possible to boost facial mimicry, which is the automatic imitation of another person's emotion. From a neuroimaging point of view, the virtual experience derived from the enfacement illusion is able to induce changes in the sensory–motor cortex [54], and in particular in those areas that are the neural basis of body image [55] and emotion processing [56–58], that is, the primary sensory (S1) and motor (M1) cortices. Interestingly, these brain areas are involved in the cerebral dimensions of pain: one representing the discriminative dimension (S1) and one representing the affective dimension (M1).

It has been indeed shown that the perception of pain can alter both facial recognition and visuospatial perception in CM compared to healthy subjects [59]. Furthermore, it has been found that by reducing the altered perception of body image in CM patients with medication overuse, it is possible to induce beneficial effects on their affective state and on their perception of pain [60]. Moreover, there is evidence that electrophysiological homeostasis is altered abnormally (allostatic load) in a migraine brain with regard to what concerns sensory–motor network interactions [61–65] as well as neurostimulation techniques applied at the right M1 or S1 which can effectively decrease migraine pain frequency, duration, and intensity [66]. Recently our research group has evaluated the effects of an intervention based on visual feedback—i.e., intended to modify pain through the perception of the body image by means of the observation of facial expressions with different emotional content [67]—on the modulation of pain perception in a sample of female CM patients [68]. Interestingly, we showed that the simple observation of a facial expression with positive emotional content, when compared to other emotional content (negative or neutral), was able to decrease pain perception. The results from this study have paved the way for the integration of new technologies, such as VR systems, for modulating body representation through the use of virtual body ownership illusions, in particular through the use of the 'enfacement illusion'. To the best of our knowledge, no study has used the enfacement illusion for the treatment of pain in patients suffering from CM.

The present study protocol presents a longitudinal randomized controlled trial (RCT) protocol, which aims to investigate whether it is possible to decrease pain perception in patients with CM by inducing the enfacement illusion of representing oneself in a happy face through a VR system (experimental group). It is expected that this effect is mediated by an improved body image perception and empathy for positive emotions. Our previous findings [68] allowed us to explore the different effects of being exposed to neutral or sad stimuli. Hence, in the present study, we used the positive emotional face as being the only one recognized as effective for pain relief in patients with CM. According to this, the main aim of this study is to enucleate specifically the effect of enfacement from the possible synergic effect of the exposure to a positive stimulus (happy face). In the control group, the patients will be subjected to a positive exposure (pleasant environment) in an immersive VR environment, which has already been demonstrated to be able to produce distracting effects on pain perception in patients with CM [69]. The rationale for choosing this control condition derives from the willingness to use another positive visual stimulus in immersive VR, which is already known to be effective in distracting individuals from pain in CM [69], that can serve to appreciate the additional effects of producing the enfacement illusion of a happy face in the experimental group. It is hypothesized that patients in the experimental group will experience greater pain relief and will improve the perception of their body image compared to the control group. Therefore, the present protocol study aims to show a possible relationship between the manipulation of the body image and pain perception and to demonstrate the effectiveness of the use of the virtual enfacement illusion as a cognitive behavioral intervention for pain relief in CM.

2. Materials and Methods

2.1. Study Design

The proposed study is a prospective double-blind RCT with two arms. A CONSORT flow chart for enrollment and randomization is shown in Figure 1. Patients fulfilling inclusion criteria, once they have signed the informed consent form, will undergo a baseline assessment (T0) using the below-listed tests and will be randomized to one of two groups: experimental and control. Both groups will be exposed to three VR sessions each lasting approximately 20 min during a one-week period. The first session will be carried out immediately after enrollment and T0, whereas the next two will be carried out in the following days when the patients will report to have a migraine attack. At T0 and at the end of the intervention (T1), the patients will fill in a questionnaire based on behavioral measures related to their emotional and psychological state and their body image perception. T1 assessment will then be carried out at the end of the last VR session. Before and after each VR session the level of pain, body image, and affective state of the patients will be assessed. Furthermore, after each VR session, the sense of embodiment (experimental group) or the sense of immersiveness (control group) will be assessed.

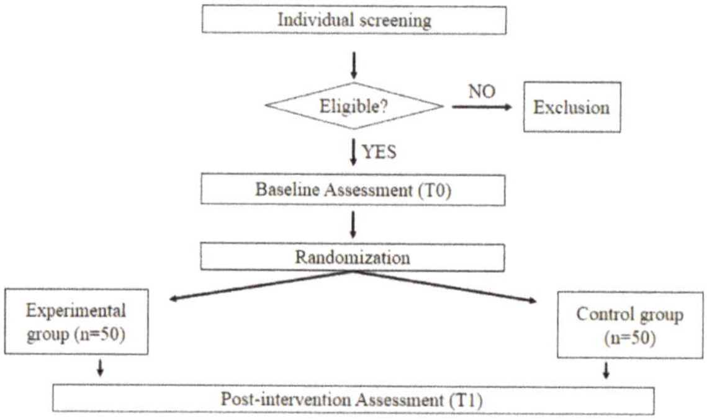

Figure 1. CONSORT flow chart for enrollment and randomization.

This study protocol conforms to the Standard Protocol Items: Recommendations for Interventional Trials (SPIRIT) guidelines (see Supplementary Table S1).

2.2. Study Setting

This trial will take place at the Headache Science and Neurorehabilitation Center of the IRCCS National Neurological Institute Mondino Foundation (Pavia), a tertiary referral center for the diagnosis and care of migraine in Northern Italy.

2.3. Participant Recruitment and Eligibility Criteria

Participants will be recruited among patients referred to the Center. An expert neurologist will verify the eligibility criteria during the recruitment process based on the participants' history, headache diaries, and neurological evaluation.

Inclusion criteria for patients will be: (a) 18–65 years of age; (b) female sex; (c) fulfilment of the ICHD-3 criteria [2] for CM (with or without medication overuse); (d) previous history of migraine as primary headache; (e) an intensity of migraine attacks between 20 and 80 on a 0–100 VAS. Only females will be included in this study because of the reported differences on pain perception between males and females [70].

Exclusion criteria will be: (a) epilepsy, psychosis, intellectual disability, pregnant women and breastfeeding women; (b) visual problems; (c) presence of chronic non-cephalic pain.

All patients will receive the advice to avoid any abortive medication during the study period. Preventive treatments will be allowed given that they are not expected to affect the outcome of this study.

In order to achieve adequate participant enrolment to reach the target sample size (see Section 2.12.1), we will provide notice of this study among patients referred to our clinic as well as in local newspapers.

2.4. Participant Evaluation

All patients will undergo the following assessment measures, as reported in Table 1, performed by a psychologist, who will be also be responsible for obtaining the informed consent form.

Table 1. Materials for participant evaluation as a function of the testing session.

Outcome Measures	T0	Session 1 Pre	Session 1 Post	Session 2 Pre	Session 2 Post	Session 3 Pre	Session 3 Post	T1
Primary outcome								
Pain Visual Analogue Scale (VAS)		x	x	x	x	x	x	
Secondary outcome								
Hospital Anxiety and Depression Scale (HADS)	x							x
Emotive Regulation Questionnaire (ERQ)	x							x
Difficulties in Emotion Regulation Scale (DERS	x							x
Body Satisfaction Scale (BSS)	x							x
Body Image Questionnaire (BIQ)		x	x	x	x	x	x	
Positive and Negative Affect Schedule (PANAS)		x	x	x	x	x	x	
Embodiment/Immersive questionnaire			x		x		x	

Note: the embodiment questionnaire is administered to the experimental group, whereas the immersive questionnaire is administered to the control group.

At T0 and T1, the participants will fill in a series of psychological questionnaires as with regards their affective and emotional state:

(a) Body Satisfaction Scale (BSS) [71] designed to measure satisfaction/dissatisfaction with 16 body parts;
(b) Hospital Anxiety and Depression Scale (HADS) [72] for anxious and depressive symptomatology;
(c) Emotive Regulation Questionnaire (ERQ) [73], which is a self-report measure of two emotion regulation strategies (i.e., cognitive reappraisal and expressive suppression);
(d) Difficulties in Emotion Regulation Scale (DERS) [74] measuring emotion regulation problems.

Moreover, within each of the three sessions, they will be also evaluated before and after the visual exposure (six times) with the following measures:

(a) Pain Visual Analogue Scale (VAS) for pain level on a 0 to 100 scale;
(b) Body Image Questionnaire (BIQ) [75] for body image perception;
(c) Positive and Negative Affect Schedule (PANAS) [76] for the positive and negative affective state.

Finally, after each visual exposure session, for a total of three times, the patients of the experimental group will fill in a questionnaire (i.e., embodiment questionnaire) related to the level of sense of belonging to the virtual body and the experience of illusion of enfacement [77]. The control group will fill in a questionnaire (i.e., immersive questionnaire) assessing the level of immersion in the virtual environment [39]. This is in order to assess the subjective strength of the two conditions to which patients will be exposed.

2.5. Randomization, Stratification, and Allocation

After T0, random numbers will be generated from a uniform distribution in the range 0–1, dividing the range in two equal intervals and assigning each patient to the group corresponding to the sampled number (1:1 ratio). Allocation of participants will be performed by an independent data manager, who will be not involved in the data collection/analysis.

2.6. Blinding

This is a double blinded study: both the patients and the clinicians collecting the data will be blinded to the group allocation. The participants do not know to what kind of VR conditions they will be exposed. On the ethics consent form, they are informed that they will be exposed in a random fashion to one of two VR conditions consisting in the exposure to a virtual environment through a head-mounted display (HMD). The clinicians coding the data are not aware of the group allocation.

2.7. Apparatus

We will use an HMD (Oculus Quest2 created by Facebook Technologies, a division of Meta, Facebook Inc., Menlo Park, CA, USA —see Figure 2), with a resolution of 1832 × 1920 pixels per eye resolution at 120 Hz to show the 360° video in the experimental group, which will be displayed through a VR video player app (Skybox VR player for Oculus, v. 1.0.0, Skybox Studio, Vancouver, BC, Canada), or the virtual environment displayed through the Calm Place app (v. 0.3.1) (Calm Inc., San Francisco, CA, USA) in the control group.

Figure 2. The HMD to be used in the experimental group and the control group.

2.8. Visual-Exposure Conditions

Each VR session will be conducted by the same experimenter (i.e., a psychologist) in order to avoid any related effects. Both visual exposure conditions will be conducted with the participant seated in a chair. In case of cyber sickness, participants will be free to discontinue the VR exposure at any moment.

2.8.1. Experimental Group

Patients in the experimental group will be exposed to the enfacement illusion condition, conducted similarly to other studies in other fields of research [47] (Figures 3 and 4). In detail, patients will see, through the HMD, a virtual body sitting in front of them in the same position showing a happy face expression. Each session will consist of four phases:

(1) Observation of the virtual facial expression and habituation to the virtual environment: the experimenter will ask patients to focus their attention on the face of the virtual body sitting in front of them for about one minute.
(2) Visuo–tactile stimulation: in order to induce the enfacement illusion in the patients, the experimenter will use a brush to apply synchronous visuo–tactile stimulation to the real face of the patients, while they will be observing a synchronous tactile stimulation on the happy face displayed in the 360° video equally applied by the experimenter in the same place and at the same time. The synchronous visuo–tactile stimulation will be applied for 2 min.
(3) The observation of the virtual facial expression and habituation to the virtual environment phase will be repeated to update habituation to the virtual environment.

(4) The synchronous visuo–tactile stimulation phase will be repeated to update the induction of the enfacement illusion.

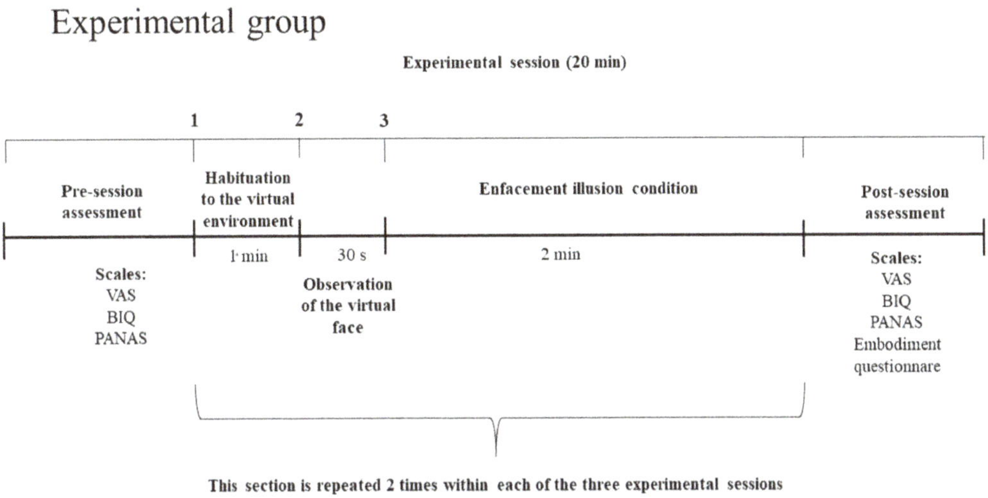

Figure 3. Timeline of each experimental session for the experimental group.

Figure 4. Caption of the 360° video while applying the face visuo–tactile stimulation to induce the enfacement illusion.

Overall, the patients will receive 4 min of synchronous visuo–tactile stimulation to induce the enfacement illusion to the happy face displayed in the 360° video through the HMD. The synchronous stimulation will be recorded with a metronome sound (60 beats per minute) in the 360° video. During the experimental session, the researcher will stimulate the face of the patients which at the same time will be synchronized with the beat sound displayed in the video. Patients will observe the same situation when they are immersed into the 360° virtual scenario: a researcher stimulating the virtual face placed in front of them. A beep sound will indicate the experimenter wants to start the stimulation, and he/she will follow the sound of the metronome for each stimulation. After exposure to the 360° video, the patients will fill in a questionnaire regarding the induction of the 'enfacement illusion' adapted from [77].

2.8.2. Control Group

Participants in the control group will be exposed to a visual stimulation by observing a pleasant immersive virtual reality environment [69] (Figures 5 and 6). As in the experimental group, there will be two minutes for the habituation to the virtual environment, where the experimenter will ask the patients to describe what they see. Then, the patients will observe the pleasant virtual environment for about 4 min.

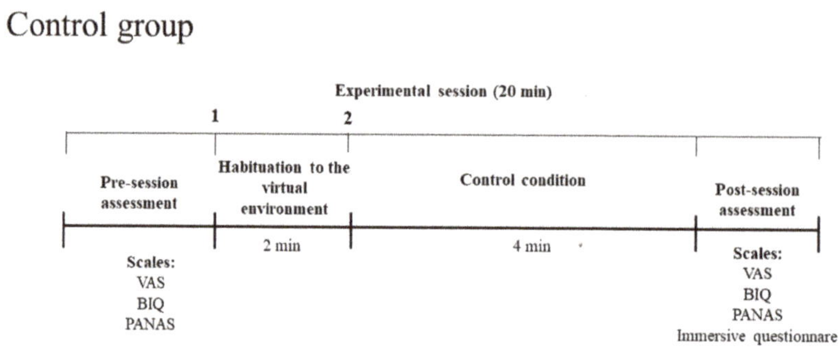

Figure 5. Timeline of each experimental session for the control group.

Figure 6. Caption of the pleasant virtual environment retrieved from the Calm Place app.

After immersion into the virtual environment, the patients will fill in a questionnaire regarding the virtual reality experience adapted from [39].

2.9. Outcome Measures

As primary outcome measure, we will consider the effects on pain perception measured on the VAS for the treatment based on the enfacement illusion compared to the control conditions across the visual-exposure sessions.

Secondary outcome measures will include:

(a) The evaluation of the effects on the perception of one's own body image and on the affective and emotional state of the treatment based on the enfacement illusion with respect to the control conditions as evaluated with the BIQ and the PANAS at the beginning and at the end of each visual exposure condition;
(b) The assessment of the virtual reality experience within each treatment condition by comparing the embodiment questionnaire (for the experimental group) and the immersive questionnaire (for the control group) across the three visual exposure sessions;
(c) The evaluation of the relationship between the affective and emotional state of patients and the change in the perception of pain and one's body image as assessed via the BSS, the HADS, the ERQ, and the DERS at T0 and T1 in the two visual exposure conditions (experimental group vs. control group).

2.10. Data Collection

Psychologists conducting evaluations will receive appropriate instruction and guidance regarding all of the outcome parameters and assessments that will be taken. The research staff collecting the data will be blinded to the group allocation.

2.11. Data Management

Study data will be recorded in a repository in an Excel file. All participants will be registered with an identification code in a random order. The repository will be kept updated to reflect the subject's status at each stage during the course of the study. The collected data, after scientific publication, will be shared in public repositories (Zenodo) according to the good practice of data sharing.

2.12. Statistical Analysis

2.12.1. Sample Size Calculation

According to the main goal of demonstrating possible changes in pain perception—as assessed on the VAS scale—in patients with CM after a non-pharmacological intervention, the number of participants needed is 100. This number was calculated in order to guarantee a statistical power of 80% and a statistical level of 95% for a one-tailed t-test in order to detect an effect size (d) = 0.5 by expecting significant differences between the two groups in terms of changes in pain perception both after each treatment session and at the end of the entire intervention in favor of patients who fall into the experimental group (delta pain for the experimental group = -40 ± 100; delta pain for the control group = 10 ± 100). With the above data, the required sample size necessary to detect significant differences is 50 subjects per group. Extra participants will be recruited in case of dropouts.

2.12.2. Planned Analysis

Statistical analysis on outcome measures will be conducted using Stata 13 (StataCorp LP, College Station, TX, USA). The data collected will be first analyzed using descriptive statistical techniques. As the primary outcome, differences in terms of VAS scores at session 1 pre assessment and session 3 post assessment in the two groups will be evaluated using ANOVA-one factor (factor: groups) (or the Kruskal–Wallis test, after a normality analysis). Finally, mixed-effects models will be implemented to examine the longitudinal aspect of the study that represent changes across the visual-exposure sessions. For secondary outcomes concerning the changes in the perception of one's own body image and on the affective and emotional state as well as the assessment of the VR experience, the analysis plan will be similar to the one planned for the primary outcome. Regarding the evaluation of the relationship between the affective and emotional state of the patients and the change in the perception of pain and one's body image, a correlation analysis will be performed between the considered scales. For all outcome analyses, an intention-to-treat (ITT) approach will be used, according to CONSORT guidelines [78,79]. An alpha level ≤ 0.05 will be considered as significant.

2.13. Ethical Issues and Dissemination Plan

This trial will involve human participants, VR-based systems, data collection, elaboration, and abstraction used for the evaluation of the two VR options. This study has been approved by the local ethics committee (IRCCS San Matteo Hospital, Pavia) and will be conducted in accordance with the Declaration of Helsinki and reported according to CONSORT guidelines [78,79]. Any subsequent modification to the protocol which may impact the study (e.g., objectives, study population, sample sizes, procedures) will be submitted as an amendment and reviewed by the IRCCS San Matteo Hospital ethics committee for approval. In addition to ethical approval, all the procedures and the data managed have been approved by the data protection officer of the IRCCS Mondino Foundation who guarantees the study's compliance to the GDPR (General Data Protection Regulation). The information provided when presenting the informed consent form to the participants will be given in a language appropriate to the individuals' level of understanding. In particular, in the consent form, participants are informed that they will receive, in a random fashion, one of two VR conditions consisting of exposure to a virtual environment through an HMD. We do not provide additional information about the content of each VR exposure in order to avoid influencing the subjective strength of the virtual reality experience, as assessed by the embodiment and immersive questionnaires. Participants will be encouraged to ask questions before signing the informed consent form and they will be free to discontinue the study at any moment. In order to improve the adherence to the protocol, the experimenter responsible for collecting the informed consent forms will highlight to the patients the opportunity to take part in this study as a way to improve the knowledge of their disease as well as to provide complementary non-pharmacological approaches in the future. Due to the low risk associated with study participation, an annual audit of the study, the Data Monitoring Committee (DMC), and interim analyses are not required. Additionally, a data safety monitoring board is not required because we are not investigating a medical product and we do not foresee any major risks associated with study participation.

To protect the privacy of patients, we will use a unique research code for each participant on all research-related documents. This enables us to identify individuals without using their names. The list linking the participant code to personal information will be kept in a secure electronic database with access limited. All electronic research-related participant information will be stored on a protected network in a secure file with limited access.

After the data analysis phase, patient privacy will be further preserved. The results obtained from the study will be described on a group level to prevent the data being traced back to a single person. Once the final report of the study is available, the results will be disseminated in the scientific community through publication in open-access, peer-reviewed scientific journals and presentations at national and international conferences.

Datasets generated and/or analyzed during the current study will be anonymized and stored on an online repository (Zenodo) according to the good practice of data sharing. External researchers may obtain access to the final trial dataset. The (intellectual) property rights with regard to the generated data will reside at the IRCCS Mondino Foundation.

To the best of our knowledge, VR-based interventions should not have any potential negative impacts on the participants. A possible adverse effect related to VR could be cyber sickness (nausea and other side effects) [80]. In order to avoid this, VR exposure will be limited to 20 min at a time and patients will be seated while using the HMD. The investigator will communicate any possible, unforeseen, adverse event to the Ministry of Health.

Regarding payment policies for participants, the compensation's amount and the method and timing of disbursement must be consistent with the laws, regulations, and guidelines of the region in which the study is conducted and must not improperly influence the decision to participate. This trial is a no-profit study, and, in Italy, the national legislation states that it is forbidden to offer or request any kind of financial benefit for participation in a clinical, experimental trial. The costs associated with the implementation of this RCT will be supported by the IRCCS Mondino Foundation.

3. Discussion and Conclusions

CM represents a life-altering condition resulting in a significant reduction in the quality of life [81]. Sufferers are usually treated with acute medications and preventive treatments, which can be poorly tolerated and present significant risks and side effects [4,5,82]. Hence, CM patients are left with few efficacious and safe therapeutic options. To this end, the technological advancements of the last few years are providing promising and novel non-pharmacological options to be adopted for treating clinical conditions, including pain states. VR systems aimed at reducing virtual BOIs can then represent new tools for the study of perceptual processes acting on body ownership [17,26] and emotional states [52,53]. In this field, synchronous multisensory stimulations, such as visuo–tactile stimulation, can be used temporarily to induce enfacement, which is the subjective illusion of ownership of another person's face [46,47]. The experimental induction of the enfacement illusion can represent an interesting application strategy for pain relief in CM.

The present RCT will provide evidence about the use of the enfacement illusion in virtual reality for pain relief in CM. It is expected that such results will arise because of the improvement in body image perception and empathy for positive emotions. Results of this RCT will advance the knowledge of this painful condition by exploring the relationship existing between internal body representation, distortion of the body image, and pain perception in CM. Furthermore, the results from this study will support the effectiveness of body ownership illusions, such as the use of the enfacement illusion, as a cognitive behavioral intervention for pain relief.

Chronic migraine's impact on society has ever been overcast by stigma, its historically obscure etiology, and the comorbidities often associated with the disease. From an economic point of view, migraine is considered as one of the costliest neurological diseases in Europe [83,84]. It is indeed characterized by diminished productivity and increased utilization of healthcare resources, translating into higher costs for both the individual and society [83,85,86]. To the best of our knowledge, this is the first study evaluating the effects of a treatment based on the enfacement illusion in reducing pain perception in this kind of patient. It is well known that CM represents a very challenging condition from a therapeutic point of view. Evidence suggests the usefulness of a multidisciplinary approach [87] in the management of difficult-to-treat primary headaches. Findings from this RCT could pave the way to the definition and testing of non-pharmacological therapies mediated by virtual BOIs in the management of pain in CM. Given the promise of virtual embodiment and enfacement illusions in reducing pain perception by means of body representation, this study will determine the extent to which VR interventions can positively affect pain perception. Furthermore, such VR interventions may alleviate this condition and provide additional alternate mechanisms for providing benefits to CM patients.

This study is a first, important step toward the evaluation of the effectiveness of the proposed virtual BOI for pain relief in CM. Larger clinical trials will be needed to confirm the findings and more behavioral studies, as well as a better understanding of this disorder, and more tailored, individual-based approaches to its treatment will be needed in the future. In this framework, the implementation of VR systems in the management of CM could be incorporated into clinical routine practices as a complementary, non-pharmacological therapy to reduce pain perception, providing promising outcomes for the patients.

Strengths and Limitations

In the field of CM, the present randomized controlled trial will allow the implementation and assessment of the effectiveness of an enfacement illusion intervention targeting pain in this condition. The availability of alternative non-pharmacological treatments will represent an expanding clinical practice and an interesting area of research. Whenever confronted with headache patients with a complex disease or those who are unwilling to accept possible drug-induced adverse events, clinicians should consider this rapidly growing armamentarium of alternative strategies of treatment and choose treatment methods based on desired the clinical indications and patient's characteristics.

This study has some limitations that need to be acknowledged. First, there are no plans to collect any functional measurements of activity changes in the pain modulatory system, which could shed light on the neural phenomena associated with the enfacement illusion. Second, this study involves only female CM participants. Even if it is known that there are differences in pain perception between males and females [70], we are aware that our choice will limit the translatability of the findings. We also decided to exclude pregnant or breastfeeding women in order to avoid the possibility of secondary headache [88] in which the effects of our intervention would be distorted by confounding variables. However, such a decision should limit the generalizability of our findings. Third, the intervention lasts for only three sessions and our primary outcome should not be considered representative for an efficacy study, according to control trial guidelines [89]. Hence, it is expected that they study's effects could be limited from a temporal point of view. Finally, we are also aware that we are not using a validated pain measure, such as the McGill pain questionnaire [90], for assessing our primary outcome. However, the VAS has been used in a large number of studies to rate the level of pain perception immediately after exposure of the experimental stimuli [91–93]. We consider that fact that as the participants have to rate their level of pain immediately after exposure to the VR conditions, an intuitive VAS assessment will be the more appropriate measure. Based on the results from this pilot clinical study, it will be possible to design further RCTs with longer intervention periods and to even investigate the possible neural correlation behind such effects as well as to provide a broad view on how the enfacement illusion could be effective in inducing benefits for migraine frequency and also for the non-painful, non-cephalic aspects of migraine (e.g., nausea, photophobia, etc.). Nonetheless, we felt that, from a research point of view and as a first step in this completely new field of research, it was important to start with a homogeneous population to control for the variables.

Supplementary Materials: The following supporting information can be downloaded at: https://www.mdpi.com/article/10.3390/jcm11226876/s1, Table S1: SPIRIT 2013 Checklist: Recommended items to address in a clinical trial protocol and related documents.

Author Contributions: S.B. and M.M.-G. developed the original concept of the trial, drafted the original protocol, developed the design, the methodology, and the analysis plan and wrote the manuscript. M.A., E.G., N.G., R.D.I., G.S. and C.T. reviewed and commented on the drafts of the protocol and the paper. All authors have read and agreed to the published version of the manuscript.

Funding: This work was supported by a grant from the Italian Ministry of Health to IRCCS Mondino Foundation (Ricerca Corrente 2021; Ricerca Corrente 2022). The funding agency had no role in the design of this study and will not have any role during its execution or analyses, the interpretation or the data, or the decision to submit the results.

Institutional Review Board Statement: This study has been approved by the local ethics committee (IRCCS San Matteo Hospital, Pavia, code: 20200075038, date of approval; 31 August 2020) and will be conducted in accordance with the Declaration of Helsinki and reported according to CONSORT guidelines [78,79].

Informed Consent Statement: All participants will be made fully aware of the aims of the research and written informed consent will be obtained from all subjects.

Data Availability Statement: Datasets generated and/or analyzed during the current study will be anonymized and stored on an online repository (Zenodo, https://zenodo.org/), according to the good practice of data sharing. External researchers may obtain access to the final trial dataset. The (intellectual) property rights with regard to the generated data will reside at the IRCCS Mondino Foundation. Anonymized results will be published in peer-reviewed journals and presented at international conferences.

Acknowledgments: The authors gratefully acknowledge the contribution that will be made by the participants of this study. Furthermore, a special thanks should be given to Rosaria Greco for her valuable suggestions.

Conflicts of Interest: The authors declare no conflict of interest.

Trial Registration: The trial was registered at clinicaltrials.gov (Clinicaltrials.gov, https://clinicaltrials.gov/ct2/show/NCT04904458, 27 May 2021).

Trial Status: This trial is currently recruiting patients. The trial is expected to end on 30 March 2024. The protocol is Version 2 dated 13 October 2021.

References

1. GBD 2015 Disease and Injury Incidence and Prevalence Collaborators. Global, Regional, and National Incidence, Prevalence, and Years Lived with Disability for 310 Diseases and Injuries, 1990–2015: A Systematic Analysis for the Global Burden of Disease Study 2015. *Lancet* **2016**, 388, 1545–1602. [CrossRef]

2. Headache Classification Committee of the International Headache Society (IHS). The International Classification of Headache Disorders, 3rd Edition. *Cephalalgia* **2018**, *38*, 1–211. [CrossRef] [PubMed]
3. Zobdeh, F.; ben Kraiem, A.; Attwood, M.M.; Chubarev, V.N.; Tarasov, V.V.; Schiöth, H.B.; Mwinyi, J. Pharmacological Treatment of Migraine: Drug Classes, Mechanisms of Action, Clinical Trials and New Treatments. *Br. J. Pharmacol.* **2021**, *178*, 4588–4607. [CrossRef] [PubMed]
4. Hepp, Z.; Dodick, D.W.; Varon, S.F.; Gillard, P.; Hansen, R.N.; Devine, E.B. Adherence to Oral Migraine-Preventive Medications among Patients with Chronic Migraine. *Cephalalgia* **2015**, *35*, 478–488. [CrossRef] [PubMed]
5. Goadsby, P.J.; Sprenger, T. Current Practice and Future Directions in the Prevention and Acute Management of Migraine. *Lancet Neurol.* **2010**, *9*, 285–298. [CrossRef]
6. Burch, R.C.; Buse, D.C.; Lipton, R.B. Migraine. *Neurol. Clin.* **2019**, *37*, 631–649. [CrossRef]
7. Bottiroli, S.; Viana, M.; Sances, G.; Ghiotto, N.; Guaschino, E.; Galli, F.; Vegni, E.; Pazzi, S.; Nappi, G.; Tassorelli, C. Psychological Factors Associated with Failure of Detoxification Treatment in Chronic Headache Associated with Medication Overuse. *Cephalalgia* **2016**, *36*, 1356–1365. [CrossRef]
8. Bottiroli, S.; Allena, M.; Sances, G.; De Icco, R.; Avenali, M.; Fadic, R.; Katsarava, Z.; Lainez, M.J.A.; Goicochea, M.T.; Bendtsen, L.; et al. Psychological, Clinical, and Therapeutic Predictors of the Outcome of Detoxification in a Large Clinical Population of Medication-Overuse Headache: A Six-Month Follow-up of the COMOESTAS Project. *Cephalalgia* **2019**, *39*, 135–147. [CrossRef]
9. Galli, F.; Caputi, M.; Sances, G.; Vegni, E.; Bottiroli, S.; Nappi, G.; Tassorelli, C. Alexithymia in Chronic and Episodic Migraine: A Comparative Study. *J. Ment. Health* **2017**, *26*, 192–196. [CrossRef]
10. Bottiroli, S.; Galli, F.; Viana, M.; Sances, G.; Tassorelli, C. Traumatic Experiences, Stressful Events, and Alexithymia in Chronic Migraine with Medication Overuse. *Front. Psychol.* **2018**, *9*, 704. [CrossRef]
11. Bottiroli, S.; Galli, F.; Ballante, E.; Pazzi, S.; Sances, G.; Guaschino, E.; Allena, M.; Tassorelli, C. Validity of the Severity of Dependence Scale for Detecting Dependence Behaviours in Chronic Migraine with Medication Overuse. *Cephalalgia* **2021**, *42*, 209–217. [CrossRef] [PubMed]
12. Bottiroli, S.; De Icco, R.; Vaghi, G.; Pazzi, S.; Guaschino, E.; Allena, M.; Ghiotto, N.; Martinelli, D.; Tassorelli, C.; Sances, G. Psychological Predictors of Negative Treatment Outcome with Erenumab in Chronic Migraine: Data from an Open Label Long-Term Prospective Study. *J. Headache Pain* **2021**, *22*, 114. [CrossRef]
13. Linde, M.; Gustavsson, A.; Stovner, L.J.; Steiner, T.J.; Barré, J.; Katsarava, Z.; Lainez, J.M.; Lampl, C.; Lantéri-Minet, M.; Rastenyte, D.; et al. The Cost of Headache Disorders in Europe: The Eurolight Project. *Eur. J. Neurol.* **2012**, *19*, 703–711. [CrossRef] [PubMed]
14. Agosti, R. Migraine Burden of Disease: From the Patient's Experience to a Socio-Economic View. *Headache J. Head Face Pain* **2018**, *58*, 17–32. [CrossRef] [PubMed]
15. Mennini, F.S.; Gitto, L.; Martelletti, P. Improving Care through Health Economics Analyses: Cost of Illness and Headache. *J. Headache Pain* **2008**, *9*, 199–206. [CrossRef]
16. Matamala-Gomez, M.; Stasolla, F.; Seinfeld, S.; Caffò, A.O.; Banakou, D.; Bottiroli, S. Editorial: Neuropsychological and Cognitive-Behavioral Assessment of Neurodegenerative Disease and Rehabilitation Using New Technologies and Virtual Reality. *Front. Psychol.* **2021**, *12*, 1850. [CrossRef]
17. Matamala-Gomez, M.; Maselli, A.; Malighetti, C.; Realdon, O.; Mantovani, F.; Riva, G. Virtual Body Ownership Illusions for Mental Health: A Narrative Review. *J. Clin. Med.* **2021**, *10*, 139. [CrossRef]
18. Matamala-Gomez, M.; Donegan, T.; Bottiroli, S.; Sandrini, G.; Sanchez-Vives, M.V.; Tassorelli, C. Immersive Virtual Reality and Virtual Embodiment for Pain Relief. *Front. Hum. Neurosci.* **2019**, *13*, 279. [CrossRef]
19. Mallari, B.; Spaeth, E.K.; Goh, H.; Boyd, B.S. Virtual Reality as an Analgesic for Acute and Chronic Pain in Adults: A Systematic Review and Meta-Analysis. *J. Pain Res.* **2019**, *12*, 2053–2085. [CrossRef]
20. Malloy, K.M.; Milling, L.S. The Effectiveness of Virtual Reality Distraction for Pain Reduction: A Systematic Review. *Clin. Psychol. Rev.* **2010**, *30*, 1011–1018. [CrossRef]
21. Hoffman, H.G.; Doctor, J.N.; Patterson, D.R.; Carrougher, G.J.; Furness, T.A. Virtual Reality as an Adjunctive Pain Control during Burn Wound Care in Adolescent Patients. *Pain* **2000**, *85*, 305–309. [CrossRef]
22. Hoffman, H.G.; Seibel, E.J.; Richards, T.L.; Furness, T.A.; Patterson, D.R.; Sharar, S.R. Virtual Reality Helmet Display Quality Influences the Magnitude of Virtual Reality Analgesia. *J. Pain* **2006**, *7*, 843–850. [CrossRef] [PubMed]
23. Carrougher, G.J.; Hoffman, H.G.; Nakamura, D.; Lezotte, D.; Soltani, M.; Leahy, L.; Engrav, L.H.; Patterson, D.R. The Effect of Virtual Reality on Pain and Range of Motion in Adults With Burn Injuries. *J. Burn Care Res.* **2009**, *30*, 785–791. [CrossRef] [PubMed]
24. Schmitt, Y.S.; Hoffman, H.G.; Blough, D.K.; Patterson, D.R.; Jensen, M.P.; Soltani, M.; Carrougher, G.J.; Nakamura, D.; Sharar, S.R. A Randomized, Controlled Trial of Immersive Virtual Reality Analgesia, during Physical Therapy for Pediatric Burns. *Burns* **2011**, *37*, 61–68. [CrossRef]
25. Hoffman, H.G.; Richards, T.L.; Van Oostrom, T.; Coda, B.A.; Jensen, M.P.; Blough, D.K.; Sharar, S.R. The Analgesic Effects of Opioids and Immersive Virtual Reality Distraction: Evidence from Subjective and Functional Brain Imaging Assessments. *Anesth. Analg.* **2007**, *105*, 1776–1783. [CrossRef] [PubMed]
26. Martini, M. Real, Rubber or Virtual: The Vision of "One's Own" Body as a Means for Pain Modulation. A Narrative Review. *Conscious. Cogn.* **2016**, *43*, 143–151. [CrossRef]

27. Sharar, S.R.; Carrougher, G.J.; Nakamura, D.; Hoffman, H.G.; Blough, D.K.; Patterson, D.R. Factors Influencing the Efficacy of Virtual Reality Distraction Analgesia During Postburn Physical Therapy: Preliminary Results from 3 Ongoing Studies. *Arch. Phys. Med. Rehabil.* **2007**, *88*, S43–S49. [CrossRef]
28. Hoffman, H.G. Interacting with Virtual Objects via Embodied Avatar Hands Reduces Pain Intensity and Diverts Attention. *Sci. Rep.* **2021**, *11*, 10672. [CrossRef]
29. Indovina, P.; Barone, D.; Gallo, L.; Chirico, A.; De Pietro, G.; Giordano, A. Virtual Reality as a Distraction Intervention to Relieve Pain and Distress During Medical Procedures. *Clin. J. Pain* **2018**, *34*, 858–877. [CrossRef]
30. Arane, K.; Behboudi, A.; Goldman, R.D. Virtual Reality for Pain and Anxiety Management in Children. *Can. Fam. Physician* **2017**, *63*, 932–934.
31. Donegan, T.; Ryan, B.E.; Swidrak, J.; Sanchez-Vives, M.V. Immersive Virtual Reality for Clinical Pain: Considerations for Effective Therapy. *Front. Virtual Real.* **2020**, *1*, 9. [CrossRef]
32. Keefe, F.J.; Huling, D.A.; Coggins, M.J.; Keefe, D.F.; Rosenthal, Z.M.; Herr, N.R.; Hoffman, H.G. Virtual Reality for Persistent Pain: A New Direction for Behavioral Pain Management. *Pain* **2012**, *153*, 2163–2166. [CrossRef]
33. Kilteni, K.; Groten, R.; Slater, M. The Sense of Embodiment in Virtual Reality. *Presence Teleoperators Virtual Environ.* **2012**, *21*, 373–387. [CrossRef]
34. Maselli, A.; Slater, M. The Building Blocks of the Full Body Ownership Illusion. *Front. Hum. Neurosci.* **2013**, *7*, 83. [CrossRef] [PubMed]
35. Gallagher, S. Dimensions of Embodiment: Body Image and Body Schema in Medical Contexts. In *Handbook of Phenomenology and Medicine*; Springer: Berlin/Heidelberg, Germany, 2001; pp. 147–175.
36. Longo, M.R.; Schüür, F.; Kammers, M.P.M.; Tsakiris, M.; Haggard, P. What Is Embodiment? A Psychometric Approach. *Cognition* **2008**, *107*, 978–998. [CrossRef] [PubMed]
37. Slater, M. Towards a Digital Body: The Virtual Arm Illusion. *Front. Hum. Neurosci.* **2008**, *2*, 6. [CrossRef]
38. Slater, M.; Sanchez-Vives, M.V. Enhancing Our Lives with Immersive Virtual Reality. *Front. Robot. AI* **2016**, *3*, 74. [CrossRef]
39. Slater, M.; Usoh, M.; Steed, A. Depth of Presence in Virtual Environments. *Presence Teleoperators Virtual Environ.* **1994**, *3*, 130–144. [CrossRef]
40. Slater, M. Immersion and the Illusion of Presence in Virtual Reality. *Br. J. Psychol.* **2018**, *109*, 431–433. [CrossRef]
41. Riva, G.; Davide, F.; IJsselsteijn, W.A. *Being There: The Experience of Presence in Mediated Environments*; IOS: Amsterdam, The Netherlands, 2003.
42. Lenggenhager, B.; Tadi, T.; Metzinger, T.; Blanke, O. Video Ergo Sum: Manipulating Bodily Self-Consciousness. *Science* **2007**, *317*, 1096–1099. [CrossRef]
43. Petkova, V.I.; Ehrsson, H.H. If I Were You: Perceptual Illusion of Body Swapping. *PLoS ONE* **2008**, *3*, 3832. [CrossRef] [PubMed]
44. Slater, M.; Perez-Marcos, D.; Ehrsson, H.H.; Sanchez-Vives, M.V. Inducing Illusory Ownership of a Virtual Body. *Front. Neurosci.* **2009**, *3*, 214–220. [CrossRef] [PubMed]
45. Kilteni, K.; Maselli, A.; Kording, K.P.; Slater, M. Over My Fake Body: Body Ownership Illusions for Studying the Multisensory Basis of Own-Body Perception. *Front. Hum. Neurosci.* **2015**, *9*, 141. [CrossRef]
46. Sforza, A.; Bufalari, I.; Haggard, P.; Aglioti, S.M. My Face in Yours: Visuo-Tactile Facial Stimulation Influences Sense of Identity. *Soc. Neurosci.* **2010**, *5*, 148–162. [CrossRef]
47. Porciello, G.; Bufalari, I.; Minio-Paluello, I.; Di Pace, E.; Aglioti, S.M. The 'Enfacement' Illusion: A Window on the Plasticity of the Self. *Cortex* **2018**, *104*, 261–275. [CrossRef] [PubMed]
48. Lotze, M.; Moseley, G.L. Role of Distorted Body Image in Pain. *Curr. Rheumatol. Rep.* **2007**, *9*, 488–496. [CrossRef] [PubMed]
49. Martínez, E.; Aira, Z.; Buesa, I.; Aizpurua, I.; Rada, D.; Azkue, J.J. Embodied Pain in Fibromyalgia: Disturbed Somatorepresentations and Increased Plasticity of the Body Schema. *PLoS ONE* **2018**, *13*, e0194534. [CrossRef]
50. Tsay, A.; Allen, T.J.; Proske, U.; Giummarra, M.J. Sensing the Body in Chronic Pain: A Review of Psychophysical Studies Implicating Altered Body Representation. *Neurosci. Biobehav. Rev.* **2015**, *52*, 221–232. [CrossRef]
51. Gonzalez-Franco, M.; Steed, A.; Hoogendyk, S.; Ofek, E. Using Facial Animation to Increase the Enfacement Illusion and Avatar Self-Identification. *IEEE Trans. Vis. Comput. Graph.* **2020**, *26*, 2023–2029. [CrossRef]
52. Ma, K.; Sellaro, R.; Lippelt, D.P.; Hommel, B. Mood Migration: How Enfacing a Smile Makes You Happier. *Cognition* **2016**, *151*, 52–62. [CrossRef]
53. Minio-Paluello, I.; Porciello, G.; Gandolfo, M.; Boukarras, S.; Aglioti, S.M. The Enfacement Illusion Boosts Facial Mimicry. *Cortex* **2020**, *123*, 113–123. [CrossRef] [PubMed]
54. Serino, A.; Sforza, A.L.; Kanayama, N.; van Elk, M.; Kaliuzhna, M.; Herbelin, B.; Blanke, O. Tuning of Temporo-Occipital Activity by Frontal Oscillations during Virtual Mirror Exposure Causes Erroneous Self-Recognition. *Eur. J. Neurosci.* **2015**, *42*, 2515–2526. [CrossRef] [PubMed]
55. Devue, C.; Brédart, S. The Neural Correlates of Visual Self-Recognition. *Conscious. Cogn.* **2011**, *20*, 40–51. [CrossRef] [PubMed]
56. Chakrabarti, B.; Bullmore, E.; Baron-Cohen, S. Empathizing with Basic Emotions: Common and Discrete Neural Substrates. *Soc. Neurosci.* **2006**, *1*, 364–384. [CrossRef] [PubMed]
57. Adolphs, R.; Damasio, H.; Tranel, D.; Damasio, A.R. Cortical Systems for the Recognition of Emotion in Facial Expressions. *J. Neurosci.* **1996**, *16*, 7678–7687. [CrossRef] [PubMed]

58. Adolphs, R.; Damasio, H.; Tranel, D.; Cooper, G.; Damasio, A.R. A Role for Somatosensory Cortices in the Visual Recognition of Emotion as Revealed by Three-Dimensional Lesion Mapping. *J. Neurosci.* **2000**, *20*, 2683–2690. [CrossRef]
59. Yetkin-Ozden, S.; Ekizoglu, E.; Baykan, B. Face Recognition in Patients with Migraine. *Pain Pract.* **2015**, *15*, 319–322. [CrossRef] [PubMed]
60. Nicolodi, M.; Sandoval, V. P012. Body Image Role in Medication-Overuse Headache Associated with Persistent Depressive Disorder. *J. Headache Pain* **2015**, *16*, A111. [CrossRef] [PubMed]
61. Borsook, D.; Maleki, N.; Becerra, L.; McEwen, B. Understanding Migraine through the Lens of Maladaptive Stress Responses: A Model Disease of Allostatic Load. *Neuron* **2012**, *73*, 219–234. [CrossRef]
62. Cauller, L. Layer I of Primary Sensory Neocortex: Where Top-down Converges upon Bottom-Up. *Behav. Brain Res.* **1995**, *71*, 163–170. [CrossRef]
63. Kim, J.H.; Kim, J.B.; Suh, S.; Seo, W.-K.; Oh, K.; Koh, S.-B. Thickening of the Somatosensory Cortex in Migraine without Aura. *Cephalalgia* **2014**, *34*, 1125–1133. [CrossRef]
64. DaSilva, A.F.M.; Granziera, C.; Snyder, J.; Hadjikhani, N. Thickening in the Somatosensory Cortex of Patients with Migraine. *Neurology* **2007**, *69*, 1990–1995. [CrossRef]
65. Soheili-Nezhad, S.; Sedghi, A.; Schweser, F.; Eslami Shahr Babaki, A.; Jahanshad, N.; Thompson, P.M.; Beckmann, C.F.; Sprooten, E.; Toghae, M. Structural and Functional Reorganization of the Brain in Migraine Without Aura. *Front. Neurol.* **2019**, *10*, 442. [CrossRef]
66. Rahimi, M.D.; Fadardi, J.S.; Saeidi, M.; Bigdeli, I.; Kashiri, R. Effectiveness of Cathodal TDCS of the Primary Motor or Sensory Cortex in Migraine: A Randomized Controlled Trial. *Brain Stimul.* **2020**, *13*, 675–682. [CrossRef]
67. Valentini, E.; Martini, M.; Lee, M.; Aglioti, S.M.; Iannetti, G. Seeing Facial Expressions Enhances Placebo Analgesia. *Pain* **2014**, *155*, 666–673. [CrossRef]
68. Matamala-Gomez, M.; Bottiroli, S.; Sances, G.; Allena, M.; De Icco, R.; Ghiotto, N.; Guaschino, E.; Sandrini, G.; Tassorelli, C. Facial Expressions Modulate Pain Perception in Patients with Chronic Migraine. *Cephalalgia* **2022**, *42*, 739–748. [CrossRef]
69. de Tommaso, M.; Calabrese, R.; Vecchio, E.; De Vito Francesco, V.; Lancioni, G.; Livrea, P. Effects of Affective Pictures on Pain Sensitivity and Cortical Responses Induced by Laser Stimuli in Healthy Subjects and Migraine Patients. *Int. J. Psychophysiol.* **2009**, *74*, 139–148. [CrossRef] [PubMed]
70. Paller, C.J.; Campbell, C.M.; Edwards, R.R.; Dobs, A.S. Sex-Based Differences in Pain Perception and Treatment. *Pain Med.* **2009**, *10*, 289–299. [CrossRef] [PubMed]
71. Slade, P.D.; Dewey, M.E.; Newton, T.; Brodie, D.; Kiemle, G. Development and Preliminary Validation of the Body Satisfaction Scale (BSS). *Psychol. Health* **1990**, *4*, 213–220. [CrossRef]
72. Costantini, M.; Musso, M.; Viterbori, P.; Bonci, F.; Del Mastro, L.; Garrone, O.; Venturini, M.; Morasso, G. Detecting Psychological Distress in Cancer Patients: Validity of the Italian Version of the Hospital Anxiety and Depression Scale. *Support. Care Cancer* **1999**, *7*, 121–127. [CrossRef] [PubMed]
73. Balzarotti, S.; John, O.P.; Gross, J.J. An Italian Adaptation of the Emotion Regulation Questionnaire. *Eur. J. Psychol. Assess.* **2010**, *26*, 61–67. [CrossRef]
74. Sighinolfi, C.; Norcini Pala, A.; Chiri, L.R.; Marchetti, I.; Sica, C. Difficulties in Emotion Regulation Scale (DERS): Traduzione e Adattamento Italiano. *Psicoter. Cogn. Comport.* **2010**, *16*, 141–170.
75. Bruchon-Schweitzer, M. Dimensionality of the Body Image. *Percept. Mot. Skills* **1987**, *65*, 887–892. [CrossRef]
76. Terracciano, A.; McCrae, R.R.; Costa, P.T. Factorial and Construct Validity of the Italian Positive and Negative Affect Schedule (PANAS). *Eur. J. Psychol. Assess.* **2003**, *19*, 131–141. [CrossRef]
77. Beck, B.; Cardini, F.; Làdavas, E.; Bertini, C. The Enfacement Illusion Is Not Affected by Negative Facial Expressions. *PLoS ONE* **2015**, *10*, e0136273. [CrossRef] [PubMed]
78. Boutron, I.; Altman, D.G.; Moher, D.; Schulz, K.F.; Ravaud, P. CONSORT Statement for Randomized Trials of Nonpharmacologic Treatments: A 2017 Update and a CONSORT Extension for Nonpharmacologic Trial Abstracts. *Ann. Intern. Med.* **2017**, *167*, 40. [CrossRef]
79. Boutron, I.; Moher, D.; Altman, D.G.; Schulz, K.F.; Ravaud, P. Extending the CONSORT Statement to Randomized Trials of Nonpharmacologic Treatment: Explanation and Elaboration. *Ann. Intern. Med.* **2008**, *148*, 295. [CrossRef]
80. Regan, C. An Investigation into Nausea and Other Side-Effects of Head-Coupled Immersive Virtual Reality. *Virtual Real.* **1995**, *1*, 17–31. [CrossRef]
81. May, A.; Schulte, L.H. Chronic Migraine: Risk Factors, Mechanisms and Treatment. *Nat. Rev. Neurol.* **2016**, *12*, 455–464. [CrossRef] [PubMed]
82. Wells, R.E.; Bertisch, S.M.; Buettner, C.; Phillips, R.S.; McCarthy, E.P. Complementary and Alternative Medicine Use among Adults with Migraines/Severe Headaches. *Headache* **2011**, *51*, 1087–1097. [CrossRef]
83. Stovner, L.; Hagen, K.; Jensen, R.; Katsarava, Z.; Lipton, R.; Scher, A.; Steiner, T.; Zwart, J.-A. The Global Burden of Headache: A Documentation of Headache Prevalence and Disability Worldwide. *Cephalalgia* **2007**, *27*, 193–210. [CrossRef]
84. Andlin-Sobocki, P.; Jonsson, B.; Wittchen, H.-U.; Olesen, J. Cost of Disorders of the Brain in Europe. *Eur. J. Neurol.* **2005**, *12*, 1–27. [CrossRef]

85. Roncolato, M.; Fabbri, L.; Recchia, G.; Cavazzuti, L.; Visona, G.; Brignoli, O.; Medea, G. An Epidemiological Study to Assess Migraine Prevalence in a Sample of Italian Population Presenting to Their GPs. *Eur. Neurol.* **2000**, *43*, 102–106. [CrossRef] [PubMed]
86. Berg, J. Economic Evidence in Migraine and Other Headaches: A Review. *Eur. J. Health Econ.* **2004**, *5*, s43–s54. [CrossRef]
87. Gaul, C.; Liesering-Latta, E.; Schäfer, B.; Fritsche, G.; Holle, D. Integrated Multidisciplinary Care of Headache Disorders: A Narrative Review. *Cephalalgia* **2016**, *36*, 1181–1191. [CrossRef] [PubMed]
88. Negro, A.; Delaruelle, Z.; Ivanova, T.A.; Khan, S.; Ornello, R.; Raffaelli, B.; Terrin, A.; Reuter, U.; Mitsikostas, D.D. Headache and Pregnancy: A Systematic Review. *J. Headache Pain* **2017**, *18*, 106. [CrossRef] [PubMed]
89. Diener, H.-C.; Tassorelli, C.; Dodick, D.W.; Silberstein, S.D.; Lipton, R.B.; Ashina, M.; Becker, W.J.; Ferrari, M.D.; Goadsby, P.J.; Pozo-Rosich, P.; et al. Guidelines of the International Headache Society for Controlled Trials of Acute Treatment of Migraine Attacks in Adults: Fourth Edition. *Cephalalgia* **2019**, *39*, 687–710. [CrossRef]
90. Melzack, R.; Torgerson, W.S. On the Language of Pain. *Anesthesiology* **1971**, *34*, 50–59. [CrossRef]
91. Miner, J.R. Randomized Double-Blind Placebo Controlled Crossover Study of Acetaminophen, Ibuprofen, Acetaminophen/Hydrocodone, and Placebo for the Relief of Pain From a Standard Painful Stimulus. *Acad. Emerg. Med.* **2009**, *16*, 911–914. [CrossRef] [PubMed]
92. Siriratna, P.; Ratanasutiranont, C.; Manissorn, T.; Santiniyom, N.; Chira-Adisai, W. Short-Term Efficacy of High-Intensity Laser Therapy in Alleviating Pain in Patients with Knee Osteoarthritis: A Single-Blind Randomised Controlled Trial. *Pain Res. Manag.* **2022**, *2022*, 1319165. [CrossRef] [PubMed]
93. Myles, P.S.; Myles, D.B.; Galagher, W.; Boyd, D.; Chew, C.; MacDonald, N.; Dennis, A. Measuring Acute Postoperative Pain Using the Visual Analog Scale: The Minimal Clinically Important Difference and Patient Acceptable Symptom State. *Br. J. Anaesth.* **2017**, *118*, 424–429. [CrossRef] [PubMed]

Journal of
Clinical Medicine

MDPI

Article

Behavioral Activation through Virtual Reality for Depression: A Single Case Experimental Design with Multiple Baselines

Desirée Colombo [1,*], Carlos Suso-Ribera [2], Isabel Ortigosa-Beltrán [3], Javier Fernández-Álvarez [2], Azucena García-Palacios [2,4] and Cristina Botella [2,4]

[1] Department of Personality, Evaluation and Psychological Treatments, Instituto Polibienestar, University of Valencia, Avd Blasco Ibañez 21, 46010 Valencia, Spain
[2] Department of Basic Psychology, Clinic and Psychobiology, Jaume I University, 12071 Castellón, Spain; susor@uji.es (C.S.-R.); fernanja@uji.es (J.F.-Á.); azucena@uji.es (A.G.-P.); botella@uji.es (C.B.)
[3] Department of Information and Communications Technologies, Pompeu Fabra University, 08002 Barcelona, Spain; isabel.ortigosa@upf.edu
[4] CIBER Fisiopatología Obesidad y Nutrición (CIBERobn), Instituto Salud Carlos III, 28029 Madrid, Spain
* Correspondence: desiree.colombo@uv.es; Tel.: +34-964-387-644

Abstract: Behavioral activation (BA) is a structured psychotherapeutic approach for the treatment of major depressive disorder (MDD), which aims at increasing the engagement in activities that might bring enjoyment and meaning to patients' lives. Although a growing body of evidence supports the effectiveness of BA, enhancing the motivation and activity level of depressed patients is often challenging. In the present study, we explored the effectiveness of a brief BA treatment supported by virtual reality (VR) to facilitate the visualization and anticipation of four pleasurable activities that we tried to re-introduce in the patients' daily routine. To do so, we conducted a single-case experimental design with multiple baselines in a sample of patients with moderate to severe depressive symptoms. Three overlap analyses across participants and across behaviors were conducted to calculate the rate of improvement of each patient after the delivery of the intervention. Across the three overlap indices, the participants generally showed moderate-to-large improvements in the level of daily activity, as well as in the time spent planning and/or engaging in one or more activities scheduled during the intervention. Furthermore, most patients also reported a moderate-to-large reduction in daily depressive symptoms and improved mood. Overall, the promising results of the present study suggest that the proposed VR-based BA intervention might represent a valid approach to behaviorally activate depressed patients. The barriers and future lines of research of this innovative field are discussed.

Keywords: virtual reality; behavioral activation; depression; single case experimental design; multiple baselines

Citation: Colombo, D.; Suso-Ribera, C.; Ortigosa-Beltrán, I.; Fernández-Álvarez, J.; García-Palacios, A.; Botella, C. Behavioral Activation through Virtual Reality for Depression: A Single Case Experimental Design with Multiple Baselines. *J. Clin. Med.* **2022**, *11*, 1262. https://doi.org/10.3390/jcm11051262

Academic Editor: Stéphane Bouchard

Received: 14 January 2022
Accepted: 24 February 2022
Published: 25 February 2022

1. Introduction

Major depressive disorder (MDD) is a debilitating condition affecting 4.4% of the general adult population [1]. MDD is characterized by the presence of mood disturbances, including reduced positive affect (PA), high negative affect (NA), and impaired ability to regulate positive and negative emotions [2]. As such, depression can affect different areas of the patients' daily functioning, thus leading to significant distress and low quality of life [3,4].

Among other symptoms, depressed patients have been shown to experience loss of interest and pleasure in daily activities, which often results in the avoidance of pleasant situations and, therefore, in high social isolation. In this vein, negatively biased expectations towards the future have been suggested as a key feature of depressive future-oriented cognition [5]. Depressed patients tend to predict and overestimate the number and intensity of future negative experiences, while anticipating fewer positive events [6–8]. As suggested in previous studies [9], this bias contributes to a maladaptive vicious cycle prolonging NA and maintaining depressive symptoms. More precisely, this negative future-oriented disposition would reinforce the avoidance of pleasurable and rewarding activities and reduce the likelihood to engage in behaviors that might contribute to increase patients' sense of accomplishment and mastery. As a result, depressed patients experience less opportunities to improve their mood, which further intensifies symptom severity [10].

So far, a wide range of evidence-based treatments have been developed to target MDD symptoms. Among others, behavioral activation (BA) is a structured psychotherapeutic intervention that aims to increase the patients' engagement in adaptive daily activities while decreasing the engagement in behaviors that potentially maintain or prolong depressive symptoms [11]. The main goal of BA is to behaviorally activate patients by promoting the re-engagement in activities that might bring pleasure and satisfaction (i.e., reinforcement) to life, according to one's personal values. With this goal in mind, patients are encouraged and supported to act from the "outside-in": that is, to act according to a structured schedule, instead of a mood [10]. In this sense, BA is a highly customized therapy, in which the alliance between the therapist and the patient is essential to recognize behavioral patterns related to one's depression, as well as to identify tailored rewarding activities to be scheduled and re-introduced into one's daily routine [10].

Over the past decades, a growing body of evidence has supported the effectiveness of BA for the treatment of MDD [12], and studies have shown that BA is as effective as other well-established psychological interventions, such as cognitive therapy and cognitive and behavioral therapy [13–15]. Besides, BA has shown its efficacy to reduce symptoms of anxiety [16], as well as to promote well-being in non-clinical populations [16]. However, as suggested by Paul et al. (2020), finding the motivation to behaviorally activate a depressed person can be quite challenging due to the intrinsic nature of the disorder. In this direction, mental imagery has been shown to be a powerful tool to boost people's motivation to engage in adaptive behaviors [17]. In their study, Renner and colleagues (2019) revealed that guiding participants through the imagination of pleasant activities enhanced their motivation and likelihood to engage in those situations. Although effective with healthy individuals, positive imagery may not be an easy task for patients suffering from MDD [18,19], who usually struggle to imagine and think about positive experiences occurring in their lives [6–8]. Consistently, the development of novel approaches to administer BA and, especially, to motivate and facilitate the anticipation of joyful experiences through imagination, represents an important challenge.

Virtual reality (VR) has been extensively used for the treatment of several psychological conditions [20–22] and, more recently, it has been implemented for the treatment of depression [23–26] and the improvement of emotion regulation skills [27]. Thanks to the immersiveness and the sense of presence [28,29], VR has been proved to be highly effective for emotional induction procedures [30]. Moreover, the possibilities offered by recent software and hardware advancements have made it possible to produce tailored experiences which are extremely close to reality [31]. Accordingly, the use of VR might represent an interesting tool in the field of BA interventions. First, VR could be used to provide a virtual spatial reference that facilitates the visualization of activities that once brought pleasure into the patients' daily lives, which might be more challenging to achieve through mental imagery only. Second, the adoption of VR for the induction of positive emotions has been shown to be highly effective [32–34], which indicates that VR might foster the anticipated pleasure and reward of an activity and, in turn, increase one's motivation. Accordingly, Chen et al. [35] tested the effectiveness of a VR-based protocol to expose depressed patients to positive scenes, showing significant decreased levels of anhedonia and depressive symptoms. Third, VR has been shown to enhance the vividness of mental simulations thanks to the feeling of "being there" and the possibility to experience the virtual environment from a first-person perspective [36]. Since the generation of more vivid mental simulations has been associated with a higher induction of positive emotions [37,38], the use of VR might represent a powerful tool to potentiate BA interventions and promote patients' engagement in personally rewarding activities. In this direction, a recent study integrated the use of 360° videos into a broader BA protocol for depression to increase motivation towards pleasurable activities [39]. Preliminary results from a case study demonstrated the feasibility and acceptability of the intervention, which was associated with reduced depressive symptoms. However, VR was only implemented as an adjunctive tool to be used by the patient alone between therapy sessions. Furthermore, the behavioral outcomes associated with the intervention were not analyzed, so the utility of VR to promote BA in depressed patients is still unclear.

The aim of this study was to test the effectiveness of a four-session, VR-assisted BA protocol for individuals with moderate-to-severe depressive symptoms. The novelty of this brief intervention relies on the use of VR to provide patients with a virtual spatial reference in which to visualize and anticipate personally pleasurable and rewarding activities to be reintroduced in their daily routines. Consistent with the ample evidence showing the effectiveness of BA to activate depressed patients [12–15], we hypothesized that our VR-based protocol would enhance patients' behavioral activation and increase daily activity levels. More specifically, we explored whether the motivation and the time spent planning or practicing the activities included in the protocol improved after the administration of the intervention, as well as whether the overall level of patients' daily activity and associated savoring increased over time. Consistent with the anticipated behavioral outcomes and with the evidence from the previous literature regarding BA efficacy [12], we also expected to observe improved daily mood and decreased depressive symptoms.

2. Materials and Methods

2.1. Study Design

In the present study, we conducted a single-case multiple baseline experimental design [40], a type of single case experimental design (SCED) in which participants are randomly assigned to different starts of the intervention phase to guarantee the internal validity of the findings. The study was conducted in accordance with the Single-Case Reporting Guidelines in Behavioral Interventions (SCRIBE) checklist for SCEDs [41].

Consistent with the guidelines [42], three different baseline lengths were adopted, each of which followed an AB design (A = baseline, B = treatment). Group 1 included 8 days of baseline (phase A) and 23 days of treatment monitoring (phase B); group 2 included 9 days of baseline and 22 days of treatment monitoring; group 3 included 12 days of baseline and 19 days of treatment monitoring. The length of the baseline and follow-up periods was chosen in order to ensure a minimum of 5 assessments per participant, as recommended for the analyses of SCEDs [43]. In total, the duration of the study was of 31 days. All participants received two intervention sessions per week over two weeks, thus resulting in a total of four sessions. During the whole study duration, participants were asked to complete a daily electronic diary sent through email using the Qualtrics platform. The daily assessment was sent at 8:30 p.m. Participants were instructed to complete each daily questionnaire on the day of receipt (i.e., not retrospectively). Participants who completed more than 30% assessments in a retrospective way were excluded from the study.

The present study was approved by the ethics committee of the Jaume I University (number: CD/103/2021). The study was registered in the clinicaltrials.gov (accessed on 14 January 2022) database (NCT05138744). Informed consent was obtained from all participants.

2.2. Inclusion and Exclusion Criteria

To be eligible for the study, participants had to meet the following criteria: being aged between 18 and 65 years, scoring more than 10 at the Patient Health Questionnaire-9 (PHQ-9) [44,45] (i.e., from moderate to severe depressive symptoms) and scoring less than 24 at the PA subscale of the Positive and Negative Affect Schedule (PANAS) [46,47] (i.e., a standard deviation below the mean of healthy individuals) [48].

Individuals who were already receiving a psychological treatment were excluded from this study. Furthermore, we excluded individuals suffering from a severe mental disorder as assessed with the Mini International Neuropsychiatric Interview Version 5.0.0 (MINI) [49], such as bipolar disorder, alcohol and/or substance dependence disorder or psychotic disorder.

2.3. Sample

The study was conducted at the Psychological Care Center of the Jaume I University (Spain). In total, eight participants meeting the inclusion criteria were recruited to take part in the study. One participant completed 45% of the daily assessments retrospectively and was therefore excluded from the analyses. The final sample included seven participants (six females and one male). According to the baseline PHQ-9 scores and existing cut-offs [45,50], three participants reported moderate depressive symptoms (i.e., a score between 10 and 14), three participants reported moderately severe symptoms (i.e., a score between 15 and 19), and only one participant reported severe depressive symptoms (i.e., a score over 20). More details about the sample are provided in Table 1.

Table 1. Characteristics of the recruited sample.

ID	Age	Sex	Medication	Group	PHQ-9	PANAS-PA
1	23	f	No	3	15	15
2	21	f	No	1	21	21
3	20	f	No	3	14	14
4	23	m	Yes	2	14	19
5	26	f	No	3	14	18
7	23	f	Yes	1	15	23
8	20	f	No	2	18	17

Group 1: 8 days of baseline (phase A), 23 days of treatment monitoring (phase B); Group 2: 9 days of baseline (phase A), 22 days of treatment monitoring (phase B); Group 3: 12 days of baseline (phase A) and 19 days of treatment monitoring (phase B). (PHQ-9 = Patient Health Questionnaire—9 items; PANAS-PA: Positive and Negative Affect Schedule—Positive Affect subscale).

All participants met the criteria for a MDD, as assessed with the MINI. Participant 4 and participant 7 were receiving a pharmacological treatment for depression at the time of the study. However, as the medication had not been introduced or changed over the last year, both participants were included in the study.

2.4. Intervention

The protocol consisted of four VR-based BA sessions, which were delivered twice a week over two weeks. Each session lasted between 30 and 45 min. Before the beginning of the study, participants were asked to select four activities from a predetermined list during a face-to-face meeting (see Appendix A), which took place the week before the intervention phase. The instructions encouraged the participants to choose activities that they liked but they no longer performed, as well as activities they would like to engage in more frequently. In line with BA guidelines [10], the therapist guided the selection of activities by helping participants to reflect on their personal goals and values and, in turn, on the behaviors and activities aligned with such goals and values to be targeted by the intervention. Each activity represented the content of one session. During this first meeting, participants also received a brief psychoeducation session regarding the theoretical framework underlying BA interventions.

The use of VR was included in the protocol to provide participants with a virtual spatial reference in which to place themselves while visualizing and virtually experiencing the chosen activities. With this aim in mind, we used the Google Earth VR application for Oculus Rift, which allows participants to travel to the place associated with a selected activity and experience the sense of "being there" from a first-person perspective. Participants were asked to identify a specific place associated with the activity to be performed in

VR (e.g., a specific place to have a walk; a specific pub to have a drink with some friends). The virtual scenario was entered by means of a head-mounted display (Oculus Rift DK2; Menlo Park, CA, USA) connected to a laptop (Alienware 17 R5 with NVIDIA GTX1070 graphics card and Intel i7 CPU; Miami, FL, USA). The setup also included two sensors and two hand-controllers, which enabled participants to move and explore the environment.

Each session was structured as follows. First, the participants were invited to wear the head-mounted display to start the VR experience. They were guided through the experience by means of a narrative (see Appendix B), which was inspired and adapted from a previous study on the use of mental imagery to envision and plan positive activities [17]. Consistent with Renner et al. (2019), the narrative was structured in order to address the following aspects: (1) focus the attention on the virtual environment to enhance the sense of presence, (2) virtually engage in the planned activity, and (3) concentrate on the positive outcomes of the activity. Subsequently, participants were invited to verbalize their thoughts and emotions in order to develop a solid rationale that justified the importance of planning the activity. Participants were, for instance, asked to recall pleasant memories associated with the activity in the past, identify possible beneficial outcomes associated with the activity or explore the potential barriers and solutions to reintroduce the activity in their lives. Following the principles of BA interventions [10], participants were finally asked to schedule the selected activity following a plan. To do so, each participant received a weekly planner to identify the steps, times and places needed to structure the activity. The same procedure was followed in each session. During the first (i.e., baseline) and last sessions (i.e., end of the treatment), participants were also invited to revise their daily diary. A graphical feedback depicting daily mood and activity level fluctuations was provided to show the connection and reciprocal influence between behavioral patterns and mood shifts. Consistently, participants were invited to reflect on the beneficial effects of engaging in pleasurable activities (or not engaging in any type of activity) on their general mood.

2.5. Measures

Behavioral outcomes: Using a Visual Analogue Scale (VAS) ranging from 0 (not at all) to 100 (extremely), participants were asked to rate their daily activity level ("To what extent have you engaged in activities and be activated today?") and the rate of savoring during the performed activities ("Today, I have been able to savor and take the most of the things I have done"). In addition, the short form [51] of the Behavioral Activation for Depression Scale (BADS-short) [52] was administrated to monitor the overall level of patients' daily behavioral activation. The short form of the BADS includes nine items, whose scores are summed to calculate two subscales: behavioral activation and avoidance. Overall, this scale has shown good internal consistency, reliability, construct validity, and predictive validity [51]. For the aim of this study, only the behavioral activation subscale was administered.

Affective outcomes: Similar to previous studies [53], participants were asked to rate their daily mood on VAS ranging from 0 (happy) to 100 (sad) ("Today, I have felt … "). Furthermore, daily depressive symptoms were assessed with the Patient Health Questionnaire–2 (PHQ-2), a two-item self-report measure of depression that has obtained good psychometric properties (i.e., construct and criterion validity) in past research [54]. Scores for each item can range between 0 (not at all) and 3 (extremely). A previous study has shown the suitability of the PHQ-2 for monitoring depressive symptoms using an electronic diary in daily life [55,56].

Specific activity-related outcomes: For each of the four activities included in the protocol, participants were asked to rate their level of motivation on a VAS ranging from 0 (not at all) to 100 (extremely) ("To what extent do you feel motivated to perform this activity?"). In the daily assessment, participants were also asked to report the time spent (i.e., minutes) practicing or planning each activity (e.g., structuring the activity, looking for information, sharing the plan with some friends, etc.).

2.6. Procedure

Participants were recruited at the Jaume I University through poster advertisements offering a VR-based brief training for depression. The individuals interested in the study were sent a web-based survey to complete the PHQ-9 and the PANAS. If inclusion criteria were met, participants were invited to attend the laboratory to further explore the exclusion criteria through the administration of the MINI. If all the criteria were satisfied, participants were asked to sign the informed consent and invited to join the study. During this first face-to-face session, participants were also guided through the selection of the personalized activities to be included in the protocol (see Appendix A). The participants were randomly allocated to one of the three baselines using an online randomizing tool.

The participants were provided with an email to get in contact with one of the researchers of the team in case of technical problems or doubts about the protocol. When missing data on two consecutive daily assessments were detected, the participants were contacted and were reminded about the importance of completing the diary. All the participants attended the four BA sessions, so no dropout was observed during the study.

At the end of the study, the participants were invited to attend the laboratory for a final debriefing session.

2.7. Data Analysis

The present study is a SCED with multiple baselines across participants (i.e., seven participants allocated to three different baseline lengths) and across behaviors (i.e., four sessions for each participant, one for each of the four activities).

To test the hypotheses related to the behavioral and affective outcomes, we performed several data overlap methods that have been widely used in the SCED literature [57], including the percent of data points exceeding the median (PEM) and the percent of all non-overlapping data (PAND), as well as the more modern non-overlap of all pairs (NAP). These analyses were conducted across participants and all of them included a comparison of baseline-to-post-treatment changes in daily measures. However, while the NAP compares each single point of the baseline phase (A) to each assessment point of the treatment phase (B), the PEM and the PAND are simpler indices that use only part of the data. Particularly, the PEM is calculated with all the points in the treatment phase but only a single point (i.e., the median) in the baseline phase, while the PAND is calculated with the data that remains after removing the minimum number of points that would eliminate all overlap between data from phases A and B [54,55]. All these non-overlap analyses allow calculation of a percentage of non-overlap (i.e., improvement) that can range from 0 to 100. However, emphasis will be made on NAP indices because they generally outperform the remaining indices [57,58], and only this index will be provided for secondary outcomes for readability reasons. In relation to the NAP scores, the median non-overlap of past studies has been proposed as a good comparison measure for interpretation [59,60]. NAP scores higher than 96% reflect very large intervention effects, while indices between 66% and 96% should be interpreted as moderate-to-large effects. For the PAND, moderate-to-large effects would be similar to the NAP (i.e., between 64% and 86%), while non-overlap cut-offs in the PEM are generally stricter and should be over 70% and as close to 100% as possible [59,61,62]. A/B outcome graphs for the visual inspection of the results have been included in the Supplementary Materials.

To test our hypotheses regarding the specific effect of the intervention on each of the four chosen activities, NAP analyses across behaviors were performed. More specifically, each session was considered as a replication of the intervention targeting a different behavior. In other words, each participant had four different baselines, representing the four activities selected at the beginning of the study. For each participant, NAP analyses for each of the four activities were performed by comparing baseline-to-post-treatment changes of the specific activity-related daily measures.

3. Results

3.1. Behavioral and Affective Outcomes

First, we performed analyses to explore whether the intervention produced a significant change in terms of both behavioral and affective measures. As shown in Table 2, all the participants showed a moderate-to-large improvement in at least one of the two behavioral measures (i.e., activity level and behavioral activation as assessed with the BADS-BA), irrespective of the overlap index used. According to the NAP, five participants improved on both outcomes, while two participants only improved on one of the two measures. Similar results were obtained with the PEM analyses, whereas the PAND index indicated a significant improvement on both variables in all the participants. Moreover, most participants (i.e., five out of seven) also reported increased daily savoring levels based on NAP and PEM analyses, which was generalized to all the participants when considering the PAND index. Overall, effect sizes and the corresponding interpretation were consistent across indices, except for participant 4, who presented a poor response to the treatment on behavioral activation and savoring according to the NAP and the PEM, and a good response based on the PAND.

Table 2. Results of the NAP, PAND and PEM analyses across-participants in relation to the behavioral outcome variables.

ID	Activity Level			BADS-BA			Savoring		
	NAP	PAND	PEM	NAP	PAND	PEM	NAP	PAND	PEM
1	80 *	80 *	87 *	74 *	72 *	67	72 *	76 *	73 *
2	76 *	71 *	79 *	76 *	76 *	75 *	72 *	71 *	75 *
3	60	67 *	64	66 *	67 *	64	61	67 *	64
4	87 *	86 *	95 *	53	77 *	30	40	70 *	33
5	80 *	82 *	100 *	83 *	79 *	85 *	85 *	79 *	82 *
7	66 *	67 *	64	75 *	76 *	86 *	78 *	76 *	71 *
8	78 *	89 *	100 *	83 *	82 *	86 *	74 *	86 *	95 *
	6/7	7/7	5/7	6/7	7/7	4/7	5/7	7/7	5/7

* = NAP indices over 66% (moderate-to-large effect); * = PAND indices over 64% (moderate-to-large effect); * = PEM indices over 70 (moderate-to-large effect). BADS-BA: Behavioral Activation for Depression Scale-Behavioral Activation subscale; NAP: non-overlap of all pairs; PAND: percentage of all non-overlapping data; PEM: percentage of data exceeding the median.

Regarding the affective measures (see Table 3), the NAP and PEM analyses indicates that six out of seven participants showed a moderate-to-large improvement in daily mood, while all participants significantly increased daily mood levels according to the PAND index. On the other hand, six out of seven participants reported a significant reduction in daily depressive symptoms according to the PAND analyses. The number of participants showing a significant clinical gain was lower when performing NAP (i.e., five out of seven participants) and PEM analyses (i.e., four out of seven participants).

Table 3. Results of the NAP, PAND and PEM analyses across-participants in relation to the affective outcome variables.

ID	Daily Mood			PHQ2		
	NAP	PAND	PEM	NAP	PAND	PEM
1	70 *	76 *	87 *	79 *	76 *	73 *
2	89 *	86 *	93 *	49	64	68
3	67 *	71 *	75 *	66 *	71 *	43
4	42	70 *	33	43	65 *	50
5	67 *	75 *	76 *	78 *	79 *	94 *
7	88 *	81 *	93 *	79 *	81 *	93 *

Table 3. *Cont.*

ID	Daily Mood			PHQ2		
	NAP	PAND	PEM	NAP	PAND	PEM
8	79 * 6/7	83 * 7/7	90 * 6/7	79 * 5/7	79 * 6/7	86 * 4/7

* = NAP indices over 66% (moderate-to-large effect); * = PAND indices over 64% (moderate-to-large effect); * = PEM indices over 70 (moderate-to-large effect). PHQ2: Patient Health Questionnaire—2; NAP: non-overlap of all pairs; PAND: percentage of all non-overlapping data; PEM: percentage of data exceeding the median.

3.2. Specific Activity-Related Outcomes

We therefore explored whether the intervention produced a significant change in the variables assessing each of the activities included in the protocol (Table 4).

Table 4. Results of the NAP analyses across-behaviors in relation to the specific activity-related outcome variables.

	Motivation				Time Spent				Time Planning			
ID	Act. 1	Act. 2	Act. 3	Act. 4	Act. 1	Act. 2	Act. 3	Act. 4	Act. 1	Act. 2	Act. 3	Act. 4
1	78 *	79 *	90 *	90 *	57	64	56	60	73 *	67 *	74 *	79 *
2	39	74 *	36	41	93 *	75 *	58	76 *	67 *	60	64	73 *
3	66 *	95 *	81 *	65	53	49	84 *	63	31	44	81 *	58
4	87 *	100 *	99 *	91 *	47	50	50	46	53	66 *	80 *	39
5	65	64	45	20	71 *	74 *	62	42	62	65	65	58
7	17	22	45	36	67 *	56	23	56	10	27	32	47
8	56	34	45	60	96 *	66 *	56	54	87 *	45	52	40

* = NAP indices over 66% (moderate-to-large effect). Act: Activity.

All participants showed a moderate-to-large improvement in the time spent performing or planning at least one of the four activities. More specifically, five out of seven participants significantly increased the daily time spent performing one or more of the selected activities. One participant reported a significant increase in the time spent practicing three of the four activities, two participants significantly increased the time spent practicing two activities, and one participant showed a significant increase in the time spent practicing one activity. Importantly, the two participants who did not report a significant increase in the time spent practicing the chosen activities (participant 1 and participant 4) did show a large-to-moderate improvement in the time spent planning four and two activities, respectively.

Regarding motivation, only four out of seven participants reported increased rates of motivation to engage in one or more of the activities planned during the intervention.

4. Discussion

So far, a growing body of research has shown the efficacy of BA for the treatment of depression. In the present study, we used the Google Earth VR application to introduce the use of VR into a brief BA-based protocol and provide participants with a virtual spatial reference in which to visualize and experience four personalized activities to be re-introduced in their daily routines.

All the participants showed a significant clinical gain on at least one of the two variables assessing daily activation level, thus suggesting the short-term effectiveness of the protocol to behaviorally activate the participants. Furthermore, most participants reported increased daily rates of savoring. In other words, the VR intervention was not only associated with an adaptive behavioral change, but also with a significant improvement in the quality and enjoyment of the daily activities in more than half participants. Importantly, these findings and those of the remaining outcomes were generally consistent regardless to the overlap index used, with the exception of one participant (i.e., participant 4). These behavioral findings are further strengthened by the secondary analyses designed to explore the behavioral changes in the specific activities included in each participant's protocol. Indeed, all participants reported a moderate-to-large improvement in the time spent planning and/or practicing one or more activities scheduled during the intervention. The fact that not all the participants significantly increased the engagement in at least one activity should not be considered as a negative outcome. Indeed, the goal of BA interventions is not to abruptly re-introduce an activity into a patient's daily routine. Rather, to gradually involve the patient in the steps needed to engage in a specific behavior, following his/her personal needs and level of confidence [10]. Considering the brief duration of our protocol, a significant increase in the time spent planning, but not practicing, an activity should be interpreted as an important clinical gain.

Besides, significant improvements in terms of mood and depressive symptoms were also observed in most patients taking part in the study, and results were generally coherent irrespective to the index used. Importantly, one participant (participant 4) did not show any significant gain in any of the affective measures according to the NAP and PEM analyses. This might be explained by the fact that this participant had the lowest average baseline daily mood (M = 29, SD = 14.99) and the lowest average baseline PHQ2 score (M = 0.89; SD = 0.78) from the whole sample (daily mood: M = 48.68, SD = 16.26; PHQ2: M = 2.43, SD = 0.96), thus being approximately 1 SD below the sample average scores. In other words, his baseline was defined by a relatively high average daily mood and very low average depressive symptoms. Accordingly, there might have been less room for clinical improvement, consistent with past research [63]. It is important to note that this finding was observed thanks to the use of a modern overlap index, the NAP, because the analyses with the PAND, a simpler but more likely to be biased method [57], wrongly supported the effectiveness of the intervention for this participant (which was not confirmed by the NAP and the PEM).

In addition to the findings on mood and depression for patient 4, we also did not observe the expected results in terms of motivation. This might be explained by the design of the study. It might be the case that, although behavioral activation did occur after the administration of the treatment, the enhancement of the patients' motivation would have required more time and practice. A more intense training over a longer period of time might have been more effective to also increase patients' motivation.

Overall, the encouraging findings of the present study suggest that our VR-based BA intervention might represent an effective tool to target depressive symptoms, at least in the short term. Unlike traditional BA treatments, the main novelty relies on the use of VR. First, the use of VR has been shown to increase patients' engagement and motivation towards a treatment which, in turn, might enhance its effectiveness and reduce dropout rates [64,65]. Even though we did not collect any acceptability data regarding the proposed intervention, no dropout was observed throughout the study. Second, VR has been found to lead to the creation of more vivid mental simulations and more intense hedonic expectations as compared to other methods, thus increasing people's likelihood to seek out those situations in real-life [36]. Our results seem to confirm this hypothesis, since all the participants significantly increased the time spent planning and/or practicing the activities included in the protocol. Third, the technology used in the present study (i.e., Google Earth VR for Oculus Rift) is easily accessible and does not require high economical investment, which makes our VA-based protocol an adequate candidate to be introduced in routine clinical practice [27]. In addition, the proposed intervention allows personalization of the protocol according to the patient's needs, thus leading to a highly tailored intervention. Finally, these preliminary results may suggest that just four sessions provided over a brief period of time could be effective to alleviate depressive symptoms and behaviorally activate patients, which may be the first step of a psychological treatment targeting depression. In this sense, future research is needed to investigate whether a more intensive training over a longer period of time might further strengthen the effectiveness of the present protocol and increase the patients' motivation to engage in more pleasurable and adaptive behaviors.

Moreover, future research should explore whether the present protocol could be introduced as a component of a broader intervention for MDD patients.

The present study is not free of limitations. First, the sample was mainly composed of female undergraduate students. Future studies are needed to replicate the present findings in a more heterogeneous sample. Additionally, although the use of VR can represent an added value, the specific use of the Google Earth VR application might have limited the possibilities offered by our intervention. Despite the high level of personalization, patients were asked to select their personally significant activities from a predetermined list, which was created based on previous studies and, most importantly, on the feasibility to virtually visualize the activity through the Google Earth VR application (i.e., outdoor activities). Third, our sample was mainly composed of individuals suffering from moderate to moderate-severe depressive symptoms, and whether our protocol could be similarly effective in patients with more severe symptoms should be further explored. Finally, further studies are needed to disentangle the role of VR in a BA intervention. This study does not allow conclusion of whether the use of VR as compared to visual imagery to anticipate a future positive activity can actually increase the motivation and likelihood to engage in that situation. In this sense, future studies are needed that focus on the specific added value of VR-based BA protocol as compared to a traditional BA intervention, as well as studies that replicate our findings using a larger number of participants and a more robust experimental design.

Supplementary Materials: The following supporting information can be downloaded at: https://www.mdpi.com/article/10.3390/jcm11051262/s1, Figure S1: Activity level outcome graph; Figure S2: BADS-BA outcome graph; Figure S3: PHQ2 outcome graph; Figure S4: Daily mood outcome graph; Figure S5: Savoring outcome graph.

Author Contributions: Conceptualization, D.C., C.S.-R., J.F.-Á. and C.B.; methodology, D.C., C.S.-R., J.F.-Á. and C.B.; formal analysis, D.C., I.O.-B. and C.S.-R.; investigation, D.C. and I.O.-B.; data curation, D.C. and C.S.-R.; writing—original draft preparation, D.C.; writing—review and editing, C.S.-R., J.F.-Á. and I.O.-B.; supervision, A.G.-P. and C.B. All authors have read and agreed to the published version of the manuscript.

Funding: This work was funded by: Juan de la Cierva—Formación postdoctoral fellowship from the Spanish MICINN (Spain; grant FJC2020-045053-I); by the Marie Sklodowska-Curie Innovative Training Networks (ITN-ETN)—Multimind (H2020 MSCA-ITN-2017, grant 765556); by CIBER of Physiopathology of Obesity and Nutrition (CIBERobn) (Instituto de Salud Carlos III, Spain, ISC III CB06 03/0052); by European Union's Horizon 2020—ehcoBUTLER project, grant 643566; and Generalitat Valenciana (PROMETEO/2018/110).

Institutional Review Board Statement: The study was conducted according to the guidelines of the Declaration of Helsinki and approved by the Ethics Committee of Jaume I University (CD/103/2021; November 2021).

Informed Consent Statement: Informed consent was obtained from all subjects involved in the study.

Data Availability Statement: The data presented in this study are available on request from the corresponding author.

Conflicts of Interest: The authors declare no conflict of interest.

Appendix A

List of the activities that the participants could choose at the beginning of the study and which were included in participants' tailored protocols. Please note that the list was inspired by previous studies on pleasant activities and BA [17,39,66]. Items were selected based on their suitability to be reproduced with the application Google Earth VR (i.e., activities that might be performed outdoors).

1. Doing outdoor physical activity, exercise, fitness (e.g., walking, running, playing tennis, etc.)

2. Buying or shopping
3. Going to social or cultural events (cinema, theatre, museum, etc.)
4. Visiting family, partner, or friends
5. Exploring a city or landscape (e.g., beach, lake, mountain, etc.)
6. Going on outings (a picnic, a barbecue, etc.)
7. Making a plan with family, partner, or friends (e.g., lunch, dinner, etc.)
8. Having family, partner, or friends come to visit
9. Reading, listening to music, playing an instrument, or writing outdoors
10. Walking a pet
11. Gardening
12. Doing outdoor photography

Table A1. Types of activities selected by each participant of the study.

ID	Activity 1	Activity 2	Activity 3	Activity 4
1	1	9	4	3
2	9	1	7	6
3	7	9	1	5
4	5	1	9	11
5	5	9	1	7
6	1	9	4	5
7	5	1	7	6

Appendix B

Narrative to guide participants during the VR experience. The instructions were inspired by a previous study exploring mental imagery of positive events [17], and partially adapted to the specific use of VR of the present study.

Introduction

"I would now like you to think about (ACTIVITY). In a few minutes, you will be able to visualize yourself doing (ACTIVITY) thanks to virtual reality. This head-mounted display will allow you to virtually travel to the place you associate with (ACTIVITY). This controller will allow you to freely move and navigate in the environment."

Start VR experience

"Now, let's think about (ACTIVITY). Just imagine (ACTIVITY) and focus on the positive aspects of (ACTIVITY). Try to visualize yourself in this environment doing (ACTIVITY), just if you were really there with your body. Focus on the most positive aspects of (ACTIVITY) and think about yourself doing the activity. Concentrate and stay focused."

Part 1: Contextual cues

"Remember to see, to hear and to feel yourself really there. As vividly as you can. Imagine it is (DATE/TIME). As you can notice, you are at (PLACE/SITUATION/CONTEXT). You have planned to (ACTIVITY). Place yourself in this situation and try to see yourself in this environment. Notice the surroundings that reminds you to engage in your planned activity. Look at the environment, focus on those contextual details which can make you feel like if you were really there, experiencing the situation and doing (ACTIVITY) with your own eyes and your own body. Try to immerse yourself completely in the experience, you can move and explore the environment as much as you want. Take a second to focus vividly on that."

Part 2: Engaging in the activity

"Now concentrate and think that you are following your plan of (ACTIVITY). Focus on the details, as if you are really doing it, as if you are really there. What you can see, hear, smell and feel with your own eyes. If you would like, go back and visualize it one more time to get it really right and just how you would like the activity to be. You are right there, at (PLACE/SITUATION/CONTEXT), and you are really doing (ACTIVITY)."

Part 3: Positive outcomes for activity

"Now focus your attention on how good it feels to be spending some time on (ACTIVITY). Focus on the most positive aspects. Take your time. Experience any pleasant feelings and sensations that you associate with (ACTIVITY). Notice how good that feels, and how valuable and pleasant it is to be right there, in this moment, spending some time doing (ACTIVITY)."

References

1. World Health Organization. *Depression and Other Common Mental Disorders: Global Health Estimates*; World Health Organization: Geneva, Switzerland, 2017; pp. 1–24.
2. Van Meter, A.R.; Youngstrom, E.A. Distinct Roles of Emotion Reactivity and Regulation in Depressive and Manic Symptoms Among Euthymic Patients. *Cognit. Ther. Res.* **2016**, *40*, 262–274. [CrossRef]
3. Katon, W.; Ciechanowski, P. Impact of major depression on chronic medical illness. *J. Psychosom. Res.* **2002**, *53*, 859–863. [CrossRef]
4. Simon, G.E. Social and economic burden of mood disorders. *Biol. Psychiatry* **2003**, *54*, 208–215. [CrossRef]
5. Marroquín, B.; Nolen-Hoeksema, S. Event prediction and affective forecasting in depressive cognition: Using emotion as information about the future. *J. Soc. Clin. Psychol.* **2015**, *34*, 117–134. [CrossRef]
6. Colombo, D.; Fernández-Álvarez, J.; Suso-Ribera, C.; Cipresso, P.; García-Palacios, A.; Riva, G.; Botella, C. Biased affective forecasting: A potential mechanism that enhances resilience and well-being. *Front. Psychol.* **2020**, *11*, 1333. [CrossRef]
7. Pyszczynski, T.; Holt, K.; Greenberg, J. Depression, Self-Focused Attention, and Expectancies for Positive and Negative Future Life Events for Self and Others. *J. Pers. Soc. Psychol.* **1987**, *52*, 994. [CrossRef]
8. Strunk, D.R.; Lopez, H.; DeRubeis, R.J. Depressive symptoms are associated with unrealistic negative predictions of future life events. *Behav. Res. Ther.* **2006**, *44*, 861–882. [CrossRef]
9. Wenze, S.J.; Gunthert, K.C.; German, R.E. Biases in Affective Forecasting and Recall in Individuals With Depression and Anxiety Symptoms. *Personal. Soc. Psychol. Bull.* **2012**, *38*, 895–906. [CrossRef]
10. Martell, C.R.; Dimidjian, S.; Herman-Dunn, R. *Behavioral Activation for Depression: A Clinician's Guide*; Guilford Press: New York, NY, USA, 2013.
11. Dimidjian, S.; Barrera, M.; Martell, C.; Muñoz, R.F.; Lewinsohn, P.M. The origins and current status of behavioral activation treatments for depression. *Annu. Rev. Clin.Psychol.* **2011**, *7*, 1–38. [CrossRef]
12. Ekers, D.; Webster, L.; Van Straten, A.; Cuijpers, P.; Richards, D.; Gilbody, S. Behavioural activation for depression; An update of meta-analysis of effectiveness and sub group analysis. *PLoS ONE* **2014**, *9*, e100100. [CrossRef]
13. Mazzucchelli, T.; Kane, R.; Rees, C. Behavioral Activation Treatments for Depression in Adults: A Meta-analysis and Review. *Clin. Psychol. Sci. Pract.* **2009**, *16*, 383–411. [CrossRef]
14. Cuijpers, P.; van Straten, A.; Warmerdam, L. Behavioral activation treatments of depression: A meta-analysis. *Clin. Psychol. Rev.* **2007**, *27*, 318–326. [CrossRef]
15. Sturmey, P. Behavioral activation is an evidence-based treatment for depression. *Behav. Modif.* **2009**, *33*, 818–829. [CrossRef]
16. Mazzucchelli, T.G.; Kane, R.T.; Rees, C.S. Behavioral activation interventions for well-being: A meta-analysis. *J. Posit. Psychol.* **2010**, *5*, 105. [CrossRef]
17. Renner, F.; Murphy, F.C.; Ji, J.L.; Manly, T.; Holmes, E.A. Mental imagery as a "motivational amplifier" to promote activities. *Behav. Res. Ther.* **2019**, *114*, 51–59. [CrossRef]
18. Blackwell, S.E.; Holmes, E.A. Brightening the Day With Flashes of Positive Mental Imagery: A Case Study of an Individual With Depression. *J. Clin. Psychol.* **2017**, *73*, 579–589. [CrossRef]
19. Blackwell, S.E.; Browning, M.; Mathews, A.; Pictet, A.; Welch, J.; Davies, J.; Watson, P.; Geddes, J.R.; Holmes, E.A. Positive imagery-based cognitive bias modification as a web-based treatment tool for depressed adults: A randomized controlled trial. *Clin. Psychol. Sci.* **2015**, *3*, 91–111. [CrossRef]
20. Botella, C.; Fernández-Álvarez, J.; Guillen, V.; Garcia-Palacios, A.; Banos, R. Recent Progress in Virtual Reality Exposure Therapy for Phobias: A Systematic Review. *Curr. Psychiatry Rep.* **2017**, *19*, 42. [CrossRef]
21. Carl, E.; Stein, A.T.; Levihn-Coon, A.; Pogue, J.R.; Rothbaum, B.; Emmelkamp, P.; Asmundson, G.J.G. Virtual reality exposure therapy for anxiety and related disorders: A meta-analysis of randomized controlled trials. *J. Anxiety Disord.* **2019**, *61*, 27–36. [CrossRef]

22. Lindner, P.; Miloff, A.; Fagernäs, S.; Andersen, J.; Sigeman, M.; Andersson, G.; Furmark, T.; Carlbring, P. Therapist-led and self-led one-session virtual reality exposure therapy for public speaking anxiety with consumer hardware and software: A randomized controlled trial. *J. Anxiety Disord.* **2019**, *61*, 45–54. [CrossRef]
23. Falconer, C.J.; Rovira, A.; King, J.A.; Gilbert, P.; Antley, A.; Fearon, P.; Ralph, N.; Slater, M.; Brewin, C.R. Embodying self-compassion within virtual reality and its effects on patients with depression. *BJPsych Open* **2016**, *2*, 74–80. [CrossRef] [PubMed]
24. Migoya-Borja, M.; Delgado-Gómez, D.; Carmona-Camacho, R.; Porras-Segovia, A.; López-Moriñigo, J.D.; Sánchez-Alonso, M.; García, L.A.; Guerra, N.; Barrigón, M.L.; Alegría, M.; et al. Feasibility of a Virtual Reality-Based Psychoeducational Tool (VRight) for Depressive Patients. *Cyberpsychology Behav. Soc. Netw.* **2020**, *23*, 246–252. [CrossRef] [PubMed]
25. Shah, L.B.I.; Torres, S.; Kannusamy, P.; Chng CML, C.M.L.H.H.G.; Klainin-Yobas, P. Efficacy of the virtual reality-based stress management program on stress-related variables in people with mood disorders: The feasibility study. *Arch. Psychiatr. Nurs.* **2015**, *29*, 6–13. [CrossRef] [PubMed]
26. Zeng, N.; Pope, Z.; Lee, J.; Gao, Z. Virtual Reality Exercise for Anxiety and Depression: A Preliminary Review of Current Research in an Emerging Field. *J. Clin. Med.* **2018**, *7*, 42. [CrossRef]
27. Colombo, D.; Díaz-García, A.; Fernandez-Álvarez, J.; Botella, C. Virtual reality for the enhancement of emotion regulation. *Clin. Psychol. Psychother.* **2021**, *28*, 519–537. [CrossRef]
28. Slater, M.; Usoh, M.; Steed, A. Depth of Presence in Virtual Environments. *Presence Teleoperators Virtual Environ.* **1994**, *3*, 130–144. [CrossRef]
29. Slater, M. Measuring Presence: A Response to the Witmer and Singer Presence Questionnaire. *Presence Teleoperators Virtual Environ.* **1999**, *8*, 560–565. [CrossRef]
30. Baños, R.M.; Liaño, V.; Botella, C.; Alcañiz, M.; Guerrero, B.; Rey, B. Changing induced moods via virtual reality. In *Persuasive Technology Lecture Notes in Computer Science (including Subser Lect Notes Artif Intell Lect Notes Bioinformatics)*; Springer: Berlin/Heidelberg, Germany, 2006; pp. 7–15.
31. Baños, R.M.; Botella, C.; Alcañiz, M.; Liaño, V.; Guerrero, B.; Rey, B. Immersion and emotion: Their impact on the sense of presence. *Cyberpsychology Behav.* **2004**, *7*, 734–741. [CrossRef]
32. Jallais, C.; Gilet, A.-L. Inducing changes in arousal and valence: Comparison of two mood induction procedures. *Behav. Res. Methods* **2010**, *42*, 318–325. [CrossRef]
33. Strack, F.; Schwarz, N.; Gschneidinger, E. Happiness and Reminiscing: The Role of Time Perspective, Affect, and Mode of Thinking. *J. Pers. Soc. Psychol.* **1985**, *49*, 1460–1469. [CrossRef]
34. Zhang, X.; Yu, H.W.; Barrett, L.F. How does this make you feel? A comparison of four affect induction procedures. *Front. Psychol.* **2014**, *5*, 689. [CrossRef]
35. Chen, K.; Barnes-Horowitz, N.; Treanor, M.; Sun, M.; Young, K.S.; Craske, M.G. Virtual Reality Reward Training for Anhedonia: A Pilot Study. *Front. Psychol.* **2021**, *11*, 3748. [CrossRef]
36. Skard, S.; Knudsen, E.S.; Sjåstad, H.; Thorbjørnsen, H. How virtual reality influences travel intentions: The role of mental imagery and happiness forecasting. *Tour. Manag.* **2021**, *87*, 104360. [CrossRef]
37. Odou, N.; Vella-Brodrick, D.A. The Efficacy of Positive Psychology Interventions to Increase Well-Being and the Role of Mental Imagery Ability. *Soc. Indic. Res.* **2013**, *110*, 111–129. [CrossRef]
38. Blackwell, S.E.; Rius-Ottenheim, N.; Schulte-van Maaren, Y.W.M.; Carlier, I.V.E.; Middelkoop, V.D.; Zitman, F.G.; Spinhoven, P.; Holmes, E.A.; Giltay, E.J. Optimism and mental imagery: A possible cognitive marker to promote well-being? *Psychiatry Res.* **2013**, *206*, 56–61. [CrossRef]
39. Paul, M.; Bullock, K.; Bailenson, J. Case Report: Virtual Reality Behavioral Activation as an Intervention for Major Depressive Disorder. *JMIR Ment. Health* **2020**, *7*. [CrossRef]
40. Kazdin, A.E. *Single-Case Research Designs: Methods for Clinical and Applied Settings*, 2nd ed.; Oxford University Press: Oxford, UK, 2011.
41. Tate, R.L.; Perdices, M.; Rosenkoetter, U.; Shadish, W.; Vohra, S.; Barlow, D.H.; Horner, R.; Kazdin, A.; Kratochwill, T.; McDonald, S. The Single-Case Reporting Guideline In BEhavioural Interventions (SCRIBE) 2016 Statement. *Remedial. Spec. Educ.* **2016**, *37*, 370–380. [CrossRef]
42. Kratochwill, T.R.; Hitchcock, J.H.; Horner, R.H.; Levin, J.R.; Odom, S.L.; Rindskopf, D.M.; Shadish, W.R. Single-Case Intervention Research Design Standards. *Remedial. Spec. Educ.* **2013**, *34*, 26–38. [CrossRef]
43. Kratochwill, T.R.; Hitchcock, J.; Horner, R.H.; Levin, J.R.; Odom, S.L.; Rindskopf, D.M.; Shadish, W.R. *Single-Case Designs Technical Documentation*; What Works Clearinghouse: Washington, DC, USA, 2010.
44. Diez-Quevedo, C.; Rangil, T.; Sanchez-Planell, L.; Kroenke, K.; Spitzer, R.L. Validation and utility of the patient health questionnaire in diagnosing mental disorders in 1003 general hospital Spanish inpatients. *Psychosom. Med.* **2001**, *63*, 679–686. [CrossRef]
45. Kroenke, K.; Spitzer, R.L.; Williams, J.B.W. The PHQ-9: Validity of a brief depression severity measure. *J. Gen. Intern. Med.* **2001**, *16*, 606–613. [CrossRef]
46. Díaz-García, A.; González-Robles, A.; Mor, S.; Mira, A.; Quero, S.; García-Palacios, A.; Baños, R.M.; Botella, C. Positive and Negative Affect Schedule (PANAS): Psychometric properties of the online Spanish version in a clinical sample with emotional disorders. *BMC Psychiatry* **2020**, *20*, 56. [CrossRef] [PubMed]

47. Watson, D.; Clark, L.A.; Tellegen, A. Development and validation of brief measures of positive and negative affect: The PANAS scales. *J. Pers. Soc. Psychol.* **1988**, *54*, 1063–1070. [CrossRef] [PubMed]
48. Sandín, B.; Chorot, P.; Lostao, L.; Joiner, T.E.; Santed, M.A.; Valiente, R.M. Escalas PANAS de afecto positivo y negativo: Validacion factorial y convergencia transcultural. *Psicothema* **1999**, *1*, 37–51.
49. Ferrando, L.; Soto, M.; Bobes, J.; Soto, O.; Franco, L.; Gibert, J. *Mini International Neuropsychiatric Interview (Spanish Version 5.0)*; Institute IAP: Madrid, Spain, 2000.
50. Kroenke, K.; Spitzer, R.L. The PHQ-9: A New Depression Diagnostic and Severity Measure. *Psychiatr. Ann.* **2002**, *32*, 509–515. [CrossRef]
51. Manos, R.C.; Kanter, J.W.; Luo, W. The behavioral activation for depression scale-short form: Development and validation. *Behav. Ther.* **2011**, *42*, 726–739. [CrossRef] [PubMed]
52. Kanter, J.W.; Mulick, P.S.; Busch, A.M.; Berlin, K.S.; Martell, C.R. The Behavioral Activation for Depression Scale (BADS): Psychometric properties and factor structure. *J. Psychopathol. Behav. Assess.* **2007**, *29*, 191–202. [CrossRef]
53. Van Rijsbergen, G.D.; Bockting, C.L.H.; Burger, H.; Spinhoven, P.; Koeter, M.W.J.; Ruhé, H.G.; Hollon, S.D.; Schene, A.H. Mood reactivity rather than cognitive reactivity is predictive of depressive relapse: A randomized study with 5.5-year follow-up. *J. Consult. Clin. Psychol.* **2013**, *81*, 508. [CrossRef] [PubMed]
54. Kroenke, K.; Spitzer, R.L.; Williams, J.B.W. The patient health questionnaire-2: Validity of a two-item depression screener. *Med. Care.* **2003**, *41*, 1284–1292. [CrossRef]
55. Bauer, A.M.; Baldwin, S.A.; Anguera, J.A.; Areán, P.A.; Atkins, D.C. Comparing approaches to mobile depression assessment for measurement-based care: Prospective study. *J. Med. Internet. Res.* **2018**, *20*, e10001. [CrossRef]
56. Fernandez-Alvarez, J.; Colombo, D.; Suso-Ribera, C.; Chirico, A.; Serino, S.; Di Lernia, D.; Palacios, A.G.; Botella, C. Using virtual reality to target positive autobiographical memory in individuals with moderate-to-moderately severe depressive symptoms: A single case experimental design. *Internet Interv.* **2021**, *25*, 100407. [CrossRef]
57. Parker, R.I.; Vannest, K. An Improved Effect Size for Single-Case Research: Nonoverlap of All Pairs. *Behav. Ther.* **2009**, *40*, 357–367. [CrossRef]
58. Parker, R.I.; Vannest, K.J.; Davis, J.L. Non-overlap analysis for single-case research in Single-case intervention research: Methodological and statistical advances. In *Single-Case Intervention Research: Methodological and Statistical Advances*; American Psychological Association: Washington, DC, USA, 2014.
59. Parker, R.I.; Vannest, K.J.; Davis, J.L. Effect size in single-case research: A review of nine nonoverlap techniques. *Behav. Modif.* **2011**, *35*, 303–322. [CrossRef]
60. Gómez-Pérez, M.C.; García-Palacios, A.; Diana, C.; Zaragozá, I.; Suso-Ribera, C. Brief Acceptance and Commitment Therapy for Fibromyalgia: Feasibility and Effectiveness of a Replicated Single-Case Design. *Pain Res. Manag.* **2020**, *2020*, 7897268. [CrossRef]
61. Ma, H.-H. The Effectiveness of Intervention on the Behavior of Individuals With Autism. *Behav. Modif.* **2009**, *33*, 339–359. [CrossRef]
62. Scruggs, T.E.; Mastropieri, M.A. Summarizing Single-Subject Research. *Behav. Modif.* **1998**, *22*, 221–242. [CrossRef]
63. Osma, J.; Peris-Baquero, O.; Suso-Ribera, C.; Sauer-Zavala, S.; Barlow, D.H. Predicting and Moderating the Response to the Unified Protocol: Do Baseline Personality and Affective Profiles Matter? *Cognit. Ther. Res.* **2021**, *45*, 817–830. [CrossRef]
64. Mouatt, B.; Smith, A.; Mellow, M.; Parfitt, G.; Smith, R.; Stanton, T. The use of virtual reality to influence engagement and enjoyment during exercise: A scoping review. *J. Sci. Med. Sport* **2019**, *22*, s98. [CrossRef]
65. Mouatt, B.; Smith, A.E.; Mellow, M.L.; Parfitt, G.; Smith, R.T.; Stanton, T.R. The Use of Virtual Reality to Influence Motivation, Affect, Enjoyment, and Engagement During Exercise: A Scoping Review. *Front. Virtual Real.* **2020**, *39*. [CrossRef]
66. MacPhillamy, D.J.; Lewinsohn, P.M. The pleasant events schedule: Studies on reliability, validity, and scale intercorrelation. *J. Consult. Clin. Psychol.* **1982**, *50*, 363. [CrossRef]

MDPI
St. Alban-Anlage 66
4052 Basel
Switzerland
www.mdpi.com

Journal of Clinical Medicine Editorial Office
E-mail: jcm@mdpi.com
www.mdpi.com/journal/jcm

www.ingramcontent.com/pod-product-compliance
Lightning Source LLC
Chambersburg PA
CBHW040753250926
51850CB00007BB/1489